WESTERN HIMALAYA

AND

TIBET

A NARRATIVE OF A JOURNEY THROUGH THE MOUNTAINS OF NORTHERN INDIA

BY

THOMAS THOMSON

GYAN

ISBN : 978-81-212-1555-8(HB)

First Published, 1852

Published, 2018

Published by

Gyan Publishing House
5, Ansari Road
Daryaganj, New Delhi-110002
Phone: 011-47034999, 9811692060
www.gyanbooks.com
E-mail: books@gyanbooks.com

Printed at: G. Print Process, Delhi.

J. W. del. W. L. Walton lithog.

Printed by Hullmandel & Walton

ISKARDO

PREFACE.

On the termination of my journey in Tibet, I submitted to the Indian Government a detailed report of my observations in that country. It was my original intention to request the permission of the Court of Directors to publish this report in the form in which it was drawn up; but after my return to England, this plan was, at the suggestion of friends, abandoned for that now followed.

At the time of my appointment to the Tibet Mission, my attention had not been specially directed to the Himalaya, but I have since had many opportunities of studying that chain of mountains. My first definite impressions of Himalayan geography were received from my fellow-travellers, Major Cunningham and Captain Henry Strachey. The latter gentleman had just completed one of the most adventurous journeys ever made in the Himalaya; and Major Cunningham's knowledge of the geography of Northern India is so accurate and extensive, that the delay in the publication of his map, although caused by the devotion of his leisure time to other branches of research, is a subject of deep regret to all who know its value. More recently I have had the good fortune to travel in the Eastern Himalaya with Dr. Hooker, and it was a source of great gratification to mé, when we met, to find that in studying these mountains at opposite extremities of the chain, the results at which we had arrived were almost identical.

My botanical collections, which were very extensive, have as yet been only roughly assorted, and the names of plants given in the present work are chiefly derived from a careful comparison of specimens with the Hookerian Herbarium at Kew,—a collection which, as is well known to Botanists, both from its extent and from the liberality with which it is thrown open to students of that science, occupies in this country the place of a national collection.

The heights of places given in the work have been derived from very various sources. Those in the earlier part are chiefly from the extremely accurate observations of the Gerards; for others I have to thank my fellow-travellers; but the greater number are calculated from my own observations of the boiling-point of water, and do not therefore pretend to great accuracy. Still the thermometer which I used (by Dollond) was a very good one, and comparisons with barometric observations, or with known heights, have given such results as satisfy me that at considerable elevations it may be depended upon to within three or four hundred feet as an extreme error.

The orthography of oriental proper names is a question of great difficulty, and grave objections may be urged against any system which has been proposed. If each European nation represents the sound of the vowels and variable consonants after the mode which prevails in its own language, then proper names must be translated, as it were, when rendered from one of these languages into another; whereas, if the mode of spelling the names remain fixed, then the value of the letters must be different in the majority of the languages from that which usually prevails. For purely popular purposes the former method would probably be the most judicious; and the English language has peculiar facilities for rendering oriental sounds, in consequence of its possessing the open sound of *u*, as in *but*, which is wanting in other European languages, though so common in Arabic, Persian, and Hindee, and all cognate tongues.

A uniform mode of spelling, however, has so many advantages, that I have been induced to give it a preference; but it will be seen that in a few instances, where the popular mode of spelling has become familiar, and as it were a portion of the English language, as in the words Punjab, Jumna, Sutlej, Kussowlee, and a few others, I have not had courage to carry out the rule.

For the plates which accompany the work I have to thank Mr. Winterbottom, who very kindly permitted me to select from a series of sketches those which I thought most suitable. This was not an easy task; but in the two views of the neighbourhood of Iskardo I found so faithful a representation of the extremely rugged scenery of the Tibetan mountains, contrasted with the level plain of Iskardo, and the lacustrine strata of the neighbourhood, that no more desirable illustrations for a journey in Tibet could be conceived. The little vignette, too, though it does not represent any part of the country through which I travelled, is precisely similar to many ravines in Rondu, and serves to show that the Gilgit valley is quite the same in general appearance with that district. I was more particularly desirous of introducing this sketch, from the very faithful representation it contains of the alluvial platforms which skirt the streams in every part of Tibet.

The map is founded principally upon Mr. Arrowsmith's large map, and his name is its best guarantee.

The districts round the Pangong lake are taken from a sketch given to me by Captain H. Strachey, and the whole of the eastern part has been revised by him. A great part of the course of the Shayuk has been laid in by Mr. Arrowsmith from my own rough survey, while the little-known district between Jamu and Zanskar, which I was not competent to survey, has been rendered as nearly as possible from the notes which I had made of the length and direction of my marches.

The sketch of the district between Nubra and the Karakoram pass, which will, I hope, be found useful as an illustration of that part of my journey, has been prepared for me by Dr. Hooker, from a rough draft of my survey, assisted by verbal explanations.

In conclusion, I have to add, that for the correction of the press, during which process many asperities by which the manuscript was disfigured have disappeared, I have to thank my kind friends, Dr. and Mrs. Hooker.

CONTENTS.

CHAPTER I.

CHAPTER II.

CHAPTER III.

CHAPTER IV.

CHAPTER V.

CHAPTER VI.

CHAPTER VII.

CHAPTER VIII.

CHAPTER IX.

CHAPTER X.

CHAPTER XI.

CHAPTER XII.

CHAPTER XIII.

CHAPTER XIV.

CHAPTER XV.

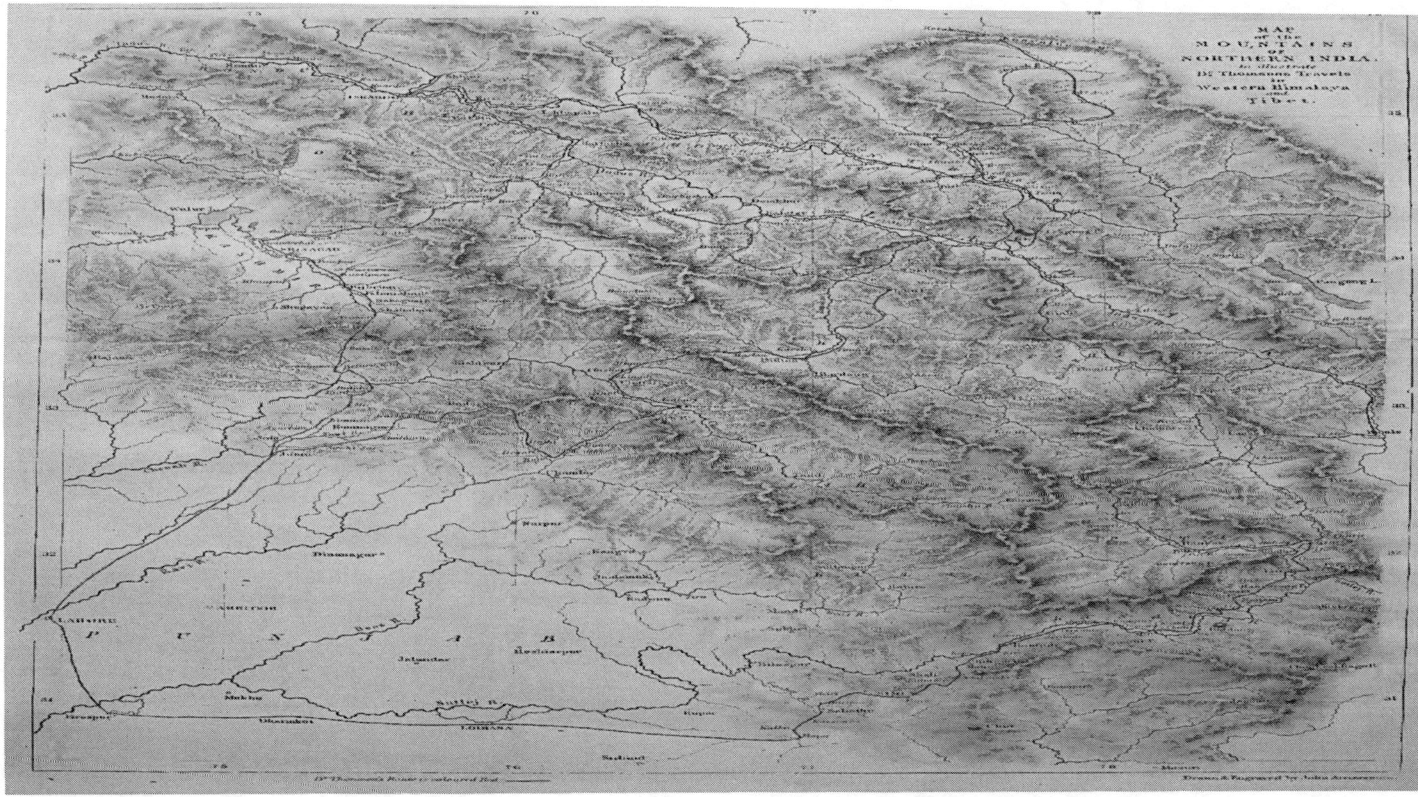
MAP
of the
MOUNTAINS
of
NORTHERN INDIA.
to illustrate
Dr Thomson's Travels
in
Western Himalaya
and
Tibet.
LAHORE
Dr Thomson's Route is coloured Red.

WESTERN HIMALAYA

AND

TIBET.

CHAPTER I.

Appointment to a Mission about to proceed to Tibet—Leave Firozpur for Simla—Approach to the Mountains—Appearance of Himalaya from Plains of India—Kalka—Ascent to Kussowlee—Vegetation of Plainward Face—Origin of Kussowlee Ridge—Climate and Vegetation of Kussowlee—Aspect of inner ranges—Road from Kussowlee to Simla—Sabathu—Cross Gambar River—Haripur—Tropical Vegetation of Basin of Gambar—Steep Ascent to Simla—its extent and situation—its Vegetation—Oak-forest—Pines—Flora of Spring Months—of Rainy Season—View from Peak of Jako—Structure of Mountain Ranges.

In the month of May, 1847, while with my Regiment at Firozpur on the south bank of the Sutlej, I received intimation that Lord Hardinge, at that time Governor-General of India, had appointed me a member of a mission which he had determined to despatch across the Himalaya Mountains into Tibet; and I was directed to proceed without delay to Simla, from which place the mission was to start, as soon as the necessary arrangements could be completed.

I left Firozpur on the evening of the 20th of May, and travelling only at night, on account of the extreme heat, I arrived at the foot of the hills, on the morning of the 24th. The greater part of the road was through a perfectly level country, and nearly parallel to the Sutlej, but without following its sinuosities. During a part of the last night's journey, I travelled among low hills, partly composed of loose sand and boulders, partly of clay and sandstone. The road enters this tract by an open valley, bounded on both sides by hills, which on the left are low and rounded. On the right they are scarped towards the plains, as well as towards the valley up which I travelled, and the strata of which they are composed, dip towards the Himalaya. The valley is traversed by a little stream descending from the mountains, one of the tributaries of the Gagar or Markanda, that remarkable river, which runs in a south-west direction, as if about to join the Indus, but ultimately loses itself in the sands of the Bikanir desert.

When viewed from the plains of India, at a distance sufficient to enable the spectator to see the most elevated part of the chain, the Himalaya appear to form several distinct parallel ranges on the horizon, rising in succession one behind another. The most distant of these is covered with perpetual snow, while the other two, usually called the middle and outer ranges, have the usual blue-grey tint of distant mountains. From very great distances in the plains, the most remote of these three apparent ranges is alone visible; and as the traveller advances towards the base of the mountains, the others rise in succession above the horizon.

The optical deception, in consequence of which, masses of mountains of every configuration resolve themselves into ranges perpendicular to the line of sight, as soon as the eye is so far removed that the outline of the different parts becomes indistinct, has given to our maps many mountain-chains, which a nearer inspection proves to have no existence. As a good instance of this, I may mention the Suliman range, west of the Indus, which, though laid down in all our maps as a mountain belt, parallel to and skirting the plain country, behind which no mountains at all are represented, evidently consists of a series of ranges, almost perpendicular to the Indus, and separated from one another by considerable rivers. The sources of these rivers lie far back, and the north and south axis from which they spring, separates all the tributaries of the Indus from a succession of streams, which run in a south-westerly direction, and appear to terminate, without reaching the sea, in the low and flat country of Seistan and western Beluchistan.

At distances of between sixty and thirty miles from the base of the Himalaya, the three parallel chains are well seen. On a nearer approach, the lower and outer mountains by degrees become more distinct, and subtend a greater angle, so as at last to conceal the more distant portions of the chain. At the same time, the uniformity of outline by which they had been characterized, insensibly disappears. Ridges become visible in the face presented to the eye, which, as the traveller continues to advance, become developed into projecting spurs, separated from the general mass by wide valleys, previously quite undistinguishable. On a still nearer approach, the elevation continuing to increase, the extent of range embraced by the eye is gradually lessened, till at last, when we arrive at the base of the mountains, a single valley with its bounding ranges of low hills is alone visible, the giant masses, so conspicuous from a greater distance, being no longer to be seen.

The low sandy or sandstone hills, which form the outskirts of the Himalaya, are not, on the road from Firozpur to Simla, anywhere of greater elevation than a few hundred feet. A few miles beyond the entrance, the valley, which has a considerable slope, widens as it approaches the more lofty mountains, and the sandstone cliffs are replaced by rounded hills, probably of a more ancient rock, covered with soil and vegetation.

At the very base of the steep mountains is situated the village of Kalka, at which, as it is the termination of palankin travelling, travellers in general stop, to arrange for the continuance of their journey. Situated close to the source of the little stream which I had been following since I had entered the hilly country, and surrounded on all sides by low hills, Kalka has an elevation of perhaps 2000 feet above the level of the sea, or 1000 feet above the plain on the outside of the sandstone hills.

The general aspect of the low hills around Kalka is barren and uninviting; it was especially so at the season of my visit, when the great heat had scorched the herbaceous vegetation, and all nature had a burnt-up appearance. The subtropical valleys are not here, as farther to the east along the base of the mountains, filled with dense forest. They are in general bare, a few scattered trees only appearing here and there. In the level part of the valley, at the very entrance, where the soil was still of some depth, *Acacia Arabica* and *Butea frondosa*, the most prevailing trees of the plains beyond, were frequent; but the stony water-courses contained little but a bamboo, and the hill-sides were covered with scattered bushes of the more ordinary shrubs of the plains of Northern India, and presented few features of interest.

Immediately on leaving Kalka, a long and steep ascent commenced, continuing for about ten miles, to the military post of Kussowlee, which occupies the crest of the ridge overlooking the Kalka valley, and can be seen throughout the greater part of the ascent, overhanging the winding road, which has been constructed along the side of the mountain. The elevation of Kussowlee is about 6500 feet, an altitude at which the climate in the Himalaya is perfectly temperate, so that during the ascent a traveller from the plains of India meets with a complete change of climate, a change, too, which in the month of May, the period of my visit, is particularly grateful, the heat below being most oppressive and disagreeable.

As the elevation increases, the view from the road becomes more extensive. The low ranges of hills to the south and west, which had obstructed the view, are by degrees overtopped, and the plains beyond become visible. Soon after leaving Kalka the road crosses a low ridge, and enters a receding bay, or steeply sloping valley beyond, at the upper extremity of which, all along the crest, are seen the houses of Kussowlee. Winding round this valley, and continuing to rise, the stream in its centre is crossed about midway, and the ascent continues on the spur which forms its western boundary. This ridge is crossed close to the point where it is given off by the main range, and the road, winding round its most projecting part, enters a fir-wood, and, turning back very abruptly in an opposite direction, proceeds eastward along the northern face of the Kussowlee range.

The plainward face of this range, along which the road from Kalka ascends, is quite devoid of forest. The lower part is covered with scattered jungle, to use a most expressive Indian word, of small shrubs, almost all of forms common in the plains. *Carissa* and *Adhatoda* are the most common, with *Rottlera tinctoria*, a plant which does not extend far into the plains, and a scandent leguminous shrub, apparently a species of *Mucuna*. Around the few houses which occur on the ascent, the bamboo occurs planted, as well as the mango, and other common cultivated trees of the Indian plains. At an elevation of about 4000 feet, an alteration in the vegetation begins to be perceptible. The thin jungle of plain shrubs disappears, the few shrubs which still occur, are generally scattered bushes of *Hamiltonia, Nyctanthes, Prinsepia, Scutellaria,* and *Rubus*, but the slopes are usually bare and grassy. Ferns and mosses appear in the crevices of the rocks, and the first individuals of those species which predominate in the temperate zone, are found in shady spots where they are sheltered from the sun. At the same elevation *Euphorbia pentagona* makes its appearance. This tree, which is confined to the hottest and driest slopes of the Himalaya, is remarkable for its peculiar shape, its thick fleshy five-angled branches, and its milky juice. It is nowhere to be met with in the plains of

Upper India, but is common throughout the subtropical belt of the Himalaya from Kamaon westward.

A glance at the map will serve to show that the great Himalayan mountain range, dividing the waters of the Sutlej from those of the Jumna, holds a nearly due east and west course in its middle part, but that at its western extremity it bends round to the south, and terminates in the Indian plain, not far from the town of Nahan, and that (among many others) the Kussowlee ridge is a branch from it, running in a north-westerly direction, and separating the waters of the more western branch of the Gambar, from the small tributaries of the Gagar, which find their way to the plains on the left hand.

The ridge upon which the station of Kussowlee is built, nowhere attains an elevation exceeding 7000 feet. It is very narrow, and often rocky and precipitous immediately below the crest on the plainward face, which dips very suddenly. The inner slope is somewhat less abrupt, and is covered from the summit to perhaps 1000 feet below it, with an open forest of a species of fir (*Pinus longifolia*), which, in general appearance and mode of growth, much resembles the Scotch fir, but is distinguished by the very great length of its leaves. The barracks for the troops and the houses of the residents are scattered over the northern slope, or perched on the narrow summit of the ridge.

The shrubby and herbaceous vegetation which occurs scattered among the fir-wood, is so markedly different from that which prevails at the base of the mountains, and during the greater part of the ascent, that the traveller appears suddenly transported into a new world.

Instead of those tribes of the vegetable kingdom which abound in the torrid zone, all the forms which now meet the eye are characteristic of a temperate climate. The moderate elevation of the range, and its proximity to the plains, tend to lessen the rapidity of the diminution of temperature; and as the greater part of the ascent lies on a bare sunny slope, the tropical flora extends towards the summit, much farther than it does on ranges which rise higher, and are clothed with shady forest. During the ascent, therefore, the traveller, though often struck with the appearance of new forms, is still accompanied by many species familiar to him as natives of tropical jungles, but on passing to the northern face of the spur, the temperate region is at once entered, and most of the tropical forms disappear.

As soon as the crest of the first slope of the Himalaya has been gained, the eye is naturally directed towards the mountains beyond, in order to ascertain their appearance and position, when viewed at a diminished distance and from so much more considerable an elevation than had previously been the case. Nor will the view from Kussowlee in favourable weather disappoint the traveller who is desirous of meeting with beautiful scenery. Immediately to the north lies a deep ravine, and beyond a single ridge is the wide valley of the Gambar, with numerous mountain spurs, which, from their comparatively lower level, are not prominently brought into view. To the south-east the main range dips abruptly to a level, nearly 1000 feet below what it attains in the station of Kussowlee itself, but again rises into the finely wooded hill on which has recently been built the Lawrence

Asylum. Still further to the south are deep dells, with bare and rugged slaty mountains, scarcely at all wooded. In the months of May and June, when the atmosphere is generally extremely hazy, the prospect is limited to the ranges more immediately in the vicinity; but occasionally even in these months, as well as in the dry intervals of the rainy season, and during the delightful autumn weather which follows the termination of the rains, a much more distant prospect is opened, stretching far up the valley of the Sutlej, to the snow-clad peaks which, on either hand, hem in that river.

In the direction of the plains of India, the view is also very remarkable. The Kussowlee ridge so completely overtops the hills which intervene between it and the level country, that from its summit they interfere very little with the commanding view of the interminable flat which, like the ocean, stretches as far as vision extends. In the usual state of the atmosphere, especially in the hot season, a dense haze overhangs the plains, and entirely obscures their more distant parts; but in the cold season, as well as at day-break in summer, and especially after heavy rains, the misty vapours are entirely dissipated, and distant objects are defined with extreme precision.

Perhaps the most striking, because the most unexpected part of the view of the inner Ḥimalaya, from Kussowlee, lies in the great depth of the valleys in the interior, and the distance of the next elevated range, of which the appearance of the mountains from the plains of India affords no indication. The extreme narrowness of the ridge, and the suddenness of the descent on both sides, is also very remarkable, and has, as already remarked, a very sensible effect on the climate, the heat of the lower mass being conveyed upwards, while the small extent of the knife-edge-like ridge, which rises above 6000 feet, exposes a minimum surface to the refrigerating influences of a rarefied atmosphere.

The distance from Kussowlee to Simla is by the road about thirty miles, though in a direct line the two places are not much more than half that distance apart. The road descends from Kussowlee almost to the level of the plains, crossing the Gambar at an elevation of a little less than 3000 feet, and ascends to Simla by following the ridge which runs parallel to that river on its right bank, the source of the Gambar being immediately below Simla. It would indeed be possible to reach Simla, by following the crest of the ridge, without descending at all into the valley of the river; but for this purpose it would be necessary to follow the Kussowlee ridge so far to the southward, in order to reach its junction with the main range, that the length of the journey would be very much greater than that now followed. The road, therefore, only keeps the ridge for a very short distance, or as far as the "col," or lower part immediately north of Kussowlee, which is quite bare of trees. It then turns abruptly to the left, descending on the north face of a spur, at first in a winding manner, afterwards for a short distance along a shady ravine, and finally through a good deal of cultivation, at an elevation of between 4000 and 5000 feet, to a considerable stream which runs towards the north to join the Gambar. The greatest part of the descent is bare of trees, except along the banks of the little stream, which are covered with a belt of wood. The cultivated lands are extensive, occupying a flattish terraced slope, such as is of very general occurrence in the mountains, the fields being adapted for the growth of rain crops, principally of rice, with a few fields of ginger and cardamoms.

After reaching the stream just mentioned, which is crossed by a ford, a suspension bridge, for which the piers are partly built, having never been erected, the road continues to descend parallel to it towards the north, passing under the military station of Sabathu, which, at the elevation of 4200 feet, occupies the crest of the ridge immediately to the east of the little river, a very short distance before its junction with the Gambar.

After passing Sabathu the road turns to the right, round the projecting ridge of the range, and descends rapidly to the valley of the Gambar river, which is crossed by a good suspension bridge at an elevation of 2700 feet above the level of the sea. It then ascends by a steep and laborious path to Haripur, a small village about 500 feet above the bed of the river. The Gambar river, where the road crosses it, flows through a narrow rocky ravine, somewhat picturesque, but quite devoid of trees. This, however, is not the general character of the river-bed, which is frequently wide, with a broad gravelly channel, and sloping though often rather steep mountains on either side. There is occasionally even a strip of flat land, capable of cultivation along the banks; and where such is the case, the water of the river is carried off in artificial channels, for the purpose of irrigation.

After attaining the crest of the ridge, and passing through the village of Haripur, the road follows the ridge parallel to the river Gambar, nearly all the way to Simla, not always on the very crest or top, which would entail a great many unnecessary ascents and descents, but generally a little on one side or other of the hill, as circumstances may render most convenient; at one time ascending rather steeply, but more generally rather gently as far as Sairi, the last stage on the way to Simla, beyond which the road is pretty level, nearly to the bottom of the mountain on which Simla stands.

The valley of the river Gambar may be regarded as an excellent specimen of a smaller Himalayan river, draining a large extent of country, and discharging its waters independently into the plains, though not, like the first-class rivers, deriving its origin from the snowy mountains. The southern border of the basin of the Gambar, is of course the main chain of the South Sutlej Himalaya; and the whole of the country between the Jutog spur, which leaves that chain at Simla, and the Kussowlee ridge, the origin of which I have already detailed, is drained by the Gambar and its tributaries. This includes an extent of country of not less than 1000 square miles, the bounding ranges of which have, throughout the greater part of their extent, an elevation varying from 8000 to about 6000 feet. Both the Kussowlee and Jutog ranges dip at last rather abruptly, so that it is only during a very short distance that they are below the last-mentioned elevation. This elevation, which is quite temperate, is however by no means that of the whole superficies of the basin, the bed of the river having, at its *débouchure* into the Sutlej, an elevation of not more than 2000 feet, and rising very gently till near its source immediately below Simla. The lateral ridges, which traverse the basin in every direction, are in general less elevated; not exceeding 5000 feet in their upper part, and sinking to 3000 or even lower, so that the mean elevation of the whole basin cannot be estimated, I should think, higher than 3500 feet.

Such being the case, it is not surprising that the general appearance of the vegetation should be tropical, and closely approximate to that of the low hills on the very exterior of the Himalaya. This is in general the case. The hills, which are generally grassy, and, though steep and frequently stony, rarely rocky or precipitous, are quite devoid of forest, or even brushwood, except in a few shady nooks with a northern exposure, and favourably situated with respect to moisture; the shrubby vegetation being thin and scattered. This total want of forest, is unquestionably caused by the dryness of the climate during the greater part of the year, which is to a certain degree increased beyond what it would otherwise be, by the proximity of the surrounding mountain ranges, to which a large proportion of the rain-clouds are no doubt attracted.

In the shady ravines north of Kussowlee, where there is the greatest approach to forest, a species of laurel is the most conspicuous tree. On the more exposed hills, *Falconeria insignis* and *Euphorbia pentagona* occur, scattered as small trees, and one small wood of *Ægle marmelos* is passed close to the village of Haripur. The most common shrubs are *Adhatoda Vasica, Carissa,* and *Zizyphus Jujuba*, species universal in the plains of upper India; *Colebrookea oppositifolia*, *Grislea*, *Bergera*, *Roylea* and *Bœhmeria nivea*, all species which are throughout the north-west Himalaya, characteristic of the lower and drier parts of the outer ranges. Two Labiate shrubs, *Plectranthus rugosus* and *Meriandra strobilifera*, are particularly abundant on the slopes between Haripur and Sairi, and strongly mark the aridity of the climate.

The herbaceous vegetation, being principally of annual growth, approaches still more closely to the plains types. At the season of my journey in May, the extreme drought had dried up almost all the smaller plants, but during, and immediately after the rainy season the herbage is very luxuriant. The steep slopes are then covered with a uniform herbage of tall grasses, which is in many places cut and preserved for hay, by the inhabitants of the scattered villages in the valleys. The most prevailing grasses are a tall sweet-scented *Cymbopogon* and *Heteropogon contortus*. A species of *Kalanchoë*, a large and conspicuous plant, with thick fleshy leaves, is very common, and the superb *Gloriosa* or *Methonica* is by no means rare.

On the highest ridges in the valley, at elevations of 5000 feet and upwards, there are frequent approaches to the temperate flora, the shady slopes on northern exposures being frequently covered with small patches of brushwood, containing species of *Berberis*, *Rubus*, *Spiræa*, etc., and numerous herbaceous species, of forms common at Simla. These, however, are quite exceptional, though no doubt with a very little more humidity the shrubby vegetation would rapidly extend, and under its shelter many small plants would be able to grow, which are now, when they attempt to vegetate, destroyed by the scorching heat of the sun.

It must also not be forgotten, that notwithstanding the general tendency to a tropical flora, the natural result of the low elevation and great aridity of these hills, a portion of the vegetation even at the lowest levels consists of plants of European forms, such as characterize the temperate vegetation of the Himalaya. I do not here refer to what may be called the cold-weather vegetation of the plains of north-western India, at which season, the temperature of the air approaching to that of the summer of the temperate zone, a considerable number of European plants make their appearance in corn-fields and along the banks of water-courses; as, for example, *Veronica Anagallis* and *agrestis*, *Anagallis*, *Medicago*, *Melilotus*, *Potentilla supina*, *Juncus bufonius*, *Arenaria serpyllifolia*, *Heliotropium Europæum*, and many others. These naturally occur at the same season, in the low valleys among the hills, in similar situations. The circumstance to which I desire to advert, is the occurrence at very low levels among the mountains, during the hot and rainy seasons, of species belonging to genera characteristic of temperate climates, and which therefore are the prevailing forms at considerable elevations on the Himalaya. As instances, I may adduce the occurrence in the valley of the Gambar, at elevations not exceeding 3000 feet, of species of *Thalictrum*, *Fragaria*, *Rosa*, *Rubus*, *Berberis*, &c., &c. This remarkable fact has been ascribed by Jacquemont* to the obscure influence of the mountains; and as the genera just enumerated never

* Voyage, etc., vol. ii. p. 6.

occur in the plains of Upper India, it appears evident that the mountainous nature of the country must be viewed as an essential element in the reasons for their descent. These, with some others which also occur at low levels in the Himalaya, appear to be in all parts of the continent of India those genera of temperate climates, which descend to the lowest altitudes. Some of them were found by Dr. Hooker on Parasnâth, a hill in upper Behar, the elevation of which does not exceed 4000 feet; and they are all natives of moderate elevations on the Nilgherries and in Ceylon, as well as on the Khasya mountains in eastern Bengal.

The ridge which runs from Haripur to Sairi, parallel to the river Gambar, is a branch from the Jutog spur, nearly north of Simla, a ridge which is given off by the main South Sutlej chain in Simla itself, and which runs directly north to the Sutlej river. The road, after following this ridge till within a few miles of Simla, leaves it on the left hand, to descend into a small stony ravine; after crossing which it mounts abruptly a very steep spur, ascending at least 1500 feet to gain the crest of the ridge, and enter Simla at its north-western extremity.

The hill station of Simla, which was originally selected as a sanatarium, or suitable residence for the servants of Government, or other Europeans, whose health had been impaired by disease, or by too long residence in a tropical climate, has of late years, in consequence of the political state of north-western India, and of the increasing number of retired officers, and of gentlemen unconnected with the public service, who have made it their residence, become a place of great importance. Besides an extensive bazaar or collection of shops, which may now almost be designated a small native town, Simla contains nearly 400 houses, scattered along the crest of different mountain ranges. Its situation is a most favourable one, on the main range of mountains south of the Sutlej river, at a point where a massive peak rises to a height of 8100 feet, and on the nearest part of the ridge to the plains of India, which is sufficiently elevated, well wooded, and situated favourably with regard to water. The greater part of the station is built on the main range, partly surrounding the peak of Jako, and partly on the ridge running north from it, at an elevation of about 7000 feet, as far as a smaller culminating point of the range, which is by the inhabitants named Prospect Point. At this point the main range turns sharply to the west, and the station is continued for nearly a mile on a spur which runs towards the north, passing through the station of Jutog. From the scattered position of the houses, the extent of Simla is much more considerable than the bare statement of the number of houses might lead one to suppose. The northern ridge extends almost four miles, and the circuit of Jako, by the principal road, which is from 500 to 1000 feet below the summit, measures five miles.

In consequence of the sudden elevation of the mountain range at the place where Simla has been built, there is a most complete and surprising change in the vegetation and general appearance of the scenery. During the last ascent on the road from the plains this is sufficiently perceptible, although from the great ravages which the proximity of so large a population has made in the oak woods, only a few stunted bushes are now left on the southern exposure. Between the plains and Simla the hills are totally devoid of trees, but immediately on gaining the top of the ridge on which the station is built, we enter a fine forest, which covers all the broader parts of the range, especially the slopes which have a northern aspect, stretching down on these in many places to the bottom of the valleys, fully 2000 feet.

The nature of the forest varies a good deal with the exposure and with the quality of the soil. By far the greater part consists of an oak and a rhododendron, both small evergreen trees, rarely exceeding thirty or forty feet, with wide-spreading arms and rugged twisted branches. A species of *Andromeda* is also very common, and a holly, an *Euonymus*, *Rhamnus*, and *Benthamia*, are the other more common trees, if we except the *Coniferæ*, of which four species occur. Of these, *Pinus longifolia* is common at the western or lower extremity of the station, and prevails, to the exclusion of any other tree, on the dry sunny spurs which run towards the south, at elevations from 7000 to 5000 feet. This species is, of all the Indian pines known to me (except its near ally *P. Khasyana*), that which is capable of enduring the most heat, and at the same time the greatest variation in amount of moisture; as it is found at elevations of not more than 1000 feet above the level of the sea, equally in the hot humid valleys of Sikkim, where it enjoys a perpetual vapour-bath, and on the dry sandstone hills of the upper Punjab, on which rain hardly ever falls. It is only, however, at low elevations, where the mean temperature is high, that it is capable of supporting a great amount of humidity, for in the damp climates of the Himalaya it is entirely wanting, except in the deepest valleys; and even in the drier districts it is always observed to select the sunnier, and therefore warmer exposures. Its upper limit is usually about 7000 feet above the level of the sea, though on Jako at Simla a few stunted trees rise as high as 7700 feet.

Pinus excelsa is also a very common species at Simla, particularly on the southern face of Mount Jako, which is the highest part of the ridge. *Abies Smithiana*, the third coniferous tree, is exceedingly rare, a few trees only occurring in a shady ravine facing the west; while the deodar, the fourth species, is common on the southern and western slopes of Jako, above 7000 feet; and again in shady groves at the bottom of the valleys on both sides of the ridge, as low as 5000 feet. This beautiful tree, the cedar of the Indian mountains, seems limited to the western half of the Himalayan range, extending from the most westerly part of Nipal, as far as the mountains of Affghanistan. It was first described by Roxburgh from specimens sent to him from Kamaon, at a time when the western Himalaya was almost inaccessible to Europeans, under the name by which it is known to the inhabitants of that province, as well as in Kashmir. It is, however, singularly enough, not known by that name in the Simla hills, where it is called *Kēlu;* another conifer, *Cupressus torulosa*, a rare tree in the district, having usurped the name, as well as the sacred character, of deodar.

In the thick woods of Simla, a large white monkey, the *Langúr* of the natives, is very common. These animals move about in large flocks, in which may be seen individuals of all sizes and ages, and seldom remain more than a few hours in one place. They are in constant motion, leaping from bough to bough and from tree to tree, chattering constantly; and, notwithstanding their great size, are in general harmless, though ready enough to defend themselves if assailed.

The forest extends in parts close up to the peak of Jako, which has an elevation of 8130 feet. The very summit, however, which is a short flat ridge, and a considerable part of the east and south face, are bare and grassy, or covered with scattered shrubs. The more common shrubby forms of the vegetation of the temperate zone, are *Salix*, *Rosa*, *Rubus*, *Lonicera*, *Viburnum*, *Berberis*, *Indigofera*, and *Prinsepia*, all, except the two last, quite European. *Indigofera* forms a remarkable exception, and one well worthy of note, as the genus is a very tropical one, although its shrubby species are particularly abundant throughout the whole of the western Himalaya. These shrubby species, however, constitute a particular section of the genus, very distinct in habit, and in the large size and bright colour of the flower, from the more ordinary forms, and they are confined to the drier parts of the mountains, being quite wanting in the humid climate of Darjeeling and Khasya, and almost entirely so in the mountains of the Peninsula.

The herbaceous vegetation of the spring months quite corresponds, in the temperate nature of its forms, with what has been found to be the case with the trees and shrubs; but during the rainy season, as has been well pointed out by Dr. Royle in his valuable essay on the distribution of Himalayan plants, this is much less markedly the case. At the commencement of spring, in April (for March is still too cold for much vegetation), the weather being generally bright, though with occasional heavy showers, the earliest flowers are species of *Viola*, *Fragaria*, *Geranium*, *Veronica*, *Valeriana*, and dandelion. From April, as summer advances, the temperature gradually rises, till towards the end of June, when the rainy season commences. These months are generally dry, and if no rain falls the heat is sometimes considerable, the thermometer rising as high as 80° in the shade. Still the flora is almost entirely temperate, the early spring plants being succeeded by many others of European families, principally *Ranunculaceæ*, *Rosaceæ*, *Labiatæ*, *Stellatæ*, *Polygonaceæ*, *Epilobiaceæ*, *Primulaceæ*, etc. I can scarcely enumerate a single spring flowering plant which does not belong to an European family, unless *Arum* be an exception, which it can hardly be considered, the flowers only being displayed during May and June, while the leaves do not make their appearance until after the rainy season has commenced. Few species are, however, identical with those of Europe, except *Stellaria media*, *Cerastium vulgatum*, *Taraxacum officinale*, *Verbascum Thapsus*, *Thymus Serpyllum*, and *Poa annua*.

The rainy season generally commences about the 20th of June, or between that date and the end of the month, and continues till the middle or end of September, with occasional intermissions, rarely exceeding a week at a time. During the rains the atmosphere is exceedingly moist, dense fogs usually prevailing when rain does not fall. The rain-fall is probably more considerable at

Simla than in the lower ranges, which are nearer the plains, for it has been observed that ranges of 7–8000 feet (which are generally for this reason well wooded), attract much moisture, and the peak of Jako and other parts of Simla are frequently observed from the stations of Sabathu and Kussowlee, to be covered with dense clouds or mist, at times when at the latter places the weather is bright and clear.

The commencement of the rainy season is the signal in the mountains, as it is very universally throughout India, wherever that season is well marked, for the appearance of a very vigorous and luxuriant growth of plants of annual growth, the seeds (or rootstocks) of which had been lying dormant in the soil awaiting the access of heavy rain. At Simla, as elsewhere in the temperate region of the Himalaya, we find at this season numerous species of Balsams, *Acanthaceæ, Orchideæ,* and *Labiatæ,* several Gentians and *Cichoraceæ,* a great many grasses and *Cyperaceæ,* and species of *Parnassia, Drosera, Pedicularis, Roscoea, Dipsacus, Thalictrum, Urtica,* etc., etc. Some of these are quite European genera, while others, as *Roscoea,* are interesting as belonging to orders whose maxima occur in very humid climates. The *Labiatæ* of the rainy season are mostly species of *Plectranthus* and *Elsholtzia,* both quite Indian genera, and very extensively distributed in mountainous districts. Balsams are quite an Indian order, and they seem everywhere, as has already been remarked by Dr. Royle and by Dr. Wight, to abound in humid shady places, either in dense forest or on the stony banks of mountain streams, in the drier districts only during the rainy season, but in more humid countries more or less throughout the year. The *Orchideæ* of Simla are entirely terrestrial, the dryness and cold of the winter months being greater than are compatible with the occurrence of epiphytical species of this natural order, and for the same reason, I presume, *Melastomaceæ*, so abundant in the Eastern Himalaya, are quite wanting.

Among the many advantages of situation by which Simla is characterized, one of the most fortunate is its position on a part of the mountain range which lies transversely to the ordinary direction of the chain, so that the view towards the plains of India, as well as up the Sutlej valley, is very much more extensive than would be obtained, had the station been situated in a less favourable position. This advantage is further enhanced by the sudden rise in elevation of the chain, which enables a resident at Simla to overlook in the direction of the plains the continuation of the range which would otherwise obstruct the view. Towards the interior of the mountains, this advantage is not possessed by Simla; for the ridge of Mahasu, which rises 1000 feet higher than the peak of Jako, obscures at least half of the snowy range, the view being limited in that direction to the course of the valley of the Sutlej, and to the mountains north of that river.

With all these advantages of situation, the view from the peak of Jako is one of the most agreeable and diversified, which occur in any part of the Himalaya; although, from the rather too level top of the mountain, and the intrusion of the forest almost to the very summit, the whole panorama cannot be embraced at once. Immediately under the eye are the numerous spurs and ridges covered with scattered houses, and the deep ravines which terminate the steep slopes below the station; towards the plains, the whole valley of the Gambar is seen, with the stations of Sabathu and Kussowlee, the church and esplanade of the former appearing low down almost within a stone's throw, while the brilliant white of the houses of Kussowlee, more nearly on a level with the eye, sparkle in the sunbeams. The ridge of Kussowlee in one place excludes the view of the plains, but to the right they may be seen stretching away in the distance, and only recognizable at last by the track of the Sutlej river, which, from the very remarkable curve close to its exit from the mountains, may be traced as far as vision can extend, a distance of 116 miles*. To the north a valley stretches from Simla as far as the Sutlej river, distant about fifteen miles, so direct that the greater part of it is seen, though the river itself is concealed. East of north a long partially wooded ridge, about four miles distant at its nearest point, running parallel to the valley just mentioned, excludes the view of the nearer part of the Sutlej valley; but the lofty ranges north of that river, covered with dense forest, and backed by masses of brilliant snow, close in the view in that direction. Due east lies the Mahasu ridge, covered on the Simla slopes with a dense forest of deodar; and to the south, across the valley of the Giri, towards which numerous rugged ridges run, is the mountain called the Chor, the highest peak of the range which separates the Giri

* In this I allow 800 feet for the height of Loodiana above the level of the sea.

from the Tons, the crest of which is upwards of 12,000 feet in height.

From the peak of Jako, the serpentine course of the range, which prevails universally throughout the Himalaya, may be well traced, as the eye of the spectator, following the direct course of the ridge, can observe numerous turns in its course, each of which, from the great foreshortening, appears much more abrupt than it really is. At each curve the range rises into a peak, while the intermediate portions are lower and excavated into "cols" or passes. In the concavity of each bend of the range is situated the head of a valley, numerous small spurs dividing the different ravines which unite to form it; while on the convex side, from the high portion of the ridge, is given off a branch of the range, forming a separation between two adjacent valleys, each of which occupies a concavity in the main range of mountain.

On my arrival at Simla on the 25th of May, I found that Major A. Cunningham, of the Bengal Engineers, and Captain Henry Strachey, of the 66th Regiment N.I., were to be my fellow-travellers, the former having been appointed the head of the mission. As Captain Strachey had to travel from Dinapore, it was evident that some time would elapse before he would arrive at Simla, nor was it till the beginning of August that the completion of the necessary preliminaries rendered it possible for us to commence our journey. I took advantage of this delay to make myself as far as possible acquainted with the physical features and vegetation of the surrounding country, though the necessary preparations for the approaching journey occupied a good deal of time, and the commencement of the rainy season rendered travelling difficult, and even out-of-door exercise unpleasant. I have already attempted to convey an idea of the general physical aspect of the scenery, which, after a short residence has made one familiar with the structure of the ridges, appears very simple. Situated on the dividing range, by which the waters of the Giri, a tributary of the Jumna, on the left, are separated from those of the tributaries of the Sutlej on the right, the spectator looks into two of the immense basins into which the Himalaya is divided by transverse ranges running parallel to the great rivers; and after a short time he finds that the chaos of mountains, which at first perplexed the eye and confused the mind, gradually resolves itself into a definite shape, each ridge being capable of being referred to its parent, and that in its turn to a branch of the main chain. From his commanding position he can also see that the main range is generally more elevated than its branches, and that each chain, by a succession of sudden sinkings, diminishes in elevation, each peak being lower than its predecessor. Nowhere in the wide tract of country visible is there the least approach to a system of parallel ridges, such as is indicated by the distant view of these mountains. On the contrary, it is seen that the great ranges are, though very irregularly, perpendicular to the general direction of the mountain mass, and that it is only the shorter spurs which have a general uniformity of direction.

Nor could I find in the structure of the mountains around Simla any confirmation of the view entertained by Humboldt of the sudden elevation of the Himalaya out of a vast fissure in the external crust of the earth.

However plausible such a view might appear when the Himalaya is contemplated as a whole (on a map), without any portion of its extent being under the eye, I found it, on the spot, quite impossible to conceive in what way, after such a sudden elevation, any power in the least analogous to existing forces could have excavated out of the solid rock those numerous valleys, so various in direction, so rugged in outline, and so vast in dimensions, which now furrow the mountain mass.

On the contrary, the conclusion has been forced upon me that these mountains have emerged extremely gradually from an ocean, of the existence of which, at very various levels, the most evident traces are, I think, discoverable. The present configuration of the surface must, I do not doubt, have been given to it during periods of rest, or of very slow elevation, the action of the sea upon submerged rocks being so very superficial that no denudation takes place at any great depth. During the period of emergence of the Himalaya, from the great length of the present valleys, which extend between parallel ranges far into the interior, the coast must have borne a strong resemblance to that of Norway at the present day, numerous promontories projecting far into the sea, and separated from one another by narrow and deep bays.

The geological structure of the Himalaya between Simla and the plains is not easily discovered by the cursory observer. The general basis of the mountains is clay-slate, occasionally very micaceous, passing into a coarse sandstone, but here and there limestone occurs interstratified. The dip is extremely variable, and the rocks, whatever their age, are evidently highly metamorphosed. The tertiary formations, so well illustrated by Falconer and Cautley, extend all along the base of the mountains, and penetrate in some places far into the valleys, for certain rocks in the neighbourhood of Sabathu have been indicated by Major Vicary, which appear to be of the same age, or perhaps of a still older tertiary epoch.

CHAPTER II.

Leave Simla—Mahasu Ridge—Pine Forest—Summit of Mahasu—Vegetation of Northern Slope—Fagu—Theog—Mattiana—Cultivated Valley—Nagkanda—Ascent of Hattu—Forest of Pine and Oak—Vegetation of Summit—View from top of Mountain—Plainward slopes bare of forest, while those facing the interior are well wooded—Cultivation at 9500 feet—Descent from Nagkanda towards Sutlej—Damp shady Ravine densely wooded—Kotgarh—Cultivation—Rapid Descent—Change of Climate—Tropical Vegetation—Rampur—Swing-bridge—Diurnal fluctuations in level of River—Gaora—Serahan—Tranda—Western boundary of Kunawar.

On the 2nd of August, 1847, every necessary preparation having been completed, and the officers of the mission having received the instructions of the Governor-General to proceed to Ladakh, and thence to take severally such direction as they should consider most conducive to the increase of our knowledge of these countries, Major Cunningham, Captain Strachey, and myself left Simla.

The route selected as most eligible, in order to reach Hangarang and Piti, to which we had been instructed in the first place to proceed, lay up the course of the Sutlej river, through Kunawar. The advanced period of the season, at which almost constant rain might be expected, rendered the river route, on which at most stages tolerable shelter is obtainable, preferable to that by the Pabar valley, and the Bruang (or Borendo) pass, which otherwise we should have preferred, from its passing through a more elevated tract of country.

From Simla the first day's journey towards the interior of the mountains is usually to Fagu, a distance of fourteen miles. Here, and for several stages farther, as far as the road lies through British territory, there are houses (bungalows, as they are termed in India) provided by Government for the accommodation of travellers, upon the payment of a small fixed sum per diem. Though often in bad repair, and therefore very uncomfortable in rainy weather, these houses (which occur also between Simla and the plains) are a very great convenience, as they enable tourists to dispense with the carriage of tents.

The difficulty of making a start, from the small number of porters procurable for our baggage, was so great that it was some time after dark before I reached the Fagu bungalow, in the midst of an extremely heavy fall of rain, which had commenced about sunset, after a fair though lowering day. The road from Simla to Fagu follows throughout the course of the main range, not always on the very crest of the ridge, but seldom at any great distance from it. After passing round the peak of Jako, it turns northward, and descends abruptly about 500 feet, to a low part of the ridge, elevated about 6800 feet, and quite bare of trees, the micaceous slaty rock being in many places exposed. The ridge continues in direction for nearly four miles, varying very little in level, only one short and rather steep ascent occurring to a peak where a spur branches off to the south, beyond which the road again slightly descends. About half-a-mile to the north of this little ridge, on the slope of the hill below the road, there is a small cluster of trees of *Cupressus torulosa*, a species of cypress, one of the rarer conifers of the Himalaya; the most favourite situation of which seems to be on very steep mountains in the interior, at elevations of from seven to nine thousand feet. It was found abundantly by Major Madden* on Shali, a peak twenty miles east of Simla, and it appears to extend thence west as far as Simla, where it occurs in several places on hot, dry, and very bare rocky hills, as low as six thousand feet.

About four miles from Simla, a sudden increase in the elevation of the range takes place, and at the same time it turns abruptly towards the south-east. The road ascends the steep face of the ridge, in a series of zigzags, rather steeply, with a deep ravine on either hand, that to the right bare, while on the left there is first a thicket of rose and willow bushes, and further on an oak-wood, of a species (*Quercus floribunda* of Wallich) different from that common at Simla, and indicative of greater elevation, though here growing with *Rhododendron* and *Andromeda*, common Simla trees. When near the top of the ascent, the road bends rapidly to the right, keeping on the south face of the ridge, and passing under but close to a small house, built on the very crest of the ridge, at an elevation of about 8000 feet. Close to this bungalow, which occupies a most excellent site, forest commences, and the

* Journal of Agr. Hort. Soc. Calc. vol. iv.

road runs for a mile through fine trees of deodar and spruce (*Abies Smithiana*), generally on the very crest of the ridge, looking down towards the east into a deep and broad valley. Right across this valley, north-east, rises the remarkable peak of Shali, a bold rocky mass sloping gently to the south, while to the north, which seems to overhang the Sutlej valley, it is cut off very abruptly. This highly beautiful mountain, the termination of a northerly spur, given off close to Mattiana, is hardly visible from Simla, its top only being seen from some of the more northerly houses.

From an elevation of about 8000 feet at its north-west end, the Mahasu ridge rises, at first gradually, to at least 9000 feet, and as it is throughout well wooded, the road along it is extremely beautiful. On the earlier part of the ridge, the forest consists chiefly of pine, *P. excelsa* and *Abies Smithiana* being abundant, and more especially the deodar, which, on the slope facing the west, may be seen in the greatest profusion, thousands of young trees springing up in dense masses, on the slopes which have been bared by the axe, or still more destructively by the fires of the hill-men.

After about five miles of what, in the Himalaya, may be called tolerably level road, another sudden ascent follows, the road inclining rather to the northern slope of the mountain, and entering a dense forest of large massive pines, intermixed with two species of sycamore, and a fine cherry, which relieve the otherwise too gloomy foliage of the coniferous trees. A magnificent climbing vine, which attaches itself to the tallest trees, rising in light green coils round their trunks, and falling in graceful festoons from the branches high over head, adds much to the elegance of the scene, and renders it, in the expressive words of Griffith, who was familiar with the rich vegetation of the humid forests of the Eastern Himalaya, the only true Himalayan forest of the western mountains.

On this ascent the road rises to about 9000 feet, the crest of the Mahasu ridge being, according to Captain Herbert, 9200 feet. The large size and dense shade of the trees, and the abundance of *Abies Smithiana*, of the sycamore, and of the gigantic vine, give the forest a totally different appearance from that of Simla, and the undergrowth presents also a considerable amount of novelty; a species of currant, a fine *Spiræa*, *Indigofera atropurpurea*, and fine species of *Rosa* and *Rubus*, forming thickets under the tall trees. This forest, indeed, from its dense shade, and great humidity, exhibits a much greater contrast to the ordinary temperate vegetation of the Himalaya, than is usually observed below 9000 feet, at which elevation the upper temperate, or subalpine vegetation, begins fairly to predominate over that which is prevalent from 5000 to 9000 feet.

On reaching the summit of the steep ascent, the road again gains the crest of the ridge, which consists of a succession of rounded knolls, covered with grass, and quite bare of trees, the forest rising almost, but not quite, to the top. On the very summit of one of the first of these knolls, is a small wooden shrine or temple, of a form common in the hills; the top of a mountain, or the summit of any very steep ascent, being usually selected as a proper spot for the erection of a sacred building by Indian mountaineers, in whose superstition every hill and grove is tenanted by supernatural beings.

The steep ascent on the northern shoulder of Mahasu, from 8000 feet, and even lower, to above 9000 feet, is the great seat of the potato cultivation in the neighbourhood of Simla. The steepest slopes seem to be preferred for this purpose, if they have only a sufficiency of soil, which is very light, loose, and stony. The undergrowth of shrubs is cleared away entirely on the spot where potatoes are planted, but the pine forest is only partially thinned, the tall straight trunks allowing of a free circulation of air below, while the thick branches above afford the amount of shade requisite for the crop. The potatoes are planted in rows in May; and, early in June, when the plants have attained a height of a few inches, the soil is earthed up round their stems in low ridges. The rains commence in the latter part of June, and during their continuance nothing is done to the crop, beyond keeping it clear of weeds. The steepness of the slope seems to afford a sufficient drainage to prevent any injury from the great rain-fall and constant humidity. The growth of the plants is exceedingly luxuriant, the foliage being tall and bushy. By the middle of October, or after the close of the rains, the potatoes are dug and ready for market, supplying not only the station of Simla, but being despatched in great quantities to the plains of India, where the potato is only cultivated as a winter crop, and where, therefore, during the cold months, none are otherwise procurable.

On the very summit of the Mahasu ridge, there are a

few trees of *Quercus semicarpifolia*, the alpine oak of the western Himalaya, an European-looking and partially deciduous species, and of *Picea Webbiana*, or *Pindrow*, the silver fir of the Indian mountains, a dark sombre-looking pine, abundant in the forests of the interior. These trees may be adopted as the characteristics of the subalpine zone, in every part of which, from 9000 to about 12,000 feet, which is the highest limit of tree vegetation in the Western Himalaya, they abound. On Mahasu they are entirely confined to the crest of the ridge, and form no part of the forest below.

The descent from the top of Mahasu to the Fagu bungalow, is at first abrupt, the road leaving the ridge to enter the forest on the northern face, and winding down, after a few hundred yards of bare stony slope, among dense forest, among which it continues for a couple of miles, rising at last rather steeply to the crest of the ridge at the point where it resumes a northerly direction. Here the bungalow of Fagu has been built, at an elevation of 8200 feet, at the very base of the steep mountain ridge behind, which rises abruptly, to a height of six or seven hundred feet. The bungalow faces the north-east, and commands a most superb view of the snowy range beyond the Sutlej, with occasional glimpses of the Jumno-Gangetic snows on the right hand.

On my arrival at Fagu, in the midst of a pelting fall of rain, I found the bungalow already occupied by my fellow-travellers, and before a bright and comfortable fire I soon forgot the discomfort of my wet ride, which indeed was not to be complained of, as it was only what might fairly have been expected in the middle of the rainy season. The confusion among our baggage, however, was so great, from its arriving irregularly and being set down hurriedly by the drenched porters, anxious to escape as soon as possible to shelter, that it was not without difficulty I procured the necessary change of clothing.

The morning of the 3rd of August was densely foggy, but without rain, and it was unanimously decided that it would be advisable to push on to the next stage, Mattiana, a distance of fifteen miles. Our anticipations of fair weather were unfortunately disappointed, for it began to rain heavily before ten o'clock, and continued to do so with little intermission till nearly two, when it cleared, and the remainder of the day was fine.

The whole day's journey lay along the ridge, which scarcely fell below 7500 feet, and nowhere rose above 9000 feet. Fagu is situated immediately above the valley of the river Giri, a large mountain stream, the most western tributary of the Jumna. A road across the Jumnetic valleys to Massuri descends abruptly towards that river, descending more than 5000 feet in little more than five miles, and crossing the river by a bridge at an elevation of 3000 feet. The mountains to the right, which dip into the valley of the Giri, are bare of forest, with a good deal of cultivation in small terraced fields on the steep sunny slopes, while scattered houses, scarcely collected into villages, are seen here and there among the fields. On the left hand, again, the deep valley which runs towards the Sutlej is full of forest, not rising however to the ridge, which is bare, or lined only with scattered jungle of *Indigofera*, *Desmodium*, *Spiræa*, roses, and brambles. It seems to be a constant rule that the depressions of the ridges are bare and open, while the more elevated portions are covered with forest. Probably the cause of this is the greater humidity of the higher slopes, which attract the rain-clouds, while the lower ranges are dry. The currents of air which sweep up the valleys may also in part be the cause of the bareness of the ridges opposite their summits.

At Theog, nearly eight miles from Fagu, there is a fort belonging to a Rana, or hill chieftain, and a small village, with a good many fields. The cultivation at this great elevation, for the fields reach to at least 8000 feet, is principally of barley, which is sown in early spring, and reaped in the beginning or middle of June, according to the season. Beyond Theog the road rises a little, and is covered with brushwood on the left hand, but bare on the right. The highest part of the road is about two miles beyond Theog, and has an elevation of about 9000 feet. The northern face of this hill is prettily wooded with the holly-leaved oak, and covered with numerous large angular boulders, whose origin is rather difficult to explain. After passing this little hill the ridge sweeps round to the left in a semicircle, ascending very gradually and gently to a low ridge, from the crest of which the bungalow of Mattiana comes into sight, at a distance of nearly two miles, the whole of which is a gentle descent. The latter part of the road has a direction nearly due north, and the bungalow is situated in a very commanding position on the top of a little eminence, a quarter of a mile from the village, which occupies the slope of the hill facing the south-east, at a considerably lower level.

The hills on both sides of the bungalow, which has an elevation of 8200 feet, are extremely steep, and descend at least 2000 feet. The valley on the left, tributary to the Sutlej, is well wooded, but that on the right is rather bare, with only a little wood here and there in the ravines, and on the more shady exposures.

The slopes below Mattiana are covered with numerous scattered houses and a good deal of cultivation. A little rice is grown during the rains, but the principal crops are barley and some wheat, sown in spring and reaped before the commencement of the rains. The opium poppy, also a spring crop, is cultivated to some extent in the lower part of the valley. It is sown in early spring, and the opium is gathered in June.

On the morning of the 4th of August we resumed our journey, proceeding as far as Nagkanda, about thirteen miles. Nagkanda, like Mattiana and Fagu, lies exactly on the crest of the main range, south of the Sutlej, and it is possible to proceed to it by a footpath along the ridge. The ascent, however, immediately north of Mattiana, where the ridge rises suddenly to nearly 10,000 feet, is so steep, rocky, and difficult, that it is quite impassable for horses, and so nearly for loaded men, that a more easy, though somewhat longer road is always preferred. I have more than once walked from Nagkanda to Mattiana by the upper road, and found it quite easy on foot, and so very beautiful as to be well worth a visit. The ascent from Mattiana is exceedingly steep, and facing nearly due south, very bare, stony, and barren; but when the higher portion of the ridge has been gained, the remainder of the road lies through beautiful forest, with much fine scenery—the earlier part steep and rocky, the remainder nearly level, till the last descent, and generally on the north face of the range.

On our present journey, however, we took the usual road, which descends from Mattiana to the valley immediately on the east, crosses it, and passes over a long spur on its eastern side, into another valley, the head of which is immediately below Nagkanda, to which place the road ascends, at last very steeply. The ravine immediately below Mattiana is crossed at an elevation probably a little above 6000 feet, as the trees of the temperate region, such as the holly-leaved and woolly oak, *Andromeda*, and *Rhododendron*, continue to the very bottom of the descent; and *Pinus excelsa* is common on the eastern slope, a little way above the stream, which descends very abruptly, like all the hill torrents near their sources, along a rocky channel, filled with large boulders. On the banks of the little stream there were a few trees of an *Acacia*, common in the lower forests, which Mr. Bentham considers a hairy variety of the *Albizzia Julibrissin* of western Asia. I observed also a Laurel, an Olive, *Rhus*, and the common Toon (*Cedrela Toona*), all indicative of the commencement of a subtropical vegetation, which no doubt must be abundant on its banks a very few miles further down. Few of the plants observed in the valley were different from those common around Simla; a species of *Caragana*, a Leguminous genus abundant in Siberia, and in the interior and more dry parts of the Himalaya, was perhaps the most interesting.

The ascent from the ravine was well wooded in its

lower part with oak and pine. A few trees of a very handsome poplar (*P. ciliata*), a tall widely-branching large-leaved tree, occurred in its lower part, as did also *Benthamia fragifera*, and a yew, apparently undistinguishable from the common European species. The upper part of the ascent was bare and grassy. The spur is a steep one, descending rapidly from the main range, and the road winding round its shoulder does not ascend beyond 7000 feet, but as soon as it has gained the eastern face continues nearly level, gradually approaching the centre of the valley, and winding along the hill-sides among numerous villages. The slopes are generally bare; here and there in the hollows or recesses along the lateral streamlets there is some very fine forest.

The appearance of this valley is considerably different from that of any of those nearer to the plains. The population is considerable, and collected into villages, some of which occupy the lower part of the valley, and are surrounded by a good deal of cultivation and numerous walnut and apricot trees, the latter of which are said, in autumn, frequently to tempt the bears from the forest, to indulge in what to them is a grateful feast. The ripening of the apricot in a valley, among forest, at an elevation of 7000 feet, indicates an undoubted diminution of the rain-fall. Very little change, however, is observable in the wild vegetation till the upper part of the last steep ascent, when a number of species make their appearance which are strangers to the more external ranges. A species of hazel, as a tree, and *Lappa*, *Achillea*, *Leonurus*, *Cheiranthus*, and *Rumex acetosa*, as herbaceous plants, may be mentioned as instances, as also a lax-paniculate *Polygonum*, with elegant panicles of white honey-scented flowers.

Nagkanda bungalow, elevated 9300 feet above the level of the sea, is situated on a depression of the main range, where it has a direction from west to east. The ridge to the west, towards Mattiana, is elevated little more than 10,000 feet, while to the east rises the peak of Hattu to a height of 10,674 feet, by the determination of the trigonometrical survey. Here the range has approached nearer to the Sutlej, now distant only about twelve miles, than at any point since leaving Simla. The valley of the Sutlej being only 3000 feet above the level of the sea, while the mountains directly opposite rise to 12,000 feet, the scenery is of the grandest description. The river itself is nowhere visible, the descent being so abrupt at the bottom that the intervening spurs entirely conceal it.

The northern slope of the ridge on which Nagkanda stands, is occupied by a very deep valley, bounded by two long spurs, which run towards the Sutlej. The whole of this valley is occupied by dense forest, a great part of which is pine, especially on the upper part of the deep receding bay which runs up nearly to the top of Hattu, the sides of which are covered with a dense sombre forest of *Picea Webbiana* (Pindrow).

On the 5th of August, a portion of our baggage, which had been left at Fagu two days before, from a deficiency of porters, not having arrived at Nagkanda, it became necessary to halt, in order to give it a chance of reaching us. The day was fortunately fine, and we availed ourselves of the opportunity to ascend Hattu, Captain

Strachey taking with him his barometers, to verify their accuracy by the trigonometrically determined height of this mountain, which was one of the stations of the Himalayan survey by Captain Herbert. As the top of the mountain is only about 1500 feet above the Nagkanda bungalow, and the distance is nearly five miles, the ascent is an easy one. The first mile is nearly level, and bare of wood on the ridge, though the forest on both sides rises within a few feet of the crest, which is bordered by brushwood. As soon as the ascent commences, the ridge becomes covered with forest, at first principally pine, spruce and silver fir (*Picea*) being the principal species. Yew is also very common, forming a fine tall tree, and the few non-coniferous trees are chiefly the alpine oak, sycamore, and cherry. The road, which at first ascends a western spur, by degrees winds round to the face of the mountain, and finally ascends to the summit from the east. The wood on the upper part is entirely oak, and more open than the pine forest lower down. The top of the mountain is steep and bare towards the east, for about five hundred feet, with precipitous rocks thirty or forty feet high towards the west, below which the slope is exceedingly steep and rocky in that direction.

The continuation of the main range towards the east is at first lower than the peak of Hattu some 600 or 700 feet, but rises again to another peak within a mile. A long spur or ridge to the south-west is, however, for nearly two miles, within a few feet of the same height as the summit of Hattu, and rises at about that distance into a point, which probably rather exceeds it. It then sinks rapidly towards the Giri river, the most easterly branch of which has its source in the ravine on the eastern face.

On the top of Hattu there are the remains of a square building, with very thick walls, I believe of native origin, and intended as a sort of fort, which, however, from the want of water, must have been quite untenable. It is now in ruins, its interior being filled with a wilderness of hemp, nettles, *Galium Aparine,* dock and other coarse plants. The grassy slopes of the summit are covered with a luxuriant herbage of *Potentillæ, Labiatæ, Gentianaceæ, Epilobium, Polygonum,* and *Anemone,* while a few stunted bushes of *Quercus semicarpifolia,* a simple-leaved *Pyrus,* and a willow, are the only shrubby vegetation. The forest, however, rises close to the base of the cliffs on the western face, and contains all the species common on the ascent of the mountain, the vegetation of the summit being in no respect peculiar, not even in early spring exhibiting any truly alpine plant. The mountain bamboo, a graceful small species of *Arundinaria,* which is extremely abundant in the woods of the upper temperate and subalpine zones, adorns the rocky hollows close to the summit.

In every direction except south, and along the ridge to the east, the view from the top of Hattu is very extensive, as it overlooks all the peaks in the immediate vicinity. To the north the mountains of Kulu, which separate the valley of the Sutlej from that of the Beas, and from the upper Chenab, are most beautifully seen, their peaks rising above one another from west to east, till they enter the region of perpetual snow. Towards the plains, in clear weather, the view must be superb; but in that direction there is so generally a hazy state of the atmosphere, that though I have ascended Hattu four times, I have never been fortunate enough to obtain a favourable day.

In looking back from the summit of Hattu towards Simla and the plains, it may be observed that the country is well wooded, though when viewed from Simla or the heights of Mahasu the same mountains had appeared almost bare. This diversity in the aspect of the country, according to the direction from which it is seen, is due to the ridges being well wooded on one face, and bare of trees on the other. The plainward face is never, except under very exceptional circumstances, at all wooded, while the northern and eastern slopes are generally covered with forest. Probably the more direct influence of the sun, and the action of the strong winds which generally blow up the valleys towards the interior of the mountains, act in concurrence in drying the atmosphere, and checking the growth of trees on the southern and western faces of the ridges.

The shrubby and herbaceous vegetation of Hattu is exceedingly luxuriant. The more open glades of the forest are filled with an undergrowth of tall balsams, annual-stemmed *Acanthaceæ*, *Dipsacus*, *Compositæ* (among which the beautiful *Calimeris* is very abundant), while in the drier pine-forest a graceful little bamboo occurs, often to the exclusion of every other plant. It grows in dense tufts, eight or ten or even twelve feet high, the diameter of the stem not exceeding a quarter of an inch. The currant of the Mahasu ridge is also common, with many of the same shrubs which are there abundant. The ridge close to Nagkanda is much drier, and has fewer peculiar plants; the resemblance to the Simla flora being there very remarkable.

On the southern slopes of this ridge, at elevations equal to that of Nagkanda bungalow, and even higher, in some places as high as 9500 feet, there are considerable patches of cultivation. Barley is probably the spring crop, but during the rains a good deal of buckwheat is cultivated. This plant will not thrive in the very humid regions, and is therefore indicative of a drier climate than that of Simla; indeed, even the occurrence of cultivation at such an elevation, during the rainy season, satisfactorily proves the existence of a more moderate rain-fall and greater warmth than on the peaks nearer the plains, as for instance on the Mahasu ridge, on which, except the potato, no cultivation whatever is attempted during the rains, though there are a few fields of wheat or barley in one spot as high as 8000 feet.

Our missing loads having arrived at Nagkanda on the evening of the 5th of August, we resumed our journey on the morning of the 6th, marching to Kotgarh, ten miles. At Nagkanda we finally left the main range, and began to descend towards the valley of the Sutlej, following, at the commencement of our journey, a spur which runs from immediately west of the bungalow directly towards the river. After about four miles we quitted this spur to descend into the valley on the right, after crossing which we ascended to Kotgarh, situated on a long spur descending from the peak of Hattu. The early part of the descent was very abrupt, through a forest of large pines, principally *P. excelsa* and spruce (*Abies Smithiana*). Some trees of the latter measured upwards of seventeen feet in circumference. Sycamore and cherry were also common in the forest, and a good many trees of *Corylus lacera*, the hazel of the north-west Himalaya, were observed. The trees were festooned with the gigantic vine already noticed in the Mahasu forest. After the first two hundred feet of descent, the forest was less dense, and chiefly pine. *Rhododendron arboreum* commenced about 1000 feet below Nagkanda, and was soon followed by the holly-leaved oak, and a little lower by *Q. incana*, the common hoary oak of Simla; and by the time we had got down to 7000 feet, the vegetation was quite similar to that of Simla. At a little below this elevation, the road leaves the crest of the ridge, which may be seen to continue in a northerly direction, partly bare and partly pine-clad, and descends rapidly to the bottom of the deep ravine on the right. Soon after leaving the ridge we entered thick forest, and at the bottom of the ravine two considerable streams are crossed within a very short distance of one another, at an elevation of about 5500 feet, the lowest level to which we descended during the day's journey. Along the banks of these streams, which have a considerable inclination of bed, the forest is very dense and shady. Few of the trees are coniferous, nor do oaks in this part of the Himalaya select such moist localities. *Lauraceæ* of several kinds, the horse-chesnut, alder, and hornbeam (*Carpinus viminea*), with Toon and *Celtis*, are the prevailing trees.

The streams which the road here crosses descend from

different parts of the ridge of Nagkanda. They occupy the bottom of deep ravines, and are in their whole course densely wooded. These ravines are, in their upper part especially, extremely steep and rocky, often with precipitous walls, and scarcely practicable even on foot. The denseness of the forest is principally due to their northern exposure, and to the consequent more equable temperature and greater humidity. They contain many trees not previously observed on the journey from Simla, though all of them, I believe even the horse-chesnut, occur in the very similar steep rocky ravines below Fagu. The alder is a common tree at 4–5000 feet in the north-western Himalaya, always in valleys and on the banks of streams.

In this shady forest I collected a considerable number of plants which do not occur at Simla. A scandent *Hydrangea*, the loosely-adhering bark of which separates in long rolls like that of the birch, and is used as a substitute for paper, was seen twining round the trunks of trees. I observed also a fine *Calanthe*, and abundance of *Adenocaulon*, a remarkable genus of *Compositæ*, which, till Mr. Edgeworth discovered a species in the Himalaya, was only known as a native of South America. In the thickest part of the forest in this ravine, I was also fortunate enough to meet with a few specimens of *Balanophora*, which here probably attains its western limit. All these plants are abundant forms in the most humid parts of Nepal and Sikkim, and their presence may, I think, be regarded as indicative of a more equable temperature throughout the year than prevails in the more open parts of the Sutlej Himalaya. The range of mountains on which Nagkanda stands certainly intercepts a great deal of moisture during the rainy season, and therefore makes the valleys on its northern aspect less humid at that period of the year. This would appear to be more than counterbalanced by the effect of the dense forest in keeping up moisture and preventing radiation during winter, for the cold and dryness of that season seem to have a much greater effect in determining the cessation of the forms characteristic of the eastern Himalaya, than the diminished rain-fall during the three months of the rainy season.

After crossing the stream at the bottom of the valley, the road advances in a northerly direction, at first gradually ascending through fine shady woods, but afterwards, turning to the right, mounting rapidly by very abrupt zigzags, up a bare dry hill-side, to the Kotgarh ridge. Here we took up our quarters for the night, in a house the property of Captain P. Gerard, a little above the village of Kotgarh, at an elevation of about 7000 feet, in a fine grove of *Pinus excelsa*.

Kotgarh, a large village, and the seat of an establishment of missionaries, was at one time a military post, and is interesting to the Himalayan traveller, from the fact of the detachment here stationed having been long commanded by one of the brothers Gerard, whose labours in these mountains, geographical and meteorological, are so well known. It has, however, long been abandoned as a military station, the peaceable state of the hill population rendering it unnecessary to keep a garrison in these mountains.

Captain Gerard's house, in which we spent the night,

is elevated several hundred feet above the upper part of the village of Kotgarh, which occupies the steep face of the ridge directly overlooking the valley of the Sutlej. One reach of the river is visible from the front of the house, and the deep roar of the rapid stream was distinctly audible, notwithstanding that we were still 4000 feet above it. On the morning of the 7th of August we resumed our journey, descending abruptly through the village of Kotgarh to the Sutlej. At first the pine-forest which surrounded our night quarters, accompanied us down the steep hill-side. It was intermixed with a few scattered deodars; and the shrubby and herbaceous vegetation was in all its features identical with that of Simla. Soon, however, the descent was on a bare hill-side, and after reaching the village, the road, inclining to the right or east, kept nearly level for about a mile, passing through much cultivation, in terraced fields on the slopes. The crops were *Kodon* (*Eleusine Coracana*) and a cylindrical-headed *Panicum*, both grains commonly cultivated in the plains of India. There were also many fields of *Amaranthus* and *Chenopodium*. The first of these is occasionally cultivated in all parts of the hills, its bright red inflorescence, in autumn, tinging with flame the bare mountain slopes. The *Chenopodium* was new to me as a cultivated grain, and is particularly interesting from its analogy with the Quinoa of South America. It is entirely a rain crop, and grows very luxuriantly, rising to a height of six or eight feet, with a perfectly straight stout very succulent green stem, and large deltoid leaves, either pale green or of a reddish tinge, and covered with grey mealiness.

The seeds, which are extremely small, are produced in great abundance on all the upper part of the plant, and are ripe in September.

For about a mile after leaving the village of Kotgarh, the descent was trifling, but the remainder of the road to the Sutlej was very steep, so that the change in the vegetation was sudden, commencing just at the point where *Quercus incana* disappeared; before which few plants indicating heat occurred. The want of wood, no doubt, assisted the rapidity of the change, for the heat soon became considerable. In the course of the descent, I noted all the new forms as they occurred; but the exact order in which each individual species makes its appearance, depends so much upon accidental and unimportant circumstances, and is so likely to be affected by errors of observation, unless many series are obtained in different aspects of the same slope, that it would lead to no advantage to enumerate the species as they were met with. Nearly 1000 feet above the bed of the river, or at an elevation of about 4000 feet, the vegetation had become quite subtropical, species of *Mollugo*, *Polanisia*, *Corchorus*, *Leucas*, *Euphorbia*, *Microrhynchus*, and the ordinary grasses and *Cyperaceæ* of the plains, being the common weeds. The descent continued very abrupt, the heat increasing rapidly, till the road reached the bank of the Sutlej, at the village of Kepu, which occupies a flat piece of land overhanging the river.

Having commenced our day's journey before daybreak, in order to complete the march before the extreme heat had commenced, we stopped here to breakfast, under the shade of a fine mango-tree. The neighbourhood of the village was well cultivated, with extensive rice-fields and a fine grove of tropical trees—mango, *Ficus Indica* and *religiosa*, *Melia Azedarach* and *Azadirachta*, *Grewia*, oranges, and plantains. Our late residence in a cool climate made us feel the heat much, though the temperature at nine in the morning was not much more than 80°. After breakfast, we continued our journey up the valley, to Nirt or Nirat, a distance of six or seven miles, and next day we reached Rampur, the capital of Basehir, twelve miles further, and still in the Sutlej valley.

The district of Basehir is an independent hill state, governed by a rajah, whose dominion also extends over Kunawar; it commences a very little north of Kotgarh, and occupies the south side of the river Sutlej and the mountain slopes above it, as far east as the confines of Kunawar. The valley of the Sutlej, in the western part of Basehir, from Rampur downwards, has an elevation of little more than 3000 feet, Rampur (140 feet above the bed of the river) being 3400 feet above the level of the sea*. The river, at the season of our journey, which was the height of the rains, at which time it is at its largest, is an impetuous torrent, of great size, but very variable in breadth, foaming along over a stony bed, with generally very precipitous rocky banks, and filled with large boulders. During the rainy season it is extremely muddy, almost milky, and deposits in tranquil parts of its course a considerable amount of white mud. The valley is generally very narrow, with steep bare hills on either side, quite devoid of trees and covered only with a few

* Gerard's 'Koonawur,' Appendix, Table 3.

scattered bushes and long coarse grass. In the bays or recesses on the mountain-sides, between the terminations of the rocky spurs which descend to the river, the valley is often filled with a hard conglomerate rock, the cement of which is calcareous, evidently (geologically) of very recent origin. These patches of conglomerate are flat-topped, and often scarped towards the river, and are frequently 200 feet and more in thickness. They differ in degree of consolidation only from ordinary alluvial deposit, so that they appear to owe their preservation from the denuding effects of river action, to the calcareous matter, which has cemented the pebbles and sand into a solid rock.

The road follows throughout the course of the river, rising sometimes 200–300 feet, to pass over rocky spurs; at other times it lies on the surface of the boulder conglomerate, and more rarely close to the river. Here and there is a small village, with a few rice-fields, but the greater part of the valley is utterly sterile. Like the valleys of the outer Himalaya, that of the Sutlej here exhibits a curious mixture of the ordinary vegetation of the plains, with forms which point out the mountainous nature of the country. The whole flora is strongly characteristic of a dry soil and an arid climate. The mountain ranges to the west and south, no doubt, intercept a good deal of rain; and the lofty mountains, 10–12,000 feet in height, which, on the right and left, rise rapidly from the river, appropriate to themselves a great part of the moisture which reaches the valley. We may, therefore, in the absence of direct meteorological observations, infer, from the physical structure of the valley, and from the nature of its vegetation, that its climate is drier than that of the valleys at the base of the Himalaya.

The Sutlej valley cannot, of course, be properly compared with the base of the mountains farther east, where luxuriant forest covers all the slopes; but when contrasted with the Pinjor valley, or the low hills above Kalka, it is only on a careful comparison that a difference is to be observed, and then, perhaps, more by the absence of forms abundant in them than by any marked addition of new ones. The ordinary shrubs of the Sutlej, at 3000 feet, are *Adhatoda Vasica, Carissa edulis, Colebrookea, Rottlera tinctoria,* and some species of *Bœhmeria,* all characteristic of the outer hills, and the two first common plains plants. The remarkable *Euphorbia pentagona* is also common. *Butea, Ægle,* and *Moringa* do not occur, nor are there any bamboos. *Flacourtia sepiaria, Capparis sepiaria,* and *Calotropis,* which are three of the commonest plants of the plains, were also not observed. A large white-flowered caper (*Capparis obovata,* Royle) and a glabrous *Zizyphus* were the most remarkable new forms. The herbaceous vegetation differed scarcely at all from that of the plains, consisting chiefly of species which, during the rainy season, spring up in the lightest and driest soils.

Mountain plants were only occasional, and mostly such as at Simla descend on the dry grassy slopes into the valleys: a berberry and bramble (*Rubus flavus*), *Plectranthus rugosus,* which is a grey and dusty-looking shrub, *Melissa umbrosa, Micromeria biflora,* a little *Geranium, Ajuga parviflora,* a *Galium, Senecio, Aplotaxis candicans,* and one or two *Umbelliferæ.* They did not, however, amount to a twentieth part of the whole vegetation, and the aspect of the flora was quite subtropical. A little *Eriophorum*, which is everywhere common in arid places at the base of the Himalaya, from Assam to the Indus, was frequent in the crevices of the rocks. Ferns were very scarce, only two or three being observed.

The town of Rampur is a considerable place, on a small level tract of ground, about a hundred feet above the bed of the river Sutlej, which it overhangs. The houses are substantially built, in the form of a square, with an open space in the centre; they are mostly one-storied, and have steeply-sloping slated roofs. The town has a good deal of trade with Tibet, principally in shawl wool, and is the seat of a small manufacture of white soft shawl-cloths. The river is here crossed by a rope suspension-bridge, of a kind very common in the lower valleys, which has often been described. It consists of nine stout ropes, which are stretched from one side of the river to the other. The width of the Sutlej at the bridge, according to Captain Gerard, by whom it was measured, is 211 feet.

During our stay at Rampur, Major Cunningham directed my attention to the alteration of the level of the river at different periods of the day, from the variable amount of solar action on the snows by which it is fed. This effect he had noticed on his former visit to the mountains, and we had frequent opportunities of observing it during our journey. At Rampur the diurnal variation was not less than three or four feet, the maximum being, I believe, during the night or early in the morning. In the immediate vicinity of snow, the streams are highest in the afternoon, but as the distance increases the period of greatest height becomes by degrees later and later.

Except on our two first days' journey, we had been extremely fortunate in weather since leaving Simla. The day of the 8th was very cloudy and oppressive, and the 9th, on which we remained stationary at Rampur to make arrangements with the Rajah for our further progress through Basehir and Kunawar, was rainy throughout. The rain, however, was light, and did not prevent the Rajah from visiting us in the afternoon, impelled, I suppose, by a desire to see our apparatus and arrangements for travelling. We were lodged in an excellent upper-roomed house of his, overhanging the Sutlej, and not far from his own residence, which lies at the east end of the town, and externally is quite without beauty, presenting to view nothing but a mass of dead walls. The Rajah seldom remains during the hot season at Rampur, as he has a second residence at Serahan, twenty miles up the river, and 7000 feet above the level of the sea, in which he usually spends the summer, though during 1847, for some reason or other, he remained during the greater part of the year at Rampur.

On the morning of the 18th of August we resumed our journey. Our direction still lay up the valley of the Sutlej, and for the first three miles the road kept parallel to the river, ascending occasionally a few hundred feet to cross spurs, when the immediate margin of the Sutlej was too rocky and precipitous to allow of a passage. This was not unfrequently the case, and after a few miles the river-bank became so rugged and difficult, that the road left it, to ascend a long ridge, descending from the mountain range to the south. The early part of the road, from the many views of the river rushing over its rocky bed, often among immense boulders, and from the general boldness of the mountain scenery, was, though bare of forest, very striking. Frequently the road overhung the river, which ran through a narrow rocky ravine many hundred feet below. At other times, it lay over the surface of the flat platforms which occupied the valley, and in several places curious excavations were noticed on the rocky surface, as if the river had formerly flowed over higher levels. One of these ancient channels was so very remarkable, that it could not be overlooked. The rocky banks on either side were at least a hundred feet apart, and the large water-worn boulders, with occasional rugged pointed rocks which filled the bed, conveyed unmistakeably the conviction that we were walking over an ancient river-bed, though the elevation could not be less than 150 feet above the present level of the river.

Three miles from Rampur the road began to ascend a long spur in a south-east direction. After we had ascended a few hundred feet, the course of the river could be seen on the left among precipitous rocks, quite impracticable. The ascent was through a well-cultivated tract, the base of the hill and lower slopes being covered with fields of rice, still only a few inches high. The road ascended rapidly, through villages with numerous fruit-trees. At first, the vegetation continued the same as in the valley, and the hills were bare, except close to the village. Within a thousand feet of the base, the cultivation ceased, and the road entered a wood of scattered firs, mixed after a little with the common oak (*Q. incana*). At about 5000 feet the steep lateral spur joined the ridge, and the road turned to the eastward, and continued along the steep sides of the ridge, which overhang the valley of the river 2000 feet below. The Sutlej was well seen, running among bare rocky hills, the pine-wood being confined to the upper parts of the steep slopes.

Had we continued our course along this ridge, it would in time have conducted us to the crest of the main range south of the Sutlej, the same which we had left at Nagkanda to descend into the Sutlej valley. It would have been necessary for this purpose to ascend to a height of between 12,000 and 13,000 feet, and to proceed to a considerable distance south; our object, however, being to keep along the river as nearly as possible, it would not have suited our purpose to ascend so far, and the road only left the banks of the Sutlej on account of the difficult nature of the ground in the bottom of the valley. We found, therefore, after continuing a mile or two on the steep slope of the ridge, that the road again began to descend, not exactly towards the Sutlej, but to the bottom of the ravine or dell, by which the spur on which we had ascended was separated from that next in succession to it.

As far as the beginning of the descent the hill-side had been bare, or only clothed with scattered pine-wood, but as soon as the eastern slope was gained, and the descent commenced, the slopes became well wooded with *Rhodo-*

dendron and Oak. The descent was probably not more than 1000 feet, perhaps scarcely so much, as the ravine sloped very abruptly to the Sutlej; on the lower part of the descent, and on the bank of the stream, the wood was principally alder, and a few subtropical grasses and *Cyperaceæ* marked the commencement of the vegetation of the lower region, while a valerian, a *Hieracium*, a species of *Datisca*, and an *Arundo* or allied grass, were the new species of plants observed; of these, perhaps the *Datisca* alone markedly indicated an approach to the interior Himalaya. After crossing the ravine the road ascended abruptly up a well-wooded slope, on the northern face of a steep spur, to the village of Gaora, at which, for the first time since leaving Simla, we encamped, no house being available for our accommodation. The morning had been fair, though dull, but soon after our arrival at Gaora it began to rain, and continued to do so all the afternoon.

Gaora is situated, according to Captain Gerard, about 3000 feet above Rampur; but from the appearance of the vegetation, and a comparison with known heights on both hands, we estimated the elevation of our encampment to be not more than 5500 feet, so that probably Captain Gerard's observations refer to some more elevated point.

On resuming our journey on the morning of the 11th of August, we continued the ascent of the spur on which the village of Gaora is situated, which is well wooded with the ordinary trees of the temperate zone of the Himalaya. There were a few rice-fields on the hill-side on cleared places above 6000 feet, and some orange-trees in the villages at about the same elevation; from both of which facts, more sun-heat and less rain during summer may be inferred, than in similar elevations on the outer Himalaya, where neither rice nor oranges occur so high. A little way higher up, the forest changed its character, the holly-leaved oak, the deodar, and the spruce, being the common trees, among which the road continued for four or five miles, without much change of level, when the forest ceased, and the road, after continuing for a short time at about the same level, descended abruptly to the ravine of the Manglâd river, a considerable stream, now swollen into a furious torrent, which rushed with impetuosity down its steep rocky bed. A great part of the descent was bare, over crumbling mica-slate rocks.

The vegetation in the bottom of the glen showed, as on former occasions, indications of a low elevation, but presented no novelty, except in the occurrence of *Melia Azedarach*, apparently wild. I have occasionally noticed this tree in the interior of the Himalaya, always at an elevation of between 4000 and 5000 feet, and invariably in the drier valleys of the mountains, but it is so commonly cultivated in India, that its occurrence can scarcely be regarded as a proof of its being indigenous, especially if we consider that it is a rare circumstance to find it in even an apparently wild state. I do not, however, know that it has a greater claim to be considered a native of any part of the world.

The ascent on the east side was long, steep, and fatiguing, up well-wooded slopes. At about 6000 feet, a single tree of *Hippophaë conferta*, with nearly ripe fruit, was observed near a spring, and a few hundred feet higher the road gained the ridge, and continued for a mile and a half of very gentle ascent, on a broad, nearly level mountain-side, to Serahan, through beautiful forest of oak and pine. Serahan, the summer residence of the Basehir Rajah, is pleasantly situated at an elevation of 7000 feet above the level of the sea, on the northern slope of the mountain range, surrounded on all sides by pine-forest. The village is small, and occupies the lower margin of an open glade of considerable extent, on which there is a good deal of cultivation, of the same plants as I have noted at Kotgarh. The latter part of our march had been through heavy rain, which continued all the evening, and the greater part of the night, but we were fortunate enough to find an empty house, capable of sheltering our servants and baggage, as well as ourselves.

Besides the *Hippophaë*, which I noted on the ascent from Manglâd, several plants appeared on this day's journey, which served to chronicle a gradual alteration in the flora, notwithstanding that the forest-trees and general character continued generally the same. Of these, the most interesting, by far, was a plant discovered by Mr. Edgeworth, in the same tract of country, and by him described as *Oxybaphus Himalayanus*, a species of a genus otherwise entirely South American. It is a rank-growing, coarse, herbaceous plant, with tumid joints, and a straggling dichotomous habit, and has small pink or rose-coloured flowers, covered with a viscid exudation. It grows in open pastures and in waste places near villages, and is an abundant species throughout the Kunawar valley.

On the morning of the 12th of August we marched to Tranda, along the mountain-side, winding a little with its sinuations, and occasionally descending to cross the little streamlets which furrow its side, and separate the lateral ridges from one another. The road lay through beautiful forest, and as the day was fine we obtained at intervals a succession of superb views, of the deep and well-wooded valleys below, and the rugged mountains north of the Sutlej. The forest-trees were still the hoary and holly-leaved oak, with deodar and spruce, though in the more shady woods along the streams, the horse-chesnut, and a fine glaucous-leaved laurel, were common. The shrubby and herbaceous vegetation was in general character the same as in the denser woods of Simla, the new species being still quite exceptional.

It soon became necessary to descend, in order to gain a place on the next range in succession to the eastward, so as not to leave the river at too great a distance. Forest continued to the bottom of the descent, which showed no signs of tropical vegetation, and was therefore not to so low a level as those of previous days. The remainder of the day's journey consisted of a succession of ascents and descents, mostly long and fatiguing, with occasionally half a mile nearly level. Many of the steeper parts were very rocky and rugged, so difficult that artificial steps were required to make them practicable, and even with their aid a horse could scarcely pass. The greater part of the road lay through forest, and two considerable streams were crossed besides the one on the early part of the march. From the last of these a long and very laborious ascent led to the crest of the

Tranda ridge, on the very top of which we halted for the night in a log hut, built for the accommodation of travellers, in the midst of a fine forest of deodar-trees.

The Tranda ridge has, till near its termination, an elevation of upwards of 8000 feet, and projects boldly forward towards the Sutlej, dipping at last extremely abruptly to the river. The Sutlej is here thrown to the north, in a sharp bend, and runs through a deep gloomy ravine. This ridge, therefore, more lofty and abrupt than any farther west, is considered as the commencement of Kunawar; and the valley to the eastward, as far as the Wangtu bridge, is generally called Lower Kunawar, to distinguish it from the upper and drier parts of that district. The rise of the bed of the river is so gradual, that the transition of climate takes place at first by almost insensible gradations; but as soon as the spurs retain a height of 8000 feet till close to the Sutlej, they exercise a powerful influence upon the climate, and the vegetation and physical aspect of the country change with groat rapidity.

CHAPTER III.

Sildang river—Fine grove of Deodars—Nachar—Fruit-trees—Vine seen for first time—Boundaries of Kulu and Kunawar—Cross Sutlej at Wangtu bridge—Vegetation of bare rocky valley—Waterfall—Chegaon—*Pinus Gerardiana*—Miru—Absence of rain—Alteration of vegetation—*Quercus Ilex*—Rogi—Willow and Poplar—Chini—Cultivated Plain—Kashbir—Pangi—Camp at upper level of trees—Junipers—Werang Pass—Alpine Vegetation—Birch and *Rhododendron*—Granite Boulders—Lipa—Alluvial Deposits—Encamp at 12,500 feet—Runang Pass—Vegetation very scanty—Stunted Forest—Sungnam.

The night we spent at Tranda was stormy, with thunder and heavy showers of rain, but the morning of the 13th was bright and beautiful, enabling us to see from our elevated position on the ridge, a single snow-peak, far to the eastward, in Kunawar. At the commencement of the day's march, the road receded from the Sutlej into a deep mountain bay, densely wooded with deodar and pine (*Pinus excelsa*). A few trees only of spruce and horse-chesnut occurred. After a mile, passing round a projecting spur, a fine view was obtained of the river Sutlej at the bottom of a deep ravine, and of the mountain range north of the river, now in several places covered with heavy snow. A little farther on, the road descended very abruptly along the face of rugged and precipitous rocks, to the valley of the Sildang river, a large stream which was crossed in two branches by two very indifferent wooden bridges. The Sildang valley, at the point where the road crosses it, has been stated by Gerard to be elevated 5800 feet above the level of the sea. It is a larger stream than any of those yet crossed since leaving Rampur, and its ravine is beautifully wooded. The ascent to the east was gentle, through woods of oak and pine, and after rising a few hundred feet, the road continued nearly level for some miles, with the Sutlej in sight below. A large village was passed on the latter part of the march, with many temples evidently of old date, and situated in a grove of very large deodar-trees, several of which were upwards of twenty feet in circumference. One large tree with a flattened trunk, as if formed by the union of two, measured, at five feet from the base, thirty-five and a-half feet round. This grove was evidently of great age, and probably consisted of old trees, at the time the village was founded, and the temples were built under its sacred shade.

Nachar, at which we took up our quarters for the night, is a very large village, by far the most considerable yet passed, with many good houses, much cultivated land, and great numbers of fine fruit-trees. Walnuts, peaches, apricots, and mulberries, were all common; and I saw one grape-vine, which bore a good many bunches of fruit. The crops cultivated were chiefly millet and buckwheat, with a good many fields of *Amaranthus* and *Chenopodium*. The fruit-trees were evidently, from their numbers and luxuriance, a very valuable part of the possessions of the inhabitants; and it was very interesting to meet with the vine, though only in small quantity, and evidently not yet in a thoroughly suitable climate. The elevation of the village, which occupied a great extent of the hill-side sloping down towards the Sutlej, now close at hand, was nearly 7000 feet.

Nearly opposite Nachar, the district of Kunawar, which had hitherto been confined to the south bank of the Sutlej, extends to both sides of the river; the province of Kulu, which had hitherto occupied the northern bank, being bounded on the east by the mountain-chain which separates the waters of the Beas river from those of the Piti, a tributary of the Sutlej. By this very lofty chain, the villages on the north side of the Sutlej, to the east of the point now reached, are entirely cut off from the valley of the Beas, and naturally become connected with the district immediately opposite to them, with which alone they have an easy communication. Kulu, till the campaign of 1846, had belonged to the Punjab; but one of the results of the Sikh war, in that year, was the transfer of that district to British rule, so that the Sutlej, in its lower course, no longer served as a boundary between hostile states. In Kunawar, the north side of the river is the most important, because it is more populous and fertile than the south, not only from its more favourable exposure, but because the chain to the south of the Sutlej continues to increase in elevation as it proceeds eastward, while that on the north becomes gradually lower as it advances towards the confluence of the Sutlej and Piti rivers.

For this reason the main road or highway through Kunawar crosses to the right bank of the Sutlej, a short way above Nachar. At starting, therefore, on the morning of the 14th of August, we began to descend towards the river. For about a mile and a half the descent was very gentle, through a good deal of cultivation. There were many fruit-trees, but very little natural wood; a few horse-chesnut trees were observed, and occasionally a scattered deodar, spruce, or pine. On the earlier part of the road the pines were *P. excelsa*, but lower down that tree gave place to *P. longifolia*. After a mile and a half, the descent became more rapid, over a rocky and bad road, which continued to the bridge, distant three miles from Nachar. On the bare, arid, and rocky hills between Nachar and the river, several very striking novelties were observed in the vegetation; but as the road had for several days been at a higher level, and generally among dense forest, it is not improbable that many of these new plants may occur on the lower parts of the hills, in the immediate vicinity of the river, further to the westward. The new species were in all about six in number, of which three—two species of *Daphne* and an olive—were very abundant, and therefore prominent features in the appearance of the country.

At the point where the bridge has been thrown across, the river Sutlej has an elevation, by the determination of Captain Gerard, of 5200 feet above the level of the sea. Its bed and the banks on both sides are very rocky and bare, and the width of the stream not more than seventy feet. The bridge is of that kind called by the mountaineers *sanga*, which means a wooden bridge or bridge of planks, contrasted with *jhula*, a rope-bridge. On the left bank the pier of the bridge is formed by an isolated rock, separated from the rocky banks by an ancient bed of the river, now quite dry, but worn smooth by the action of the current. This former channel is stated by Gerard to have been blocked up by a fall of rocks from above; previous to which occurrence, the isolated rock must have stood as an island in the centre of the stream. The construction of the bridge is singular, but simple, and only adapted for very little traffic. Six stout trunks of trees are laid alongside of one another on the pier, so that the end towards the river is a little higher than the other; above these are placed in succession two similar layers of trunks, each projecting several feet beyond the one below it, and the whole of these are kept in position by a substantial stone building, through which the roadway runs. A similar structure on the opposite bank narrows the distance to be spanned, at the same time that it affords support to the central portion of the bridge, which consists of two strong pine-trees fifty feet in length, placed about two feet apart, and supporting stout cross planking. The whole forms a bridge quite strong enough to support foot-passengers or lightly laden horses, the only purpose for which it is required.

In spite of the considerable elevation which the Sutlej valley had now acquired, a number of plants of tropical character occurred in the neighbourhood of the Wangtu bridge. These were mostly common grasses and *Cyperaceæ*, *Polycarpæa corymbosa*, *Achyranthes aspera*, and a few other species, all common mountain-plants at low elevations, which here, from the great heat caused by the

F 2

lessened rain and the concentration of the sun's rays, at the bottom of a deep bare valley, surmounted on both sides by mountains 10,000 feet above its level, enjoy a congenial climate. They are, however, confined to the most exposed places, and to the lower levels only. A few rugged pine-trees are scattered on the steep rocks, both *Pinus excelsa*, which does not descend quite to the base of the hills, and *Pinus longifolia*, which has here reached nearly its eastern limits, the elevation of the river-bed soon becoming greater than that at which it will grow. Close to the Wangtu bridge, on the right bank, a considerable stream joins the Sutlej from the north, and is crossed by the road not far from its junction with the great river. The lower part of this tributary exhibits a succession of fine rapids and a waterfall, now much swollen by the melting of the snow; and which, notwithstanding the want of trees and consequent bareness of the accessories, formed a picture such as often greets the eye of the traveller in the alpine districts of Himalaya, but which no amount of repetition renders less grand and magnificent. Captain Gerard has, in his little 'Tour in Kunawar,' described this torrent in strong language, which showed that he felt the beauty of the scene. For this he has been condemned by Jacquemont, who sneeringly says that he describes it "comme si c'était le Niagara," an expression which induced me to turn on the spot to Gerard's book, so that I can testify to the accuracy and absence of exaggeration of his description.

After crossing this stream, the road ascends the spur which runs parallel to it, to an elevation of about 1000 feet above the Sutlej, but only to descend again to its banks, the ascent being caused by the impracticable nature of the rocky banks of the river. The spur was bare of trees, but with scattered brushwood, in which the olive and white *Daphne*, observed on the descent from Nachar, still abounded, with several other novelties, among which a *Clematis*, *Silene*, *Stellaria*, and *Selaginella*, all previously-described Kunawar species, were the most remarkable. Several of the grasses of the plains of India, such as a *Panicum* (perhaps *P. paludosum*), *Eleusine Indica*, and *Heteropogon contortus*, occurred on the hot dry pastures among the rocks, up to above 6000 feet. The rock was everywhere gneiss, but varied much in appearance and texture, and contained many granite veins.

After regaining the river, the road ran along its bank, or on low spurs not more than a few hundred feet above it, through a dry treeless tract, till about two miles from the end of the day's journey, when a long steep ascent led to Chegaon, a large village situated on a stream with steep rocky banks, the houses as usual being surrounded with fruit-trees. Here we encamped after a march of at least fourteen miles, at an elevation of 7000 feet above the level of the sea, or nearly 1800 feet above the valley of the Sutlej.

Next day our journey was a short one, not more than five and a half miles, to the village of Miru. It began by a rapid ascent for two miles to the crest of the ridge, advancing all the time towards the Sutlej, which wound round the base of the steep spur 2000 feet below. The ascent was bare (as the slopes facing the west generally are), and the hill-side almost precipitous; but as soon as the crest of the ridge, at an elevation of about 8000 feet, had been gained, scattered trees appeared of a species not previously seen. This was *P. Gerardiana*, the pine of Kunawar and the other dry regions of the Western Himalaya, from the back parts of Garhwal (where it has been seen by Dr. Jameson) to the valleys of the Upper Chenab. The first trees met with were small, and in appearance quite distinct from *P. longifolia* and *excelsa*, being more compact, with much shorter leaves and a very peculiar bark, falling off in large patches, so as to leave the trunk nearly smooth.

Beyond the crest of the ridge, from which the view into the Sutlej valley, and towards the mountains across the river, was superb, the road on the east slope again receded from the river, entering an oak-wood, through which it continued nearly level for more than a mile, but soon began to descend slightly towards the stream, which ran at the bottom of a deep ravine, down to which the road plunged abruptly, to ascend again as steeply on the other side; after which a steep ascent of upwards of a mile led to Miru, a large village in which we encamped, at an elevation of 8500 feet.

At this delightful elevation, in a climate where the periodical rains of the Himalaya are scarcely felt, embosomed in extensive orchards of luxuriant fruit-trees, and facing the south, so that it has the full benefit of the sun's rays to mature its grain-crops, Miru is one of the most delightful villages of Kunawar, being rivalled only by Rogi and Chini, beyond which the climate becomes too arid for beauty. The crops at Miru, both of grain and fruit, were most luxuriant, and the vine thrives to perfection. The principal vineyards, however, are lower down, at elevations of between 6000 and 7000 feet, at which level the sun has more power in autumn to ripen the grape.

The scenery around Miru is indescribably beautiful, as it almost overhangs the Sutlej 3000 feet below, while beyond the river the mountain-slopes are densely wooded, yet often rocky and with every variation of form. A single peak, still streaked with snow, but too steep for much to lie, rises almost due opposite; behind which the summits of the chain south of the Sutlej rise to an elevation of upwards of 18,000 feet.

At Miru we found that we had completely left the rainy region of the mountains, and henceforward the weather continued beautiful. The change had been very gradual. At Serahan we had heavy rain; a rainy night at Tranda was succeeded by a brilliant day, till the afternoon, when it rained smartly for an hour. The next day was again fine, and at Miru, though the afternoon was cloudy, and a heavy storm was visible among the mountains across the Sutlej, only a few drops of rain fell. The transition from a rainy to a dry climate had thus been apparently very sudden, four days having brought us from Serahan, where the periodical rains were falling heavily, to a place at which there were only light showers. This was in part, of course, accident. Fine weather may, perhaps, have set-in in the interval in all parts of the mountains. In very rainy seasons, when the rain-fall in the outer Himalaya is considerably above the mean, heavy showers extend into Kunawar, at least as far as Chini; and careful meteorological observations would probably show that the transition of climate is a very gradual one, the snowy mountains and the great spurs which run towards the Sutlej collecting and condensing, as they increase in elevation, more and more of the moisture which is brought by the south-east winds from the Bay of Bengal.

Jacquemont, in the valuable journal of his tour in India, which has been published by the French Government, has observed that the passage of the ridge between Chegaon and Miru may be considered as producing a marked change in the vegetation. This change, as we have seen during our journey up the Sutlej, had long been going on, though very gradually and almost insensibly. Several circumstances combine to make the transition appear at this point more sudden than a careful calculation of the number of new species will prove to be the case. It is the first wooded ridge on the north side of the Sutlej over which the road passes, and it rises higher than any other part of the route east of Nagkanda. A considerable effect is also produced by several new arboreous or shrubby species making their appearance, as well as by the fact that the new forms, which day by day have insensibly been increasing in number, have at last begun to form a prominent feature in the country.

I find among my notes a list of all the species of plants which came under my observation during the walk from Chegaon to Miru. Their number is rather above 150 species, of which number about 120 are common Simla plants. Of the remaining thirty, eleven were quite new to me, ten had occurred only the day before, and nine had been common for some days past. These numbers convey a very different idea of the amount of change from that produced at the time, but the latter must be admitted to be very fallacious, the eye of the botanist being so naturally attracted by novelty, to the utter disregard of what is common, that it is difficult to preserve the degree of attention requisite to observe properly.

Pinus Gerardiana produces a very large cone, containing, like the stone-pine of Europe, eatable nuts, of an elongated oblong form, which, when roasted like chesnuts, are agreeable to the taste, though with a little flavour of turpentine. This tree has been repeatedly tried in the rainy districts of the Himalaya, but will not succeed, a dry climate being essential to it. Besides Gerard's pine, a new species of oak was the most conspicuous tree, forming a thick dry wood on western exposures. This oak, the only species of the genus which grows in the interior of Kunawar, is the *Quercus Ilex*. The specimens which I collected quite agree with the European plant, and belong to that form of the evergreen oak, which has been called *Q. Ballota*. The same tree is common in some parts of Affghanistan, where it is called *Balút*. A small graceful ash was also common, and species of *Stellaria, Lychnis, Dianthus, Herniaria, Cruciferæ, Senecio,* and *Valeriana,* which, with several *Chenopodiaceæ* and *Artemisiæ,* were the new species observed.

On the morning of the 16th of August, we proceeded to Rogi, eight and a half miles. On leaving Miru the road at first ascended gradually through a pretty wood of deodar and Gerard's pine. The common pear-tree of the Himalaya, and many of the more ordinary Simla shrubs, species of *Desmodium, Indigofera, Spiræa, Buddleia,* and *Plectranthus,* were common under the shade of the pine-forest. As the elevation increased, the trees gradually diminished in number, and the road continued to rise along the side of a rocky hill, with only a few scattered deodars. A very pretty reach of the Sutlej now came into sight. The river was broader than usual, and seemed to flow with a gentle stream along an even bed, without interruption from rocks. Opposite the junction of the Miru tributary, which was in sight at the end of the reach, the Sutlej was particularly wide, and its channel was divided into several branches, which enclosed a number of gravelly islands, immediately beyond which the stream again contracted in width, and resumed its usual rocky character.

From the top of the steep ascent, which must have exceeded 9000 feet in elevation, the road continued along the side of the hill, without much change of level. The slopes were nearly bare, a few trees of the deodar and Gerard's pine only occurring occasionally. The latter tree was more common, and larger than the day before. It is a compact small tree, with much-twisted ascending branches, and a mottled grey bark, quite smooth from the decortication of the outer layers. It bore abundance of large pendulous cones, the size of a small pine-apple, still quite green.

A little more than two miles from Miru, the road descended to pass a stream, which was crossed in two branches. Immediately afterwards another long ascent commenced, at first steep and bare, with a western exposure, then more gradual through an open wood of deodar and *Pinus excelsa*. The highest elevation attained was almost 11,000 feet, and close to the summit a most superb view was seen to the south. The valley of the Sutlej was not in sight, but the whole course of the Baspa, except its junction with the Sutlej, and a great extent of fine snowy range beyond, were beautifully seen. The Burang or Borendo pass, elevated 16,000 feet, which leads from the Baspa valley to the upper part of the Pabar or Tons river, a branch of the Jumna, was very conspicuous, with many large patches of grey dirty-looking snow on the hills near it, but its summit seemingly bare. At the highest elevation attained the face of the hill was a mass of precipitous rocks. A fine peak, which had long been visible across the Sutlej, was now almost opposite. This mountain, the termination of the range to the east of the Baspa river, when viewed from the west and north-west, has the appearance of a vast precipice, rocky and bare of trees, commencing within little more than a thousand feet of the Sutlej. The north-east face, which comes into view for the first time from the heights above Miru, is covered throughout with magnificent forest, rising to an elevation considerably higher than that at which I stood.

The elevation we had now attained was higher than any previous part of our journey, being 200 feet above the peak of Hattu. A cold westerly wind was blowing up the valley of the Sutlej, evidently bringing a good deal of moisture along with it, for thin wreaths of mist were occasionally condensed, for a few minutes obscuring the distant view, and then melting again into transparent vapour. The vegetation was less different from that below, than I had expected, and much more luxuriant than I could have supposed, with nothing of an alpine character. Many of the species were identical with those of Nagkanda and the crest of Hattu; but there was no bamboo, nor any of the *Acanthaceæ*, so common in the more shady and humid forest further east. Balsams, however, were abundant and large, *Potentillæ*, *Salvia nubicola*, and *Nepetæ*, *Polygona*, *Achilleæ*, *Gnaphalia*, and several species of *Pedicularis* and *Ophelia*, formed a thick and rank growth. The most remarkable forms observed were Astragalinæ, of which several species, one a spinous *Caragana*, were abundant. A pretty little *Veronica* and *Bupleurum*, and several new *Cichoraceæ*, were also collected, as well as an *Orobanche*, parasitical upon the roots of the common thyme (*Thymus Serpyllum*).

From the crest, the remainder of the road consists of a succession of short ascents and descents, along the face of a very rocky hill, till within a mile of Rogi, when it descends very abruptly down the side of a rugged ravine to that village, which, though elevated 9000 feet, lies low down on the mountain-side, and has the appearance of being in a hollow. At Rogi we found the grapes quite ripe, and extremely abundant, but all from vineyards at lower levels. The commonest grape is globular, and of a deep, nearly black colour; but many varieties are cultivated. The apricots were also ripe, and had been gathered from the trees. The flat tops of the houses were now covered with them, drying in the sun. They are split up the middle and dried, the stones being taken out. In this state they keep well, and form a considerable article of export to India. Peach and walnut trees are also common at Rogi, and I saw a few apple-trees. A species of willow, which, in shape of leaf and general appearance, closely resembles a common English willow (*Salix alba*), is commonly planted along with a glabrous poplar, a small, rather spreading tree, which is frequent throughout Tibet, and seems to be the balsam poplar of Siberia and North America. The English henbane (*Hyoscyamus niger*) abounds in waste places. This also is a common Tibetan plant, and extends into the drier valleys of the Himalaya, such as Kunawar and Kashmir, but not into the outer mountains, where the periodical rains are heavy.

On the 17th of August we proceeded to Pangi, nine miles farther, passing on the road the village of Chini, the largest inhabited place and most fertile tract of Kunawar, of which it may therefore be considered the capital. From Rogi we had to make a considerable ascent to regain the road, that village lying lower than the direct route from Miru. The ascent lay first through the cultivated lands of the village, and afterwards through open wood. After regaining the road, the ascent continued through a gloomy forest of large deodar-trees for about a mile, terminating at about 10,000 feet of elevation, at which height, turning round a corner on the crest of the ridge, we found ourselves on the upper part of a precipitous cliff, which descends sheer down to the Sutlej. Unfortunately the morning was very misty, a dense fog, condensed from the steadily blowing west wind, enveloping everything, till after ten o'clock, by which time we had long passed the precipitous part of the road. We were told, however, that the cliff was absolutely impracticable below, and, indeed, even where we passed, no little engineering skill was displayed, as the road led along the face of an absolute precipice, on ledges scarcely three feet broad, or just as often over wooden planking, supported at intervals by large upright pieces of timber, whose resting-places were invisible in the dense mist by which we were surrounded.

As soon as this rocky projection was passed, the road descended rapidly, but over good level ground for half a mile, through a forest of deodar, in which some of the trees were of large size, one of them measuring nineteen feet eight inches in circumference. At the bottom of this descent, after passing a projecting rocky ridge, the village of Chini came in sight, straggling along the side of a sloping hill. Chini occupies the most level, and therefore the most fertile, valley in Kunawar. The village is prettily situated among deodar-trees, while below, and on either side of it, the slopes are disposed in a succession of terraces, some of them of considerable extent, richly cultivated with wheat, barley, and buckwheat. Through this fertile tract, the road was quite level, winding among the stone enclosures of the fields, and often bordered on both sides by grassy pastures, or patches of beautiful green turf, where the little rills, which served to irrigate the fields, had overflowed their banks, and converted the flat land into swampy meadows. Near Chini, we passed a single vineyard of small extent, at an elevation of 7000 feet, the fruit still quite unripe, though for several days we had been plentifully supplied with ripe grapes from the lower vineyards. The vines are supported by erect poles, about four feet high, placed about three feet apart, and connected by horizontal ones laid across them, on which the vines twine.

A little further we passed the small village of Kashbir, consisting of two or three houses only; beyond which a pleasant forest of deodar and Gerard's pine was entered, quite dry, and almost devoid of undergrowth; a few bushes of *Daphne*, occasionally a small ash-tree, two or three stunted oaks, and quantities of withered grass and dried-up *Artemisia*, being the only plants observed. Everything looked arid, notwithstanding the eastern exposure, and showed strikingly the rapid change of climate which was taking place. Some of the trees of *Pinus Gerardiana*, which seemed to thrive more in this arid wood than further west, were between fifty and sixty feet in height, and one of the largest of them which I noticed was nearly twelve feet in circumference. Through this forest the road continued nearly level, till it reached a ravine, on the opposite bank of which was situated the village of Pangi. A very steep descent of half a mile brought us to the stream; and an ascent of more than a mile, in the course of which we rose about 1000 feet vertically, terminated the day's journey. Pangi is a large village, 9000 feet above the level of the sea, with much cultivation and magnificent orchards of apricots, peaches, and walnuts.

From Chegaon to Pangi we had passed through the finest and most fertile part of Kunawar, which is, however, by no means confined to the north bank of the Sutlej; many large villages having been seen on the opposite side of the valley, with almost as much cultivation as those through which we had passed. The communication across the Sutlej is kept up by paths which lead through the lower cultivation and vineyards to the bank of the river, which is spanned in several places by rope-bridges, one of which only, we saw at a distance. During these three days' journey, the weather was most beautiful, and we could never sufficiently admire the ever-changing beauties of the scenery, which, probably, for variety and magnificence, is nowhere surpassed. The great peak of Raldang, a culminating point of the south Sutlej Himalaya, lies nearly opposite to Chini, and, from a great part of the Kunawar valley, is a prominent feature from almost every point of view. It forms a rugged rocky mass, and the ravines on its slopes are filled with large masses of snow, the lowest beds at this season of a dirty grey colour, and evidently still rapidly receding under the influence of the powerful autumn sun. No glaciers were anywhere in sight.

We were now about to enter upon a very troublesome part of our journey, the crossing of the various ridges which are given off by the mountain range north of the Sutlej, at the great bend of that river where it is joined by the almost equally large Piti river, from the north. These long ranges, given off by an axis 18,000 feet in height, slope at first gently towards these rivers, but at last dip extremely abruptly into the enormous ravine, at the bottom of which the Piti and Sutlej rivers run. Occasionally a rugged and difficult footpath may be found to lead among these precipices, by frequent steep ascents and descents, at no great distance above the river. These paths are always most laborious, and often very dangerous, and the usual road into the valley of the Piti river leads across the higher part of all these ridges, where they are no longer precipitous, but slope at a gentle inclination.

During the journey from Simla, I had been able to acquire very little information regarding the geology of the valley of the Sutlej; the quantity of forest, and the rapidity with which we travelled, being unfavourable to the determination of the nature of the rocks. In the earlier part of our journey argillaceous schist, often highly micaceous, predominated. In Kunawar, from Wangtu eastward, gneiss and mica-schist were almost the only rocks which I observed. These appeared to alternate again and again as we advanced, but I obtained no certainty regarding their relative position. Veins of granite occurred occasionally in the gneiss, especially at Wangtu, and probably, from the number of boulders, the axis of the range north of the Sutlej is composed of granite.

Behind Pangi is the Werang ridge, crossed by the pass of that name at a point where its height is 13,200 feet above the sea. This ridge, as will be seen by the map, separates the valley east of Pangi from that of Lipa, the next in succession to the eastward, through which a large tributary flows to join the Sutlej. From Pangi to Lipa, the distance, though considerable, is not too much for an active man to accomplish in one day. It would, however, have been a very long march, allowing of no delay on the way, or on the top of the pass. We therefore divided the distance into two days' journey, ascending on the 18th of August to the upper limit of tree vegetation on the west side of the ridge, and leaving the remainder of the ascent and the whole descent for the next day.

At daybreak we were on foot, preparing for the ascent. The morning was, as usual for some days past, thickly foggy, and a heavy dew had fallen during the night. At starting we ascended gently through a dry pine-wood, towards the face of the mountain ridge of which Pangi occupies the western slope. This ridge, like that above Rogi, on the previous day's journey, is very precipitous towards the Sutlej; and the road leads among rocks, and sometimes over planks of wood, ascending gradually as we advanced. After about a mile and a half, rounding the most projecting part of the ridge, we began to recede from the Sutlej on the eastern slope of the range, along the western side of a beautifully wooded open valley, at the bottom of which ran a large rapid stream, evidently descending from snow. Without descending at all, we continued to advance for a mile and a half through fine forest, till we nearly met the stream, which we crossed after a slight abrupt descent. Immediately after crossing, a steep fatiguing ascent of not less than three miles commenced, continuing, with scarcely any intermission, till we reached the spot selected for our encampment, inclining all the way in the direction of the course of the stream, and therefore towards the Sutlej; so that when we stopped, we almost overlooked that river, and had a fine view of the peak of Raldang, covered with a dazzling coat of fresh snow.

The forest at the base of this ascent was principally composed of deodar and Gerard's pine. The former continued abundant till within a quarter of a mile of the top, when it suddenly disappeared. *Pinus Gerardiana* gradually diminished in number during the ascent, and at last disappeared about the same time as the deodar. *Pinus excelsa* was not seen at the bottom, and was scarce on the earlier part of the ascent, but became more abundant as we increased our elevation, and was the only tree seen round our encampment. At this point the trees were straggling and distant, but very tall and luxuriant, being well sheltered by rocks. Above our encampment, which was, according to Captain Strachey's barometer, 11,800 feet, there were only a very few stunted trees on a rocky ridge behind. Excepting in the occurrence of a few new species of *Astragalus* and *Artemisia*, now quite typical forms, the vegetation during the greater part of the ascent was the same as on the higher levels east of Miru, and it was only above 11,000 feet that any considerable change was observed. Here three species of juniper made their appearance, all stunted bushes, though one of them was *J. excelsa*, which, in more favourable circumstances, grows to a small tree. The second species was *J. squamosa*, a depressed shrub, with rigid twisted branches, and the third was undistinguishable from the common juniper of Europe. A thorny species of *Ribes*, very like the common gooseberry, a strongly scented Labiate, *Dictamnus Himalayanus*, several *Compositæ*, one of which was a large-flowered thistle, and European-looking *Junci* and grasses, were all observed above 11,000 feet. A beautiful Rose (*R. Webbiana*) was common all the way from the stream.

During the ascent, after crossing the ravine, the rock was throughout gneiss, passing sometimes into a curious dark slaty rock. It was often very fine-grained; and in one place a granite vein was observed, entirely without stratification, and about a foot thick. Throughout the ascent the surface was strewed with erratic blocks of granite, evidently transported from a distance.

The slope below our camp, for several hundred feet, was cultivated with barley, but the crops were indifferent. Lower down, the mountain-side was too steep to admit of tillage. There were no houses, the fields being the property of the inhabitants of a village a long way below, to the east of Pangi.

The morning of the 19th, before sunrise, was a good deal clearer than the two last had been, but mist began to collect soon after sunrise, and did not entirely disappear for about two hours. Immediately after starting, the last trees of *Pinus excelsa* were left behind, and the ascent to the crest of the pass was gentle, over rough stony ground, covered with tufts of juniper, a shrubby *Artemisia*, and *Pteris aquilina*. The pass, which has an elevation of 13,200 feet, occupies a low part of the ridge, the slope to the left descending gently, but rising again into a sharp rocky peak, five or six hundred feet higher. The crest of the pass is a vast mass of loose rocks, and the slopes of the hill on the right are likewise covered with a mass of fragments. These angular boulders are all granite, none of which occurs *in situ;* the rocks throughout the ascent, so far as I could observe, being gneiss and mica-slate, the latter in one place containing large crystals of cyanite in great abundance.

In the crevices of the loose stones which covered

the pass, a very luxuriant vegetation was found; the same plants grew on the hill to the right, and were especially abundant among its rocky recesses. The forms were, for the first time on our journey, quite alpine, very few of the plants being even shrubby, while the great majority were small herbs. A willow, a very small *Rhododendron*, and *Andromeda fastigiata*, were almost the only shrubby plants, and the majority of forms were those common on the Alps of Europe, and comprised species of *Astragalus*, *Stellaria*, *Anemone*, *Ranunculus*, *Meconopsis*, *Saxifraga*, *Sedum*, several *Umbelliferæ*, *Pedicularis*, *Gentiana*, *Gnaphalium*, *Dolomiæa*, *Saussurea*, *Artemisia*, *Ligularia*, *Morina*, *Galium*, *Valeriana*, and many others. I added to my collection in all about thirty new species in a very short time. I had, however, never before been at so great an elevation in the Himalaya, so that almost every plant I met was new to me.

The view from the top of the pass was only remarkable for its barrenness. In the direction we had ascended, the prospect was not striking; and to the north-east, the valley in advance and hills beyond were almost bare, scattered bushes and very little forest being visible. The wind blew over the pass from the Indian side, and continued throughout the day to blow on our backs strongly as we descended.

From the crest of the pass, the descent to Lipa was long and steep, the distance being about five miles. At about 500 feet or rather more (of perpendicular height) below the pass, the first tree, a large birch, stood quite alone, with a stout erect trunk. A little further down, a small grove of the same trees was passed, in which every individual had its trunk bent in the direction of the slope, probably by the weight of the winter's snow. No birches had been seen on the south face of the pass, nor did the dwarf *Rhododendron* and little *Andromeda* appear till the summit had been gained, though they were abundant on the northern face. *Rhododendron campanulatum* was the next plant observed, forming bushes four or five feet in height, and growing in large green patches, along with the willow, which I had found on the top, and the same rose common on the southern side. About 1200 feet below the summit, that is, about 12,000 feet above the sea, pine-trees commenced—*Pinus excelsa* and *Picea* making their appearance together, the deodar not till a considerably lower level had been reached. The trees of silver fir were small, with smaller and shorter leaves than the common tree of the forests in the outer Himalaya, and were therefore the true *Picea Webbiana* of Royle, the more common long-leaved form being the *Picea Pindrow* of that author*.

* I have carefully compared, since my return to England, a great many specimens of the Himalayan *Picea*, and am sorry to be obliged to dissent from the opinion of their distinctness, which has been expressed by many excellent observers. Great variations occur in length of leaf, which is either green on both sides, or very glaucous below. All have notched leaves, but the notch varies much in depth and form. There are also differences in the form of the cones and the shape of the scales. The long green-leaved state is that of the moist Himalaya; in the driest regions the very short glaucous-leaved form occurs. There are, however, among the specimens collected by Wallich, Strachey, and myself, so many intermediate forms of leaf, that I feel satisfied that all must be considered states of one species, varying, like most *Coniferæ*, with climate and other accidental circumstances.

At an elevation of 11,000 feet, at a rough estimate, we passed the first deodars, and at the same height cultivation commenced. The first fields were wheat, now nearly ripe. With the cultivation many plants of lower elevation began to appear, which had disappeared on the upper part of the mountain, but many were missed which had been common, and the general aspect of the vegetation was strikingly altered, the diminution affecting at once the number, the abundance, and the luxuriance of the plants. Juniper was frequent till some time after the first corn-fields were passed, and Gerard's pine was common on the lower part of the descent. Throughout the whole distance from the crest to the Lipa stream, the road lay along a ravine, which was very rough and uneven, and covered with numerous and often very large boulders of granite* scattered irregularly over the surface of the valley. Towards the end of the day's march, we reached the Lipa stream, which was of large size; and we continued along its right bank, through a dry fir-wood, till close to the village, when we crossed by a substantial wooden bridge to enter Lipa, which is situate on a flattish piece of ground on the left bank of the stream, and very little above its level. It is a small village, with some cultivation, and a rather odd-looking little temple, close to which are two fine trees of *Juniperus excelsa*, the sacred

* I have now no doubt that the whole of this descent was over an ancient glacier moraine, but I was not at the time familiar with glaciers or their moraines by personal experience; and though on this and other similar occasions my notes show that I was much puzzled by the numerous transported blocks, the idea of this explanation did not suggest itself to me till I had an opportunity of seeing the connection of such phenomena with actual moraines.

juniper of the Kunawarees and Tibetans. We were accommodated with a room close to the temple, which afforded us sufficiently comfortable quarters.

At the back of the village a thick bank of alluvial clay was observed resting on the rocks behind, and vast masses of the same extended up the valley for a considerable distance. This was the first occurrence of a very common feature of Tibetan valleys, so common as to be almost universal; and as I shall have many opportunities of referring to it again, and shall find it necessary to try to give some explanation, or rather to attempt some conjectures as to its cause, I shall only here pause to observe that the first time of its occurrence coincided with the first entrance into an extremely dry climate; the passage of the Werang ridge having effected a greater change in the aspect of the country than had been seen during very many previous days—the change from luxuriant forest, not indeed to treelessness, but to thin and stunted woods.

In the valley of Lipa I met with a species of caper, apparently the same which I had collected at Rampur on the Sutlej, on hot rocky places close to the river, but which had not been met with in the intermediate parts of the journey. This little prickly shrub I afterwards found to be a common Tibetan plant, which (like most of its tribe) prefers the hottest and driest exposures, expanding its large white blossoms on dry stony ground, or among rocks where hardly any other plant will vegetate.

Lipa is situated at no great distance from the Sutlej, at an elevation of 8000 feet above the level of the sea. The next range to the eastward is that of Runang, separating the Lipa valley from that of the Ruskalau, on which is situated the village of Sungnam. As in the former instance, we divided the passage into two days' journey, encamping on the 20th of August at an elevation of 12,500 feet. The road began to ascend as soon as we left Lipa. At first we took the direction of the stream, gradually rising along the face of a rocky hill composed of a dark clay-slate, which had now taken the place of the gneiss of the lower part of the Sutlej; but turning to the left, to ascend the ridge, as soon as its crest had been gained. The surface was everywhere barren and dried up. A few scattered pine-trees occurred at intervals, but nothing approaching to forest, and the parched stony ground was quite destitute of any covering of turf or of herbaceous vegetation in sufficient quantity to attract the notice of the general observer. The ascent on the ridge was steep and uninterrupted; but as the general direction of the day's journey was down the range, or towards the Sutlej, we had to pass from one ridge to the next in succession, across the ravine by which the two were separated. Here the road was nearly level, and took a long curve in the receding hollow of the hill, turning round a belt of green which occupied the middle of the hollow.

On the left hand, above the road, there was not a trace of verdure in the ravine; but just below the road a small spring burst out from the stony ground. For three or four yards the banks of the little streamlet were quite bare, but at about that distance from its source they were fringed with luxuriant marsh-plants, *Veronica Beccabunga* and *Anagallis*, rushes, and several kinds of grasses, which gradually increased in abundance. Within a hundred yards of its origin a thicket of willows bordered the stream, and a rich vegetation grew under their shade. From this it would appear that the barrenness of the country cannot be ascribed to any fault of temperature or of altitude, but solely to the deficiency of moisture.

On the next ridge beyond this little green spot, the ascent continued steep, over loose shingly soil, among scattered trees of deodar, and occasionally a fine tree of *Pinus Gerardiana;* a spinous *Astragalus,* and several species of *Artemisia,* formed almost all the scanty vegetation. Higher up there was, in one place, a good view of the Sutlej to the south-east, with a very lofty snowy mountain beyond. A little further on, the pines ceased to grow, and no tree but juniper was seen, the vegetation becoming more and more wretched in appearance, though the same *Astragalus* and *Artemisiæ* predominated. Above 12,000 feet, two or three alpine species made their appearance; these were a *Polygonum,* a *Mulgedium,* and a little shrubby *Potentilla.* Except these, however, not one of the numerous alpine forms observed on the Werang pass two days before were to be seen.

We encamped at an elevation of 12,500 feet on the north-east slope of the ridge, overhanging a deep wide valley, in which there were several patches of cultivation still green, at an elevation which I estimated at about 1000 feet below the level of our tents. By this wide valley, (in the lower part of which, on its east side, is the village of Kanam,) we were still separated from the central range on which the Runang pass is situated. The hills all round had a desolate aspect. They were rounded in outline, and appeared quite smooth and destitute of herbage, excepting large dark-green patches of juniper, by which they were mottled. A single stunted tree of *Pinus excelsa* stood within a short distance of our encampment, and four or five hundred feet lower was a small grove, apparently of birch. During the afternoon a furious west wind blew without intermission. The morning had been quite calm, but before noon the wind had begun to blow, and gradually increased in violence till late in the afternoon; after dark it became calm.

The next morning was clear, with scarcely any wind, but the mountains above us were partly shrouded in mist. For the first time during our journey we had *Zobos* furnished for the conveyance of our tents. These animals, which are mules between a Yak bull and Indian cow, are intermediate between the two, having most of the peculiarities by which the Yak is distinguished, though in a much less degree. Their colour varies much,—black, white, and iron-grey being all common. They have coarse long shaggy hair, much shorter than in the Yak, a stout rounded body, and the tail has a small tuft at the end, quite similar in miniature to that of the Yak. These mules are exceedingly common in Upper Kunawar and Hangarang, and are much preferred as beasts of burden to the Yak, being more docile, and less sensitive to climatic influences.

The first half-mile of the ascent to the pass was very gentle, till we passed round the hollow of the valley which lay below our encampment. The hill-sides were covered with stones, among which grew a few tufts of thyme, a large-leaved saxifrage, a yellow *Scorzonera*, a curious

Polygonum, and an *Oxyria*, the same in appearance with that of the Alps of Europe. Two or three little rills of water trickled across the road, but their margins had no trace of green. The remainder of the ascent was more rapid, but nowhere fatiguing, and I reached the top about 9 A.M. Nothing can be conceived more dreary and bare than the aspect of the pass and the mountains all around. The hills, which at a distance appeared smooth and rounded, were now seen to be covered with loose stones piled upon one another, in the crevices of which a few plants found an attachment for their roots. The elevation was about 14,500 feet, but there was no appearance of snow. To the north-east a wide and straight valley ran from the crest, at the end of which, far below and perhaps eight miles off, was seen the village of Sungnam, beyond which another lofty range of equally rounded mountains, apparently smooth, ran parallel to that on which I stood. On this range, at a level, to the eye sensibly the same as that of the Runang pass, an evident track indicated the pass of Hangarang, over which lay the continuation of our journey.

I spent a considerable time on the top of the pass, and by close searching, in the crevices of the stones, especially on the hill which rose to the south-east, I succeeded in collecting a considerable number of species of plants, though very much fewer than on the Werang pass two days before. From our morning's camp to the top of the pass the whole number of species which I met with was only forty-six, not half of which were observed on the summit. The number gathered on the former pass was nearly three times as great. It must not be forgotten, however, in comparing the two ranges, that the Werang pass is 1300 feet lower than that of Runang, and ought therefore, independent of climate, to be more productive. The species which were observed for the first time on the summit of the Runang pass were not more than six, and were all forms which I have since found to be abundant throughout the higher parts of Tibet. A little willow, creeping among the stones, and scarcely more luxuriant than *Salix herbacea*, was the only shrubby plant. The others were *Oxytropis chiliophylla*, *Biebersteinia odora*, a *Draba*, *Lamium rhomboideum* of Bentham, and a species of rhubarb, of which I found only a few leaves and one or two panicles, from which the ripe fruit had nearly fallen away.

The descent from the pass to Sungnam was even more barren and desolate than the other side. The valley was open and almost straight, and the slope gradual. Till nearly half-way not a drop of water occurred on the road, and for miles almost the only vegetation on the hill-sides was an erect branched *Polygonum*, never more than a foot in height. At an elevation of about 10,000 feet, a few deodars occurred, all miserably stunted in height, though often with trunks of considerable diameter. Gerard's pine, and the ash of Tibet, also appeared a little lower, but in very small numbers. During the greater part of the descent, the white houses of Sungnam were in sight, to all appearance at the end of the valley down which we were proceeding; but when near the bottom, we discovered that we were still separated from them by a wide and level plain, that of the Ruskalan river. On the opposite side of this plain, on the side of a hill just sufficiently high to terminate the vista down the valley by which we descended from the pass, stands the town of Sungnam; while the cultivated lands, which form a wide belt, scarcely higher than the level of the river, were entirely out of sight till we arrived close to the precipitous bank parallel to the river. Here the descent was abrupt to the bed of the Ruskalan. The bank was alluvial, with enormous boulders, and was covered with tufts of *Ephedra*, a remarkable leafless plant with rod-like branches, which is abundant in every part of northern Tibet, especially in the driest and hottest exposures. It extends also occasionally into the partially rainy district, being found in Kunawar nearly as far west as the bridge of Wangtu.

Sungnam is one of the principal places of Kunawar, dividing with Kanam, which we did not visit, the claim to be the principal seat in the Sutlej valley of the Buddhist religion. It contains numerous temples and monasteries, with also a considerable industrial population. Cultivation occupies a great part of the valley, and extends up the course of the stream to a considerable distance. The level tract along the river has in many places a breadth of nearly a quarter of a mile, and the town occupies a ridge on the mountain side, to which a gently-sloping road leads from the bridge by which we crossed the Ruskalan.

The elevation of Sungnam above the level of the sea is 9000 feet. Still the vine thrives well, the steep slopes facing the river being covered with vineyards: the grapes were not yet ripe. The principal fruit-trees are apricots and apples. Willows and poplars are also frequent in the village; a new species of the latter being for the first time observed, with leaves white and downy underneath, which appears in no way to differ from *Populus alba*, the common white poplar of Europe.

CHAPTER IV.

Hangarang ridge separates Kunawar from Piti—Ascent to Hangarang Pass—Alluvial deposit—Steep ascent—View of valley—Limestone rocks—*Caragana versicolor*, or *Dama*—Camp at 14,000 feet—Top of pass—View from pass—Vegetation of summit—Descent to Hango—Cultivation round the village—Luxuriant wild plants—Road to Lio—*Crambe*—Ravine of Piti river—Lio—Bridge over Piti river—Ascent to Nako—Nako—Cultivation of the village—Buddhist temple—Transported blocks—Chango—Changar—Stopped by villagers on Chinese frontier—Natural bridge—Kyuri—Alluvium—Clay deposit with shells—Lari—Ramifications of mountain ranges—Alluvial platforms—Pok—Dankar—Lara—Rangrig—Upper part of Piti—Climate—Saline exudations.

THE Hangarang ridge, as we may conveniently call that mountain range on which the pass of Hangarang is situated, forms the boundary between the districts of Kunawar and Hangarang. As this range terminates at or close to the point where the Sutlej is joined by the Piti river, this division is geographically convenient. It has also a marked physical signification, forming the absolute limit of the deodar and Gerard's pine; and indeed, if we except the juniper, of all tree vegetation.

On the 22nd of August, our party left Sungnam to ascend towards the Hangarang pass, encamping, as on the two previous occasions, on the upper part of the ascent, so as to get to the summit of the pass at an early hour next day. Our road lay up a narrow ravine, through which a small stream descended from the vicinity of the Hangarang pass, to join the Ruskalan immediately below Sungnam. We followed for a long time the course of this rivulet, so that the ascent was by no means fatiguing. A very few stunted deodars, and a single tree of *Pinus Gerardiana*, were the only trees met with. A little shrubby vegetation was now and then seen, consisting of an ash, rose, *Colutea*, *Lonicera*, and *Spiræa*. The banks of the ravine were everywhere composed of a conglomerate of angular stones, in general imbedded in soft clay, though the matrix was not unfrequently calcareous, and in several places even composed of crystalline carbonate of lime.

The hard calcareous conglomerates are, I think, of different origin from the clayey ones. Indeed, I was induced to believe from what I saw in the neighbourhood of Sungnam, and occasionally in other districts (as I shall have again occasion to notice), that the calcareous conglomerates, which only occur in the neighbourhood of the limestone formation, and therefore where calcareous springs are common, are formed by the infiltration of water containing lime among beds of loose shingle which have accumulated along the base of the steep hills. These calcareous conglomerates are quite local, never very extensive, and are often covered with an incrustation of lime, showing the continued existence of the calcareous springs, by the action of which I suppose them to have been formed.

The clay beds, on the other hand, are continuous and

uniform in appearance. They vary much in thickness, but are on the whole much thicker and more remarkable in the upper part of the ravine, where (on the east side) a mass of clay, not less than five or six hundred feet in thickness, has accumulated, forming steep sloping or quite perpendicular banks, which at the top are worn away into pinnacles, and excavated into deep grooves and hollows, I presume by the action of melting snow. The fragments of rock which it contained were all angular, or at most a very little worn at the edges.

Five or six miles from Sungnam, the road left the course of the ravine, and began rapidly to ascend the steep spur which bounded it on the left. At first we followed a fissure in the clay conglomerate, which still had a thickness of nearly two hundred feet. Above, the ridge was rocky and very steep. When we had attained a sufficient height to overlook the valley by which we had ascended from Sungnam, I was able to estimate better than while in the ravine, the extent of the clay deposit. It was now seen to occupy both sides of the valley, and to be pretty equally diffused throughout, but certainly thicker on the left or eastern side,—in the upper part at least, for low down, just behind Sungnam, it capped a round sloping hill of considerable elevation to the right of the little streamlet and of the road. The valley did not narrow at the lower extremity, where it debouched into that of the Ruskalan, so much as to give any reason for supposing that it could have been closed by a barrier, so as to form a lake. Indeed, the absolute elevation of the conglomerate was so great at the upper end of the valley, that it would be necessary to suppose a barrier several thousand feet above the bed of the Ruskalan to produce such an effect. The greater thickness of the conglomerate in the upper part of the ravine, and the almost complete angularity of the fragments, were equally opposed to such a view. Nor was I able to form any probable conjecture as to the mode in which these accumulations had been formed.

In the earlier part of the day's journey, the rock, where exposed, was invariably clay-slate, not different in appearance from that which, commencing at Lipa, had been observed on every part of the Runang ridge. It dipped generally at a high angle, but was often much contorted. In the upper part of the ravine, thick beds of a hard cherty quartz rock alternated with the slate; and in the course of the last steep ascent, at an elevation of about 13,500 feet, the first limestone was observed. It was of a dark blue colour, very hard, coarsely stratified, and much veined with white calcareous spar. It seemed to dip at a high angle towards the north-east.

The ridge by which we ascended was quite bare of trees and exceedingly barren, producing very little vegetation of any sort, and no novelty, till we had almost attained an elevation of 14,000 feet. We then observed bushes of a species of *Caragana* (*C. versicolor*), the *Dama* of the Tibetans, a very curious stunted shrub, which is very extensively distributed at elevations which no other woody plants attain, and which, therefore, is much prized and extensively used as fuel. I had not met with it before, nor does it appear to extend at all into the wooded region of the Himalaya. We encamped on a flat piece of ground at 14,000 feet. Notwithstanding the elevation, the heat of the sun was very great during the day, but the evening and night were extremely cold.

Early next morning a short steep ascent of about 800 feet brought us to the top of the pass, which has an elevation of 14,800 feet above the sea. The *Dama*, in green patches from two to four feet in diameter, was abundant till near the summit. The pass occupies a hollow in the ridge, which rises considerably on both sides. To the north-west, on the northern exposure, there was at a short distance one small patch of snow, from which the pass and surrounding mountains were otherwise quite free. No remarkable difficulty of breathing was experienced by any of the party, except immediately after any exertion. The ascent was latterly so steep, that it was necessary to stop frequently to take breath, and the pulse was found to be very considerably accelerated when counted immediately after walking. There was, however, a great difference according to the individual; in one case it rose as high as 136; but a few minutes' rest restored it nearly to the usual standard.

At the crest of the pass, the rock was a hard bluish-grey limestone, traversed in every direction by numerous crystalline veins. I ascended the hill to the south-east, to an elevation of nearly 16,000 feet, which was within a few hundred feet of the summit. At that height it was composed of a mass of loose fragments of black slate, perfectly moveable, and so steep, that it was difficult to progress in an upward direction. Vegetation had almost disappeared; more, however, from the moveable shingly soil than from the elevation attained, for wherever a solid rock peeped out, straggling plants still lingered: the rhubarb, *Biebersteinia*, a minute saxifrage, and a yellow lichen, were the species which attained the greatest altitude.

The view from the summit of the pass, and the steep hill above it, was extensive, but very desolate. In the direction of our previous journey, the rounded outline of the Runang range bounded the view, but in front a much wider and more diversified extent of country was embraced. To the eastward, the lofty mountain of Porgyul was seen almost to its base; its upper part a magnificent mass of snow, the summit being upwards of 22,000 feet in height. To the north of Porgyul, where the valley of the Piti river allowed the distant mountains to be seen, a succession of ranges rose one beyond another, the furthest evidently at a great distance, and covered with heavy snow*.

The vegetation at the summit of the ridge was even more scanty than on the Runang pass. There was, however, more novelty in species than I had met with there. A grass, several saxifrages, *Potentillæ* and *Seda*, a little *Thermopsis*, an *Anemone*, and a beautiful *Delphinium* (*D. Brunonianum*, Royle), were the new species observed; and these, I believe, (as was indeed to be expected from the minuteness with which the country had

* The distant snowy mountains seen from the top of the Hangarang pass are probably those due north of Zungsam and east of the Parang pass, which Major Cunningham, from some angles obtained on our journey, estimated (I believe, but quote from memory) at nearly 24,000 feet.

been investigated by Dr. Royle's collectors,) were all previously described species.

From the pass the descent was pretty steep all the way to Hango, a small village, elevated 11,500 feet. The road lay on the side of a ravine, keeping the hills on the left hand, and the channel of the stream on the right. The *Dama*, which had disappeared at the summit, was again plentiful on the northern slope; and a shrubby species of *Potentilla*, quite new to me, was exceedingly common. Otherwise, little change was visible. The road was good, but the hills were dry and stony.

The village of Hango, notwithstanding its great elevation, has a considerable extent of cultivation, though I think the corn was less luxuriant than at lower levels. The wheat was still green, and rather scanty, a good deal of a wild oat (perhaps *Avena fatua*) being mixed with it; but the barley was stronger and more productive. There was also a number of fields of *Hordeum Ægiceras*, that curious awnless monstrous barley, which seems peculiar to the higher regions of Tibet, where it is very frequently cultivated. This grain was much further advanced than the wheat, being nearly ripe. The arable lands of Hango are nearly destitute of trees, a few willows being the only arboreous vegetation. They are abundantly supplied with water, circulating in copious rills among the different fields, which are disposed in terraces one above another, faced by walls about three feet in height. On the margins of the cultivation, stimulated by the moisture derived from the irrigation, there was a very abundant growth of shrubs, and of luxuriant herbaceous plants. The gooseberry, *Hippophaë*, and rose, were the shrubs, and several large *Umbelliferæ*, one of which was closely allied to the *Assafœtida*, a tall *Thalictrum*, a yellow-flowered *Medicago*, *Verbascum Thapsus*, two species of thistle, the common henbane, dock, mint, *Plantago*, and various species of *Artemisia*, were the most common herbaceous plants.

On the 24th of August we proceeded to Lio, a village on the right or west bank of the Piti river. The road crosses the small stream which runs past Hango, a little below the village, and gradually ascends the slope of the hill on its left bank. Close to the stream there is a bank of clayey alluvium, with stones, and traces of it may be seen at intervals for some distance down the valley, but it is nowhere of any great thickness. The hill along which the road lay was composed of a cherty sandstone of a light-blue colour, often nearly white; in fragments, and especially when pulverized, it was quite so; and being extremely brittle, the slopes were covered with fine white dust, the glare of which, in the bright sunshine, was very unpleasant. On this gravelly ascent the vegetation was equally scanty, and much the same in character as at moderate elevations on the two previous days; a large thistle, species of *Artemisia*, *Chenopodiaceæ*, and a spinous *Astragalus*, being the most abundant plants.

The road continued to ascend gently for about half a mile, rapidly increasing its height above the stream, which had a considerable slope. The next two miles were tolerably level, over a good but stony road, at an elevation a little under 12,000 feet. A species of *Crambe*, with a long fusiform root, smelling somewhat like a turnip, was common along this part of the road. The young leaves of this plant are used by the Tibetans as a pot-herb, and are said to be well-flavoured. A species of currant (*R. glandulosum*), with viscid, glandular, very aromatic-smelling leaves, was also met with; its fruit, now ripe, had a sweetish taste, but no flavour. It is a common Tibetan species, extending on the Indus as low down as 6500 feet.

An abrupt descent followed, of not less than seven or eight hundred feet, into a wide steeply-sloping valley, descending from the north to join that of Hango. On the surface of this hollow, the road passed among a multitude of large angular boulders of limestone, irregularly scattered over the surface. This limestone was much like that of the Hangarang pass, and as it nowhere occurred *in situ* on the road, the boulders must have come from the hills on the upper part of the lateral ravine. A small spring of water and a solitary willow marked the centre of the valley, beyond which the road again ascended slightly, till on rounding a corner, the Piti river came into view, at the bottom of a most remarkable rocky ravine. Full in front, just beyond the river, was a scarped rock of great height; it was of a dark grey colour, and was traversed in every direction by immense white veins. Round this precipice, which seemed to project beyond the general mass, the river swept in a deep curve, of which the convexity was towards me.

The mountains on the right bank of the river, which formed the termination of the range on which I stood, seemed not less steep than those opposite, for the road, general of passing those them without change of level, rose rapidly as it turned to the left, till it had attained an elevation of at least 12,000 feet, at which height it wound among precipitous rocks of hard dark slate, covered with bushes of *Ephedra*, and scattered trees of *Juniperus excelsa*. When fairly round the rocky projecting range, the village of Lio was discovered more than 2000 feet below, in a narrow ravine, on the bank of a small stream descending from the north-west, and close to its junction with the Piti river. The descent was very abrupt, in a rocky ravine among large boulders, partly of slate, partly of granite. This rock occurred in thick veins in the clay-slate, most abundantly on the lower part of the precipices which rose on the left hand during the descent.

Lio, at an elevation of 9600 feet above the sea, is a considerable village, with a large tract of cultivation, disposed in terraces from three to six feet above one another. The crops of wheat and barley had been all cut, but there were many fields of buckwheat in full flower, and of millet (*Panicum miliaceum*) still quite green. Numerous apricot-trees, from which the fruit had long been gathered, were interspersed among the cultivated lands. Surrounded on all sides by very precipitous mountains, which reflect the sun's rays, Lio appears to enjoy a great amount of heat, and the weeds which bordered the corn-fields were rank and abundant, and included many species which had not been seen at the higher villages. *Salvia glutinosa*, almost the only remaining Simla plant, burdock, sow-thistle, lucerne, and melilot, were the commonest weeds. A little *Cuscuta* was common on these latter. Lio the of any kind occurred in the valley, nor on the slopes on either side. Elevation could not be the cause of this, the height being much lower than the line of upper limit of tree vegetation in the outer Himalaya, and the temperature of the valley, as was evident from the kinds of grain cultivated, very much greater than it would have been at the same level, in the more rainy climates nearer the plains of India.

The ravine through which the Lio stream runs is narrow and rocky, and contains a great number of transported blocks of various sizes, scattered irregularly over the surface. Close to the village there is a curious isolated rock, separated by the stream from the mountain mass with which it has evidently once been connected.

On the 25th of August we crossed the Piti river, a little above Lio, and ascended to the village of Nako, on a very steep ridge, which descended from the great mountain Porgyul. After leaving the cultivated lands of Lio, which extend for half a mile from the upper part of the village, we ascended the right bank of the Piti river for nearly a mile, to a bridge, by which it is crossed. The river ran here in an extremely narrow ravine, precipitous mountains rising on either side. Its banks were steep, and covered with loose shingle, the *débris* of the precipices above. The stream is of considerable size, but much inferior to the Sutlej where we had last observed it close at hand, though I believe it is nearly as large as that river, at the point of junction of the two. The Piti runs in this part of its course with great rapidity, and is probably of considerable depth.

The bridge was situated at a bend of the river, where

the rocky banks contract more than usual. It was similar in structure to that over the Sútlej at Wangtu, but much smaller, and in so dilapidated a state, that it could scarcely be expected to last another year. The ascent to Nako was throughout steep, the difference of elevation being about 2500 feet, and the distance not more than two miles and a half. When at a sufficient height above the narrow dell in which the Piti runs, a good view was obtained of the mountains by which we were surrounded, which rose on all sides in rugged precipices. The steepness of the cliffs allowed their geological structure to be well seen. The fundamental rock, wherever I saw it, appeared to be clay-slate, sometimes passing into chert or quartzy sandstone. This basal rock was everywhere traversed by innumerable veins of quartz and granite, which exhibited no signs of parallelism, but ramified in every direction. These veins were often of great thickness. Not unfrequently, indeed, the mass of granite much exceeded the slaty beds between which it was interposed; but its connection with other veins of more moderate size rendered it evident that it had been injected into the slate.

Behind the village of Lio a thick deposit of alluvial clay was discernible, which seemed to suggest the idea of the valley having formerly been a lake; and at no place where I had seen these clayey accumulations was this hypothesis so plausible, for the precipices south of the junction of the Lio stream, rose almost perpendicularly for more than 1000 feet above the Piti river, and approached so close to one another, that their disruption was at least a possible contingency.

The slopes, as we ascended, were covered with boulders of granite in countless profusion, and the vegetation was extremely scanty, *Ephedra* being the most abundant plant observed. On the upper part of the ascent the road crossed a little streamlet, which was conducted in an artificial channel to irrigate a few fields of wheat. The margins of this little stream, and a belt a few feet in width on both sides, where the ground was swampy, were covered with a dense thicket of *Hippophaë* and rose-bushes, among which grew thickly and luxuriantly a scandent *Clematis*, and *Rubia cordifolia*, mint, dock, and thistles. The number of species altogether was scarcely more than a dozen, but the brilliant green formed so delightful a contrast with the prevailing monotony, that what in a more fertile country would have been passed as a mere thicket of thorns, to my eyes appeared a most beautiful grove of graceful shrubs; and I lingered in the swampy ground, till I had traversed it repeatedly in every direction, and completely exhausted the flora.

Nako is a smaller village than Lio, and from its elevation (12,000 feet) has no fruit-trees; but at the base of the cultivation, which is extensive, there was a copse of willows and poplars. The predominant crop was barley, now quite ripe, and being cut; the species was the common one, not *H. Ægiceras*, but the ears were very short, and the return must, I should think, have been very small. There was abundance of water, which ran in every direction through the fields. The little streamlets had a narrow belt of green on their margins, consisting of small grasses, several gentians, and *Potentillæ*, one of which I could not distinguish from *P. anserina*, a *Polygonum* very like *P. viviparum*, and, most remarkable of all, a small orchideous plant, which seemed to be a species of *Herminium*.

At Nako, we had a most satisfactory proof of the little estimation in which the lamas, or priests of the Buddhist religion, hold their religious buildings, the apartments furnished to us in the village being the different parts of the temple, surrounded with full-sized figures of the different incarnations of Buddha, in sitting posture, each with his hands in the position which is conventionally used to indicate the individual. The remarkable forms and system of the Buddhist religion, as practised in Kunawar and Ladak, have been so often and accurately described, that it would be useless for me to attempt to give any account of what I could, from want of previous knowledge, very imperfectly understand, and from my other occupations scarcely at all inquire into. The gradual transition, in ascending the Sutlej, from Hinduism to Buddhism, is very remarkable, and not the less so because it is accompanied by an equally gradual change in the physical aspect of the inhabitants, the Hindus of the lower Sutlej appearing to pass by insensible gradations as we advance from village to village, till at last we arrive at a pure Tartar population. The people of upper Piti have quite the Tartar physiognomy, the small stature and stout build of the inhabitants of Ladak, to whom also they closely approximate in dress. To what extent mere climatic influences may cause these differences, and how far they depend on an intermixture of races, I do not pretend to decide. It is impossible, however, to avoid being struck by the coincidence between these physical and moral changes in the human race, and the gradual alteration in the forms of the vegetable world, which are observable as we advance from a wet to a dry climate.

From Nako we proceeded, on the 26th of August, nearly due north, to Chango, about ten miles up the Piti valley. Nako is situated on the shoulder of the great mountain Porgyul, which rises to a height of 10,000 feet above that village, and Chango is at the very extremity of a long spur given off by that mountain further east: it is therefore separated from the Nako spur by a valley of considerable size, which descends abruptly towards the Piti river. Our road lay in a long sweep round the deep bay formed by this valley, at an elevation not lower than that of Nako, crossing in the most receding part a foaming torrent which descends from the perpetual snows of the mountain behind. Half a mile from Nako, and scarcely lower than that place, is a patch of cultivation, watered, as I was surprised to find, by a conduit brought more than a mile along the side of the hill from the stream which occupies the mid-valley; the water of which was collected into several ponds, one above another, in which it was kept in reserve till required for irrigation. The crops cultivated were buckwheat and a species of *Brassica*, both in flower. A number of poplars and willows were planted along the stream, but no fruit-trees.

Beyond this cultivated tract, the road, till we reached Chango, was entirely barren. For several miles we continued to pass through a most extraordinary accumulation of transported blocks, scattered irregularly on the gently sloping sides of the mountains. They covered a very large area, and occurred in such almost incredible profusion, that the road seemed to lie in a hollow among fragments of rock on all sides. They were all angular; and at so considerable an elevation as 12,000 feet, I have now no hesitation in referring them to glacier action. The rock *in situ* was clay-slate, with copious granite veins, and the boulders were in general the same. In one place, however, a dark mica-slate, with large crystals of cyanite, was the predominating rock of the erratic blocks, which no doubt might have been traced to its source in the ravine above, as I nowhere saw it *in situ* during the day.

After passing the torrent which occupies the centre of the valley, the road very gradually approaches the Piti river, from which it had at first receded considerably. We could now observe that the mountains which overhung the river in this part of its course were much less precipitous, and the valley wider and more open, than around Lio. Alluvial beds of great thickness everywhere rested on the ancient rocks, assuming the most diversified forms, but in general thicker and higher on the sides of the hills, at some distance from the river, than in the centre of the valley. About a mile and a half from Chango, the road began to descend rather rapidly along a dry water-course filled with huge boulders. It then crossed a stream, which had cut for itself a very deep channel through the alluvial conglomerate, and ascended slightly to the village of Chango. Close to the last stream was a bed of very fine clay, which had a thickness of at least twenty-five feet, and did not appear to contain any stones, pebbles, or fragments of rock. This clay had quite a different appearance from the alluvial conglomerate, which covered it, without appearing to pass into it. It occurred extensively in several places in the neighbourhood of Chango, and had entirely the appearance of having been deposited in a very tranquil lake, while the alluvium which rested upon it, and, therefore, was of more recent formation, contained so many fragments of rock, all seemingly angular, that its origin could scarcely be assigned to deposition under water, unless under some very peculiar circumstances.

Chango is situated in the middle of an open, nearly level tract of considerable size, which slopes very gently towards the Piti river. The cultivation is extensive, water being more than usually abundant, so that much of the ground is swampy from its waste, and covered with tufts of a small *Iris* and a species of *Equisetum*. The barley had been all cut, as well as the beans, which are here grown to some extent. Buckwheat and rapeseed (a species of *Brassica*) were still in flower, and the millet quite green. Apricot-trees were still common, though the elevation of Chango is about 10,500 feet. The village lies nearly opposite to Shialkar, but separated from it by the Piti river, which, at the bridge of that place, is elevated exactly 10,000 feet above the level of the sea.

A little way above Shialkar and Chango, two very considerable rivers unite to form the Piti river. The larger of these, descending from the north-west, is known by the same name. The other, which flows from the north-east, may be called the Parang river, by which name it is known in the upper part of its course; lower down, it seems to be usually called Zungsam. The direct road from Hangarang to the Indus lies up this river, which unfortunately flows for several days' journey through districts which are included within the Chinese frontier. It was our wish to proceed by the most expeditious route, and at the same time that nearest the line of boundary, to Hanle. It was, therefore, our object to effect, if possible, a passage up the Zungsam river, though, as we knew that Captain Gerard and M. Jacquemont had both been stopped upon the frontier, we had no reason to anticipate any more favourable result.

We therefore took, on leaving Chango, a north-easterly direction, proceeding, on the 27th of August, to a village on the left bank of the Parang or Zungsam river, called Changar, the same place which, by Gerard and Jacquemont, is named Changrezing. Leaving the cultivated lands of Chango, and crossing the stream which skirts the plain, we immediately commenced a steep zigzag ascent over a barren shingly road, to the heights which overhang the village to the north-east. After a very fatiguing climb of not less than 1300 feet, we attained the summit of the ridge, and advanced along it for some distance without much change of level, but still gradually ascending among low-topped gravelly hills. A very steep ascent followed to the summit of the pass, which was called Changrang La*, and could not be much under 13,000 feet. The whole ascent was ex-

* La, in Western Tibet, seems to mean always a *pass*. To the eastward it is often translated *mountain*.

tremely barren, the arid slopes producing a minimum of vegetation. A fleshy Cruciferous plant, with a strong pungent taste not unlike horse-radish (*Christolea* of Decaisne in Jacquemont), a fine *Nepeta* (*N. floccosa*, Benth.), and a little *Stipa*, were the only novelties; and these, with the *Ephedra*, a little *Lactuca*, an aromatic species of *Chenopodium* (*C. Botrys*), the Tibetan *Euphorbia*, and a shrubby white-flowered spinous *Astragalus*, were almost all the plants observed.

From the summit of the pass, the road descended abruptly into a deep ravine, which originated in a snowy mountain to the south. At the bottom of this ravine, between rocky precipitous banks, ran a considerable torrent, which was crossed by a very frail wooden bridge. Immediately after crossing, the road began to ascend rapidly, rising to an elevation only a few hundred feet lower than the pass from which we had descended, after which, half a mile of nearly level road brought us to our camp at Changar, a small village on a stony hill, of which only one house seemed habitable. A few fields of barley, not yet ripe, separated our tents from the village; these were irrigated by a small streamlet, whose source was a spring on the rocky hill-side a few hundred yards off, shaded by a few rose-bushes and a small clump of juniper-trees.

We remained one day stationary at Changar, to complete some arrangements which were required previous to our leaving the district of Hangarang; and on the 29th we proceeded to ascend the valley of the Zungsam river, intending, if no obstacles were offered, to follow its course and the regular road to Hanle; but in case of obstruction, which there was every reason to apprehend, to adopt the plan which had been already followed both by Gerard and Jacquemont, of crossing the river, encamping on its north bank, and proceeding in a westerly direction along the course of the Piti river to the Parang pass, in which direction we could effect a passage to Hanle without the necessity of entering on the territories under Chinese control.

Our road, for about three miles, was undulating, with rather a tendency to descend, but without any abrupt change of level. It lay along the gently sloping side of the ridge, and crossed a good many little ravines. To the right was the crest of the ridge; to the left, the valley of the Zungsam river, which was nearly 2000 feet below, the slope being very precipitous. In many of the ravines, where there was a stream of water, there was a dense jungle of shrubs, which contrasted strongly with the barrenness of the hills. A willow, rose, *Lonicera*, a shrubby *Astragalus*, an *Artemisia*, a *Potentilla* of large size, and a black currant, closely resembling that of our gardens, were the principal shrubs; and the herbaceous vegetation was the same as in similar places since entering the Tibetan region. The currant, which occurred here for the first time, was quite a new species: its ripe fruit was quite black, and had the size and flavour of the common black currant, with, however, a considerable degree of acidity.

About three miles from Changar, an abrupt descent led from the platform on which we had been travelling, to the level of the banks of the river, more than 1000 feet lower. The path by which we descended was steep, rocky, and difficult. The rock was still clay-slate, with granite veins. The granite in general very much exceeded in quantity the rock into which it had been injected, as was well seen on several precipitous cliffs along the course of the stream, in which the stratification of the slaty rock and the ramifications of the granite could be examined in detail. The banks of the river were adorned with a species of *Myricaria*, a small tree, with very delicate graceful foliage and beautiful rose-coloured flowers.

On reaching the small streamlet which forms the frontier of the Chinese dominions, we found, as indeed we expected, that there was no intention of permitting us to proceed by the direct road to Hanle; and all arguments to induce a compliance with our wish proving ineffectual, we agreed to take the route up the Piti river by Dankar, and were then permitted to proceed about a mile, to the village of Kyuri, where we encamped for the day. I have now no doubt that if we had resolutely advanced, no serious opposition to our progress would have been made; but our instructions were so precise that we should not have been justified in using the smallest degree of force, or incurring any risk of a collision.

To reach Kyuri*, we crossed the Zungsam river by a very remarkable natural bridge, composed of an enormous block of granite, which has in some way been placed across the stream, at a spot where it is much contracted in width, flowing in a deep rocky fissure from fifteen to twenty-five feet in width, evidently of great depth. At

* Jacquemont writes this name *Khiri*. I follow the orthography which I find in my notes made at the time.

this point a considerable number of boulders of large size are piled on both banks, of which the one that spans the channel is eighty-five feet in length and probably not less than forty in width and twenty in depth; it is placed obliquely across the stream, its left or southern extremity being lower, and inclined at so considerable an angle that the passage is one of some difficulty for horses and loaded cattle, though for men, with ordinary care, it is quite easy. The higher end is so much elevated above the surface on which it rests, that a rudely constructed stair of stones is necessary to enable travellers to descend.

Our encamping ground at Kyuri was on a gently sloping barren plain, seven or eight hundred feet above the valley of the Zungsam, and was reached by a short steep ascent from the bridge. There was no cultivation; but about a mile to the east, a long sloping tract of alluvium interposed between the mountains and the river was covered with green fields, though it had only two houses and not a single tree. Alluvium abounded in every direction, forming steep sloping banks, often much worn away by running water, and occasionally from two to three hundred feet in thickness. The plain on which we were encamped was also of recent origin; it consisted of a fine clay, curiously worn into cliffs and narrow ridges. A few layers of fine sand were included in the clay, and by a careful search I found three or four small fresh-water shells in the clay, belonging to at least two species—one a *Lymnæa,* the other a *Planorbis.* The shells were, however, very scarce, and all found near one spot, nor did any other portion of the deposit seem fossiliferous. The clay was in front of and below our encampment, and was covered by coarse alluvial conglomerate.

The road up the valley of the Parang river being tabooed to us by the jealousy of the Chinese Government, it became necessary to make a very considerable *détour*, no practicable road being known in the mountains north of Piti, between that which we were thus prevented from following, and the Parang pass, to reach which we had to make five or six marches up the Piti river before turning to the north. On leaving Kyuri, on the 30th of August, we ascended gently on a bare gravelly hill for several hundred feet, and then proceeded for two miles to the westward, along the steep side of the mountain. The road was rocky and very barren, the caper and an *Astragalus* being almost the only plants seen. We then descended rapidly, so as to reach the bank of the Piti river, at the place where it makes its great bend and assumes a southerly direction. Here it is joined by the Giu (Gumdo of Jacquemont), a considerable stream, which has its source in the lofty and inaccessible range to the north. This torrent had excavated a deep channel in the alluvial beds, which were composed of alternations of coarse incoherent conglomerate and fine clay. In this ravine, which sheltered them from the bleak winds of the more exposed slopes, I found a luxuriant growth of shrubs; of which the commonest forms were the rose, ash, *Colutea*, *Rhamnus*, *Myricaria*, *Capparis*, *Ephedra*, and *Artemisiæ*. As soon as the stream was passed, a steep ascent commenced, but the luxuriant vegetation at once disappeared, and the road was as barren, dusty, and stony as usual. We ascended only to descend again, and encamped on a small level spot forty or fifty feet above the Piti river, destitute of cultivation or inhabitants, but known to the people of the district by the name of Huling.

On our next day's journey, the country at first presented the same general character. The mountains along the road were lofty and rugged, and sloped steeply to the river. A mass of alluvial deposit generally rested on their bases, and the road lay at no great distance above the river, rising a few hundred feet to pass over the spurs, and again descending on their western sides. The steep slopes were in several places covered with an incrustation of hard angular breccia, with a calcareous matrix, the origin of which I conceive to have been the same as that of the breccia noticed in the vicinity of Sungnam. Across the river there was a considerable tract of level ground, covered with cultivation surrounding a small village, with a few poplar and willow trees; but the left bank, on which we travelled, was entirely barren. Nearly opposite this village, the bank of the river becoming steep and precipitous, we ascended about a thousand feet, and continued at that elevation till the difficulty was passed, after which we returned to the river-side. At this elevation two or three springs broke out on the steep face of the hill, and, trickling down among the rocks below, promoted the growth of a few willows and rose-bushes, and a small thicket of *Hippophaë*. Round the springs the ground was covered with a slight saline exudation.

The village of Lari, at which we encamped, is elevated 11,200 feet. It occupies a large extent of alluvial surface, sloping at a very small angle from the base of the mountains to the river, at a place where a stream issued from among the mountains. The cultivated lands are extensive, but very bare of trees when compared with the villages in Kunawar, or even in Hangarang. One apricot-tree only could be seen in the village lands, but there were still a few willows and poplars. The flora of the cultivated tracts had not altered. The little *Iris*, first seen at Chango, was very common, and the gentians, *Potentillæ*, *Astragali*, and other small plants, were the same as had been common since crossing the Hangarang pass; the season, however, was so far advanced, that much of the luxuriant vegetation had withered away. The crops of wheat and barley were quite ripe, and had been partly cut; but a few fields of millet were still green.

In the neighbourhood of Lari, the Piti valley is considerably more open than lower down. It had, indeed, been gradually expanding since we joined it at Lio. The mountains now recede considerably from the river, a long sloping surface of alluvium being interposed, which is at one time largely developed on the north side of the river, in which case the southern spur generally projects. A little further on, the northern mountains send down a projecting spur, and an open tract is seen to the south. The mountains behind the alluvial platforms rise very abruptly, and present towards the plain, steep, almost perpendicular slopes, which, from the peculiar nature of the rock, a very fragile slate, are covered by a steeply-sloping mass of *débris* almost to the top. This talus, indeed, on some of the cliffs behind Lari, seems to rise to the very summit of the ridges.

It is not easy to convey an idea in words of the mode in which these mountains are arranged, unless it is recollected that it is an universal rule that all mountains are ramifications of an axis, giving off branches on both sides, and that each branch is again divided in a similar manner, till the ultimate divisions are arrived at. All mountainous districts are in this respect similar to one another, and differ principally in the proportion borne by the altitude to the superficial extent of the ranges of which they are composed. An examination of the map will show that the axis of the range which lies north of the Piti valley, passes through the Parang pass, and in fact occupies the midway between the Piti and Parang rivers, terminating in the great bend of the latter, to the east of its junction with the Piti. The whole of this range is of great altitude, and it seems to rise in elevation to the eastward, no passage being known further east than the Parang pass. The primary branches of this chain, descending towards the Piti valley, are separated by considerable tributaries which discharge themselves into that river. In general, these lateral streams have, in the lower part of their course, very rugged rocky channels, but they rise rapidly, and, at a distance of a few miles from the main river, their ravines expand into open valleys, three or four thousand feet above its level. The ramifications of the primary branches are, as might be expected, in their upper part concealed among the mountains, but those near their termination abut upon the main valley, in a series of ridges separated by little streamlets. We have, therefore, as we ascend the Piti river, not a wall of mountain, parallel to its course, but a succession of ridges, more or less perpendicular to it, all descending from a great elevation, and rapidly diminishing in height. The result is necessarily a great degree of irregularity, the width of the alluvial belt varying much, while the direction of the ridges, and of the cliffs by which they are bounded, is constantly changing.

Leaving Lari on the 1st of September, we continued our journey up the Piti valley. The road lay partly on the platforms of alluvial conglomerate, and partly over the steep shingly talus which rested on the hills where they were not separated by alluvium from the river. One alluvial plain, about two miles from Lari, was well cultivated with the usual crops, the barley being quite ripe, the wheat very nearly so, the oil-seed and buckwheat out of flower, and the millet, of which there were only a few fields, still green. The platforms of alluvium have, in general, an irregularly triangular form, the base resting on the river, the apex at the termination of a mountain ravine, down which a stream runs. This stream, instead of bisecting the platform, usually runs in a hollow channel on one side or other between the mountains and the alluvium, and is, where practicable, carried off in small artificial conduits for the purposes of irrigation. The platforms always slope gently from their apex to the river, and they are generally cut off in a cliff at the lower end. These cliffs always show marks of stratification, sensibly parallel to the river, and the pebbles which the alluvium contains, are (and have been for the last two days) usually rounded.

I ought not to omit to mention, that I use the word

alluvium merely as a convenient mode of expression, without meaning to convey an idea of the mode in which these beds originate. No equally suitable word suggests itself, and the phenomena occur so frequently, that it is necessary to have some short expression by which to describe them. The origin of these alluvia is certainly very puzzling. At first sight, in any particular spot, the most natural suggestion is, that they have been deposited under water, and probably therefore in a lake. Their occurrence day after day, notwithstanding the greatest changes of altitude, their enormous thickness in many places, and the peculiar position in which they occur, soon dispel this idea, and throw the observer into a maze of doubt and difficulty, at last leading him to the conclusion, that no one cause is sufficient to explain the highly-variable phenomena which he observes, and that a lengthened series of patient observations will be necessary before the subject can be understood. These observations have yet to be supplied, but I believe I shall best serve future observers, by detailing as fully as possible the points which attracted my attention, without attempting for the present to speculate upon the causes of the phenomena. The suggestions which I have to offer to the reader, will be best understood when I have detailed all the facts upon which they are founded.

It is especially necessary to distinguish between three forms of alluvium, all of which have already occurred in Piti. These are, first, the fine clay; secondly, the platforms, such as I have described in the last paragraph; and thirdly, the enormous masses, which are without any definite limits, and do not seem referable to any present valley system.

We encamped at Pok, a large village nearly nine miles from Lari. Here we found again an extensive alluvial platform, covered with much cultivation; and on the mountain ravine above the village there was a considerable grove of young juniper-trees. A week or two before, I should have considered them as scattered trees; now they had quite the appearance of a forest, so bare had the country been since crossing Hangarang.

West of Pok, our journey of the 2nd of September was over the alluvial platform, which continued for two miles beyond the cultivation of the village, gradually contracting in width by the encroachment of successive spurs, which at last advanced close to the river. The road now ascended by a short steep path on the mountain-side, to a higher level. At the base of this ascent there were a great many angular masses of limestone, evidently transported from the valleys behind. These fragments were very numerous, and many of them of great size. They continued abundant during a great part of the day, but no limestone was seen *in situ*. I have not preserved any record of the exact position of these angular fragments with regard to the valleys behind, but I have little doubt that they will be found to be of glacial origin, such being certainly the case in many other similar instances. The limestone was very compact, of a blue or grey colour, and many of the fragments were almost full of coralline remains. I collected many fossiliferous specimens, which were afterwards despatched from Hanle to Simla by a messenger, on whom we thought we could rely, but they never reached their destination*.

We encamped at Dankar, after travelling ten miles. This place is the principal village of the Piti valley, and is 13,000 feet above the level of the sea. The valley of the Piti is here very wide, and divided into numerous channels, which are separated by low gravelly islands, the whole width of the river being not less than half a mile. Here the alluvium is very highly developed, lying in patches on the face of the steep hills. The village of Dankar, though 1000 feet above the river, occupies both sides of a steep ridge entirely composed of alluvium. Nor is this its utmost limit; for several hundred feet above the houses, similar alluvial masses occur. These beds are not, however, continuous from these great elevations, down to the level of the river: they rest, on the contrary, on the ancient rocks, which are here very steep, and the clay may be seen in isolated projecting masses, capping the most prominent ridges†.

The village of Dankar is built on arid barren soil, but the cultivated lands stretch from about the level of the village almost to the river, on a very steep slope. Thickets of *Hippophaë* were scattered among the cultivation, where the ground was swampy; and notwithstanding the great altitude, the exposure being favourable, the crops seemed good, and the wild plants were more luxuriant

* This limestone will, I believe, turn out to be the counterpart of the limestones of Silurian age, which form one of the most interesting results of the labours of Captain R. Strachey, in Kumaon and Garhwal.

† A very excellent sketch of the fort and village of Dankar, by Mr. Trebeck, is given in Moorcroft's Travels, in which the appearance and position of the alluvial masses is well represented.

than usual. One of the new species observed was a pretty gentian (*G. Moorcroftiana*, Wall.), interesting as having been one of the few plants sent from the Tibetan country by the unfortunate traveller whose name it bears. It is also a common species in the valley of Dras, in which, perhaps, Mr. Moorcroft's specimens were collected, unless, indeed, they were obtained in Piti by Mr. Trebeck, during his journey to that valley from Ladak.

Leaving Dankar on the morning of the 3rd of September, we ascended the heights behind the village to the side of the main ridge behind, along which we proceeded without change of level. The mountain was almost precipitous, and extremely barren, but commanded a fine view of the open flat plain of the Piti river, descending from the north-west; and of the course of the Pin, a large tributary which descends from the south-west, at the source of which there is a pass, by which it is possible to descend upon the Sutlej at Wangtu. The mountain range interposed between the Sutlej and Piti valleys was, from the elevation at which we now stood, seen to great advantage. These mountains are, indeed, in the terse words of Jacquemont, "d'une affreuse stérilité;" yet, in their varied outline, massive forms, and snow-sprinkled summits, there is no doubt a degree of grandeur, which produces a powerful impression.

At about a mile and a half from Dankar, during which we had, with the ridge, gradually approached the river, the road began to descend, and we at last reached the bank of the river, close to which, and sometimes even on its gravelly bed, we continued for several miles. Where the banks were lowest, and the gravel was moist, there were thickets of low shrubs, *Hippophaë*, *Myricaria*, *Ribes*, and willow; elsewhere, the gravel was barren and unproductive. We encamped at Lara, a village nine miles from Dankar, at which there were only two poplar-trees, and a very small extent of arable ground. The wheat was ripe and very luxuriant, the ears being large and well filled.

On the 4th of September, we continued our progress up the Piti valley, which had quite the same aspect as on the day before, encamping on the left bank of the river, opposite to the village of Rangrig, on a desert spot among limestone rocks, at an elevation of 12,300 feet. Here we had attained our furthest limit in a north-westerly direction, our road now turning to the right, and ascending a considerable valley towards the Parang pass, in a direction which promised much novelty and interest, as it had only been traversed by one traveller, the unfortunate Trebeck, who, in the year 1822, travelled from Le to Dankar by this route. The further course of the Piti river, which, as we learn from Moorcroft's travels, was visited in 1822 by Captain Mercer, was afterwards surveyed by Captain Broome. It communicates with Lahul, which is the upper part of the valley of the Chandrabhaga or Chenab river, by the Kulzum pass, a depression in that great branch of the trans-Sutlej Himalaya, by which the waters of the Sutlej and its tributaries on the east, are separated from those of the Chenab and Beas.

During our journey through the district of Piti, the weather had been almost uniformly dry and serene, though we were now in the very height of the Indian rainy season. The only exception occurred while we were encamped at Changar, on the lower part of the Parang river, about the 29th of August, when the sky was for two days very cloudy, and on one night it rained gently for nearly half an hour. The clouds were, however, high, and never dense, and the unsettled state of the atmosphere was of very short continuance. While it lasted, it was accompanied by violent wind, very irregular in direction.

In every part of Piti we found the margins of springs, and the grassy turf which grew on low swampy spots along the river, covered with a saline incrustation, in the form of a dry efflorescence, which encrusted the blades of grass. It appeared to be confined to the vicinity of water, the barren rocky tracts being destitute of it. This saline matter, as elsewhere in Tibet, consists of sesquicarbonate of soda, and, as a consequence of the abundance of that alkali, soda-producing plants were common, especially *Chenopodiaceæ*, among which the common *Salsola Kali* was very abundant.

The district of Piti, which was formerly almost independent, but paid tribute to, or exchanged presents with, all the Tibetan countries in its neighbourhood, namely, with Garu, Ladak, and Lahul, as well as with Kunawar, followed in 1846 the fortunes of Lahul in being transferred to British rule. It is a very thinly populated valley, the villages being small and distant, and the arable tracts of no great extent. The mountains on its southern border, by which it is separated from Kunawar, are so very elevated that they entirely intercept all access of humidity from the districts to the northward of them, and render the climate entirely rainless. The houses are in consequence very generally built of unburnt bricks, made of the fine lacustrine clay so common in the valleys, and their flat roofs are thickly covered with a layer of the same material.

CHAPTER V.

Leave Valley of Piti river—Kibar—Cultivation above 14,000 feet—Vegetation of mountains—Rocky gorge—Encampment at 17,000 feet—Parang Pass—Snow-bed and glacier—First plants at 16,500 feet—Parang valley—Gorge leading to Chumoreri Lake—Kiang, or wild horse—Chumurti—Remarkable grassy plain—Lanak Pass—Granite boulders—Plants above 18,000 feet—Undulating hilly country—Hanle plain—Vegetation—Monastery of Hanle.

Our last occupation in the valley of the Piti river was to make the necessary arrangements for the transport of our baggage through the deserts which were to be traversed before we should again arrive at inhabited tracts. The principal part of our effects were carried by men, but our party was so large that it was not easy to provide porters for the necessary amount of food during a journey of a week in an uninhabited country. A motley group of ponies, asses, and yaks therefore formed part of the train which accompanied us into the desert country between Piti and the Indus.

Three miles north-west of our encamping ground opposite Rangrig, we left the Piti river on the morning of the 5th of September, turning up the valley of a considerable stream which here joined the main river. The platform of alluvium on which we had been travelling continued for about half a mile up the lateral valley, and was covered with large boulders of angular fragments. The rock was limestone, the same as had occurred everywhere since leaving Lara. A little village called Ki, and a large monastery, situated on a curious, seemingly isolated, conical hill above the village, were passed on the right hand. Soon after, the ascent became rapid on a steep ridge to the east of the stream, and the Piti valley was completely shut out from view as we got in among the mountains. The ridge by which we ascended was barren and stony, and produced little vegetation. A curious broad-leaved *Allium* was the only novelty. We continued to ascend along the stream till we reached the village of Kibar, at which we encamped, at an elevation of 13,800 feet, in a narrow valley surrounded on all sides by lofty mountains.

Kibar is rather a pleasing-looking village, remarkable for its houses being all built of stone, instead of the mud or unburnt brick so commonly used in the valley of Piti. It is situated on the summit of a limestone rock, on the right bank of the stream. Our tents were on a patch of green-sward on the opposite bank, separated from the village by a deep ravine. Crossing this on the morning of the 6th, we ascended the slope of the hill above the village, among cultivation which rose on the hill-side fully 300 feet higher. Except one field of oil-seed, the crops were all barley, which was ripe, and partly cut: it was apparently very poor, being thin and deficient in ear. After leaving the cultivation, we continued to ascend on the ridge, till we attained an elevation of nearly 15,000 feet, at which height the road wound round the sides of hills, without any considerable change of level, for two or three miles. It was still early morning, and the air was very frosty. Every little rill was covered with a thick coating of ice, and some small swamps which we passed were crisp with frost.

Notwithstanding the considerable elevation, I noticed but little in the vegetation different from that common in Piti. The forms were by no means so alpine as on the passes between Kunawar and Hangarang, though the elevation was greater than on any of these. It was probably owing to the aridity of the climate that the flora, at elevations of 15,000 feet, instead of being composed of delicate alpine plants, was much the same as it had been 4000 feet lower. The rose, the common *Rhamnus* of Piti, a little shrubby *Potentilla*, a spinous *Astragalus*, and several *Artemisiæ*, were the common shrubs, and two species of rhubarb grew abundantly on the dry hills above Kibar. The *Dama*, which shuns the level country, the *Allium* first observed the day before, and *Lamium rhomboideum* of the Hangarang pass, were almost the only striking plants observed; all the others were those of the ordinary flora of the dry hills and gravelly plains of the Piti valley. It is necessary, of course, in comparing this vegetation with that of the passes, to recollect that we were here in a valley, on slopes surrounded on all sides by lofty ridges, not on the summit of a range overlooking everything around, or only surpassed a very little by the continuation of the same ridge; so that the temperature of the summer months must be considerably higher than on the more exposed though less elevated passes.

Further on, the road descended rapidly to the stream, which flowed in a rocky gorge, through which we held our course for three miles. A few willows, and stunted shrubs of *Myricaria*, occurred on the descent, and the willow was found occasionally on the banks of the stream in the gorge, which was enclosed by high and steep limestone rocks on both sides. These gradually contracted as we advanced, but again expanded at the point where we encamped, which was close to the bank of the stream. The ravine being now more open, we could see the hills to better advantage, and were struck with astonishment at the desolation by which we were surrounded. We were, in truth, in a wilderness of rocks, which to the south closed together, so as to shut in the ravine by which we had ascended. High walls of cliffs rose on either hand to an elevation of at least 1500 feet, displaying a natural section of a multitude of strata, which seemed to be repeated again and again in a succession of beds of limestone and slate. The elevation of our encampment was 14,800 feet.

On the 7th of September, the wish of our guides and porters according with our own, we did not cross the Parang pass, which was still five miles distant, and nearly 4000 feet above us, but contented ourselves by ascending to the highest water, perhaps 1500 feet below the summit. We ascended on a steep shingly ridge to the right of the stream where we had passed the night. Tufts of *Lamium rhomboideum* grew among the loose shingle, but no other plant seemed to vegetate in such an ungenial soil. When we had passed from the shingle, which was confined to the base of the ascent, the ridge was dry and gravelly, with tufts of *Dama* and of a species of nettle. Above 16,500 feet, the spur was rocky and uneven, and some alpine vegetation was observed, for which I conjecture that the melting of the snow had probably supplied moisture, as lower down the sterility had been complete. About fifteen species were collected, two *Potentillæ*, *Biebersteinia odora*, a *Lychnis*, a little tufted saxifrage, and species of *Nepeta*, *Artemisia*, *Gnaphalium*, *Saussurea*, *Allardia*, *Polygonum*, *Rheum*, *Blitum*, one grass, and a fern. Three or four lichens grew on the stones, and I obtained one specimen of a moss without fructification. The *Allardia*, a pretty little rose-coloured flower, with an agreeable smell, was the only new species; all the others were already familiar to me. They grew in the crevices of the rocks, in extremely small quantity, struggling as it were for existence against the unfavourable circumstances to which they were exposed.

A stony ravine, elevated about 17,000 feet, was the place selected for our encampment. A small stream, supplied by a patch of snow a little way above, trickled down under the angular gravel. The ascent had been extremely fatiguing, because almost without intermission, and we were glad of rest on reaching that elevation. During the day, however, I ascended a ridge of rugged rocks, which rose above our tents to a height of more than 500 feet, being desirous of ascertaining to what elevation I should find vegetation. An *Alsine* was common among the gravel, with two small plants which were not in a determinable state; and on the rocks, to the highest level to which I succeeded in ascending (probably 17,600 feet), the little *Allardia* continued to occur occasionally. The ridge afforded a good view of the mountains round.

The range to the north, which we had still to cross, lay in a semicircle behind; to the east was the continuation of the ridge by which we ascended; and a deep hollow lay to the west. Rugged rock everywhere met the view. The slates which alternated with the limestone were so very brittle that they everywhere formed piles of angular fragments, which filled all the hollows, and formed a sloping talus against every precipice. The view was one not to be forgotten, its desolation far surpassing any conception of waste and utter barrenness which I could have formed.

During the whole day I was never free from a dull headache, evidently caused by the great elevation. Rest relieved it, but the least exertion brought it back again. It continued all evening, as long as I was awake, and still remained in the morning of the 8th, when I rose soon after daybreak to prepare for the journey. A few paces took us beyond the shingly ravine in which we had been encamped, and the remainder of the ascent was throughout over loose angular fragments, the *débris* of the cliffs on the right. Under the latter we passed, winding round the side of the semicircular bay, till we got to about its centre, when the ascent became excessively steep and toilsome. The exertion of raising the body was very fatiguing, and the last few hundred yards were only accomplished after many pauses. A few large patches of snow lay in hollows along the road; but up to the very crest of the pass there was no trace of perpetual snow, nor even any continuous snow-bed.

The summit of the Parang pass is a narrow ridge, covered with large blocks of stone. To the north lay a large field of snow, sloping downwards at a very gentle angle. In this direction the view was limited within two miles by steep rugged mountains, which closed in on both sides. To the right and left also, the pass was overlooked by ridges close at hand. The only direction in which a distant view was obtained was south, where the mountains beyond the Piti river were beautifully seen: from the great elevation at which we stood, their summits were everywhere in view; their elevation was surprisingly uniform, and the whole range was capped with snow. The mountains close at hand presented much the same appearance as I had seen from the rocks above our encampment the day before.

I reached the summit of the pass, which has an elevation of 18,500 feet, at a quarter before eight in the morning. At that time the temperature was 28°; and a cold southerly wind blew with considerable violence, making us seek the shelter of the blocks which lay around. A small red lichen, (*Lecanora miniata*,) on the fragments of rock, was the only vegetable production I observed. After an hour's rest, we commenced the descent over the snow-bed, proceeding towards a gap which was visible in the mountains. The snow was hard frozen, and crisp under the feet. Descending steadily without any fatigue, we were soon evidently on a snow-covered glacier. A few fissures were passed, but mostly not above a few inches wide, and none that we could not with ease step over, the widest not exceeding two feet. At a distance of about a mile and a half from the crest, the mountains, which on both sides surrounded the snow-bed in the form of a circle, had so much approached to one another, that they formed a narrow valley, down which the snowy mass continued in the form of a rugged glacier. We now left the surface of the ice, and proceeded along the stony side of the ravine, with the glacier on our left hand, and steep limestone rocks on our right. Blocks of limestone strewed our path as we descended, and numerous small fragments of the same rock covered the edge of the glacier.

About three miles from the summit of the pass the glacier terminated abruptly in a bluff precipice, the height of which was more than 100 feet. Little rills of water were, at the time we passed (9½ A.M.), trickling from every part of the surface, and a small streamlet ran along the edge of the glacier under an arch of ice. The structure was here very evident: broad white bands, and narrower ones of a dirty colour, from the earthy matter which they had absorbed, ran parallel to the slope of the ravine, the arches or loops (so well explained by Professor Forbes in his delightful work on the glaciers of the Alps) being drawn out to a great length.

At the termination of the glacier, we descended from the steep mountain-side, along which we had hitherto travelled, to the flat plain, the continuation of the surface on which the glacier rested. On this descent the first vegetation appeared at an elevation of about 16,500 feet. Two small grasses, *Biebersteinia odora*, a *Lychnis*, and a little villous *Astragalus*, were the plants observed: they grew in the crevices of the rock, and scarcely rose above the ground. None of the species were different from those collected in the mountains of Piti.

When we had reached the middle of the valley, so as

to be exactly in face of the glacier, we found that a large stream issued from a vaulted cavity at its termination. For some hundred feet the stream ran among large masses of ice, as if the glacier had very recently extended further, and had melted away irregularly, leaving these masses standing. Leaving the glacier, we still followed the valley, which was confined on both sides by steep cliffs. We kept close to the stream, walking over its gravelly bed, and I collected a few more plants as I descended; none, however, new to me. A little *Nepeta*, four species of *Potentilla*, a *Gnaphalium*, several grasses and *Carices*, and a very small fern, were the species. About three miles from the end of the glacier we found our tents pitched on a small plain, connected with a lateral ravine, and covered with tufts of *Dama*, and a little species of *Alsine* in flat tufts, which was quite new to me. The elevation of our encampment was 16,000 feet.

We followed the course of the valley into which we had thus descended, for three days, without meeting with any inhabitants, and through so uniform a country, that it is unnecessary to detail each day's journey. Rugged and rocky mountains, of moderate elevation, principally limestone, bounded the view on both sides. In front we seldom saw more than a few miles; and behind, the view was in general equally limited, though occasionally we could see, up a lateral valley, the peak of a snowy mountain. The valley was almost invariably wide and level, once or twice only interrupted by projecting ridges of low rocks advancing to its centre. Low platforms of alluvium, like those of Piti, occupied the wider parts, their upper angles resting (as in Piti) on the opening of lateral ravines, while their bases were cut into cliffs by the stream.

During these three days we descended from 16,000 to about 14,800 feet. The surrounding mountains were quite barren and desolate. The gravelly plains were covered with tufts of *Dama* and of the curious tufted *Alsine*, which formed dense flattened hassock-like masses, of considerable size. The soil was very saline, and as we descended it gradually became more so. In the earlier part of the descent, the alpine forms were the same as those to the south of the Parang pass, and the plants were few in number and much scattered. Lower down, however, more novelty was met with. A little willow was the first shrubby plant, and was followed by *Ephedra*, *Myricaria*, and *Hippophaë*, all much stunted. Still lower there were large patches of green-sward along the stream, generally swampy, and always covered with a saline incrustation. *Artemisiæ*, *Astragali*, *Gentianæ*, and *Potentillæ*, were the commonest forms, with a number of saline plants, chiefly *Chenopodiaceæ*, which abounded on the lowest spots.

On the 11th, the last of these three days, the vegetation had quite lost its alpine character, notwithstanding that the elevation was still 15,000 feet. No *Biebersteinia* was seen, and the little species of *Potentilla*, *Alsine*, *Saxifraga*, *Cruciferæ*, and *Parnassia*, were no longer met with. The large *Hyoscyamus* of Piti (*Belenia* of Decaisne) had made its appearance, with tall *Artemisiæ*, a *Clematis*, a rank-growing *Corydalis*, *Cicer Soongaricum*, and other plants in no way alpine. I was much surprised to observe so complete a change in so moderate a descent, and very much interested to find that the alpine flora had so completely disappeared. I regret that I am as yet unable to give my results in more perfect form, the necessary comparison and determination of the species collected still remaining to be done.

During our descent we had gradually taken a more easterly course, and on the 11th our direction was nearly due east. On this day we passed the gorge in the mountains, up which the road turns to the Chumoreri lake, by which Mr. Trebeck had travelled to and from Ladakh. This would have been our most direct route to Le, but we were desirous of visiting the more eastern districts, so as to reach the Indus as soon as possible. The mountains in this gorge suddenly lowered; a wide gravelly plain sloped gently up to a low ridge, which did not appear to rise higher than two or three hundred feet above the level of the Parang river. Beyond this ridge, on the assurance of our guides, confirmed by Major Cunningham, who had on a former occasion travelled along the Chumoreri lake as far as its southern extremity, lies the lake, without any more considerable elevation separating it from the Parang river.

It is much to be regretted that the late period of the season, and the other important objects which we had to accomplish, should have prevented us from crossing this narrow neck of land. It would probably have thrown much light upon the question of the origin and nature of the salt lakes, which are, as is well known, scattered over Tibet, Central Asia, and Siberia. The Chumoreri lake has certainly no outlet, but from the nature of the surrounding mountains, everywhere steep and lofty, there can be no doubt that at one period its waters were discharged at its south end by the narrow valley which we saw from the south side of the Parang river*. An accurate determination of the height of the separating ridge above the present surface of the lake, a careful examination of the configuration of the surface at its southern end, and an analysis of the water, which is described as sufficiently brackish to be unpleasant though not absolutely undrinkable, would certainly enable conclusions to be drawn as to the nature of the cause which has lowered the level of the waters of the lake, and so put an end to its discharge.

In the plain which sloped gently upwards from the Parang river towards the Chumoreri lake, we saw for the first time a Kiang, or wild horse, but at too great a distance to enable his shape and appearance to be distinctly made out; and the river, which was interposed between us, prevented our approaching nearer. We afterwards frequently saw these animals, but from their extreme wariness, and the open nature of the country, we were never fortunate enough, notwithstanding repeated trials, to get within gunshot distance of them. They appear to abound at elevations between 14,000 and 16,000 feet, on the open undulating tracts on the summits of the mountain ranges, and to avoid valleys and rocky districts, where they would be liable to surprise.

* I state these facts on the authority of Major Cunningham. Captain H. Strachey visited this district in 1848, and will, I hope, soon make public his observations. He has ascertained that the surface of the lake is 15,200 feet above the level of the sea.

To the eastward of the former outlet of the lake, the valley of the Parang river was more contracted than it had been in any previous part of its course. Rocky hills, projecting from the southern mountains, advanced so close to the river, that no passage was practicable along their base, and the road several times ascended several hundred feet to cross these ridges. This obstruction was, however, but temporary, lasting only for a few miles, beyond which the valley expanded into a very wide plain, extending for five or six miles in an easterly direction, by about half that distance from north to south. The borders of this wide expanse were very low platforms, almost horizontal, and not more than from six to ten feet above the river. The middle portion was a plain of gravel, scarcely higher than the level of the stream, and evidently occasionally submerged. Here the river bends rapidly round towards the south-east. The district at which we had now arrived is called Chumurti, and about eight or ten miles to the east of our encampment on the 11th of September, is a village or assemblage of tents called Chumur, from which we obtained a supply of porters, to relieve the party who had accompanied us from Piti. Here also, in accordance with the instructions we had received on leaving Simla, Captain Strachey left us, with the intention of following the course of the Parang river, as far as he conveniently could, and then turning to the left across one of the passes of the great trans-Sutlej chain to the Indus. Major Cunningham and myself, on the other hand, proposed to proceed by the direct, and equally unknown, route to Hanle, and thence to visit the Indus, and proceed to Le.

The Parang river, whose source is in the mountains immediately north of the Parang pass, has, as we have seen, at first a northerly direction, but gradually bends more and more to the eastward and southward, and finally has a nearly south-west course, where it joins the Piti river, nearly opposite Shialkar. Its source, as well as its confluence with the Piti river, are within the British territory; but the most important, because the most populous, part of its course lies within the Chinese border. The boundary of the Chinese district runs nearly from north-east to south-west, passing a little to the west of Rodok, and crossing the Indus at the village of Chibra, where Mr. Trebeck was stopped in his attempt to penetrate up the Indus; thence a little south of Haule, and across the course of the Parang river. It then bends more towards the south, and again crosses the Parang at the point where we were stopped in the end of August, whence its direction is nearly due south as far as Nilang, on the Jahnavi branch of the Ganges.

The Parang river being a tributary of the Sutlej, by crossing the great chain at the Parang pass we had not reached the Indus valley, but had descended into a lateral valley still connected with the drainage of the Sutlej. The great line of watershed between the Indus and Sutlej lay still before us. This chain, which is the prolongation of Kailas, must be called the trans-Sutlej Himalaya, unless the name Himalaya be restricted to the chain south of the Sutlej, in which case the mountains of Lahul, Kishtawar, and Kashmir, would lose their claim to that appellation.

Towards this chain, which we were to cross by the

Lanak pass, we commenced our journey on the morning of the 12th of September. Our road lay across the Parang river, which flowed in several channels among the wide expanse of gravel which here formed its bed. The morning was bitterly cold, and the water almost icy, to the great discomfort of our porters. The largest stream was perhaps twenty-five feet wide and two and a half deep, with a moderately rapid current. After crossing the river we took a northerly direction, leaving the valley or plain of the Parang river, and ascending an open, almost level valley, bounded by low hills. The mountains on the left, which were interposed between our route and the Chumoreri lake, were the most rugged in sight. In the centre of the plain was the channel of a stream, very shingly, but without water, along which, or on alluvial banks only a few feet higher, we gradually advanced. The level of our camp on the Parang river had been 14,800 feet; and from this we were now gradually but imperceptibly rising. The hills on either hand were rounded and low, but increased in height as we receded from the Parang river. The soil was very barren, and showed many indications of salt. Scattered plants of *Salsola* were common, with *Christolea*, a pretty Cruciferous plant, with purple flowers and fleshy wedge-shaped leaves, tasting strongly of horse-radish, which has been described by Decaisne from specimens collected by Jacquemont in Piti. A little white *Alyssum*, which I had not previously met with, was also very common.

Four miles from the Parang river we reached a flat grassy plain of considerable extent, with deep black soil, in which meandered a very slowly running stream, perhaps twelve feet wide, which seemed to have an outlet by an open valley on our right, and to join the Parang some miles to the east of where we left it. A great part of this plain was swampy, the turf rising in little knolls, but round the edges and in all the higher parts it was covered with a thick incrustation of white efflorescent salt. To the north and east, low gently-sloping hills as barren as ever rose from the edge of the green plain; and in the north-east corner, close to the foot of the hills, a large fountain, discharging copiously clear tasteless cold water, was evidently the source of the stream which flowed over the plain. The grassy turf produced a considerable number of plants, not a few of which were new to me. An *Umbellifera*, an *Aster* with large purple flowers, a *Saussurea*, and two species of *Pedicularis*, one with white, the other with yellow flowers, were very common, as were also a species of *Triglochin*, a white *Juncus*, several *Carices*, and three or four very beautiful grasses. In the shallow water of the pools scattered over the plain, a species of alga was common, floating without attachment. It was a broad foliaceous green plant, and has been determined by the Rev. M. J. Berkeley to be a species of *Nostoc*, closely allied to, if not identical with *N. commune*, a species which occurs in all parts of the globe.

After crossing this plain, and stopping to rest by the fountain, we began to ascend the long slopes of the hills, partly on a level ridge, partly along the wide sloping valleys by which the low hills were separated. Both hills and plain were frightfully arid, the aspect of the country being of an uniform grey colour; and coarse gravel, with scattered stones of larger size, everywhere covered the surface. The ascent was very inconsiderable till towards the end of the day's journey. The distance travelled was about ten miles, and we encamped at about 15,800 feet, on the left bank of a small stream which descended from the north, the borders of which were swampy and covered with green turf, in which the common plants of the country occurred, such as little gentians, *Ranunculi*, *Parnassia*, several *Polygona* and *Potentillæ*, *Carices*, and grasses. On the west bank of the stream was a low ridge of clay-slate rocks, while on the right and in the valley was a heap of granite boulders; no doubt an ancient moraine, for the fragments were piled on one another to a great height, and rose far above the stream as well as the ordinary level of the plain.

On the 13th of September we crossed the Lanak pass, which lay before us at a distance of about five miles. From our encampment the mountains appeared easy of access and rounded in outline, and we commenced the ascent by a nearly level walk across the gravelly plain. After a mile and a half we rejoined the stream, and kept along it for a little way. Its banks were green with a narrow belt of turf; and the bed was often rocky, the rock being still clay-slate, notwithstanding the granite boulders everywhere scattered about. The edges of the stream were frozen, spiculæ of thin ice adhering to the herbage. The vegetation was quite alpine, the elevation being certainly above 16,000 feet. A *Delphinium*, which seemed the same as the *D. Brunonianum* of the Hangarang pass, a little yellow saxifrage, and a white-flowered species of the same genus, which I believe to be the Scottish alpine *S. cernua*, an entire-leaved yellow *Ranunculus*, a *Pedicularis* with purple flowers, and some grasses, were the most remarkable plants observed.

After a mile, we left the ravine and ascended to the open gently-sloping ground on its left, still rising sensibly as we advanced. The surface was, as usual, dry and gravelly, and *Oxytropis chiliophylla* and a little *Stipa* were almost the only plants. We continued nearly parallel to the ravine, and crossed it again a little further on. It was now dry, and its steep stony banks were covered with bushes of *Dama*. Still gradually ascending, we crossed the same ravine a third time, where its bed was upwards of 17,000 feet. There was again no water visible, but the ground was still moist, the streamlet probably, as is very general in these arid regions, trickling under the surface among the loose gravel. The little alpine nettle, which I had first found on the northern spurs of Porgyul, near Changar, and again on the southern face of the Parang pass, was here common, as were two species of *Alsine*, which formed dense tufts. A little saxifrage and the *Delphinium* were also still observed, but all the other plants had disappeared.

Leaving the ravine for the last time, we continued the ascent, which became steeper as we advanced. A rounded ridge lay to our right hand, and we rose nearer and nearer to its crest. Fragments of granite, piled on one another in increasing numbers, covered the steep slopes. Rock *in situ* was only to be seen in one place; it was still clay-slate, containing a good deal of mica. The top of the pass was nearly level for several hundred yards, and covered with boulders, principally of granite, but a few of quartz and of a trappean rock, quite black and homogeneous. The outline of the mountains was generally rounded, and they rose gradually in both directions above the pass, which had an elevation of 18,100 feet. The view, both towards the direction in which we had come and that in which we were proceeding, was rather extensive, but from the prevailing uniformity of outline and colour it was more striking than beautiful. There were no trees or villages, no variation of surface greater than an occasional grey rock, but everywhere the same dreary sterile uniformity. Nothing could be seen of Lake Chumoreri, which lies at least fifteen miles westward, and is surrounded by mountains, everywhere (except in the direction of the former outlet) higher than that on which we stood.

The occurrence of great accumulations of boulders, of a rock different from that which occurs *in situ* on the very summit of the pass, was quite conformable to what I had observed on some of the passes between Kunawar and Hangarang. It was not, however, on this account the less puzzling, nor was it till I crossed the Sassar pass, in August, 1848, that I could at all conceive in what way it was to be explained. On this pass, as I shall afterwards relate in detail, a glacier occupies the crest of the pass, descending from higher mountains to the north, and presenting a bluff termination in two directions.

On the summit of the pass I collected specimens of three phenogamous plants, probably nourished by a recently melted patch of snow; for though there was none on the pass itself, nor on the descent on either side, a steep mountain, half a mile to the right, in a due northern exposure, was still covered with snow to at least five hundred feet below the level of the pass. The small quantity of snow seen in the distant view was very remarkable, and the more so as there was no indication of diminished elevation; ridge rising beyond ridge, and peak behind peak, to the utmost limits of view. The three plants which were observed were a little *Arenaria* or *Stellaria*, and two Cruciferous plants, one of which only was in fruit. A red lichen, the same as that seen on the Parang pass, covered the stones.

The descent from the Lanak pass was at first gentle, but very soon became steep, to the bottom of a valley in which a small stream of water was running, derived, I suppose, from some small snow-beds in a lateral ravine out of sight, for it almost immediately disappeared under the gravel. Soon after leaving the crest of the pass, we came upon clay-slate rock finely laminated, and dipping south-south-west at a high angle. The valley by which we descended gradually contracted into a rocky ravine, at last very narrow, with high precipitous walls, and full of large boulders. We encamped for the night at its junction with a large stream descending in a rocky dell from the west. Around our camp, on both sides of the stream, there was an outbreak of greenstone, which had upheaved the clay-slate rocks.

On the 14th of September we proceeded along the stream close to which we had encamped the day before. High mountains, whose summits could not be seen from the bottom of the narrow ravine, rose on both sides.

The rock on both banks was clay-slate, much altered by heat, often very hard, and with numerous quartz veins; no more greenstone was observed. The stream, copious when we started, gradually disappeared as the ravine widened, and water soon lay only in pools along the gravelly bed. Boulders of granite were abundant all along. After three miles the ravine opened into a wide gravelly plain, skirted by rounded hills of considerable elevation, to which the alluvial platforms sloped very gently on both sides. *Christolea*, a little shrubby *Artemisia*, and a small *Stipa*, were the plants which grew among the gravel.

After about a mile and a half, the direction of the plain trending to the south more than was suited to our purpose, we turned to the left, to cross the ridge which ran parallel to it on the north-east. A long gravelly plain, sloping almost imperceptibly upwards, led us to the summit of the ridge, which was not more than two or three hundred feet above the plain we had left. From this pass, for such it was, though an insignificant one, an open valley, skirted on both sides by low rounded hills, ran to the north-east for nearly five miles. The appearance of the country was very remarkable. The hills were all very gentle in slope, and quite rounded in outline, so that the surface was almost undulating. It required reflection on the fact that we were traversing a tract in which the bottoms of the valleys were from 15,000 to 15,500 feet above the level of the sea, to make us aware of the very mountainous nature of the country we were passing through, which was, if any part of Tibet (which I have seen) may be so called, the

Table Land north of the Himalaya. The height of the mountains, too, was in fact greater than we had at first been inclined to believe, the gentleness of the slopes making us think the ridges nearer than they really were, and therefore leading to a false estimate of their height. In general they were from 1000 to 2000 feet in height, and their summits therefore from 16,000 to 17,000 feet above the level of the sea.

The open valley along which we now proceeded was remarkable in another point of view. It was quite waterless, and seemed hemmed in on both sides by hills, so that its drainage must take place in the direction of its long axis; at least, no lateral depression could be perceived on either side. About a mile from its eastern end, this plain was lower than in any other part. We had been descending along it from west to east, and we could see that beyond that point it rose gently to the eastward. The surface of the lowest part was covered with a hard shining white clay, without any of the fine gravel which abounded elsewhere. A few tufts of an *Eurotia* were the only plant which it produced. It was evident that the winter snows which fall on this isolated spot, when melted in summer, finding no exit, form a small lake, till they completely disappear by evaporation.

After crossing this low clayey tract, we ascended gently for nearly a mile in an easterly direction, when the valley terminated very abruptly and unexpectedly in a precipitous descent of four or five hundred feet, the clay-slate rocks emerging suddenly from beneath the gravel at the very edge of the precipice. The road descended in a narrow gorge, which had apparently been worn by aqueous action in the almost perpendicular cliff. On emerging from this gorge, we found ourselves on the border of a very extensive perfectly level tract, seemingly surrounded by hills, and approaching in shape to a circle, though its outline, from projecting ranges of hills, was very irregular. The margins of this plain were dry and gravelly; the centre, as seen from a distance, was green, but in many places encrusted with a saline efflorescence.

Skirting this plain, which lay on our right, while ranges of hills, separated by wide gravelly valleys, occupied the left, we reached Hanle, a Buddhist monastery inhabited by about twenty lamas, built on the summit of a steep hill which rises abruptly out of the plain. We encamped in a ravine at the foot of the hill on which the monastery is built, in which the tents of the wandering population are erected when they bring their flocks into this neighbourhood.

The plain of Hanle, which is not, I think, less than six or eight miles in diameter, resembles very much that curious flat tract which we passed on the 12th of September, on the south side of the Lanak pass; it is, however, much larger in dimensions. Several streams, very tortuous and sluggish, wind over its surface. These were frequently three feet or more in depth, and contained multitudes of small fish, usually about six inches in length, but growing to eight or ten inches at least. They were a species of carp. We tried to eat them, but, though sweet and well-tasted, the bones were so numerous and troublesome that we relinquished the attempt. We were much interested at the occurrence of fish at an elevation of 14,300 feet, a height at which, *à priori*, it would scarcely have been expected that they would have existed.

The surface of the plain was very saline, and, where not swampy, covered with coarse grasses and *Cyperaceæ*. It was very uneven, hummocks or knolls being scattered over the surface, which made walking very difficult. These, I presume, were caused by the gradual growth of plants, which, in process of time, formed heaps in spots not covered by water during the melting of the snow in spring. In some parts there were extensive patches of *Dama*. A species of *Elymus* and a *Blysmus* were very abundant. The ground in the vicinity of the streams was swampy, and the coarse grasses of the drier parts were replaced by little *Potentillæ*, *Glaux maritima*, *Taraxacum*, *Aster*, and a number of Chenopodiaceous plants. In the running waters a *Potamogeton* and *Ranunculus aquatilis* were plentiful. The streams, which must, I believe, as in the case of the plain of the 12th, principally derive their supply from springs which break out on the edge of the flat country, all converge to a point at the north-east end of the plain, and, uniting into one, continue their course down an open valley in a northerly direction towards the Indus.

As no section of the bed of this remarkable plain is anywhere to be seen, it is not possible to form an estimate of the depth of its boggy soil, or of the nature of the subjacent deposit. It can scarcely be doubted that it has at one time been a lake, which has been gradually silted up; but it is not easy to conjecture the length of time which has elapsed since it became dry land, in the absence of any knowledge of the nature and contents of the deposits which occur beneath the surface. As an outlet for the waters of the plain exists to the northward, we may infer that the waters of the lake were always fresh.

We remained two days at Hanle, to effect a change of porters, a matter which cannot be accomplished in a hurry in an almost uninhabited country, without unnecessary hardships on individuals. There is no settled population except the monks or lamas; a few stone huts without roofs, which were scattered about the foot of the rock, having no tenants. To the east of the monastery, on the border of the plain, watered by an artificial channel brought with considerable labour from the river, we observed two or three small fields. The grain, which was barley, had been cut and carried away, so that harvest at Hanle was over. The view from the top of the monastery was extensive, as we overlooked the whole plain to the south, and the valley of the Hanle river on the east. The mountains were highest to the east, where a very lofty, steep, and irregular range, with a good deal of snow in some places, separated Hanle from the Indus. To the south and west, the mountains, though high, were rounded.

The rock on which the monastery is built is wholly igneous, but varies from a coarse-grained granite, rapidly decaying, to a dark-coloured greenstone, with large crystals scattered through it. Close to the foot of the hill, the clay-slate was in a few places visible, considerably altered by igneous action, as was to be expected from its proximity to the greenstone.

CHAPTER VI.

Descend Hanle river—Unsettled weather—Encamp on banks of Indus —Upper course of Indus—Pugha ravine—Forest of Myricaria-trees —Borax plain—Hot springs—Borax lakes of Eastern Tibet—Sulphur mine — Pulokanka Pass — Salt lake — Lacustrine clays with shells — Ancient water-mark — Rupchu — Tunglung Pass — Fall of snow — Alluvial conglomerate — Giah — Narrow ravine — Miru — Upshi—Indus valley—Marsilang—Richly cultivated plain of Chashut—Bridge over Indus—Le—Buddhist edifices.

On the 17th of September we left Hanle, *en route* to Le. Our road lay down the left bank of the river by which the waters of the lake-plain are discharged into the Indus. The valley through which it flowed was open and level, and its slope imperceptible. On the left lay a low range of hills, an irregular mass increasing much in width, as well as in height, as we proceeded northwards, the Hanle extremity being the termination where it slopes into the plain. On the right, a very lofty range, some of the peaks of which were certainly not less than 21,000 feet in elevation, ran parallel to our course, separating the open valley of the Hanle river from the Indus.

The width of the valley varied from one to three miles. The stream was very winding, crossing from side to side, and often pressing the road close to the spurs of the range on the left. The range on this side was principally clay-slate, with occasional outbreaks of trap, which had in many places converted the stratified rock into a hard red or green jasper. From the immediate proximity of the igneous rock the stratified masses were very much contorted, and no regular dip was observable.

Saline efflorescence occurred everywhere in great quantity in the vicinity of the stream; as a consequence, Chenopodiaceous plants were more than usually abundant, and I collected at least three species of that family which I had not previously observed. The banks of the stream were everywhere bordered by a belt of green herbage, more or less broad, in which the usual species of *Ranunculus, Gentiana, Pedicularis, Juncus, Cyperaceæ,* and grasses were common. *Glaux maritima* also occurred abundantly. Two other European plants were found in the swamps along the course of the river, which were very interesting as a proof of the extremely European nature of the flora: these were *Hippuris vulgaris* and *Limosella lacustris.* Towards the end of the day's journey, *Caragana versicolor* (*Dama*) became very common, covering a large extent of surface, and growing to a much greater size than I had ever before seen, with an upright stem nearly six feet in height. I could scarcely persuade myself that the species was the same as the little depressed shrubs which grew on the passes further south. Two species of *Myricaria,* both of which I had seen in Piti, also reappeared during the day, so that we were evidently approaching a lower level and more genial climate.

Banks of alluvial conglomerate occurred on the sides

of the valley, in the spaces between the projecting spurs of the range on the left hand, on the latter part of the day. The beds were distinctly stratified and very sandy, more or less full of rounded stones, and often passing into pure sand, which was interstratified with the coarser beds. The day was very cloudy and threatening, and a few drops of rain fell for the first time since the 29th of August, the weather during the whole of that interval having been brilliant and quite dry. We encamped eleven miles from Hanle, on a gravelly plain close to the river.

During the night the weather did not improve, but continued very cloudy, and on the morning of the 18th the mountains on the right side of the valley were covered with snow, down to within 1500 feet of the plain. The wind blew strongly from the northward, and the day, which was still very cloudy, was bitterly cold, and, to our feelings, extremely uncomfortable. We continued to follow the course of the Hanle river, passing over long gravel flats, which alternated with turfy saline meadows. Several low spurs from the mountains on the left, which projected far into the plain, making the river bend much to the right, were crossed as we proceeded. About ten miles from our morning's camp, we left the course of the river, which turned to the right and entered a rocky mountain gorge, while our road kept its northerly direction. An open valley led us to the crest of a low ridge of trap and slate, from which a very long stony monotonous valley descended to an extensive plain covered with fine mud and saline exudation, on which the only vegetation was a few tufts of *Suæda* and coarse grass. Crossing this plain, on which the dry clay was in many places deeply cracked and fissured, as if it had till within a short time been under water, or at least swampy, we encamped, at an elevation of 13,800 feet, on the banks of the Indus, here a muddy torpid stream, without any apparent current, about four feet deep and twenty or twenty-five feet wide. There was, however, another channel, separated from that on which we were encamped by a small island.

So sluggish was the stream at the point where we joined it, that we were for a long time uncertain in which direction the current was flowing; and though we were prepared to find the Indus at the end of our day's journey, the river on whose banks we were encamped was so much less than our anticipations, that we were very unwilling to be convinced that we had really arrived at the great river, to which we had so long looked forward as one of the most interesting objects of our journey. The island in the centre of the channel was a bank of very fine sand or mud, on which large flocks of wild-fowl were resting; it was very little elevated above the surface of the water, which must frequently, I should think, rise sufficiently to cover it. The bank on which we were encamped, though rather higher, was not more than four feet above the water; it was quite vertical, and composed of fine clay, without any intermixture of stones or gravel.

The course of the river Indus, from its source to Le, has hitherto been less known than any other part in Tibet; but as Captain Strachey, a month or two after our visit, descended along it from the Chinese frontier, as far as Le, the unknown portion is now very much reduced. It rises in the mountains north of the lakes of Mansarawer and Rawan Rhad, and runs in general towards the north-east. Moorcroft has described its appearance at Garu or Gartop, where it is a very insignificant stream; but the intervening country is so little known, except by native report, that we can scarcely be said to have an exact knowledge of the upper part of its course. There is in some maps an eastern branch laid down, but of that we have no definite information. From the arid and snowless nature of the country through which it must flow, it is probably a very small stream, but its length may be considerable.

Immediately above the open plain in which we joined the Indus, it would appear to have a very rocky and rugged channel. Such, at least, was the description given to us by our guides of the lower course of the Hanle river, which we left only a few miles before it joined the Indus; and as the mountains to the south-west appeared to close in very abruptly within a very short distance of our encampment, we could not doubt that the open and level plain which we found in this portion of the river's course was of limited extent, and quite an exceptional feature in the character of the country through which the Indus flows. From the great elevation and abrupt slope of the range which runs parallel to the Hanle river on the east, there can be no doubt that the spurs which it sends down on its north-east slope, towards the Indus, must be bold and rocky; and though the hills on the left bank of the Hanle river are much less elevated, yet they rise as they advance to the eastward. The descent of this river too, though very gentle in the upper part of its course, while its valley is broad, is probably very abrupt in the last few miles, where its channel is rocky and its ravine narrow. The elevation of its junction with the Indus is, I believe, about 13,800 feet above the level of the sea.

On the 19th of September our road lay in a westerly direction down the Indus. The weather was still extremely unsettled, the sky being cloudy and a violent north or north-west wind continuing to blow in frequent gusts. No rain, however, fell. The plain gradually narrowed as we advanced, and the mountains on the left approached by degrees close to the river. Low grassy plains, covered with a saline incrustation, quite dry, and without any brushwood or tall herbaceous vegetation, skirted the river, the course of which we followed very closely. Indeed, notwithstanding the considerable diminution of altitude, the aspect of the valley of the Indus was more dreary and barren than we had for some days been accustomed to. The rocky spurs were quite bare; and even on the level tracts no vegetation was seen, excepting on the very lowest banks, which were moistened by the river. This utter sterility was no doubt due to the absence of lateral rivulets, the hills which rose on our left hand being stony and steep, and not rising to a sufficient elevation to be covered with perpetual snow, or to accumulate and retain snow-beds in their ravines till a late period of the year.

The rock on the left-hand mountains during the day was quite different from any that had hitherto occurred, being a conglomerate, with rounded stones of various sizes, many of them granite. The matrix was of a very dark colour, and generally extremely hard; more rarely it was a coarse sand, crumbling to pieces. This conglomerate was everywhere stratified, the beds dipping to the south-west, at an angle of about forty-five degrees. During the day the river varied much in width, being seldom less than twenty-five yards, and sometimes as much as eighty. The stream was generally very gentle, not exceeding two miles an hour, except in a few rapids, and the river was in most places fordable. We encamped on the left bank, in a place where it was shallow and wide.

On the 20th of September we continued at first to follow the left bank of the Indus, which gradually assumed a more northerly direction. The mountains on both sides approached much more closely to the river than they had done the day before, and those on the right continued extremely lofty. The river now flowed more rapidly, and was often wider and more shallow; one rapid was not less than 150 yards in width. Banks of alluvial clayey conglomerate were usually interposed between the mountains and the river, forming cliffs which attained not unfrequently an elevation of fifty feet. These were separated by projecting spurs, over which the road passed wherever they advanced so close to the centre of the valley as to prevent a passage along the level plain. Some small streamlets were crossed during the day, and in consequence the vegetation was at times more varied, and at the same time more luxuriant, than it had been the day before. A few bushes of *Myricaria* were seen on the bank of the river; and in the lateral ravines the ordinary shrubs and herbaceous vegetation were common. The only new plant was a species of *Labiatæ*, a coarse-growing under-shrub, probably a species of *Ballota*.

The hard conglomerate of the day before did not again occur, various forms of clay-slate being the prevailing rock. The steep slopes were, however, very frequently covered with a talus of angular fragments, which obscured the structure of the lower portions of the mountains, at the same time that it revealed the nature of the higher strata, which would otherwise have been inaccessible. Red and green jaspery rocks, very hard and brittle, were abundant, with various forms of greenstone, at times closely resembling syenite. These were evidently the same rocks as had been met with in the neighbourhood of Hanle, and along the river for some way below that town. Their recurrence here, therefore, tended to confirm what had for some time appeared to me to be the prevailing strike of these formations, namely, from S.S.E. to N.N.W.

After following the course of the Indus for about eight miles, we turned abruptly to the left, ascending a narrow gorge, in which a considerable stream flowed from the south-west. The slope was, from the first, considerable, and the course of the ravine very winding. Steep rocky cliffs rose precipitously on both sides, and generally approached so close to one another that their tops could not be seen. The channel of the stream was at first stony and quite bare, but after a mile bushes of the *Myricaria* became common, fringing the stream, but nowhere growing at any distance from it. These gradually increased in size and abundance, and at our camping place, three miles from the commencement of the ravine, they were generally small trees, many of them not less than fifteen feet in height, with stout erect trunks five or six inches in diameter.

The morning of the 21st of September was bright and clear, and intensely frosty, the unsettled weather which had continued since our leaving Hanle having quite disappeared. Our road still lay up the gorge, which had quite the same appearance as on the previous day. High precipices, or very steep banks, hemmed in the stream on both sides. Small trees of *Myricaria* still continued abundant in the immediate vicinity of the water; elsewhere, all was as desolate as ever. Some of these trees were not less than a foot in diameter; the trunk was generally very short, often branching within a foot of the base. At intervals there was a good deal of alluvium, partly in the shape of coarse conglomerate, partly a fine micaceous sand, filling up the recesses at the bends of the ravine. After three miles, the ravine suddenly expanded into a narrow plain, the surface of which was irregularly undulating, and completely encrusted with salt. As this plain was interesting in consequence of the production of borax, we encamped on the bank of the little stream about a mile from the end of the gorge, and remained stationary the next day in order to examine the nature of the locality in which the borax is found.

As the day's journey was a very short one, we arrived at the salt plain by eight o'clock A.M. The air was still quite frosty. While our tents were being pitched on a dry bank a little way above the stream, we proceeded to its bank, and were not a little surprised to find the water quite tepid, notwithstanding the extreme cold of the air. On procuring a thermometer, it was found to have a temperature of 69°. Advancing up the stream, we found that numerous hot springs rose on its banks, and sometimes under the water. The hottest of these had a temperature of 174°. From these springs gas was copiously evolved, smelling strongly of sulphur; and in their immediate neighbourhood the water of the little river had a faintly sulphurous taste, though elsewhere it was quite pure and good. The stream, which was perhaps twenty feet wide, was usually rather deep. Dense masses of aquatic weeds, chiefly species of *Zannichellia* and *Potamogeton*, grew in the water, and along the margins their dead stems, mixed with mud, formed immense banks, scarcely strong enough to bear the weight of a man, and yet seemingly quite solid. A small crustaceous animal was common among the weeds, but though I searched with care I could find no shells. The stream was full of fish, which swarmed among the weeds, and darted backwards and forwards in the tepid water in immense shoals. They were generally about six inches in length, and appeared to my inexperienced eye to belong to two or three species, all different from those which had been seen at Hanle. In the hottest water of the hot springs I collected three species of *Conferva*.

The existence of the tree *Myricaria* in the gorges between Pugha and the Indus, which had appeared to us at the time very remarkable, was fully explained by the occurrence of the hot springs, and the consequent high temperature of the water of the stream, and was peculiarly interesting as an illustration of the influence of temperature upon vegetation. It may fairly be considered, I think, as a proof, that arboreous vegetation does not cease at great elevations in consequence of the rarefaction of the air, but only on account of the diminution of temperature which usually accompanies increased elevation. The trees of *Myricaria,* it must be observed, came abruptly to an end with the ravine, none occurring on the open plain. We cannot suppose that the trifling increased elevation caused their disappearance; it seems probable that the narrow walls of the gorge, by concentrating the heat, prevented its escape, and that, therefore, the temperature was more elevated than in the open plain, where the action of winds and free radiation combined to lower it. The occurrence of fish in the water of Pugha, at an elevation of nearly 15,500 feet above the level of the sea, is also very remarkable, and still more strikingly demonstrative of the same fact, inasmuch as it would certainly not have been very surprising that air at that elevation should, from its rarity, be insufficient for the support of life in animals breathing by gills.

At the gorge, where the narrow ravine expands into the lake plain of Pugha, the rock is clay-slate, but the hills which skirt the open plain are micaceous schist, varying much in appearance, often with large crystals of garnet, and crumbling rapidly to decay. On the surface of the plain lay many scattered boulders of a peculiar kind of granite, evidently transported from a considerable distance along the stream; and in all the central parts of the plain, a very remarkable conglomerate in horizontal strata, consisting of angular fragments of the surrounding rocks, cemented together by calcareous matter, was observed.

The whole of the plain is covered, to the depth of several feet at least, with white salt, principally borax, which is obtained in a tolerably pure state by digging, the superficial layer, which contains a little mixture of other saline matters, being rejected. There is at present little export of borax from Pugha, the demand for the salt in Upper India being very limited, and the export to Europe almost at an end.

It has long been known that borax is produced naturally in different parts of Tibet, and the salt imported thence into India was at one time the principal source of supply of the European market. I am not aware that any of the places in which the borax is met with had previously been visited by any European traveller, but the nature of the localities in which it occurs has been the subject of frequent inquiry, and several more or less detailed accounts have been made public. These differ considerably from one another, and no description that I have met with accords with that of the Pugha valley. Mr. Saunders* describes (from hearsay) the borax lake north of Jigatzi as twenty miles in circumference, and says that the borax is dug from its margins, the deeper and more central parts producing common salt. From the account of Mr. Blane†, who describes, from the information of the natives, the borax district north of Lucknow, and, therefore, in the more western part of the course of the Sanpu, it would appear that the lake there contains boracic acid, and that the borax is artificially prepared by

* Turner's Tibet, p. 406. † Phil. Tr. 1787, p. 297.

saturating the sesquicarbonate of soda, which is so universally produced on the surface of Tibet, with the acid. At least, the statement that the production of borax is dependent on the amount of soda, leads to this conclusion. The whole description, however, (as is, indeed, to be expected in a native account of a chemical process,) is very obscure, and not to be depended upon. Mr. Saunders does not notice any hot springs in the neighbourhood of the borax; but in the more western district described by Mr. Blane, hot springs seem to accompany the borax lake as at Pugha.

It is not impossible that the three districts in which the occurrence of borax has been noticed, which are only a very small portion of those which exist, may represent three stages of one and the same phenomenon. The boracic acid lake may, by the gradual influx of soda, be gradually converted into borax, which, from its great insolubility, will be deposited as it is formed. On the drainage or drying-up of such a lake, a borax plain, similar to that of Pugha, would be left behind*.

From Pugha, two roads towards Le were open to us. We might either return to the Indus, and follow the valley of that river throughout, or proceed by a more direct route across the mountains to join the road from Lake Chumoreri to Le, by which Mr. Trebeck had travelled on his way to Piti. As we knew that the Indus route would be surveyed by Captain Strachey, who was desirous of following the course of the river as far as prac-

* I have made over all my specimens of the borax and other saline products of Tibet to Dr. R. D. Thomson, of Glasgow, who is at present engaged in examining them.

ticable, we preferred the more mountainous road, and, therefore, on leaving our encampment at Pugha, on the morning of the 23rd of September, we continued to ascend the valley of the little stream, on the banks of which we had been encamped. For the first two miles the plain was nearly level, and similar in character to what has just been described, hot springs being observed at intervals.

Two miles from our encampment, we stopped and examined the spot whence sulphur is obtained, at the base of the mountain slope on the north side of the valley. Ascending a few feet over a loose talus of shingle, which skirted the bottom of the hill, we found two narrow caverns in the slaty rock, apparently natural, or only a little widened by art, roughly circular, and less than three feet in diameter at the mouth. One of these caverns continued a long way inwards, nearly horizontally, but it contracted considerably in diameter, and was so dark that we could not penetrate far. The rock was principally gypsum, interstratified with very friable mica-slate. Sometimes the gypsum was amorphous and powdery, at other times in needles two or three inches long, perpendicular to the strata of slate. The sulphur was in small quantities, scattered among the gypsum, and was more abundant in the lower beds. It was frequently in very perfect crystals, not, however, of any great size.

The air which issued from these funnel-shaped apertures was very sensibly warm, and had a strongly sulphurous odour. Unfortunately, we had not anticipated the necessity for observing the temperature, which was not by any means oppressive, and was only remarkable in contrast with the extreme cold of the external air.

In the neighbourhood of the sulphur-pits, the hot springs along the course of the stream were very numerous, evolving much gas. A little higher they ceased altogether, and the upper part of the plain was without any springs, as was evident from the quantity of ice by which it was covered. For more than a mile it was a dead level, and very swampy; but afterwards the valley became gently sloping and gravelly, the little stream being often hidden under the pebbles. Large boulders of the same granite which we had observed the day before, were scattered over the surface. The vegetation in this valley was extremely scanty, a few scattered tufts of *Dama*, and some shrubby *Artemisiæ*, were occasionally seen, but the herbaceous vegetation had been almost entirely destroyed by the intense morning frosts, which had for some time been of daily occurrence. On the latter part of the day's journey the rock on the mountain-side changed from mica-slate to gneiss, of which very lofty scarped cliffs rose abruptly on the right hand. We encamped on a level spot, after ten miles of almost imperceptible ascent.

Next morning we continued to ascend the valley, which was now very rugged, from masses of boulders, which were heaped one on another to a very great thickness. The stream had cut for itself a narrow channel, nearly a hundred feet in depth, the walls of which were entirely composed of huge incoherent masses of rock, all more or less angular. A walk of three miles brought us to the crest of the pass, which was nearly level and grassy for about a mile; its elevation was about 16,500 feet. The pass (Pulokanka La) is a very deep depression in the axis of the chain, which runs parallel to the left bank of the Indus, separating the waters tributary to that river from those which join the Zanskar river, some of the feeders of the latter springing from the valleys on the western slopes of these mountains. The hills right and left of the pass rise very boldly into rugged masses, contrasting strongly with the level plain which constitutes the pass, in which the watershed is scarcely perceptible.

From the pass the descent was considerably more abrupt than the ascent had been. The valley to the right was bare and stony, watered by a small streamlet, which had, as on the eastern face of the pass, cut a deep channel for itself among boulders. On descending, we turned gradually to the right, and a lake by degrees came in view, towards the southern extremity of which the road advanced over undulating hills of fine clay, full of fresh-water shells, almost entirely of one species of *Lymnæa*, of which the specimens were extremely numerous. This lake is the Thogji Chumo of Mr. Trebeck, who travelled along it on his journey from Le to Piti.

I was much surprised, and not a little pleased, to find that the clay-beds contained fossils; as, except on one occasion in Piti, where I found one or two specimens of a small *Planorbis*, I had in vain sought in the clayey beds for any trace of organized beings. Here, however, shells were in prodigious abundance, and as the species was a large one, they were very conspicuous. The clay formation was horizontally stratified, and quite impalpable.

The uppermost beds were at least a hundred feet above the level of the lake; and as the valley by which we descended was in its lower part almost horizontal, the lacustrine beds extended to a considerable distance from the lake, forming a slightly undulating surface, over which the road ran.

After reaching the banks of the lake, the road kept its eastern shore throughout its whole length, which was about three miles, and we encamped close to its north end, on the edge of a level salt plain. Our elevation was about 15,500 feet. The margins of the lake, which was intensely saline, were generally very shallow, and its banks often swampy, and covered with saline plants, especially *Chenopodiaceæ;* a species of *Suæda*, with cylindrical fleshy leaves, was especially abundant, growing in the soft mud close to the banks of the lake. A *Blysmus*, several grasses, and *Ranunculus Cymbalaria* were also common along the banks of the lake. No shells could be seen in the water. The surrounding hills were not very lofty, but often rose abruptly several hundred feet, and were in general rugged and rocky. At the height of perhaps 150 feet above the lake, a weathered mark could be traced on the face of the mountains, wherever they were rocky, everywhere quite horizontal. This was most conspicuous from a distance, and became indistinct on a near approach. It appeared to indicate, as I shall hereafter show, the level of the surface of the lake at some former period.

On the morning of the 25th of September, our day's journey commenced by rounding the north end of the lake, keeping at some distance from its margin to avoid swamp. For about two miles from the northern end, the ground continued almost level, and contained great masses of the lacustrine clay quite horizontally stratified, and very little higher than the surface of the water, but here quite without shells. A wide valley, rising gently towards the north, lay beyond this level plain; but our road, passing across the end of the lake, ascended another valley, which ran in a north-west direction from its north-west corner. The slope of this valley was very gentle. It was bounded by low undulating or rocky hills, on which, where the surface was suitable, the same remarkable water-mark could be traced continuously, and still, to all appearance, quite horizontal. The centre of the valley was occupied by clay, at first non-fossiliferous, but a little further on containing a great abundance of shells, the same as in the bed seen the day before. A few specimens of a very small bivalve, seemingly a species of *Cyclas*, were also met with; but they were so very rare, that they bore an infinitesimally small proportion to the *Lymnæa*.

For several miles the ancient water-mark could be traced along the sides of the hills, appearing to descend gradually, as the valley slightly rose in elevation. Beds of clay continued to occupy the middle of the valley nearly as long as the water-mark remained visible. At last it disappeared where a depression on the left, leading to the valley of Rukchin, seemed to indicate the former drainage of the lake, at a time when its waters occupied a much higher level, and contained in a living state the large mollusca of which the shelly coverings still remain in such vast abundance in the clay. As it was at the very edge of the lacustrine clay formation that the shells were so abundant, while the masses of clay in the vicinity of our encampment of the 25th, at the north-east extremity of the lake, were without any, it would appear that the species was quite littoral, while in the more central parts fine mud was deposited, without shells. The outlet was indicated to me by Major Cunningham, who in a previous journey had travelled along a part of the Rukchin valley in descending from the Lachalang pass towards the salt lake. As it may fairly be inferred that the lake was quite fresh at the time when it was inhabited by *Lymnææ* and *Cyclades*, it is satisfactory to know that so very small an increase of the height of the surface of the water, as about 150 feet, would be sufficient to admit of its discharging its waters along the course of an open valley into one of the tributaries of the Zanskar river.

Our road, after passing the ravine on the left, along which I suppose the discharge of the lake at its original level to have been effected, turned still more towards the north, and ascending an open valley to the right, crossed a low *col*, or pass, and descended into a small basin surrounded by hills, which was evidently at some former period the bed of a small lake, for it was filled with pure fine clay, in which, however, I could not observe any shells. From this plain we passed into another open valley, up which we ascended in a northerly direction for five or six miles, encamping where the mountains on both sides began to close in a circle. Throughout the day we had been gradually but very gently ascending, and the height of our encampment was probably about 16,500 feet. We were about two miles from the Tunglung pass, a depression in the range parallel to the Indus, the same ridge which we had crossed before descending to the salt lake. The axis of the range had been very near us on the right hand since we had crossed it on the 24th, and had sent down a succession of spurs, separated by wide valleys, along which we had been travelling. These separating ridges appeared usually to rise to an elevation of from one to two thousand feet above the nearly level valleys which lay at their bases, and were, though often rocky, less remarkably so than in many previous parts of our journey.

The elevated country surrounding the sources of the Parang and Hanle rivers, and those of the more eastern branches of the Zanskar, as well as that encircling Lake Chumoreri, constitutes as near an approach to what Humboldt has denominated a knot (*nœud*) of mountains, as any part of the Himalaya which I have visited; not that I conceive there is any reason to suppose that we have in this part of the chain an intersection of two mountain masses of different ages, to which cause the distinguished geographer is disposed to assign those aggregations of mountains which he has so designated. There is, however, as indicated by the origin of so many considerable streams in a confined area, an extensive tract of highly elevated land, in which the valleys have a very gentle slope, while the surrounding mountains are not much elevated above them. The whole tract is nevertheless eminently mountainous, if contrasted, not with the still more rugged districts by which it is on every side surrounded, but with the hilly districts of less alpine countries.

In the elevated district which we had been traversing

since crossing the Parang pass, there is little or no cultivation, a field or two at Hanle and at the monastery on the banks of Lake Chumoreri (as I am informed by Major Cunningham) being the only exceptions. The district, however, is much frequented by a nomade population of shepherds, who, living in tents, move about with their flocks as the abundance of food or their own caprice may lead them. Clusters of black tents were now and then seen by us at intervals, especially in Rupchu, by which name the districts round the salt lake are known to the wandering inhabitants.

During the whole of the 25th of September, a furious north wind had continued to blow, accompanied by a cloudy sky, and all the indications of extremely unsettled weather, such as had been met with in the neighbourhood of Hanle only a week before. It was evident that, as winter approached, these periods of disturbance recurred more and more frequently. This time the fury of the blast increased as the day advanced, and after dark the cold in our tents was very severe. About 10 P.M. it began to snow slightly, and at daybreak on the 26th the ground was covered with snow to a depth of between two and three inches. As we had a prospect of arriving in milder regions by diminishing our elevation during the day, we hastened our departure as much as possible. A mile and a half of level ground brought us directly under the pass, the ascent to which was at last very steep. The road was very stony and rugged, but everything being covered with snow a good deal deeper than on the open plain on which we had encamped, we did not linger at the summit. The wind still blew strongly from the north, driving in our faces the still falling snow, and opposing our progress towards the crest, which was very rocky, being composed of a mass of hard stratified quartz. The elevation of the summit was about 17,500 feet.

The descent from the pass was very rapid. After a few paces, we were in a narrow and steep ravine, in which we continued to descend very abruptly, without obtaining any view of the surrounding country. Three miles from the summit, at perhaps 2000 feet lower level, snow ceased to lie on the ground, but it continued to fall lightly till the afternoon. Large rounded tufts of an Alsinaceous plant were common on the upper part of the descent, conspicuous under the snow. Lower down, the remains of species of *Corydalis* and *Saussurea* were discoverable in crevices of the rocks, the only remains of the alpine vegetation. The rock on both sides was clay-slate.

Continuing to descend rapidly, the ravine widened a little, and became filled with a most extensive development of alluvial conglomerate, forming thick masses, worn into pinnacles and fantastic shapes, like the similar deposits above Sungnam in Kunawar. This was particularly conspicuous where a lateral valley joined that along which we descended, a flat-topped promontory of alluvium there projecting far beyond the primitive rocks.

After a descent of about 4000 feet of perpendicular height, we arrived at Giah, elevated 13,400 feet above the sea, not a little glad to be among houses, in a more temperate region than it had been for some time our lot to travel in. We took up our quarters in the upper room of a two-storied house, which had been prepared for our reception, and willingly agreed to halt a day in order to give time for arrangements, for a change of porters, and a rest to our servants and guides. Giah will be recollected, by those acquainted with Moorcroft's travels, as the place where he entered the Tibetan country, and where he was for some time kept in considerable uncertainty as to the nature of the reception he would meet with. Since that time the supremacy of the Sikhs has entirely changed the state of the country; and though the king (Gylpo) of Giah still exists, he does not even exercise a nominal sovereignty, but lives a pensioner on the Sikh government, without power and with a very limited income.

The influence of the Sikhs has, however, produced little change in the character of the people, as their occupation of the country, except in Le itself, and at one or two military posts, is entirely nominal, and only maintained by the moral influence of their known superiority in resources and military skill. The gumpa, or monastery, as in Moorcroft's time, crowns a rocky hill on the right bank of the Giah stream, while the town, or more properly village, on the left bank, is built on the steep alluvial banks high above the stream. There was a considerable extent of cultivation round the village, barley and peas being the chief crops; both had been cut, but were still lying in small heaps in the fields. Notwithstanding the great elevation, a number of poplar-trees, of the large cordate-leaved species (which seems identical with *P. balsamifera*), occur in the village, several of which attain a considerable size.

On the morning of the 28th of September we resumed

our journey towards Le. By crossing the Tunglung pass, we had again gained the eastern slope of the ridge dividing the waters of the Zanskar from those of the Indus. The Giah stream flows towards the latter river with a north-easterly course, and two marches of little more than seven miles each, brought us to the banks of the Indus at a village called Upshi. For the first mile after leaving Giah, the valley was somewhat open, with steep banks of alluvial conglomerate; it then contracted rather suddenly into a narrow ravine, with steep rocky walls, composed of highly inclined strata of conglomerate and sandstone. Owing to the diminished elevation, the vegetation was considerably more recognizable than it had been for the last week, and several shrubby plants were seen which had long been absent. *Ephedra* was common in the crevices of the rocks, and the Tibetan rose and a small shrubby *Lonicera* grew on the gravelly banks of the little stream.

At Miru, a considerable village where we encamped, the valley expanded into a little plain, filled as usual with alluvium, and covered with cultivation. A few poplar-trees occurred in the village. The ravine contracted immediately below this place, and was, if possible, more narrow and rocky than the day before, as the little stream had to be crossed not less than four or five times in as many miles, on small wooden bridges of rough planks. A very beautiful Labiate shrub, a species of *Perowskia*, with bright blue flowers, which I afterwards found very abundant in the Indus valley from 12,000 to 8000 feet, was here met with for the first time. Close to its junction with the Indus, the ravine expanded into an open plain, well covered with houses and enclosures, with scattered poplar and willow trees, as well as a few apricots, and traversed by canals of irrigation conducted from the little Giah rivulet. The Indus is here not more than forty feet wide, flowing swiftly over large boulders, and quite unfordable.

Throughout the whole course of this very remarkable gorge by which we descended from Giah, the rock continued to be conglomerate, alternating with strata of sandstone and of a very friable slate. The conglomerate was extremely hard, and generally of a dark brown colour. The matrix, which had often a semi-vitrified appearance, was not less hard than the enclosed stones, which were all rounded and very various in size and composition, jasper rock, granite, and quartz being all seen. The sandstone which accompanied the conglomerate varied much in colour, various shades of red, brown, and green being predominant. It was also extremely hard. These strata, which were highly inclined, often nearly vertical, were in general well marked, in consequence of the beds of hard sandstone and conglomerate being thrown out in relief by the more rapid decay of the soft slates with which they alternated. The dip was everywhere very variable, and several very distinct sections were displayed, where it was evident that the strata were curved and sinuated. The curves observed were convex below; the strike of the strata was nearly perpendicular to the general direction of the ravine, or from north-west to south-east.

From Upshi, our course lay down the Indus valley in a direction west of north. The width of the Indus, which was a rapid stream, varied from thirty or forty to a hundred feet. Platforms of alluvium, almost level-topped, and often attaining a thickness of a hundred feet, were interposed between the river and the mountains, which, still composed of highly inclined strata of conglomerate and its associated rocks, advanced in a succession of spurs towards the centre of the valley. These platforms were quite bare of vegetation, a few tufts of a prickly *Echinops* being the only plant worthy of note which I observed. No villages were passed till we reached Marsilang, at which we encamped after a journey of about ten miles. Here there was very extensive cultivation on the surface of the platform, on both sides of a deep ravine, cut in the alluvium by a considerable stream, which descended from the west. The plantations of willow and poplar were very luxuriant. The willows were planted in rows, and were frequently pollarded, their twigs being in great demand for baskets and other useful purposes in so treeless a country. When allowed to grow their full size, they spread much, and attain a length of upwards of thirty feet. The cultivated willows of Tibet are mostly European forms; *Salix fragilis* and *S. alba* are the most common. The poplars are of two sorts: one a spreading tree with large cordate leaves, which was first seen in Upper Kunawar, and is common in all the Tibetan villages, up to the highest limit of tree cultivation; it is quite identical with *Populus balsamifera*, which I cannot distinguish in the herbarium from *P. laurifolia*, of Ledebour. The other, which I had not before seen in Tibet, was a tall, erect, and slender tree, with much darker foliage and smaller leaves; it seems, so far as my specimens enable me to decide, to be the common black poplar (*P. nigra*) of Europe.

At Marsilang the Indus is crossed by a good wooden bridge, thirty-four paces in length, which enables its inhabitants to communicate with the large villages and extensive cultivated tracts on the east bank of the river. As soon as we left the cultivated lands of Marsilang, on the morning of the 1st of October, we found ourselves again on a platform of alluvium; but after a few miles we reached another village, with extensive cultivation, and on the latter part of the day's journey passed through a succession of villages separated by gradually shorter intervals of unprofitable and barren land. These cultivated tracts were everywhere well irrigated; indeed, every spot, where irrigation was easy of execution, seemed to be under cultivation. Each village had its plantation of poplars and willows, not, however, so plentiful as at Marsilang. The grain had everywhere been cut and housed, the operations of harvest being seemingly quite at an end. The whole of this richly-cultivated district is called Chashut.

Our journey of the 2nd of October was for about six miles through an uninterrupted tract of cultivation, very little elevated above the level of the river, the alluvial platforms being here of inconsiderable thickness. The direction of the valley was also much more westerly, and the mountains on both sides had receded considerably from the river, leaving an open plain of five or six miles in width. Numerous irrigation channels intersected the fields, which gradually, as we proceeded, united one to another, till at last they all combined into one large and deep canal, by which the superfluous waters were conveyed to the Indus. Crossing this canal, we reached the river, which we crossed by a bridge twenty-five paces in length. A few houses, and a small patch of cultivation, lay on the right bank of the river, immediately beyond the bridge, but no extent of fertile country; low spurs of rocky hills descending from the north, close down upon the Indus. After crossing the bridge we turned up a wide and gravelly valley between two of these ridges, the course of which we followed, ascending very gradually among large boulders, strewed over the surface, for about three miles. We then turned abruptly to the left, through a narrow ravine in the low granitic hills by which the valley was on that side bounded. Emerging from this, we entered a quite similar and parallel valley, and obtained our first view of the town of Le, covering the top and slopes of a steep hill by which the valley was apparently terminated, about two miles beyond the point at which we entered it.

Le, the capital of the province of Ladak, and the most important place, and only town, of Western Tibet, is situated about three miles from the Indus, in the upper part of an open valley, which rises gradually as it recedes from the river, so that the town is rather more than 1200 feet above its level, or about 11,800 feet above the sea. The town occupies the slope, and surrounds the base of a low spur, on the left or east side of the valley, while the centre and right side are occupied by extensive tracts of cultivation, the fields rising in terraces one above another, and watered by little rills drawn from a stream which descends in the centre of the valley.

The aspect of the town, which is very peculiar, is faithfully represented in the frontispiece to the second volume of Moorcroft's Travels, from a sketch by Mr. Trebeck.

In the neighbourhood of the town there are several small enclosures, planted with poplar and willow trees, in one of which we pitched our tents. These plantations were all young, a very fine garden of old trees having been, it was said, destroyed at the time of the Sikh invasion. The governor of Ladak, a deputy of Maharaja Gulab Singh, the ruler of Kashmir, to whom the rule of Ladak has devolved as a dependency of the latter country, resides in the town; but the detachment of troops, amounting to about 150 men, who form the military garrison of the place, occupy a small square fort on the west side of the valley, about a mile from the town of Le.

The peculiarities of the Buddhist religion, as practised in Tibet, which are everywhere conspicuous in all parts of Ladak, are especially remarkable in the capital. The principal monasteries in the neighbourhood of Le are at some distance from the town in the vicinity of villages both up and down the Indus; but religious edifices, of the many kinds which are everywhere so common in Tibet, are seen all round Le in great numbers. Along the road by which we approached the town, there is a very long building, of the kind called *Mané*, extending for more than half a mile. It consists of two parallel walls, twelve or fifteen feet apart, and nearly six feet high, the intervals between which are filled up with stones and rubbish, and the whole covered with a sloping roof, which rises at a gentle angle to the central ridge, midway between the two walls. On the roof are laid large slabs of slate, every one of which is covered with Tibetan letters, or more rarely with a rude drawing of a temple. The words on these stones are (I believe, invariably) a repetition of the mystical Buddhist prayer, from one of the words of which these curious, and apparently useless, erections take their name. The Mane seems one of the most indispensable accompaniments of a Tibetan village, and they may occasionally be seen even in desert tracts; so that the amount of labour which has been expended in their construction must have been very great, some of the largest containing many millions of repetitions of the words *Om Mane Padme Hom.* In the smaller villages they are often very inferior in size, sometimes not more than twenty or thirty feet in length, and three feet high. Every traveller has constant occasion to notice that in passing these walls the Tibetans always leave them on the right hand, considering it both wrong and unlucky to do otherwise; those proceeding in contrary directions therefore take opposite sides.

Equally conspicuous in the environs of Le are the urn-like buildings, called Chokten or Chosten, which are, I believe, erected over the ashes of Lamas, or priests, and are, therefore, in a country where a third or fourth part of the male population adopt a monastic life, particularly abundant. Long rows of these, consisting of twenty or more urns of various sizes, may often be seen in conspicuous places above the villages, forming, from the brilliant whitewash with which they are covered when new, very prominent objects. Many of those near Lè are of large size, and ornamented with rude paintings of dragons and other mythological animals of uncouth form.

The religion of Tibet, from the remarkable nature of its institutions and ceremonies, has of late years attracted much attention; but as, from the hurried nature of my journey, I had no opportunity of acquiring any information regarding it which has not already been made public, it is not necessary for me to dwell upon it at any length. Throughout the whole of Western Tibet, the monasteries are very poor, in comparison with those in the neighbourhood of Lassa, of which we read such gorgeous descriptions; all their wealth in silver and gold having been plundered by the Sikhs, during their short possession of the country as far east as Garu and Taklakhar. Still the number of Lamas does not seem to have much diminished, though they are more dependent upon the cultivation of the soil than in Eastern Tibet, where some of the monasteries are said to contain thousands of priests.

The town of Le is said to contain about 3000 inhabitants. Many of the houses are very high, the former residence of the king containing seven stories. They are usually built of unburnt brick, formed from the fine lacustrine clay of the neighbourhood. The Sikh Thannadar has lately built for himself a house of stone, but he found it necessary to bring lime from Nubra, a distance of nearly forty miles, none being procurable so near in the valley of the Indus. The timber used in the construction of the houses is all poplar or willow, both of which are found to last a very long time in the arid climate of Tibet. The beams are laid perhaps two feet apart, and covered sometimes with small planking, but more generally with brushwood, over which is laid a thick coating of clay, so as to form a flat roof, to which there is usually access by a small stair or ladder.

The mountain ranges which bound the valley in which the town of Le is situated, though not lofty, are very generally rocky and inaccessible. They consist partly of distinctly stratified gneiss, but principally of a fine white granite, which decays with great rapidity, and contains many irregular nodules of an iron grey colour, much finer in the grain than the rest. The width of the fertile plain of Chashut, over which I made the last two marches down the Indus, had prevented me from ascertaining the nature of the rocks on the mountains to the left, so that I cannot fix the exact point where the granitic eruption comes in contact with the slates and conglomerates of the Giah ravine.

CHAPTER VII.

Departure from Le—Sabu Valley—Pass between Le and Nubra—Snow —Encamp at 15,500 feet—Digar—Valley of Shayuk—Alluvium— *Populus Euphratica*—Tsatti—Nubra river—District of Nubra— Villages—Irrigation—Saline soil—Isolated rocks—Chirasa—Panamik—Lower Nubra—Platforms of Alluvium—Traces of a great flood—Unmaru—Kuru—Great contraction of valley—Mountain pass of Waris—Boghdan ravine—Chorbat—Mahommedan population—Villages—Outburst of granite—Siksa—Khapalu—Open plain of Khapalu—Junction of Shayuk and Indus—Nar—Iskardo plain— Description of Iskardo—Aqueduct—Fort—Lacustrine clay formation —Vegetation.

WHILE we were at Le there was a good deal of unsettled weather, and two very slight falls of snow. On the 9th of October we had an opportunity of observing an eclipse of the sun, which was welcomed by the inhabitants of the town with a most discordant beating of drums, intended to frighten away the demons who had taken possession of the sun. After a week's halt, Major Cunningham and myself started in different directions; Major Cunningham following the course of the Indus, and proceeding by Dras to Kashmir, while I crossed the range of mountains to the north into the valley of the Shayuk, and descended along that river to its junction with the Indus. The mountain range which separates these two rivers barely rises into the region of perpetual snow, a very few peaks only retaining any snow throughout the year. It is therefore crossed by passes at the head of each valley; but the pass nearest to Le having a small but very steep glacier on its northern face, is difficult and dangerous in autumn, after the snow has entirely melted from the surface of the ice. I was, therefore, recommended to cross into Nubra, by a pass a few miles further east, at the head of the valley of Sabu, which is separated from that in which the town of Le lies, by a steep ridge of granite hills.

I left Le on the morning of the 11th of October. The road to the Sabu valley enters the granite range close to the town, ascending a narrow stony valley in an easterly direction, and crossing by a short steep ascent a depression in the ridge, to descend into a narrow ravine which has a south-east course into the Sabu valley, up which the road led. The hills were very stony and bare, or covered with the large *Echinops* of the Indus valley, of which the heads of fruit were falling to pieces. I encamped for the night in the valley of Sabu, which is very like that of Le, with pretty extensive cultivation, but few trees.

Next day I crossed the pass. The ascent was very long and fatiguing, and, from the lateness of the season, very uninteresting. A cold bleak wind blew from the north in strong gusts, and the sky was overcast with light clouds. The valley contracted into a rocky ravine before the road left it to ascend rapidly the steep mountain-sides, which were covered with masses of boulders, heaped together in great confusion. The upper part of the ascent, which was very steep, was covered with snow, which lay on the loose stones of the crest to the depth of about a foot. It was late in the evening before I reached the top of the pass, the distance being much greater than I had been led to anticipate. The elevation of the summit, by the observations of Captain Strachey, is about 18,300 feet.

On the north face of the pass snow lay thickly for two miles or rather more, and more scantily for a mile further. As evening had begun to close before I reached the summit, I hurried my descent as much as possible. Fortunately, a great part of my baggage porters were in advance, but it had been for some time quite dark before I reached a spot sufficiently free of snow to be suitable for an encampment. The night was intensely cold, the sky being clear; and next morning, at half-past six o'clock, the thermometer stood at 15°. At the same time I found that water boiled at 184°, indicating an elevation of upwards of 15,500 feet.

In the morning I made a short march to the village of Digar, which I ought to have reached the day before, had not the darkness prevented me. The distance was not more than four miles, and the descent about 2500 feet, Digar being rather more than 13,000 feet above the level of the sea. The general direction of the valley in which I was encamped was north-east, and it was surrounded on all sides by extremely rugged mountains, now much covered with snow, down to about 14,000 feet. Throughout the descent, vast piles of boulders, heaped one on another, and forming steep banks, evidently moraines, occupied the flanks of the valley. The village of Digar, though small, and possessing only two small trees, had a considerable extent of cultivation, and seemed prosperous. It was situated on the left side of the valley, or rather on the slope of the mountains on that side opposite a lateral ravine, from which a stream of boulders had at one time descended. The centre of the valley was much lower, being excavated out of the alluvium which had once filled the whole.

On the morning of the 14th of October, I descended to the valley of the Shayuk, making a march of fifteen miles to the village of Tsatti, on the right bank of that river. The road skirted the steep stony hills on the left side of the valley, parallel to the Digar stream, for about two miles, descending rapidly, but still high above the bottom of the dell. The Digar ravine, before reaching the Shayuk, joined a wider one which descends from the south-east, and the united valley has a nearly due north direction. As the road turned by degrees to the left, round a spur of the mountains, the Shayuk valley came in sight, 1500 feet below. It was of considerable width, and very stony, barren, and desolate. Mountains of black slate, very lofty and rugged, in many places too steep for snow to lie, were seen to the north-east, from among which the river appeared to issue into the more open tract immediately below.

The road did not descend at once to the level of the river, but, turning abruptly to the left, proceeded along a platform of alluvium, at least a thousand feet in thickness, for more than a mile, before it descended, which it did at last very abruptly down a steep sandy slope. The mass of alluvium was, in many places, almost pure sand, but in general many pebbles and boulders were mixed with it. Towards the river it presented scarped cliffs, in which its composition was well seen.

The Shayuk, where I descended to it, flowed through a wide gravelly plain, varying in breadth from one to two miles, and quite destitute of vegetation. Rocky spurs of black slate and conglomerate, with many granite veins, projecting from the mountains on the south, occasionally narrowed the valley, while the recesses were generally filled with a mass of alluvium. The river was occasionally divided into several branches. In some of the recesses small trees of a peculiar species of poplar (*P. Euphratica*) were not uncommon, growing in pure sand. This tree is remarkable for its extended distribution. Originally discovered on the banks of the Euphrates, it has been found by Griffith, and more recently by Dr. Stocks and others, to be abundant on the banks of the Indus, in Sind and Multan. It occurs also at intervals along the valley of the Indus, within the mountains, but appears to be far from common, and to confine itself to hot sandy places. In several parts of Nubra it is common enough, but only, so far as I have observed, on the south side of the Shayuk. This poplar is also remarkable for the very changeable shape of its leaves, which vary from broadly deltoid and coarsely toothed, to narrow-linear and quite entire. The leaves of the full-grown tree are generally broad and much toothed, while young plants have very narrow leaves; the shoots of pollarded plants, which are common, the tree being much used for fuel, are also narrow.

After proceeding parallel to the river for six or seven miles, I crossed to the right bank. The stream was undivided, and about a hundred yards broad. It had a considerable velocity, and was about three feet deep in the centre. Its bed was full of large waterworn boulders and gravel, and the banks on both sides were, for a great distance from the river, of similar structure, and so little elevated above its surface, that a very slight rise of the water would have been sufficient to submerge them.

From the village of Tsatti, at which I encamped on the 14th of October, I followed the course of the Shayuk to its junction with a large stream descending from the north, which, from the name of the district in which the junction is situated, is commonly called the Nubra river. Thence I ascended the latter stream for about twenty miles, with the intention of making an attempt to penetrate to the north-east, across the mountains to the Nubra Chu of Vigne; but the lateness of the season, and especially the occurrence of several falls of snow, which extended down the mountain slopes almost as far as the plain, induced me to place reliance on the assurances of the people of the valley, that the difficulties of the road would be quite insurmountable.

The district of Nubra includes the whole course of the Shayuk river, from its great bend to the eastward of the point where I joined it below Digar, till it again contracts nine or ten miles below the village of Unmaru; and also the lower part of the valley of the Nubra river, as far up, indeed, as population and cultivation extend. The place of junction of the two rivers is elevated, according to my observation of the boiling-point of water, about

10,600 feet above the level of the sea. This may be considered as the mean elevation of the whole district; for the cultivated tracts nowhere rise to any height above the bed of the rivers, which have everywhere a very gentle and apparently uniform inclination.

The valley of the Shayuk is widest at the point of its junction with the Nubra river. At this place the level plain, including the gently sloping alluvium on each side, has a breadth of about six miles. The width of the valley gradually diminishes as we recede from the centre, the mountains encroaching more and more, till at last they hem in the river, leaving no space for villages or cultivation, and the valley ceases to be inhabited. The centre of the plain is uniformly occupied by a flat gravelly expanse, one to three miles in width, scarcely raised above the surface of the river, which, when flooded, covers a great part of it. On both sides of this gravelly bed, low platforms of alluvium, in the form of triangles, with their apices resting on the mountain ravines, slope very gently towards the base of mountains, which rise abruptly and precipitously on both sides of the valley, to a height of three or four thousand feet. Some of the more projecting spurs, even where the width of the valley is greatest, advance so far into the open plain as to abut upon the river and compel the traveller to ascend their slopes, in order to cross them in travelling from village to village.

The gravelly plain over which the Shayuk flows, is usually quite devoid of vegetation. A few scattered bushes of *Tamarix* and *Myricaria* appear, indeed, near its junction with the Nubra river, but further up the gravel is absolutely bare: in this it contrasts strongly with similar portions in the valley of the Nubra river, which are densely wooded. The cause of this difference seems to lie in the frequent floods which have, at different periods, devastated the whole course of the Shayuk valley, from the glaciers of Sassar. These floods, which appear to be due to the blocking-up of the upper course of the river by the ice, have been most destructive to the prosperity of the valley.

Throughout Nubra, the villages, with scarcely an exception, occupy the surface of the low platforms of alluvium which fill up the funnel-shaped terminations of the ravines. In Tibet the size of the villages, and the extent of cultivation by which they are surrounded, entirely depend on the supply of water and on the facility with which it can be diverted from its bed for purposes of irrigation; and as, in this district, the width and horizontality of the alluvial tracts are very favourable to the industry of man, the villages are in general large and surrounded with much cultivation. Indeed, a super-abundance of water is in general indicated by the swampy banks of the irrigation canals, as the water, oozing through the loose gravel of the platforms, produces a dense jungle of *Hippophaë* scrub, which makes the cultivated tracts conspicuous, even in winter, when the trees are bare of leaves and the fields of crops.

This copious supply of water no doubt depends on the great elevation of the surrounding mountains, which everywhere rise, if not above, yet almost to the level of perpetual snow, which is about 18,000 feet, so that at the head of each little stream there is either a glacier, or a snow-bed which does not entirely melt till the latter end of autumn, affording therefore a nearly perennial supply of water. Even in the hottest months slight falls of snow are of occasional occurrence at all elevations above 16,000 feet; and as every range rises much above that height, a small addition to the supply is thus obtained.

The villages have generally a few fruit-trees, as well as a good many poplars and willows, which yield almost the only timber the inhabitants can command. The walnut and *Elæagnus*, both of which trees find their upper limit in Nubra, are so extremely scarce that they are not available for such purposes.

In most parts of Nubra the soil is very generally saline, the dry grassy plains which are common on the banks of the streams being generally covered with a copious efflorescence of carbonate of soda; while the abundance of *Salsolæ* and other Chenopodiaceous plants on the dry alluvial plains, and even on the rocky hills, seems to prove that the saline matter is not confined to the immediate vicinity of water, or to the lowest levels, but is very generally diffused over the surface.

The valley of the Nubra river, for upwards of twenty miles, is very similar in general character to that of the Shayuk. The same wide gravelly expanse occupies its centre, forming a plain of one or two miles in width, through which the river runs in many branches. A great part of this gravelly plain, particularly on the right side of the valley, is covered by a dense thicket of *Hippophaë*, extending continuously for four or five miles, usually impervious, except in certain beaten tracts, and tenanted by vast numbers of hares. The gravel on which this jungle grows is almost on a level with the river, so that it is very generally swampy, and traversed here and there by little streamlets of water. The *Hippophaë* is here a small tree, attaining a height of fifteen feet, with a short thick trunk and stiff crooked spinous branches.

In several parts of the course of the Nubra river, low hills rise in the valley, isolated, or nearly so, from the mountain ranges behind, and forming, therefore, a remarkable feature. On one of these, on the right bank of the river, is situated the little fort and village of Chirasa, a considerable mass of houses, of a class a little better than those usual in the district, and conspicuous from their elevated position. The rock on which they stand is composed of a hard porphyry, which has been injected from below, and has displaced the black slate, which is the more usual rock in the lower part of this valley.

In the lower part of the ravine behind the town of Chirasa, the alluvium is more extensively developed than usual in this valley, where aqueous action seems in a great measure to have removed the accumulation of detritus, which once, no doubt, occupied the whole valley. Beds of gravelly conglomerate, at times passing into fine clay, may here be seen, at a height of perhaps 1000 feet, on the mountain-sides in isolated patches, generally faced by cliffs, in which a tendency to horizontal stratification is observable.

The lower part of the Nubra valley is very fertile, and on the east side cultivation extends, with little interruption, from Tirit as far as Panamik, in a belt varying in width from a few hundred feet to nearly a mile. The villages are large, and seem populous. Many of the houses are very substantially built, and the long sacred walls, called Mané, are numerous, and of great length and size. Several watercourses, which are carried along the sides of the hills at an elevation of several hundred feet above the cultivation, and are easily recognizable by the fringe of *Hippophaë* bushes, which forms an impenetrable belt along their margins, indicate a degree of industry and energy very unusual in Tibet, where, however, the amount of cultivable land is seldom sufficient to promise much reward to any extensive and elaborate system of irrigation.

As the advanced period of the year rendered exploration at great elevations scarcely practicable, and made it desirable to reach a lower level as soon as possible, I did not remain more than a week in Nubra. On the 22nd of October I started from Lyakjung, at the mouth of the Nubra river, towards Iskardo, following the course of the Shayuk river. The district of Nubra extends about thirty miles below the junction of the river of that name with the Shayuk; but I found the level valley gradually to diminish in width as I descended. On the 22nd of October I encamped at Hundar; on the 23rd, at Tertse; and on the 24th at Unmaru, beyond which village there is no cultivation, and the valley becomes extremely narrow. On the 25th of October I reached an encamping ground called Kuru, at the termination of the Nubra district, where the mountains, which for three days had gradually been encroaching on the valley, completely closed in, and the river entered a deep gorge, walled in on both sides by lofty and almost perpendicular cliffs of black slate.

The general aspect of the lower part of Nubra requires no particular description, as it presents much the same features as the other parts of the district. The mountains on both sides of the valley are not less steep, barren, and inaccessible than elsewhere in Tibet. The alluvial platforms, which were everywhere present, increased remarkably in thickness as they diminished in size. Widely spread out in the broadest parts of the valley, they were not more than from twenty to forty feet thick where cut across by the river, and sloped very gently. In the narrower parts of the valley they were often not less than a hundred feet high along the river. In structure these platforms varied much. The greater part certainly consisted of gravel and clay, quite unstratified, but the lower beds were very frequently fine clay, or fine sand, or alternations of these two. The superposition of the coarse beds to the fine was nearly uniformly observed, though occasionally, above the fine clays, alternations of gravel with thin beds of sand or clay were met with. In one place, on the north side of the river, nearly opposite to the village of Tertse, I found these beds to contain fresh-water shells. The fossiliferous bed was elevated very little above the present level of the river, and was composed of a fine somewhat sandy clay, stratified horizontally, and covered with upwards of fifty feet of coarse conglomerate. The shells, which were all small, were species of *Planorbis* and *Lymnæa*, apparently identical with those afterwards found in the neighbourhood of Iskardo, but quite different from those of the salt lake of Thogji.

The villages of Lower Nubra are not numerous, but some of them possess very extensive cultivation. Hundar in particular, at the mouth of a large ravine, by which a considerable tributary stream descends from the south (at the source of which there is a pass across the range into the valley of the Indus), is a very large village (probably the most populous in Nubra), with very fine orchards of apricot-trees. Walnut, mulberry, and *Elæagnus* became common at Unmaru, on the north bank of the river. Perhaps the gradual narrowing of the valley may have a considerable effect in modifying the climate, for the diminution of elevation is very inconsiderable, the river at Kuru being nearly 10,300 feet above the sea, or not more than 300 feet lower than the junction of the Shayuk and Nubra rivers.

In this part of its course, and at this advanced season, when the great summer floods are over, the Shayuk appears to be everywhere fordable. It is, however, a noble stream, with a rapid current; and is usually divided into many channels. Above Hundar, where I forded it, one branch was not less than 300 feet wide, and was from one to two feet deep. Opposite Tertse, again, I found the stream running in seven branches, of which three were from 100 to 150 feet wide, and had an average depth of about two feet, increased in the centre to about three. The other branches were, however, much smaller.

In several places between Hundar and Tertse, on the

gravelly plain which skirted the river, I observed manifest traces of a flood, consisting of such rejectamenta as are usually seen deposited by swollen streams, fragments of wood and twigs, straw, sheep's dung, and other light materials, forming a bed two or three feet wide, continuous in many places for hundreds of yards, at a distance of not less than half a mile from the river. To my inquiries as to the nature of the flood which had deposited these reliquiæ, the invariable reply was, that a great flood had taken place five years before, by the bursting of a lake called Khundan Chu, at which time the whole course of the river was devastated, and much destruction of property, sometimes even life, ensued, particularly in the narrower parts of the valley. In most parts of the world the preservation of such insignificant vestiges of a flood for so long a period would have been impossible; but here, where rain is almost unknown, and where the winter falls of snow seldom exceed one or two inches, there are no disturbing causes which could prevent them from remaining till carried away or altered in position by another similar flood. I should, therefore, have had no difficulty in attaching credence to the testimony of the inhabitants of the country, even had I not, in my journey down the river, received the most abundant proofs that the flood was everywhere well known, at least as far as Iskardo.

The vegetation of Lower Nubra had so entirely disappeared, that I could form scarcely any idea of its character; but, as the general aspect of the country was unaltered, I had no reason to look for any change. In the gravelly bed of the river, bushes of *Myricaria* and *Tamarix* were common; thickets of *Hippophaë*, loaded with very acid yellow berries, lined the watercourses, forming an impenetrable barrier. Little bushes of *Artemisia*, *Lycium*, *Perowskia*, and *Ephedra*, were also occasionally seen on the rocks, but the herbaceous vegetation had quite withered away. In the villages, the cultivated trees were also rapidly shedding their leaves; constant night frosts, and frequent falls of snow on the mountain-sides, having so far reduced the temperature that winter was evidently at hand.

Below the village of Unmaru, the width of the valley had so much diminished that many of the lateral spurs advanced close to the river. Several of these prominent spurs consisted of trap rocks, various forms of basalt and greenstone occurring, with not unfrequently veins of coarse serpentine. Stratified rocks, however, still continued, but the hard black slate was often with difficulty distinguishable from the basalt.

My encamping ground at Kuru was on the north side of the river, and close to the gorge into which the Shayuk disappeared among rocks of black slate, which rise almost perpendicularly from the river. A small tributary, descending from the north, ran parallel and close to the rugged mountain spur which formed the barrier of the valley; and immediately above, a deep bay or recess in the mountains was entirely filled with beds of loose sand, resting on the alluvial clay formation. The appearance of the place was altogether most singular. Much of the light sandy beds were evidently of very recent origin, probably referable to the great flood five years before, at which time the waters, suddenly checked at the gorge, after having spread out *ad libitum* in the open valley of

Nubra, rose to a height of not less than fifty feet above their usual level, and required several days to subside. The beds of clay under the loose sand were all stratified, and were, no doubt, referable to the same lacustrine formation as the fossiliferous beds observed higher up the valley of the Shayuk.

From Kuru there is no road along the bank of the river, the rocks being on both sides too precipitous to permit of a passage, and the river too deep to be forded. In winter, when the river is frozen, travellers are able to continue their course along its bed by proceeding on the ice in those places where the steepness of the rocks obstructs the passage; but at other seasons it is necessary to make a long *détour*, and to ascend a lateral ravine for eight miles before a point is reached where the steep ridge is capable of being crossed. Leaving Kuru on the morning of the 26th of October, I encamped at the village of Waris, elevated 12,400 feet, among a few fields from which the crops had long been cleared. The few huts which formed the village contained no inhabitants, being abandoned, as soon as the harvest has been reaped and housed, for the more temperate climate of the river valley.

The ravine by which I ascended from Kuru was very narrow and rugged. The road generally lay at a considerable height on the steep slopes of the hills, but three times crossed the stream; once by a natural bridge composed of a huge mass of rock lying across a very narrow part of the stream, where it had worn out in the solid rock a channel not more than from three to twelve feet wide. The steep sloping banks of the ravine were usually shingly and devoid of vegetation; but on the margin of the little stream there were a good many shrubs, principally willows, and occasionally the cordate-leaved poplar so commonly cultivated in the Tibetan villages, which here appeared quite indigenous.

The geological structure of this rocky ravine was very intricate, from the great mass of igneous rock, granite, greenstone, and amygdaloid, which everywhere occurred. A very hard conglomerate, similar in character to that of the upper Indus and of the Giah ravine, was also observed at intervals, alternating with very highly metamorphic slates. After about five miles, the road left the main ravine to ascend into a lateral branch, much more steep than the former. Here masses of alluvial conglomerate of great thickness rested on the sides of the mountains, many hundred feet above the bed of the stream. During the day the weather had been very cloudy and threatening, and a little snow fell in the afternoon at my encamping ground at Waris.

During the night more snow fell, and on the morning of the 27th it was four or five inches deep. From my camp I ascended at once, very steeply, to the crest of the ridge on the left, which I then followed in a succession of undulations in a westerly direction. As soon as I had gained the summit, a reach of the Shayuk was seen, distant perhaps a mile and a half, flowing among steep black rocks, with here and there banks of gravel at the bends. The view from the ridge was very striking, the dark colour of the rocks below contrasting strongly with the snowy whiteness of the upper parts of the mountains, which, on the south side of the Shayuk, rise very abruptly to a height of perhaps 18,000 feet.

The summit of the ridge was not less than 14,700 feet above the sea. At this elevation, the snow, on southern exposures, had, by eleven A.M., quite melted, under the influence of a bright sun. Along the ridge, tufts of a prickly *Statice*, still displaying the remains of flowers, were very common, and a few stunted trees of juniper occurred at intervals. The descent from the ridge was exceedingly abrupt (three thousand feet in less than a mile), into a narrow valley, in which I encamped among the fields of a summer village named Boghdan, now, like the one I had left in the morning, deserted by its inhabitants, who had gone for the winter to the village of Chulungka, nine miles distant, on the banks of the Shayuk. I was now in the district of Chorbat, the ridge which I had just crossed being the boundary of Nubra on the west.

The Boghdan ravine, though very narrow and tortuous, is well wooded with small trees of poplar and willow, and with shrubs, chiefly of *Hippophaë* and *Myricaria*. These plants are entirely confined to the level bottom of the ravine, forming a belt, ten or twenty feet wide, on each side of the little stream. After a descent of three miles, I again joined the Shayuk, along which a journey of four days brought me to Siksa, the principal village of Chorbat, encamping on the way at the villages of Chulungka, Turtuk, and Pranu.

The district of Chorbat is a dependency of the government of Iskardo, which, like that of Le, is subject to Kashmir. The desert country by which Nubra and

Chorbat are separated has, for the present, acted as a barrier to the further extension eastward of the Mahommedan religion, which is now universally that of the people of the whole of the Iskardo (or Balti) district, as well as of Dras. On the Indus, and in the valleys south of it, there is no uninhabited tract between the two, so that the Mahommedan and Buddhist population are in direct contact. The result is, that Mahommedanism is in that part gradually, though very slowly, extending to the eastward.

In this part of its course the Shayuk river is in general very rapid, and is hemmed in so closely by the mountains on both sides, that little space is left for the accumulation of alluvium, except where considerable lateral streams join the main river. The barrier by which Chorbat is separated from Nubra is the most contracted part of the valley, and the general ruggedness by degrees becomes less marked as we continue to descend the river. The mountains, everywhere steep, rocky, and inaccessible, close in general to within a quarter of a mile of one another, and their projecting spurs, at short intervals, advance quite to the centre of the valley, forming deep bays, either filled with sand or occasionally occupied by platforms of conglomerate, on the top of which, where water is procurable, there is generally a village. The river, winding from one side of its channel to the other, washes the foot of each rocky spur, so that the road frequently quits the level of the river to ascend abruptly the rocky hills, which are often so steep as to be only accessible by means of scaffoldings of wood, propped up against the face of the perpendicular cliffs by trunks of trees. Once or twice the road lay at a great height above the river for several miles, without descending at all to its level.

The channel of the Shayuk is generally formed of coarse gravel or large rolled stones, and immense boulders are everywhere scattered on the level banks. The stream is rapid and deep, and the fall much more considerable than in Nubra,. Siksa being only about 9000 feet above the sea. It is nowhere in the whole distance fordable; and as the villages lie alternately on opposite sides of the river, I had occasion to cross it three times before reaching Siksa. In every case a narrow and rapid part of the river is selected, the bridges being composed of poplar trunks, stretching from bank to bank, with a light and rude hand-rail of hurdles to give support. Opposite Turtuk, the bridge, which rests upon piers projecting on each side eight feet into the river, measures twenty-five paces, so that the river is not more than eighty feet wide.

Where platforms of alluvium occupy the lateral ravines, they attain a very great thickness, seldom less than two hundred feet, and occasionally at least twice as much. They are generally cut off in steep cliffs by the river, beautifully showing the structure of the alluvium. In the sections of these masses of boulders and clay, I several times observed that the strata, instead of being horizontal, were highest in the middle and sloped gently downwards on either side. This would indicate, I think, a local origin of these deposits, which probably commenced under water, close to a ravine on the mountain-side, and gradually extended, by the addition of successive layers, till they met similar accumulations, derived from the opposite side of the valley.

In the upper part of the district of Chorbat, the villages are few and very insignificant, but lower down several are of great extent. Chulungka, the highest village, consists of three or four houses, on a small platform about fifty feet above the river. This village stood formerly on the low ground close to the Shayuk, but the cultivable soil at the lower level was entirely swept away by the flood of 1842, so that the inhabitants were obliged to change the position of their houses. The first considerable village is Turtuk, on the south side of the river. Pranu, on the north side, is remarkable for the great extent of its cultivation, and for several isolated rocks, behind which the alluvium has accumulated to a thickness of at least six or seven hundred feet.

All the villages are surrounded by fine orchards of apricot-trees. Walnut and mulberry trees are also common; and at Turtuk I saw a few vines; these latter are, however, by no means generally cultivated in the district. Willows are less frequent than in Nubra, but there are plenty of poplars. The black poplar is the common species, but a white downy-leaved species (*P. alba*), which is cultivated also in Kunawar, and which seems to be indigenous in some of the Himalayan valleys south of Kashmir, occurs for the first time at Turtuk. The fields are everywhere terraced, and water seems to be very abundant.

A very remarkable outburst of granite commences at the junction of the Boghdan ravine with the Shayuk, and continues as far as Siksa, altering the secondary rocks so that they can scarcely be recognized. The granite is frequently in great mass, and usually occupies the lowest part of the valley, sending out gigantic veins or branches into the overlying slates, which are often transformed into a coarse serpentine. The hard conglomerate which is associated with the slate, seems the same as occurs in Lower Nubra, so that probably the slates are also a continuation of the same series, and the whole may even be connected with the conglomerates and slates of the Giah valley and of the Indus below Le, the strike of which to the N.W. or N.N.W. would carry them nearly in the direction of Chorbat. Here the intrusion of the granite renders both dip and strike obscure, the beds being frequently quite vertical.

From Siksa, close to which there is a small fort or castle on an isolated rock, a road leads across the Hanu pass into the valley of the Indus. By this route Mr. Vigne proceeded when he abandoned his intention of penetrating by the Shayuk to Nubra, and it has since been crossed by several travellers at different times. It is, indeed, a route very commonly adopted in travelling from Iskardo to Le, as the lower part of the Shayuk is more open and practicable than the Indus below the junction of the river of Dras.

Below Siksa, the valley of the Shayuk continues narrow for eight or ten miles. It then begins again to expand, and its width continues to increase as far as Khapalu, which is situated near the centre of a wide plain similar to that of Nubra, and, like that, coincident with the junction of a large river from the north. It is certainly worthy of note, that it is always at the point of junction of large tributaries that the valley of the Shayuk is widest, and that the evidences of the former existence of lakes are most evident, while in the intermediate parts of its course the valley is narrow and rugged, and shows no certain indications of having been at any period lacustrine.

The great axis of the plain of Khapalu is from south-east to north-west, in the direction of the river Machulu, which runs through a very open and wide gravelly plain, apparently for a considerable distance. This stream, which is probably at least as large as the Nubra river, has its source in heavily-snowed mountains to the north. The general surface of the plain is gravelly, and its appearance on the whole is so similar to that of Nubra that no detailed description is necessary. The river divides in the open gravelly plain into numerous branches, which separate to a considerable distance from one another, and ramify very irregularly. There is not much alluvial accumulation in this plain, except in the immediate vicinity of Khapalu, where a very curious isolated rock of black slate rises abruptly in the middle of the plain, its base being washed by one branch of the Shayuk, now (after its junction with the Machulu) too deep to be forded. Behind this rock there is an accumulation of alluvium, forming a steep ridge six or seven hundred feet in height; which it is necessary to cross in travelling from Surmu to Khapalu, as the abruptness with which the clay-slate rock rises out of the water, completely prevents a passage along the margin of the river.

On the 2nd of November I forded the Shayuk a little below the village of Abadan, where it runs in two branches, each about a hundred yards wide, and with an average depth of about two feet. A little further down it is joined by the Machulu, and it does not appear to be anywhere fordable in its further course, even in winter, so that probably the influx of water brought by that stream is very considerable. I did not, however, see the junction, which is situated on the north side of the plain, quite out of the direct road towards the town of Khapalu.

Where the valley is widest, the mountain ranges on both sides of the river are well seen. The range south of the Shayuk rises close at hand into a very steep mountain mass, now much snowed. A pass which leads from Khapalu to Kartash was (I was informed) already shut up by snow, and impracticable for travellers. To the north, up the wide valley of the Machulu, the mountains are more distant, and the main chain of the Muztagh is evidently fully in sight; the absence of hills close at hand allowing a considerable extent of it to be seen; it was very heavily snowed. The nearest, and apparently loftiest peak, bore N. 13 W. (Magn.) from Surmu.

The principal villages of this open tract are Surmu and Khapalu, both on the south side of the Shayuk, and separated from one another by a high alluvial ridge, which rests on a bold scarped rock rising immediately out of the river. Surmu has a very long and narrow tract of cultivation, skirting the gravelly river-bed. It occupies the slopes of a projecting platform of alluvium of no great height. In this village many fields, on a level with the river, have evidently been destroyed by the flood of 1842, as fruit-trees were still standing among the gravel and shingle of the river-beds. Khapalu, on the other hand, which is situated at the point of junction of a considerable stream, occupies the surface of a thick bed of alluvium of great extent, sloping very steeply from the apex of the triangle in a recess among the mountains to its base, which is formed by the Shayuk. The fort of Khapalu is perched at a great height on a remarkable projecting scarped rock, just at the mouth of the ravine behind the village. The cultivation has a width of not less than two miles, and, as it abounds in fruit-trees, it must in summer, when the fields are green and the trees are in leaf, be a place (for Tibet) of considerable beauty. From the abruptness of the slope of the alluvial platform, the terrace-walls of the fields are very high, often as much as six feet. The fruit-trees are the same as those commonly cultivated in Nubra and Chorbat; the elm and *Elæagnus* of Nubra are also common, as well as the white poplar. At Khapalu there are also a few plane-trees, which do not extend further east.

The *Lycium* of Nubra, which had entirely disappeared in the narrow and rocky parts of the Shayuk, reappeared as soon as the valley spread out into a gravelly plain, being common at Abadan, and abundant at Surmu and Khapalu. A species of berberry, a genus wanting in the higher parts of the Shayuk (except in the mountains, where a small alpine species is occasionally seen), was found in Surmu. The species was apparently identical with the common berberry of Europe, which extends even into the drier valleys of the Himalaya. I also recognized a few other new plants—a small, almost herbaceous *Sophora* was one of these, and, still more remarkable,

Peganum Harmala, a species which extends from the Mediterranean flora as far east as the Punjab, and which indicates a very considerable amount of summer heat.

The shrubby *Hippophaë* is still very plentiful, but, either from more careful cultivation, or because the nature of the slopes prevents the formation of swampy margins to the little irrigation streams, it does not spread to so great an extent over the cultivated tracts, which, therefore, in the winter season look considerably more bare than those around the villages of Nubra.

The height of the bed of the Shayuk at Khapalu may be roughly estimated at about 8000 feet, as the determination of the boiling-point of water at my tent, which was high up in the village, gave an elevation of 8300 feet. I arrived at Khapalu from Surmu on the 3rd of November, and remained there during the 4th. The weather, which for some days had been very unsettled and disagreeable, suddenly cleared up on the 2nd of November, and continued for nearly a week very fine, the days being uniformly bright and sunny, with a gentle wind blowing up the valley of the Shayuk. The temperature in the sun was extremely agreeable, though the shade maximum was never much higher than 50°. The nights were clear and cold, the thermometer falling at Khapalu more than 14° below the freezing-point.

A little below Khapalu I found a number of people washing the sand of the Indus for gold; but the produce seemed to be very trifling, and the work is only carried on during winter, when labour is of no value for other purposes. I purchased for a rupee (paying, I believe, a good deal more than the value) the produce in gold-dust of one man's labour for three weeks. I suppose, however, he only worked occasionally.

Below Khapalu the valley of the Shayuk again begins to contract, but the open plain may be considered to extend for some way below the village of Braghar, where a large tributary joins from the north, and to which place there is a great deal of cultivation, especially on the right bank. Immediately below Braghar, there is a remarkable saline grassy plain, very swampy, and traversed by numerous small streamlets, in which a *Chara* and a linear-leaved *Potamogeton* were abundant. Below this plain the mountain spurs close in upon the river, contracting its channel very much, and frequently preventing all passage along the bank. The narrow portion of the river extends within a few miles of Iskardo, or for at least thirty miles of river distance. Throughout this tract the valley is very similar to that between Nubra and Chorbat. Villages are numerous, occupying very elevated platforms, on which there is frequently luxuriant cultivation. In many of the narrowest and most rugged places there is no passage along the river, and the road crosses spurs of considerable elevation.

Between Kunes and Kuru the narrowness of the river is probably at its maximum, as the road lies altogether along a ridge, elevated perhaps a thousand feet, to which the ascents and descents are extremely abrupt. Many parts of this ridge are capped with alluvium, which occurs in many places along this part of the course of the Shayuk in very great quantity. The largest village on this part of the river is Kiris, situated just above the junction of the Shayuk and Indus, on a nearly level alluvial platform of large size. Round Kiris there is a very extensive deposit of lacustrine clay, very fine, and horizontally stratified. Good sections of this, sometimes at least fifty feet in thickness, are exposed east of Kiris, not far from the Shayuk. I did not observe any fossils; but in so cursory an inspection as I was able to make, it is very probable that I may have overlooked them.

The junction of the Shayuk and Indus rivers takes place a little way below Kiris. The Shayuk is considerably wider and more rapid than the Indus, but much less deep, so that neither river so decidedly preponderates over the other as to enable their relative size to be determined at a glance. Probably the discharge of the two will be found nearly equal. The direction of the united streams is the same as that of the Shayuk, which the Indus joins nearly at a right angle.

The granitic and slate rocks of the district of Chorbat are continued unaltered as far as the junction of the Indus and Shayuk. In many places the granite so predominates as to form almost the whole mass of the mountains, but more generally there is also a good deal of slate. The schists are of very various appearance; a very hard black slate is the most common, but in contact with and near the granite many portions of the slaty mass are quite undistinguishable from gneiss. The direction and inclination of the dip vary extremely. In general the granitic veins appear to be parallel to the strata of schist, but instances are not unfrequent where vertical strata of schist are cut through by horizontal veins of granite.

On the 9th of November I encamped at Kiris, and next day I passed the junction of the Indus and Shayuk. The direction of the united streams soon becomes nearly due north, and it flows for many miles through a very narrow ravine, along which the road is of a most difficult nature, partly high on the mountains, partly on platforms of alluvium, and occasionally over angular blocks of rock, which are piled in enormous heaps along the banks of the river. At the most northerly point of the river, where the ravine is narrowest, I passed through the cultivated lands of the village of Nar, which extend for more than two miles on the surface of an alluvial platform many hundred feet above the bottom of the valley. Leaving this village, I continued to ascend, and entirely lost sight of the Indus, which flowed to the south-west, while the road kept winding among rocky hills, gradually ascending to the crest of a low pass, among rocks of black slate, which entirely prevented me from seeing the nature of the surrounding country. From the summit of the ascent I descended gradually down a narrow valley, and emerging at last rather suddenly on an open plain, I found myself in sight of the valley of Iskardo, which presented to the eye an expanse of level ground much greater than I had seen since leaving Khapalu, to which and to Nubra the district round Iskardo bears a very close resemblance.

When the road entered the open country, at the north-east corner of the plain of Iskardo, it lay for miles over loose sand, utterly barren, forming low undulating hills, which rested upon a deposit of pure white clay. Three miles from Iskardo, a spur from the northern mountains advances close to the river, and the road skirting the latter is for a short distance rocky and uneven. Soon, however, it again enters a tract of bare sand, which extends as far as the ferry immediately above the town of Iskardo. The river, being here unfordable, is crossed by means of a flat-bottomed boat.

The plain of Iskardo, which surrounds the junction of the Shigar river with the Indus, is nearly twenty miles in length, and has an average breadth of about five miles. It is elevated about 7200 feet above the level of the sea. In its very centre, on the south bank of the Indus, and opposite to the junction of the Shigar river, an isolated rock of black slate rises to the height of nearly a thousand feet, directly overhanging the Indus, parallel to which it stretches for nearly a mile. It is faced on all sides by perpendicular cliffs, inaccessible except at the west end, where a steep and difficult path leads to the summit, which is a long narrow ridge.

The name Iskardo is a Mahommedan corruption of a Tibetan name Skardo, or Kardo, as it is very commonly pronounced; but as the first-mentioned name is most familiar to foreigners, and is likely to become universal, as well from the inhabitants of the district being all Mahommedans, as from the country being now subject to Kashmir, it is better, I think, to retain it, than to attempt to substitute the more pure Tibetan pronunciation.

The mountains which surround the Iskardo plain rise at once with great abruptness, and are very steep and bare. Those on the south side, derived from the range which separates the Indus from the table-land of Deotsu,

Pl. II.

J.W. del. W. L. Walton, Lithog.

Printed by Hullmandel & Walton

ISKARDO

From South-east of the Valley.

the axis of which is not more than ten or fifteen miles distant, rise very abruptly in rocky pinnacles, covered, at the time I reached the valley, with much snow. Two spurs from this range run forward to the Indus, one five miles east of Iskardo, the other about three miles to the west of it, dividing the whole south side of the valley into three deep bays, each watered by a considerable stream, whose source is in the southern mountains. The mountains on the north side, the terminal spurs of two great branches of the Kuenlun or Muztagh, which flank the Shigar river, are considerably lower, but equally barren and desolate.

The river Indus traverses the open valley in an extremely winding course. At one time it washes the base of the cliffs which terminate the projecting mountain spurs; at another it flows between high banks of alluvial conglomerate or of fine clay. Not unfrequently these clayey cliffs recede to a considerable distance from the river, in which case the intervening space is generally sandy. A small branch of the stream, at times little more than a chain of pools, often runs close to the cliffs, indicating a former channel of the river; and when this is the case, the low ground between the two channels is often swampy and grassy.

The bed of the Indus in this part of its course is very little inclined, the stream flowing in general very gently over a sandy bed, its surface quite smooth and tranquil, occasionally only a little rippled in turning round a projecting rocky spur, where its bottom is gravelly and the inclination perhaps a little greater. Opposite Iskardo the Indus is even in the depth of winter a noble stream, often more than 500 feet wide, and nine or ten feet deep in the centre.

Iskardo occupies a nearly level plain of fine alluvial clay elevated fifty or sixty feet above the river, and extending from the isolated rock which overhangs the Indus towards the mountains on the south side of the valley. To the right and left of the rocky hill, two small streams have excavated for themselves out of the soft clay deep and wide ravines, which are covered with coarse gravel, and are faced by more or less steep banks of clay or sand. The surface of the platform on which all the cultivated ground lies is watered by means of artificial canals, brought from a distance of nearly two miles, from the point where the streams issue from among the hills.

The neighbourhood of the rock of Iskardo was doubtless selected as the site of the principal town of the kingdom of Balti, from the advantages which it afforded as a place of defence; and in the days of the independence of the country a fortified palace occupied its eastern extremity, while the western and more accessible end was apparently protected by a series of rude works. The principal buildings of the palace seem to have been at the very base of the rock. A mass of ruins, showing large blocks of well-hewn stone, fragments of marble fountains, and some solid walls supporting terraces, which appear at one time to have been gardens, alone remain to show the former magnificence of the place. A mausoleum, raised to the memory of the last independent king, Ahmed Shah, perched on a rock perhaps 300 feet above the plain, is still untouched and uninjured.

An aqueduct or canal extends in a direct line from the palace towards the mountains, a distance of at least a mile. It is an exceedingly massive work, consisting of two walls raised perhaps fifteen feet above the level of the plain, and built of very large blocks of hewn stone. The intervening space is filled with earth. At present, a small conduit, a foot or so wide, brings all the water which is required for the use of the inhabitants of Iskardo; but a very large quantity might be conveyed along the aqueduct, and the work is so strong and substantial that very little repair would be requisite to restore it to its original condition.

The fortified post of the present rulers of the country is built on the margin of the platform of alluvium, on the right bank of the little stream which joins the Indus to the east of the rock of Iskardo, and is separated by a hollow from the palace and the principal part of the village. It is built of unburnt brick, and is extremely irregular in shape, with rounded bastions at the angles.

The houses of Iskardo are very much scattered over a large extent of surface, so that there is no appearance of a town; nor is the population in the immediate neighbourhood of the rock so extensive as that of some of the more remote villages in the valley, and especially of those on the banks of the Shigar river, which are very richly cultivated. Many of the Iskardo houses, however, are very good, being often of two stories, and built of unburnt bricks in a framework of wood. Latticed windows, covered with paper or small plates of mica, are also common. The roofs are all flat, and covered with mud beaten hard.

The lacustrine clay formation occurs in great quantity throughout the valley of Iskardo, and is nowhere seen in greater perfection than in the immediate neighbourhood of the town, where the cliffs facing the Indus, and those along the little lateral streams which descend from the south, exhibit an abundance of sections of these beds. The height of the cliffs is very variable; but it is seldom less than thirty feet, and to the east of the town is as much as a hundred feet. The clay formation varies much in appearance, being most commonly a very fine unctuous cream-coloured clay, stratified quite horizontally, but occasionally gritty and mixed with numerous particles of mica. Now and then thin beds of sand and of small waterworn pebbles alternate with the finer clays. In many places near the rock of Iskardo, the beds are very irregular, undulating a good deal, and at times exhibiting very remarkable flexures, as if the isolated rocky mass (which must have once been under water) had formed eddies in the lake, and prevented that regularity of deposition which is elsewhere so universal.

Fossils are very rare in these clays, but occurred in several different localities. Close to Iskardo I once found a very few small specimens of a *Lymnæa* and *Planorbis*, but after repeatedly searching carefully did not succeed in obtaining any more. I was more fortunate in two places east of Iskardo, where fresh-water shells are sufficiently common in one or two thin seams of very fine clay, mixed with a good deal of apparently vegetable matter. The great mass of the clay is, however, quite non-fossiliferous.

The surface of the clay formation round Iskardo is

very undulating, and is often covered with masses of large boulders. Opposite two of the ravines which penetrate the mountains on the southern side of the valley, two very remarkable banks of boulders project forward into the valley. They consist of very large fragments of rock, angular or more or less rounded, piled on one another to a height of forty or fifty feet. They terminate abruptly, and are, I think, evidently moraines.

On the very top of the isolated rock, in the middle of the Iskardo plain, horizontal beds of coarse sandstone rest upon the hard clay-slate of which the rock is composed. This sandstone crumbles with great ease in the hand, the particles of which it is composed being very slightly coherent. These beds, in which I could find no traces of shells or of vegetable remains, are elevated at least 800 or 1000 feet above the level of the Indus. The sandstone seems to cap the whole hill, but is exposed only in a few places, being in a great measure covered by the loose drift or alluvium which has been deposited above it.

The vegetation of Iskardo had so entirely disappeared, that I was able to form very little idea of its nature. A few shrubby species, and some withered fragments of autumn flowering plants, alone remained. On the whole, I was struck with the similarity of the few plants which I recognized with those of Nubra and Le. *Artemisiæ* and *Chenopodiaceæ* were still abundant. *Hippophaë* was the universal shrub along all the streamlets, and *Lycium* was common in sandy places; a berberry (the same already seen at Khapalu) was also frequent. The few novelties were Kashmir plants. *Lycopsis arvensis, Pru-*

nella vulgaris, a thistle, a species of *Sium*, some gentians, and *Ranunculus aquatilis*, were the most Indian forms which I met with. From the mountains I procured specimens of a juniper (*J. excelsa*), and of the alpine birch of the Himalaya, which skirts the southern borders of the Tibetan region, without extending into the driest parts of that country.

CHAPTER VIII.

Leave Iskardo in the direction of Kashmir—First march through snow to Turgu—Lacustrine clay—it extends into narrow valleys beyond Nar—Gol—Junction of Indus and Shayuk—Parkuta—Tolti—Kartash—Extensive lacustrine deposits—Tarkata—Road turns up the Dras river—Ulding Thung—Fall of snow—Hardas—Karbu—Continued snow—Dras—Find pass in front shut by deep snow—Obliged to return to Iskardo—Rafts and rope-bridges on Indus—*Elæagnus* and Apricot apparently wild—Winter at Iskardo.

On the 2nd of December I left Iskardo, in the direction of Kashmir, by way of Dras, all other routes being shut with snow. My first march was to Turgu, seven miles. The ground was all the way covered with snow which had fallen during the night, but it thawed a good deal during the day, making the journey rather unpleasant. The road lay along the south bank of the river, at first over the level platform of lacustrine clay, among large boulders, which were scattered over its surface, but soon descending by a narrow and steep footpath, on the face of the clayey cliff, to the level of the river, to cross a deep bay, from which the clay formation has been entirely removed, to a large village three miles from Iskardo, through the cultivation of which the road ascended gradually, and proceeded on the barren stony slopes behind. About five miles from Iskardo, a spur, from the mountain range on the south, which abuts in a scarped cliff upon the river, has been taken advantage of by the inhabitants to build a small gateway, through which the road is made to run. The extreme steepness of the mountain mass which lies to the south and east, makes it scarcely possible to approach Iskardo along the south bank of the river from these directions, without passing through this gateway, and, therefore, a small party of soldiers is kept on this rocky pass by the Sikh rulers of the country. A species of *Daphne* was very common on the rocky hills about this pass, apparently an evergreen, as it was in full leaf in the midst of the snow. From the higher parts of the road, and from the rocky pass which overhangs the river, there is an extensive view over the barren sandy waste on the north bank of the river. The lacustrine clay is, at this end of the valley, very thick and but little excavated, forming cliffs which rise close to the river, which has, as it were, worn for itself a narrow channel in the clay formation. The banks or cliffs are of very different heights, and many of them consist of alluvial gravel and boulders, overlying and quite obscuring the clays. Behind Turgu, and in many places on the last part of the march, there are great masses of angular fragments of rock piled into a steeply sloping mass, as if they had fallen from the mountains behind, but so mixed with smaller fragments and with gravel, that it seems probable that they were accumulated under water.

The next day's march, from Turgu to Gol, round the great bend of the Indus, was entirely barren. On the western side of the curve several rocky spurs were crossed, but after the road turns to the south it runs generally on the surface of very elevated platforms of coarse alluvial debris, covered in many places with enormous boulders, partly derived, in all probability, from the fall of masses of rock from the cliffs above, but in more than one place so curiously arranged, at the apertures of lateral ravines, as to be, I think, almost certainly of glacial origin. Many of the large boulders which occurred in the alluvium were observed to be much waterworn, spherical cavities being worn out in them. Similar waterworn rocks were also seen *in situ* at great heights above the river, in places to which no water has at present access, and where it is difficult to understand in what way the effect was produced. Behind the alluvial platforms, which are generally one or two hundred feet above the level of the river, the mountains rise precipitously, in cliffs of granite, which has now replaced the slate rocks of Iskardo.

At the point where the river changes its direction from north to south-west, the mountains on the southern bank advance quite to the river, and on the north side also they approach very near. It would therefore, at first sight, appear that the lake, in which the clay formation of Iskardo has been deposited, had here terminated to the eastward, no clay being seen in the narrow ravine above Nar, or near the river anywhere between Nar and Gol. I had at first no doubt that I had reached the eastern extremity of the lake; but some time after passing the most northerly point of the ravine I observed a patch of very fine cream-coloured clay, quite similar to the finest portions of the Iskardo formation, clinging in a remarkable position on the flank of a very steep rocky cliff, not less than 1000 or 1200 feet above the river. Several other patches came into sight soon after, all high up on the mountain-sides; one above the village of Golochu, and others at intervals all the way to the junction of the Indus and Shayuk. I cannot, therefore, doubt that the lake in which the clay beds of Kiris were deposited, was the same as that which occupied the Iskardo basin; nor does it seem easy to fix its exact boundaries. The great height of the patches of clay, in the narrow channel above Nar, show that the depth of the lake had been very considerable; and if we assume a depth of 1500 feet, which seems necessary, and at the same time admit the arrangement of the ancient rocks to have been the same as at present, we must either suppose some great barrier to have existed in the narrow passage below Khapalu, or must admit that the Khapalu lake was also continuous with that of Iskardo. I did not, however, observe any beds of fine clay higher up than Kuru, in the narrow part of the ravine of the Shuyak, which would warrant the drawing such a conclusion; although vast masses of alluvium certainly abound there, piled at great heights above the river. Is it possible that these may at one time have been continuous, and have blocked up the whole valley, and that the portions now seen capping ridges, whose origin is otherwise inexplicable, are the last remnants of a continuous mass which occupied the whole interspace? and if so, to what are we to ascribe the deposition of such an enormous mass of alluvium-like accumulation?

To the eastward of the village of Gol the valley of

the Indus again becomes a little wider, an open sandy plain extending round the junction of the two rivers. The cultivation round Gol is on a high platform of alluvium; but the road descends, soon after leaving the village, nearly to the level of the river, and continues over the low ground, skirting the mountains of the southern bank, till it reaches the junction of the two rivers, where it turns abruptly to the south, ascending the left bank of the Indus, which runs nearly due north in a narrow rocky ravine. A bluff projecting ridge of granite, sixty or eighty feet high, polished on the surface by aqueous action, and of a brilliantly brown-black colour, so that the nature of the rock is only discoverable by breaking it, here advances close to the river, and is crossed by a steep sinuous path, eked out by flights of steps, with wooden supports, where it would otherwise be impracticable. The Indus is here very narrow and deep, and runs with an extremely rapid current. The path, after crossing this ridge, again descends to the level of the river. Even in this narrow ravine I was surprised to find the fine cream-coloured clay of the lacustrine formation, similar to many of the beds of the same deposit round Iskardo. It was here quite on a level with the river.

The mountains rise on both sides of the Indus very abruptly, being almost always precipitous. From the narrowness of the valley the great elevation of these is not seen, and the lesser height of those on the right bank of the Indus, which form the termination of the chain separating that river from the Shayuk, is not brought prominently to notice. For more than two miles, the ravine continues very narrow, and several steep spurs are crossed. It then becomes gradually a little wider, narrow platforms of conglomerate skirting the stream, and changes its direction from nearly due south to south-east. The right bank is stony and unproductive the whole way, but on the left there is one small village, three miles from the junction of the Shayuk, and thence after three miles of desert, a succession of small villages continuing with little intermission on the surface of alluvial platforms as far as Parkuta, at which I encamped. In one of the villages a good many small juniper-trees were seen.

The lacustrine clay formation, though not continuous throughout the whole of this day's march, may be traced in patches, with so little interval that its former continuity cannot be doubted. The spots in which I observed its presence in the narrow ravine were all close to the river, the low level of the road not permitting an extended view of the higher slopes of the mountains. Further up, however, patches were in my subsequent April journey seen at considerable elevations, but in December the slopes were covered with snow to within a thousand feet of the river. In several places the clay formed cliffs, which rose perpendicularly from the Indus, and could be seen to be covered with modern alluvium deposited during floods, just as the ancient rocks are in other places. The clay appeared everywhere extremely fine, without any intermixture of sand or micaceous grains. I saw no appearance of fossils, which I think never occur in the very fine cream-coloured clays, but seem always to accompany more sandy, or at least gritty varieties, as if the influx of a small stream, and probably the proximity of land, were requisite to the existence of testaceous mollusks; while the central part of the lake, in which the very finest clays were deposited, was quite devoid of them.

Parkuta is a very large village, three or four hundred feet above the river, occupying both slopes of a deep ravine cut in the thick mass of alluvium by a large stream from the south. The alluvium is scarped towards the Indus, and a low granitic hill, the cause of its accumulation to such a height, just rises above the general surface of the platform. This is covered with a mass of buildings, formerly the residence of the Rajah of Parkuta, a branch of the same family who ruled at Iskardo, and dependent on them while that state remained independent; he has, however, been removed by the Sikhs, and his house is at present untenanted. The village is large, with extensive cultivation, and many fine fruit-trees. Vines are plentiful, climbing over the poplars.

On the 5th of December my day's journey carried me to Tolti, a distance of twelve miles. The valley continuéd narrow, and the mountains rose precipitously on both sides. On the early part of the march there were many villages, and much cultivation on the left bank, The village of Urdi, three or four miles from Parkuta, seemed very populous, and extended for a great distance along the river. It was remarkable for an aqueduct supported on pillars of stone, which crossed a ravine immediately above the village. At this spot the cultivation terminated abruptly, and the alluvial platform was for more than a mile, during which space it gradually narrowed by the encroachments of the cliffs, covered with an accumulation of very large granitic boulders, which seemed to have fallen on it from the mountains behind.

As I approached Tolti the valley of the Indus became much more rugged and narrow. A long gentle ascent to a ridge more than a thousand feet above the bottom of the valley, but which dipped abruptly to the river, occupied the latter part of the march. At Tolti the belt of cultivation is very narrow, just skirting the river on very narrow platforms of alluvium, which are irrigated by artificial canals carried with considerable labour between the fields and the mountains. Tolti was the most gloomy village which I had yet seen, the precipitous mountains forming a circle all round it, and almost shutting out the light of day. The bird's-nest fort in the ravine behind the village, perched on the top of a rock (in a most untenable position, though probably well suited for defence against sudden attack), accorded well with the gloomy aspect of the place. The temperature was here considerably lower than in the more open valley, as large patches of snow lay still unmelted in the fields, though four days had elapsed since its fall. At Gol, two days before, it had quite melted. On a bank a mile or two below Tolti, I saw a few trees of *Populus Euphratica*, just recognizable by a few withered leaves which still remained on the tree.

From Tolti, I made three marches to Tarkata, a small village on the Indus, six miles below its junction with the river of Dras. The general aspect of the valley of the

Indus was but little changed in this distance, notwithstanding a very long and remarkable bend of the river above Kartash, in which its direction is to the eastward of north. From Tolti, the easiest road in an upward direction crosses the Indus, and proceeds on the right bank; but to avoid the labour of crossing, I suppose, my guides conducted me by a road on the left bank. On this side, the lower part of the valley is so steep as to be impracticable; and I found it necessary to ascend at once from Tolti on a stony ridge, almost directly away from the river. The ascent was long and fatiguing; the ridge being capped, in the same manner as that above Kunes on the Shayuk, with masses of alluvium. The ridge was more than 1500 feet above the river, and its upper part was covered with snow, through which the path lay for four or five miles, after which it descended very abruptly to the river, which had been in sight almost all the way, generally running among precipitous rocks, but with a few villages scattered at intervals on the northern bank. After regaining the bank of the river, the road was for five or six miles nearly level, passing opposite the village of Kartash, with a fort on a hill. Here still resides the Rajah Ali Sher Khan, the most intelligent of the princes of Balti; though now past the prime of life, he still retains the intelligence and kind hospitality for which he is so deservedly praised by Vigne.

Kartash being situated at the northern or lower end of the great bend of the Indus, and in an extremely narrow part of the ravine, is a most sombre-looking place. It is possible, however, that in summer, when the villages are green with cultivation and fruit-trees, the appearance of this and other places may be less gloomy, and that, from having only seen this part of Tibet in the depth of winter, I may be disposed to regard it in too unfavourable a point of view. The abrupt and precipitous rise of the mountains on all sides must undoubtedly tend strongly to modify the summer temperature, which, from the want of rain, and the reflection from masses of bare rock, would otherwise be oppressive. The fort seems to have some good buildings, and to be kept in excellent order, and the village looked extensive and prosperous.

All along the narrow ravine, from Tolti nearly as far as Tarkata, deposits of alluvium were very extensively developed, not only in the valley of the river, but at considerable heights on the ridges. There was, however, I believe, none of the lacustrine clay, as contradistinguished from the coarser alluvium. I speak here with considerable hesitation, as I find with regret that I have not in my notes attended with sufficient care to the distinction between the two, not having at the time sufficiently adverted to their probably different origin. I am now disposed to think that in the narrow ravine above Tolti was situated the barrier which bounded on the east the lake basin of Iskardo, a vast inland sea, which must have extended thence in a north-westerly direction as far as Rondu. This barrier, if my supposition be correct, must have consisted of a mass of coarse drift or alluvium, entirely blocking up the narrow ravine to a height of three thousand feet or more above the present level of the Indus.

The mountains all along this ravine are extremely elevated, the peaks above Kartash (from which a pass leads to Khapalu on the Shayuk) being, I should think, not less than 18,000 feet. The bareness and desolation of their sides exceeded anything I had seen since leaving Iskardo, and quite equalled the most rugged parts of Tibet which I had yet visited. They consisted of large masses of rock, split and fractured in every direction, often very precipitous, without a vestige of soil, and with scarcely the slightest traces of vegetation. Immense tracts, both along the river and on the slopes of the ravines descending from the mountains, were covered with boulders or with angular fragments of rock, strewed irregularly on the surface, or piled in masses one on another. Granite formed the great mass of the mountains, mixed with stratified rocks, which were always highly metamorphic, but extremely variable in appearance, sometimes, though rarely, having the appearance of ordinary gneiss. A singular porphyritic rock appeared (as boulders) along the river in one place only.

About two miles west of Tarkata, the Indus resumes its more usual direction, and, at the same time, its valley becomes somewhat more open, the mountains, without any diminution of elevation, receding considerably from the river. Their lower slopes present a very different aspect from those in other parts of the Indus, being composed not of primitive rock, but of a soft and almost incoherent sandstone, alternating irregularly and without any definite order with boulder conglomerate, and fine clay. These beds, which are very extensively developed on both sides of the river, around the village of Tarkata, for some distance in both directions, attain a thickness of at least six or seven hundred feet. They are, however, very irregular, forming a succession of ridges separated by deep ravines or gullies, on the sides of which fine sections of the strata are generally exposed, showing them to be uniformly horizontal, and to consist of a great many alternations of sand, clay, and drift. Above Tarkata, very fine clays were abundant.

The sandstone, of which a greater part of these curious deposits consists, is formed principally of coarse grains of quartz, which only cohere very slightly, and easily crumble under pressure. It is quite similar in appearance to the sandstone which occurs on the summit of the rock of Iskardo, differing only in being very much more extensively developed than that is, and in being associated and alternating with the very fine clays resembling those which occupy the lower levels of the valley of Iskardo. The sandstones of Tarkata did not appear to be fossiliferous, nor did I, in the slight examination I was able to give them, discover any shells in the fine clays in this neighbourhood. The general similarity, however, of these deposits to the lacustrine clays of the Iskardo valley, makes it nearly certain that their origin is similar, while the association of the sandstones and the fine clays in the neighbourhood of Tarkata, renders it probable that I am right in assuming the arenaceous beds of the summit of the rock of Iskardo to be lacustrine.

Ever since leaving Iskardo, the weather had been very unsettled, but no more snow had fallen. The sky had been pretty generally overcast with light clouds, and during the day the wind had almost invariably blown down the river, generally with great violence, and, especially in the narrowest parts of the valley, in furious gusts, against which it was most laborious to make any progress. The mornings had been always frosty, but the temperature rose in the middle of the day several degrees above 32°. On the 8th of December, a sudden increase of cold seemed to take place, the temperature not rising above the freezing-point. Large cakes of ice, which appeared early on the morning of that day, floating down the river, indicated an evident commencement of very severe weather in the upper part of its course, and the descent of such masses of ice, in cakes of from one to ten feet in diameter, tended very much to lower the temperature of all parts of the river to which they extended. The elevation of Tarkata I found to be 7800 feet above the sea.

The road from Iskardo to Kashmir leaves the valley of the Indus at the junction of the river of Dras, and follows the course of that river almost to its source. The lower part of the valley of Dras is a deep and narrow rocky ravine, bordered by precipices of granite, which are so steep that the bottom of the valley is quite inaccessible. In passing from the Indus into the valley of Dras, the road crosses the granitic spur which separates the two rivers, at an elevation of about 2000 feet above the Indus, ascending to this height very rapidly along a steep spur, which recedes almost in a perpendicular direction from that river. From the shoulder of this ridge, which was elevated probably about 10,000 feet, the course of the Indus was visible for some distance above the junction of the river of Dras. It appeared to be hemmed in very closely by rocky mountain spurs. A good many patches of fine lacustrine clay were in sight, on both banks.

From the same ridge, the view up the Dras valley was very remarkable. The river of that name, which formed many deep pools and was partially frozen, ran at the bottom of a deep gorge. On the right bank opposite to where I stood, a sheer precipice rose nearly to a level with my eye. Between the ridge on which I stood and the next in succession up the Dras valley, an open and shallow valley, everywhere strewed with enormous blocks of granite, sloped gently till it approached the brink of the almost perpendicular cliffs which overhang the Dras river. Crossing this open valley, and the low spur beyond it, I encamped at a small village called Ulding Thung, situated at the point of junction of the Dras river, with a considerable tributary descending from the west.

This little village occupies the gentle slope of a hill-side, but I encamped at the lowest part of it, which was a small level plain surrounded by a number of giant boulders, resting on the upper edge of a very steep slope, and evidently, I think, of glacial origin. They were quite angular, and not less than from twenty to thirty feet in length.

On the slope of the hill above my encampment at Ulding, the lacustrine clay formation again occurred in great quantity. It was a very fine impalpable clay, without fossils, and was here (as is not uncommon elsewhere) dug out by the inhabitants for the purpose of extracting its salt, which is obtained in a state of brine by simply washing the clay with water. The elevation of this clay formation was probably a good deal more than 8500 feet, but not greater than that of many of the hills and patches of similar deposit around Tarkata in the valley of the Indus.

At daybreak on the morning of the 18th of December I found that between three and four inches of snow had fallen during the night. It had ceased snowing at that time; and during the day, which was stormy and often very cloudy, no more fell. There was a good deal of thaw during the day, and towards evening the snow, except in sheltered spots, was nearly melted. My day's journey was about ten miles, to the village of Hardas, on the left bank of the Dras river; passing about two miles before the end of the march the river of Kargyl or Pashkyum, a very large stream which descends from the south-east. During the earlier part of this day, the road was extremely bad. It descended from Ulding abruptly to the level of the Dras river, to cross at its point of junction a large tributary whose source is in the eastern slopes of Deotsu. A succession of steep ascents and descents followed for four or five miles, throughout which distance the ravine through which the river ran was narrow and precipitous and quite without villages. Further up, the valley widened a little, the mountains rose less steeply, and left narrow strips of level ground along the margin of the stream.

Very early on the morning of the 11th of December, it began again to snow, and continued with little intermission throughout the day. I marched ten miles to Karbu, crossing the river three miles above Hardas, and keeping on the right bank during the remainder of the day. I could see that the valley was wider than the day before, but the incessant snow made the appearance of the country undistinguishable. The margins of the stream were occasionally fringed with bushes of poplar and willow. Karbu is a village high up a steep lateral valley, with scattered groves of juniper on the sides of the hills above the cultivation. By evening the depth of snow was about fifteen inches.

On the 12th of December, after marching five miles through a heavy fall of snow to the village of Tashgang, crossing the river by a wooden bridge close to the village, a violent storm of wind and snow-drift, blowing directly down the valley, compelled me to halt for the night. The snow-storm continued till about eight P.M., when the weather cleared, and the night was clear and starlight. Next morning, the weather continuing fine, I was able to proceed to Dras. The depth of snow had increased to about two feet; and the labour of progressing through this depth of untrodden snow was much increased by the shortness of the steps of the porters, treading exactly after one another, so as to form pits in the snow, not more than a foot apart, and alternately on the right and left.

I reached the Sikh fort at Dras, which was distant eleven miles, about two o'clock; the road was pretty level and the valley open, with low hills on either hand. The depth of snow increased as I advanced, and was three feet in the plain round the fort. Here I was greeted by the most unwelcome tidings, that my advance so far was fruitless, the pass in front being blocked up with snow. For this I was quite unprepared, having been led to believe that the road to Kashmir in this direction was always open, and no hint having been given me at Iskardo that my delay there might in the least prevent my reaching Kashmir. The heavy snow-fall of the last three or four days seemed to have been something quite unusual; and it had accumulated, as I was told, on the pass to a depth which quite precluded all possibility of a passage for many days to come.

Notwithstanding all these assurances, I should certainly have tried to advance at least as far as Maten, had I not found at Dras one of the principal inhabitants of Kargyl, who had returned the day before from that place, after attempting in the morning to advance towards the pass, which is ten miles further on, and being stopped by finding the snow ten and twelve feet deep, and quite soft. After the assurances of this traveller, I should not have been justified in taking so many porters across the pass, supposing them to have acceded to my wishes to make the attempt; I therefore very reluctantly gave up the idea of proceeding.

It then became a question what I should do. It might and would probably be many weeks before the pass would be practicable for loaded men. To have remained at Dras so long would have been impossible. The demands of my party for fuel were found very difficult to supply, even for a day, the faggots of brushwood, which alone are there available, being soon consumed, and, therefore, unwillingly parted with; I therefore resolved to return to Iskardo, and remain there till the return of spring should enable me to resume my travels, and to visit the district further down the Indus, before crossing into Kashmir.

My return journey, being from a severe to a milder climate, was sufficiently agreeable. At first a succession of bright and clear days reduced the temperature very much. The thermometer fell to zero in the mornings, and the frost throughout the day was intense. I was no longer able to inhabit my tent, which I had continued to occupy up to the period of my arrival at Dras, where, in the Sikh fort, I found, rather to my surprise, a room, with a fire-place and chimney, allotted for my accommodation by the kindness of the commandant. In descending again towards the Indus, I took shelter in the villages, occupying, if possible, a cow-house in preference to one used by the inhabitants. The houses are generally built of waterworn stones, without cement, but plastered with mud outside and inside. The roofs are flat; the rafters are unsawn trees or branches of poplar, covered with willow twigs, over which is laid a thick coating of mud. A hole in the centre of the roof serves for a chimney, the fire being made in the centre of the floor. In some of the poorer villages the houses were less elaborate, consisting merely of wattle-work of willow twigs, covered with a thin coating of clay.

In the open plain below Dras I observed many withered stems of *Prangos*, the celebrated Umbelliferous plant so much valued by the inhabitants of Dras as a food for their sheep, still bearing ripe seeds. Juniper, too, was common, even along the bank of the stream. As I descended the river, I found that a very few days had made a great change in the temperature. The river was everywhere hard frozen, and all the little streams which ran down the mountain-sides were coated with a thick shell of ice. More than once I saw a waterfall with a covering, perhaps a yard in thickness, of clear blue ice, under which the little streamlet could be distinctly seen. At Ulding, though the cold was severe, I found the ground partially free of snow, so that the amount of fall, at that distance from the central chain of mountains, had been quite insignificant.

On the 19th of December, on which day I regained the valley of the Indus, it was again snowing heavily, after an interval of exactly seven days. The river was now entirely frozen over, and so solid, that one of my servants, a native of India, losing his way in the snow-storm, instead of turning to the left on arriving at the Indus, walked across the river to a village on the right bank, without being aware that he had quitted the proper road.

Instead of keeping the left bank of the river, as I had done in my upward course, I crossed it on the ice about three or four miles above the village of Kartash, or Karmang, as it is also called, and kept on the north side till within a mile of Tolti. About two miles below Kartash, there are a succession of rapids in the stream, which extend, without much intermission, considerably more than a mile, and must produce a very considerable change in the elevation of its bed. The river was nowhere frozen between Kartash and Tolti, the stream being too rapid to freeze readily. In crossing to the left bank I made use of a raft of skins, which consisted of a light frame-work of willow rods, six feet square, resting on about a dozen inflated sheep or goat skins. This flimsy contrivance just floated on the water when loaded with three or four people.

At Tolti and at Karmang are the only rope-bridges which I saw on the Indus, above Iskardo. The cables used in their construction are here made of willow twigs, twisted into a thick rope. Seven such ropes on each side are combined to form the parallel lateral cables, about a yard apart, from which the road way of the bridge is suspended. These bridges are perfectly safe, though, from their open structure, rather formidable to those who are not accustomed to use them. The principle on which they are made is the same as one which is in use in all the hill provinces of India, from the Khasya mountains and Butan, as far west as the Indus; but the material differs with each particular locality, cane being used in the most eastern parts, rope (often of grass or *Eriophorum*) in the Western Himalaya; and in Tibet, where even that material is not available, willow twigs are employed as a substitute.

In many parts of the Indus valley, even in the most rugged and desolate spots, I noticed, occasionally, trees of the *Elæagnus* and of apricot, growing in rocky places along the river, where it was very evident that they had never been planted. The *Elæagnus* is always conspicuous, even in mid-winter, in consequence of the withered leaves remaining attached to the tree instead of falling at the end of autumn. Occasionally, no doubt, the occurrence of these trees was due to the former existence of villages in the vicinity of the places in which they were observed, but they also seemed sometimes to occur in places where no cultivation could ever have existed. Their occurrence, however, must, I think, be considered purely accidental: they were too few in number to be regarded as really indigenous; nor is it surprising that these trees, which are so extensively cultivated round all the villages of Baltistan, and so universally used as food by the inhabitants, should occasionally vegetate at a great distance from their usual place of growth.

I reached Iskardo on the evening of the 25th of December, and succeeded, without difficulty, in hiring a house sufficiently large to accommodate all my party. As I remained stationary at this place for two months, I was able to make some observations of the thermometer, and to watch the state of the weather during the whole of that period. The elevation of Iskardo above the level of the sea is about 7200 feet. Winter may be said to have commenced on the 28th of November, on which day the first snow fell. From that date, falls of snow recurred constantly at intervals, which varied from two or three days to a week. The earlier falls were very slight, not more than an inch or two in depth, but the quantity gradually increased, until each fall was from four to six inches. The entire depth of the snow in the middle of February, beyond which time the fresh falls were insignificant, was from fifteen to eighteen inches.

After each fall of snow, the weather usually became bright and calm, with a serene cloudless sky. The sun

R 2

shone out brightly, and was agreeably warm to the feel, while the temperature of the air rose nearly to, or a little above, the freezing-point. In the earlier part of the winter, the snow melted rapidly, and the ground in the open valley was generally nearly free of it before the next fall. After the beginning of January, however, the cold increased, and the snow lay permanently, except on the most sunny slopes. The sun seemed to have much less power, and little thaw took place except on rocks and beaten paths. The diminution in the quantity of snow by evaporation was often considerable.

The greatest cold which was registered at Iskardo was at daybreak on the 8th of February, when Fahrenheit's thermometer stood at half a degree above zero. The mean temperature at sunrise during the whole winter was 19½°, and that at two P.M. 33¾°. The mean temperature during the period from the 28th of December to the 31st of January was 27½°, and from the 1st to the 24th of February 25¾°. The increase of cold was principally by the depression of the night temperature, the mean highest temperature being within a fraction of a degree the same during both periods.

On the first or second day of clear weather after a fall of snow, the temperature in the morning was often very low, with abundant hoar-frost, which, except at such times, was not seen at all. The surface of the plain was covered with a dense fog, which remained till nearly noon before the sun was able to dispel it. On the second or third day the sky would become hazy, the sun being partly obscured by a thin stratum of cloud at a great elevation. During the continuance of this haze, the temperature was always more elevated than when the sky was clear. The hazy weather was once or twice dissipated by violent winds, without any fall of snow on the open plain; but more generally it increased gradually, till the sky was completely and densely overcast, and snow began again to fall, perhaps most frequently during the night.

During the greater part of the winter the snow was invariably in extremely minute grains. It was not till the latter part of February, when spring was rapidly approaching, that large flakes fell. I more than once observed the phenomenon of small quantities of extremely fine-grained snow falling when the sky was quite clear, and the air at the surface of the earth quite motionless. During clear weather very little thaw took place, the cold produced by radiation appearing to counteract the sun's action; at the same time the snow diminished rapidly by evaporation, which was not the case when the sky was overcast.

The fall of snow was evidently much less considerable in the open plain than on the mountains round Iskardo. During the heavier falls, the snow on the steep mountain slopes often slipped downwards. It was but rarely that these avalanches were visible, but the noise of the snow in motion was heard like distant thunder, often many times a day, and the bare spots which it had left could be seen after the snow-storm had ceased. When the weather was settled, the wind was in general very gentle, and blew up the valley of the Indus; during snow-storms it was usually violent, and very irregular in direction. The storms came mostly from the south-west, a moisture-bringing upper current of air from that direction being condensed by the dry and cold north wind.

My collections had accumulated to such an extent, and got into such confusion, during five months of almost incessant travelling, that I was very glad to have an opportunity of devoting some time to their arrangement, and found, without difficulty, occupation for all my time during two months of rest. The snow was never so deep as to prevent me from taking regular exercise, so that I was soon familiar with all the roads in the neighbourhood of the town, and examined the cliffs of clay in every direction in search of fossils, without discovering (as I had some hopes of doing) any mammalian remains. The communication with Le was open all winter; I was therefore able to correspond with Captain Strachey, who, after examining the course of the Indus from the Chinese boundary downwards, was spending the winter there. By his assistance I succeeded in replenishing my store of tea and sugar, both of which were exhausted. The sugar which I procured from Le was very good, and the brick tea, though not superexcellent in quality, was, in the absence of better, quite good enough for use. Other supplies I had no difficulty in procuring at Iskardo, sheep and flour being abundant. The wood supplied for fuel was almost entirely *Elæagnus*, no wild timber occurring in the country.

The Thannadar of Iskardo, who is the deputy of Maharajah Gulab Singh of Kashmir, is the governor of all Balti, but he rules by means of native Mahommedan chiefs or rajahs. In some instances, where no opposition was made to the Sikh invasion, the former ruler was allowed to retain his position; in other cases a change was made. At Iskardo, Mahommed Shah, the present Rajah, had been an exile in Kashmir, from being on bad terms with his father. He is a feeble and sickly young man, without the energy of his father, M. Vigne's host in Iskardo. The inhabitants of Balti, though Tibetan in language and appearance, are all Mahommedans, and differ from the more eastern Tibetans of Le (who call themselves Bhotias, or inhabitants of Bhot) by being taller and less stoutly made. Their language, I am told, differs considerably from that of Le, but only as one dialect differs from another.

CHAPTER IX.

Leave Iskardo for Rondu—Insurrection in Gilgit—Koardu—Kamar—Enter narrow part of Indus valley—Difficult road—Range of mountains south of Indus—Description of Rondu—Thawar—Avalanches—Alluvium—Swing bridge—Villages—Juniper—*Pinus excelsa*—Rocks—Vegetation—Return to Iskardo—Agriculture of Balti—Game of Chaugan—Chakor hunting—Shigar valley—Journey towards Kashmir—Dras valley—Karbu—Dras fort—Maten—Cross pass into Kashmir—Baltal—Valley of Sind river—Sonamarg—Gagangir—Gond—Gangan—Ganderbal—Enter main valley of Kashmir—Town of Kashmir—Description of Kashmir—Lacustrine formation—Trap hills—Lake—Climate—Vegetation.

It was not till the 25th of February that the approach of spring was sufficiently decided to permit me to make a move with any chance of fair weather. On that day I started from Iskardo, with the intention of making eight or ten days' journey down the Indus in the direction of Rondu. The district of Rondu may be understood to comprise the whole of the narrow part of the Indus valley, from the western end of the Iskardo plain to the great bend of that river, where it assumes a southerly direction. It is only during the winter season that the route along the valley of the Indus is much frequented, as it is quite impracticable for horses, and so very bad even for travellers on foot, that the road over the passes towards Hasora is always preferred in summer. At the season of my journey I had no option, the passes being still covered with heavy snow.

Unfortunately for my objects, the inhabitants of Gilgit had since the beginning of winter been in a state of open insurrection, and had besieged the garrison placed by Gulab Singh in one of the forts of the valley. Attempts had been made by the Thannadar of Iskardo to send a force to their relief, but the garrison of that place was too weak to enable him to detach more than a very small portion of it; and the forced levies of Balti men, collected in all the districts of the country, had evidently no desire to fight against the more active inhabitants of Gilgit and the robber tribes of the higher valleys of Hunza and Nagyr. Large parties of fifty and a hundred were continually arriving during the winter at Iskardo, and were as soon as possible despatched towards the disturbed country; but the greater number of them, I was told, managed to desert, and to return to their villages, or to hiding-places elsewhere, long before the detachment arrived at the end of its journey.

Crossing the Indus in the ferry-boat, a little below the rock of Iskardo, my road lay along the north bank of the river, through extensive tracts of cultivation. There was much less snow on the surface of the fields in the village of Koardu, the first through which I passed on the north bank, than in the town of Iskardo, owing to the more favourable exposure. The villagers were busy sprinkling a thin layer of earth over the snow to hasten its melting. This village, which is about five miles distant from Iskardo, is backed by very high masses of clay conglomerate and clay, forming very irregular, often precipitous banks, resting on the ancient rocks behind. From Iskardo these beds are very conspicuous, but in the village itself only a very small portion can be seen at a time.

West of Koardu, a ridge of mica-slate, containing abundance of garnets, advances close to the river, which here runs on the northern side of the valley. The road up the valley skirts the base of this projecting spur, and then passes over level platforms for about four miles. The level tracts were still covered with snow, but in rocky places, and on all slopes facing the south, the ground was quite bare. Four miles from Koardu I passed the very large village of Kamar, the fields rising in terraces one behind another on a steeply sloping platform, which skirts the plain for nearly two miles. Behind the village, the same system of conglomerate and clay-beds, as at Koardu, rises in steep banks.

About a mile beyond Kamar, which is the last village on the north side of the Iskardo plain, the valley of the Indus contracts very suddenly, the mountains closing in upon the river. The beds of lacustrine clay extend without any diminution to the end of the open valley, and are covered, when close to the mountains, by numerous boulders of all sizes, many of which are of great dimensions. The fine clay at the termination of the open plain appears to underlie a great mass of boulder conglomerate, which is continued into the narrow part of the river valley.

Where the river passes from the open plain into the narrow ravine, the inclination of its bed seems increased, and the rapidity of its motion becomes much greater. This result is quite in accordance with what has been observed in the Nubra and Khapalu plains. Indeed, narrow valleys are so generally steeply sloping, and wide valleys so generally nearly level, that it can scarcely be doubted that the inclination of the surface is in some way connected with the width or amount of excavation of the valley.

For a mile or two beyond the end of the Iskardo plain, the mountains are sufficiently far apart to allow of the interposition of a narrow platform of conglomerate, over which the road runs. Soon, however, even this disappears, and thenceforward, as far as I went, the Indus runs through a narrow ravine of very uniform character. The mountains on both sides of the river are extremely steep, and, so far as I could judge at so early a season, almost uniformly rocky and precipitous. At distant intervals a small platform of alluvium is interposed between the cliffs and the river, but much more frequently precipices directly overhang the stream, or steep bare rocks, only not absolutely precipitous, rise from its margin. It is but seldom that the stony bed of the river or the alluvial platforms overhanging it, afford a level road for a few hundred yards at a time. In general the path continually ascends and descends over each successive ridge; the elevation to which it is required to ascend to find a practicable passage, varying from a few hundred to several thousand feet above the bottom of the valley. In at least eight or ten places between Iskardo and Rondu, the path ascends or descends by means of ladders placed against the face of a perpendicular wall of rock, or crosses fissures in the cliffs by planks laid horizontally over them. This road is therefore quite impracticable for beasts of burden or horses, and is never used except in winter, when no other route is open to the traveller.

As the road lies altogether on the north or right bank of the Indus, the elevation and appearance of the mountains on that side cannot well be seen. This range separates the Indus valley from that of Shigar, which is in no part of Rondu more than twenty-five miles distant, and is crossed in several places by passes at the head of the larger ravines. These passes being still blocked up with snow, I could not cross them, nor ascertain their elevation, which is perhaps nowhere less than fourteen or fifteen thousand feet, except at the very eastern extremity of the ridge.

From the higher parts of the road, where it attained an elevation of eight and nine thousand feet, the mountain ranges on the south of the Indus could be well seen. They were covered with snow from base to summit, and in general rose so very abruptly, that the nearer spurs completely concealed from view the main range, except when a more open valley than usual permitted the view to extend backwards. Occasionally very lofty peaks were seen, which appeared to attain a height of at least eighteen or twenty thousand feet; but, as the whole landscape was covered with snow, distances could not be estimated with any accuracy. As the ridge to the south of the Indus keeps very close to the river, it is probable that the highest summits seen in that direction were situated beyond the valley of Hasora.

The villages of Rondu are not numerous, and are of very small extent; still every available spot seems to be occupied by a small patch of cultivation. The platforms are generally high above the river. In the lower part of the district, where the lateral ravines are of greater length, they open out above the very steep slope, by which they debouche into the Indus, into gently sloping open valleys. The villages of Thawar and Murdu, being situated in these open valleys, are much more extensive than any of those close to the Indus. The fort of Rondu is on the left bank of the river, on a platform perhaps two hundred feet above its level, nearly opposite the end of the Thawar valley, and not far from the termination of a valley which descends from the southern mountains, along which there is a road across a pass to Hasora.

From Iskardo to Thawar, a large village in a lateral ravine on the north side of the Indus, almost opposite to the fort of Rondu, the road distance is about forty miles. As five days were employed in traversing this distance, the average day's journey was only eight miles; and yet, from the difficult nature of the road, all the marches appeared long, and were felt to be very fatiguing. A great part of the road being at an elevation much more considerable than that the Iskardo plain, I met with much snow on all the higher parts of the mountains. In the valley of the Indus thaw made rapid progress, and by the beginning of March, in favourable exposures, there was no snow below 8000 feet.

The progress of the thaw occasioned constant avalanches, the snow slipping from the steep sides of the ravines, and when once in motion, advancing with constantly increasing momentum till it reached the lowest level. All day long the mountains echoed with the sound of falling snow; the avalanches were not often visible, as they took place in the ravines, but now and then (where the ravines terminated in precipices) they were seen pouring in cataracts of snow over the face of the cliffs. In each large ravine which joined the Indus I found one of these gigantic avalanches, and was enabled to see that they were composed of a congeries of balls of snow, varying in diameter from one to six feet, and often containing fragments of rock in their centre. Many of these snow-streams were not less than forty or fifty feet thick. At the level of the Indus they were now very soft, and evidently thawing rapidly.

In many parts of Rondu are to be seen very distinct indications of the boulder conglomerate, by which the ravine was *perhaps* at one period entirely filled; though from the very steep slopes of the mountains in most places, there is not often a resting-place for it. The platforms on which the villages are built are all formed of this alluvium, and are often covered with transported blocks of vast size. Between Siri and Baicha I saw several which were not less than sixty feet in length. In the upper part of the valley of Thawar, which is more level than the ravines higher up the Indus, a great accumulation of clay and boulders is seen attaining a height of at least 8000 feet above the level of the sea, as it forms hills a thousand feet above the village, which is at least as much above the Indus.

The valley in which the village of Thawar is situated

slopes gently towards the Indus till near its termination, when it descends extremely abruptly down a very steep inclined bank of boulders, which appears to block up the whole of the end of the valley. The slope of this steep bank was so great that it was only possible to descend by a very devious route. Between the lower part of the cultivation and the commencement of the steep slope, the valley was very irregular, and filled with heaps of boulders, forming long low hills. The appearance of the mass of debris in this valley was very remarkable, and had much the appearance of an old moraine deposited by a glacier, which had extended as far as the end of the present cultivation, and had shot forward the boulders by which it had been covered into the abyss below.

The Indus is crossed by a swing-bridge of willow twigs, which leads from the villages on the north bank to the fort of Rondu. From Thawar I descended to this bridge, in order to ascertain the boiling-point of water, so as to get an approximation to the elevation of the bed of the river. It is thrown across a remarkably contracted part of the river, where it flows between perpendicular rocks rising several hundred feet out of the water, and the path by which the bridge is reached from Thawar descends the scarped face of the precipice by a succession of ladders.

From the boiling-point of water I estimated the elevation of the bridge, which was more than a hundred feet above the river, at 6200 feet. This would indicate a fall of about 1000 feet since leaving Iskardo, or, as the river flows very tranquilly till it leaves the Iskardo plain, from the commencement of Rondu, a distance by the road of twenty-nine miles, but not, I should think, more than twenty along the course of the river, as the road winds very much in crossing ridges. This is equivalent to a fall of about fifty feet per mile, which, for a stream discharging so vast a volume of water, is very considerable indeed, but not more than is indicated by the general turbulent course of the river.

The villages of Rondu, though mostly small, have abundance of fruit-trees. The apricot is still the commonest of these; but there are also many fine walnuts, and plenty of vines climbing up the trees, and remarkable for the great size of their trunks. Willows are very common, and two kinds of poplar, and now and then there occurs a plane-tree of enormous girth and stature, which must, no doubt, afford a most welcome shade from the rays of the too-powerful sun of summer, the heat of which, in so deep and rocky a ravine, must be very oppressive. The willow and poplar had already begun to show signs of vitality, the flower-buds being almost ready to expand; the other trees seemed still quite inert.

All over the hills of Rondu the juniper* is rather common, and seemingly quite at home both on the

* This juniper has a very extended range in altitude, being common in the drier parts of the Himalaya at elevations of 12–13,000 feet, and in some parts of Tibet, where it meets with a higher summer temperature, even as high as 14–15,000 feet. It is the *Juniperus excelsa* of Wallich, and, so far as the point can be decided by dried specimens, seems identical with specimens in the Hookerian Herbarium, collected in Karabagh and Sakitschiwan by Szowitz, and communicated to Sir W. J. Hooker by Fischer. The Taurian specimens of *J. excelsa* from Bieberstein are, however, a good deal different, and are perhaps only a form of *J. Sabina*.

higher ridges, and in the bottom of the ravine close to the river. It forms generally a low bush, but occasionally I saw small trees, and once, in a level tract close to the river and near a village, a considerable tree perhaps forty feet high. The young plants had made considerable shoots, and were covered with longish acicular patent leaves, very different from the short adpressed scaly leaves of the adult plant.

Rondu is remarkable for producing another Coniferous tree, indeed a true pine, namely, *Pinus excelsa,* which occurs in small groves in several places on the south side of the river, at elevations from eight to ten thousand feet above the sea. It was first observed opposite the village of Siri, but is more plentiful above the fort of Rondu. One or two trees occur close to the river, and on the north side, so that I was enabled to get specimens and ascertain the species. The occurrence of this tree must be considered to indicate a greater degree of humidity than exists in the upper parts of the Indus valley, so that Rondu is the place of transition between the Tibetan climate and that of the eastern Punjab, into which the Indus passes at its point of exit from the mountains.

The mountains of Rondu contain much granite, which occurs in great mass at the bridge opposite the fort. In this place the granite occupies the lower part of the ravine, close to the river, while the higher parts of the mountains are composed of gneiss or clay-slate, sometimes passing into sandstone, or of a highly crystalline magnesian rock. The granite consists chiefly of quartz and mica, the former, as well as the felspar, white, the mica black and highly crystalline. The stratified rocks are always highly metamorphic, and are shattered and dislocated by the intrusion of the granite to a very great extent.

Below Thawar and the fort of Rondu, the valley of the Indus continues extremely narrow and difficult, and ceases to be inhabited at the village and fortified post of Tok, at which place a few soldiers are stationed, to keep up the communication with Gilgit, and to give notice of any incursions from that side. Thence, as far as the mountain range which bounds the Gilgit valley on the east, the valley is said to be quite desert. The disturbed state of Gilgit had made me abandon my original intention of continuing my journey in that direction; I therefore made only one march to the westward of Thawar, and found the ravine, along which the river flowed, so barren and uninteresting, that I did not consider it necessary to visit Tok, but retraced my steps towards Iskardo, which I reached on the 11th of March.

I should have been glad to have had an opportunity of observing the nature of the vegetation of the valley of Rondu, but the season of the year was unfortunately not favourable for that purpose. The cultivated plants were not different from those of Iskardo, and much of the shrubby vegetation was the same as that common higher up the Indus. An ash, of which the flowers were just expanded, but which was still quite leafless, appeared a novelty; but it was probably the same species which I had already collected in Kunawar and Piti. The only subtropical plants of which I saw any traces, were *Linaria ramosissima*, a shrubby *Plectranthus*, now leafless, but which I guessed to be *P. rugosus*, and some withered stems of tall reedy grasses, species of *Saccharum* and *Erianthus*. In summer, no doubt, many more would have occurred, and a complete list of the plants of Rondu would be of very great interest, as illustrative of the connection between the alpine flora of Ladak, which passes into that of Siberia, and the vegetation of the mountains of Affghanistan, the plants of which are in a great measure the same as those of Persia and Asia Minor. There is also a transition through this country, down the valley of the Indus, to a third flora, that of the hot dry plains of the Punjab and of Sind, which extends with little variation along the littoral districts of Beluchistan and Persia, into Arabia and Egypt.

On my return to Iskardo, I found the plain almost free from snow, a little only remaining on banks facing the north. The mountains on the south side of the valley were, however, still snow-clad to the very base, and the fruit-trees had scarcely begun to show any signs of vegetation. Along the watercourses there was more appearance of spring; a little gentian and *Hutchinsia* were already in flower, and most of the spring plants had begun to grow rapidly.

The return of spring set the whole population of the district to work in their fields; and both in Rondu and in the neighbourhood of Iskardo, I had an opportunity of seeing the mode in which the processes of agriculture are carried on. As soon as the ground is clear of snow, the manure, which has been accumulated during the preceding year, consisting of the contents of the cowhouse and stable, mixed with every sort of refuse, is carried in small baskets to the fields, on which it is deposited in small heaps. It is then spread uniformly over the surface by hand. Occasionally the field has had a previous ploughing, but it is more usually just in the state in which it had been left after the harvesting of the previous crop.

After the manure has been spread, it is ploughed into the land. The plough is usually drawn by a pair of bullocks, and is formed entirely of wood, the front part being blunted and hollow. The ploughshare, a sharp and hard piece of wood, is passed through the hollow, beyond which it projects several inches. This moveable piece of wood does the principal work, and is easily replaced when it has sustained injury. After the ploughing, the seed is sown broadcast, and the field is then harrowed. The harrow is a frame-work of wood, weighted with stones, but without spikes; or a heavy board, weighted; or occasionally only a thorny bush, with several large stones laid upon it. It is generally drawn by one man, who assists its action by breaking with his feet the clods which would otherwise be too bulky to be crushed by it. The harrowing is repeated till the soil is reduced to a sufficient fineness, an operation which is much facilitated by the dryness of the atmosphere. The field is then laid out into small square beds, for convenience of irrigation, and water is supplied to it at intervals throughout the summer.

About the middle of March, an assembly of all the principal inhabitants of the district took place at Iskardo, on some occasion of ceremony or festivity, the nature of which I have forgotten. I was thus fortunate enough to be a witness of the national game of the Chaugan, which is derived from Persia, and has been described by Mr. Vigne as hockey on horseback, a definition so exact, as to render a further detail unnecessary. Large quadrangular enclosed meadows for this game may be seen in all the larger villages of Balti, often surrounded by rows of beautiful willow and poplar trees.

About the same time, I was invited by the Thannadar of Iskardo to be present at a hunting party, which he had arranged for the capture of the *chakor*, or painted partridge, by surrounding a spot of ground, in which these birds are numerous, with a ring of men, who, approaching from all directions, gradually form a dense circle of perhaps a hundred yards in diameter. When the partridges are disturbed by a horseman in this enclosure, they naturally fly towards the living wall by which they are surrounded. Loud shouts, and the beating of drums and waving of caps and cloaks, turn them back, and they are driven from side to side, till at last, exhausted with fatigue, and stupid from the noise and confusion, they sink to the ground, and allow themselves to be caught by hand. The scene was a very striking one. The spot selected was a deep dell, full of rocks, but without trees. The sport, however, did not seem so successful as usual, six or eight birds only being captured. The chakor is an extremely common bird in all parts of the valley of the Indus, and indeed throughout Tibet. In winter, when the hills are covered with snow, they are to be found in great numbers close to the river, even in the immediate neighbourhood of the villages; and in general, when approached, they lie very close among the crevices of the stones.

Before finally leaving Iskardo, I devoted three days to a visit to the valley of Shigar, which is watered by a very large tributary which joins the Indus opposite the rock of Iskardo. The terminal ridges of the mountain ranges on both sides of the Shigar river, advance close to the centre of the valley where the stream enters the Indus. The road to Shigar from Iskardo, therefore, crosses low hills of dark schistose rocks, winding among dry valleys which are occupied by great masses of alluvium. A coarse sandstone, horizontally stratified, formed beds of fifty feet thick, alternating with and capped by beds of clay conglomerate containing numerous angular fragments. The sandstone was very similar to that which I had previously seen on the top of the rock of Iskardo, and rested upon thinner strata of a bluish-grey indurated clay, quite non-fossiliferous, and different in appearance from any deposit which I had seen in Tibet. These lacustrine strata occupied both sides of the valley along which the road lay. From the summit of the low range of hills, the road descended rapidly to the level of the cultivation of the Shigar plain. The Shigar river flows through a wide gravelly channel in many branches; and low, grassy, and swampy tracts skirt the stream. Fifty feet above these are the platforms of alluvium, which extend along the left bank of the river uninterruptedly for five or six miles, and vary in width from a quarter of a mile to a mile or more. They are almost entirely covered with arable land, formed into terraces which rise gradually one above another, and a succession of small villages are scattered among the fields. Numerous little streams descend from the mountains, and irrigation canals ramify in every direction. Ploughing was the universal occupation of the villagers; and the yellow flowers of *Tussilago Farfara* were everywhere seen expanding on the clayey banks of the rivulets.

The fort of Shigar is close to the mountains on the east side of the valley, where a considerable stream makes its exit from them. By this stream, Mr. Vigne ascended to a pass on the high range to the eastward, and descended upon the Shayuk at the village of Braghar. Where it terminates in the Shigar plain, this valley is for a few hundred yards very narrow; but a little above its entrance it widens considerably, and the flanks of the mountains are covered with a great accumulation of the alluvial deposits, clinging to the face of the rocks on both sides, certainly as high as a thousand feet above the stream. The beds were sometimes, but rarely, stratified, and were very variable in appearance. Coarse conglomerates, at one time with angular boulders, at others, with rounded stones, alternated with coarse and fine sand and finely laminated clays. No fossils of any kind were observed.

In summer, the discharge of the Shigar river, which descends from the snowy masses of the Muztagh or Kouen-lun, must be immense, as prodigious glaciers descend very low among the valleys of its different branches. Up one of the streams a practicable road exists towards Yarkand over an enormous glacier. I met with one or two people at Iskardo who had traversed it; but it is now not at all frequented, being very unsafe, in consequence of the marauding propensities of the wild Mahommedan tribes who inhabited the Hunza valley. It was described to me as an exceedingly difficult road, lying for several days over the surface of the glacier.

On the 31st of March, I left Iskardo for the last time. It was expected that the pass between Dras and Kashmir would be easily accessible by the time I should reach it. My road as far as Dras was the same as that along which I had twice travelled in December, and, except from the indications of returning spring, was much the same as it had then been. The crops of wheat and barley in the fields in the Iskardo plain were an inch or two high, the buds of the apricot were just beginning to swell, and the willows had almost expanded their flowers.

At Gol and Nar, where the valley is narrow and the heat therefore more concentrated, the corn was considerably further advanced, and in some of the apricot flowers the petals had begun to expand. Wild flowers had also begun to vegetate: a violet was in flower on the banks of streamlets, as well as a *Primula* and an *Androsace*. Above Parkuta, again, the season was more backward. Large snow-banks, which had descended in avalanches, still remained in all the larger furrows on the mountain-sides. The river had been discoloured since the day I left Iskardo, and on the 4th of April, the day I reached Kartash, it became very much so, and was said to be rising rapidly.

On the 6th of April, I entered the Dras valley, and

encamped at Ulding Thung, where there were still a few patches of snow. On the 7th, I marched to Hardas, ten miles. Here, at about 9000 feet, spring had scarcely commenced. The fruit-trees showed no signs of vitality; and though the fields had been ploughed, the grain had not yet begun to vegetate. The valley of the Dras river begins to expand at the village of Bilergu, four or five miles above Ulding. As soon as there is enough of level space, beds of conglomerate, and more rarely of fine clay, appear along the river. Round the village of Bilergu, the poplars, willows, and apricots are as numerous as in the valley of the Indus; but beyond it, the inclination of the valley is considerable, and at Hardas there were but few trees. Above Bilergu the quantity of snow increased considerably, and the contrast between the sides of the valley was very striking: at Hardas, the shady slope was quite white, while that facing the south had only a few patches of snow.

On the 8th of April, I marched to Karbu, eight miles. As I advanced, I found much more snow; but the road was in general free, except in the ravines where snow-slips had descended. On the latter part of the day, these were universal in all the ravines, and were frequently of great depth, and so soft as to be difficult to cross: on the least deviation from the beaten path, I sank to the middle at every step. These avalanches were cut off abruptly by the river, forming cliffs of snow fifteen or twenty feet high, in which the structure and development of the mass by successive slips, alternating with falls of snow, could be distinctly made out. One or two of them still crossed the river, which flowed below the bridge of ice. Three miles below Karbu, the granite, which had been the rock ever since entering Dras, was replaced by a peculiar slate, apparently magnesian, and perhaps hornblende slate, passing into or containing beds of a coarse sandstone.

At Karbu, where I was detained a day, the Thannadar not having expected me so soon, and my porters not being ready, the weather was very unsettled, and in the evening, and during the nights of the 8th and 9th of April, there was a good deal of rain, especially on the 9th. The wind during the storm was very irregular in direction. The ground was still covered to the depth of more than a foot with snow. The morning of the 10th was gloomy, but as the day advanced the clouds broke, and the afternoon was bright and beautiful, with a gentle air down the valley.

On the 11th of April I reached the fort of Dras. For the last ten miles the snow lay continuously, and two or three feet deep, but there was always a clear path. The temperature being much above the freezing-point, the thaw proceeded rapidly. A good deal of *Prangos*, which is evidently a common wild plant (as it is also in many parts of Kashmir), was seen; the withered inflorescence projecting through the snow. I observed it also very abundantly in the hay, which is preserved in the villages, and seems to consist of all the plants of the meadows cut indiscriminately, and not of *Prangos* alone, as I had erroneously imagined.

My former journey having terminated at Dras, the road in advance was new to me; but the whole country being still covered with snow, I could see little of the nature of the surface. The fort of Dras is about 10,000 feet above the sea: it is situated in an open, nearly level plain of some width, skirted by low hills. The higher mountains, which are several miles distant on both sides, are very steep. Several villages are scattered over the plain, at some distance from the fort, which stands alone, on the bank of a little stream, just before it joins the Dras river. Beyond Dras, the road to the pass having scarcely been used, there was no beaten path. In the morning the snow was hard and firm, and even in the afternoon, notwithstanding the warmth of the midday sun, the foot did not sink more than three or four inches. The depth of snow increased rapidly as I advanced. Two miles above the fort the plain contracts into a narrow valley, and the channel of the river becomes very rocky; the stream is also very rapid, and the slope of its bed evidently considerable. The valley again expands around the village of Pain Dras. Immediately beyond this I crossed the river on a bridge of snow, at least forty feet thick, which covered the river for more than a hundred yards. This snow-bed, which was continuous with the general level of the surface, was to all appearance quite solid. After a march of ten miles I encamped at Maten, the last village of Dras, a small group of stone huts half a mile from the river on its eastern bank, and immediately at the base of a very steep scarped mountain, which rises in precipices several thousand feet above the village. Maten I estimated, from the boiling-point of water, to be 10,700 feet above the sea.

On the 13th of April I crossed the pass into Kashmir,

starting, as the distance was said to be considerable, at about half-past two o'clock in the morning. The evening before had been dull, with irregular squalls of wind, so that the weather did not promise very favourably. It was very dark and quite calm at two A.M., and when I started it snowed slightly, but not enough to induce me to stop, as I hoped it would cease with daylight. Unfortunately, on the contrary, it increased rapidly, and by four o'clock was snowing heavily, and continued to do so till the afternoon. There was no wind, and the air was very mild, so that I suffered no inconvenience from cold. The surface of the snow, even in the morning, was a little soft, the cloudy night having prevented it from freezing. After four o'clock it snowed so heavily that the accumulation of fresh snow soon amounted to several feet, and we sank above the knee at every step. There was scarcely any slope, the road appearing quite horizontal. Before daylight my guides managed to lose their way, and we wandered for more than half an hour puzzled by our own footsteps. The compass was of no use, as I did not know the direction in which we ought to proceed, nor was it till after dawn that we recovered the road.

After daylight there was no improvement in any respect, as the heavy snow completely obscured the view. The leaders of the party, however, seemed to recognize the outlines of the hills, as they held their course without hesitation. The valley was quite full of snow, which completely covered all irregularities of surface. The river was often quite covered by the mass of snow for distances of more than a furlong without interruption.

Our path often crossed it; and, latterly, for several miles before gaining the crest of the pass, the stream was completely concealed.

About noon the snow fell more lightly, and we could see around. The width of the valley was from half a mile to a mile, and steep mountains rose on both sides to a considerable height, the peaks being, I should think, at least 16,000 feet. Patches of willow and juniper were seen on the sides of the hills. Still the road was to appearance quite level. The valley made several bends, and we turned finally to the right, before gaining the crest of the pass, to which there was a barely perceptible rise.

The descent was at first gradual, but soon became very steep, down a bank of snow, which filled the whole of a narrow ravine. The rocky walls on either side were at first bare, but soon became sprinkled with birch and pine. For two thousand feet below the summit of the pass the descent was uninterrupted, till I reached the banks of the Sind river, which flows through the northernmost valley of Kashmir, and is separated from the main valley by a lofty range of mountains. Here, on a level space separated by a little stream from pine-forest, I found a log-hut buried up to the roof in snow, which was heaped up round the building, probably from having been thrown off the roof. The snow at Baltal—for so this first halting-place on the Kashmir side of the Zoji pass is called—was not deep, probably little more than what had fallen during the day.

My whole party took possession of the log-hut; but not liking the smoke which, in an instant, filled it, so that there was no seeing across its width, I had a space cleared for my tent. It rained smartly in the evening, but soon after dark it again began to snow, and long before morning I was awoke by the cracking of the ridge-pole of my tent, which had given way under the pressure of a foot and a half of snow. Had it fallen at once I should probably have been buried till morning, as I was too distant to make myself heard, and had to rise to summon assistance, to move my bed into the log-hut.

All day on the 14th it snowed unceasingly, and my people would not continue the journey; but on the 15th it was fair, and I gladly made a move, as the log-hut of Baltal was a most uncomfortable resting-place. The road lay along the Sind river, which ran to the south-west, through a deep but rather open valley, only partially wooded. The forest consists partly of pines, partly of deciduous-leaved trees. Of these I could recognize birch, poplar, and willow, which formed the mass of the woods, but there were no doubt many others. The pines were principally *Pinus excelsa;* silver fir and spruce also occurred, but I saw no deodar nor Gerard's pine. The trees grew in well defined masses of forest, separated by much open ground, in the level plain which skirted the river on the south side of the valley; on this side they also rose high on the mountains, but the slopes on the north side were bare.

Seven or eight miles from Baltal, I found an uninhabited house, at a place called Sonamarg*, where a bridge crosses the Sind river. Snow had been continuous all

* In Moorcroft's time, this place was a small village.

the way, diminishing in depth as we descended the river. A mile or two before reaching Sonamarg, the stream approaches close to the mountains on the north side of the valley, barely leaving a passage for the road, which for some distance skirted the base of steep cliffs. In one of the ravines which here furrowed the mountain slopes, I had an opportunity of seeing the descent of an avalanche. While crossing the ravine I was warned by the sound that a snow-slip was approaching, but had abundance of time to retreat to a place of safety before it came near. When the avalanche came into sight, the ravine, which was narrow and deep, was completely filled by balls of snow of various dimensions, which continued to flow past for several minutes. The snow-slip terminated in the river, which was speedily blocked up for two-thirds of its width with an immense accumulation of snow.

At Sonamarg the Sind river bends abruptly towards the south, and enters a rocky gorge, down which its stream advances with great rapidity, over a steeply inclined bed, very rocky and much interrupted by rapids. Leaving Sonamarg on the morning of the 16th of April, I crossed the river, and after a mile and a half of level ground bare of trees, still covered with snow, I entered a thin forest of pine and silver fir, which continued to the entrance of the gorge. The silver fir (*Picea Webbiana*) was a fine straight tree, with short horizontal or drooping branches, and its leaves were very variable in length.

When I had fairly entered the narrow gorge of the river, I found that it was in many places still blocked up with snow, which had descended in avalanches down the narrow ravines, and had accumulated in the bed of the stream. We crossed the river three times on snow-beds. From the rapidity of the descent, however, the climate changed rapidly. After four or five miles there was no snow, except in ravines, where it had accumulated in avalanches, and at last even these had almost entirely melted away. Still snow lay in patches on the right bank of the river, in the village of Gagangir, at which I halted for the day; and on the left bank, which faced the north, and was therefore in shade, snow still covered the whole surface down to the bank of the river.

At the village of Gagangir the Sind river resumes its south-westerly direction, and its valley becomes more open, and the descent of its bed less abrupt. The elevation of the village is about 7900 feet above the level of the sea, so that the descent from Sonamarg is probably not less than a thousand feet in a distance of nine miles—a very considerable fall. On the latter part of the day's journey, a very considerable change was observable in the aspect of the vegetation. Birch and willow continued common throughout, but were mixed latterly with many other trees and shrubs, all of which were beginning to show symptoms of vitality. The hazel (*Corylus lacera*) and a species of *Viburnum* were in full flower, both still devoid of leaves; a few herbaceous plants were also in flower in open places, the most abundant of which were a species of *Colchicum*, remarkable for its bright orange-coloured flowers, and a pretty little rose-purple *Corydalis*, very closely allied to, if not the same as, a species of eastern Europe. Still the general aspect of the country was very wintry, as there were few pines, and the forest was therefore quite bare of leaves, while the signs of progress, though evident on a near inspection, did not attract attention in the general view.

At Gagangir, which is the first village of Kashmir by the route along which I was travelling, I was enabled to relieve my Dras porters, who had accompanied me so far. The discharge and payment of these men occupied me a great part of the 17th of April; and as the day was rainy I did not leave Gagangir till the 18th, when I marched to Gond, seven miles. The road still followed the course of the Sind river, which I crossed twice during the day. The width of the valley was considerable all along, with much arable land, and a good many villages in ruins on both sides. The mountains on the right hand were uniformly bare of trees, and often rocky; on the left they were well wooded to the summit, the forest being most dense above. Early in the day several of the ravines were still full of snow; and on the shady side a good deal lay in patches. Further on, the snow in the valley had quite disappeared, but on the mountain slopes there was still plenty. As I advanced the cultivated land increased in extent, and the appearance of the valley became exceedingly picturesque, the centre being occupied by a broad belt of fields and orchards, while the hills on both sides rose abruptly to a great elevation. The fruit-trees were principally walnuts, apples, and apricots. Groves of poplar occurred occasionally along the river, but I saw no birch during the day. Many more spring plants were in flower than on the previous day; *Cruciferæ* were the prevailing family, but I also collected species of *Nepeta* and *Gagea*, and a pretty little tulip. On the latter part of the march, a small shrubby species of *Amygdalus* was very abundant; and *Fothergilla involucrata* of Falconer, a plant of the natural order *Hamamelideæ*, which was just bursting into flower, formed a dense coppice on the hills on the north bank of the river. Though the greater part of the plants was new to me, still I recognized a number of species which occur in the valley of the Indus. *Juniperus excelsa* was common in rocky places, and the *Ribes* and rose were the same as those common at Iskardo.

On the 19th, the road still followed the course of the Sind river, now a rapid torrent, much swollen by the heavy rains, flowing through an open valley. A good deal of level ground was interposed between the mountains and the stream, and was laid out in terraced fields evidently adapted for rice cultivation, but now quite bare. I met with many very interesting plants. *Tussilago Farfara* was abundant, growing in gravelly places along the river. In shady woods a species of *Hepatica*, with a small white flower, first discovered by Dr. Falconer, was common. In more sunny places a *Primula* and *Androsace* were in full flower. On open sandy soil a species of the curious Siberian genus *Ceratocephalus* was a very striking novelty. On the higher hills there was still dense forest of *Pinus excelsa*, spruce, silver fir, and deodar, mixed with yew and *Juniperus excelsa*, and with many deciduous-leaved trees, few of which were recognizable. After travelling twelve miles I encamped at Gangan, which is elevated about 6000 feet.

Next day I remained stationary; but on the 21st I continued my journey to Ganderbal, nine miles further and close to the point where the Sind valley expands into the open plain of Kashmir. As I advanced, the valley gradually widened, and turned more to the south. There were several platforms, or steppes, as it were, of nearly level arable land, one above another, and below them the river flowed through a wide stony plain. The mountains on the right, high and snow-topped, receded to a considerable distance; those on the left gradually diminished in elevation, became less covered with forest, and at last terminated in low ranges of hills covered only with brush-wood. The road was extremely pretty. At first it lay along the right bank of the river, through fine underwood, and among beautiful meadows, which skirted the bank of the stream; it then crossed to the left bank, and, ascending the lower hills, entered a fine wood, in which apricot, pear, and cherry trees, all bursting into flower, were common, and to all appearance wild, though they had probably spread into these woods from the neighbouring villages. Latterly we emerged upon a somewhat elevated platform sloping to the south, covered with bushes and many fruit-trees, with here and there a village, and a great deal of cultivated ground. Where the Sind valley joined the plain of Kashmir, it was several miles in width, and evidently richly cultivated. The expanse of the plain of Kashmir was much greater than I had anticipated; the mountains on its south side, which were still covered with snow, were in sight, but at a considerable distance.

Above Gond the valley of the Sind river is very poorly

inhabited, and deserted villages and abandoned cultivation showed that the population is diminishing. The lower part of the valley, however, is very populous. The villages are numerous and large, and the houses good: they are usually built entirely or partially of wood, with high sloping roofs, which are either thatched or covered with wood. The cultivated lands all rest upon platforms or banks of alluvium, which are probably analogous to those of the Tibetan valleys, though, as they are generally faced by sloping banks covered with bush-jungle, their structure is not so easily determined as that of the platforms of that more barren country.

On the morning of the 22nd of April, after following the base of the low hills for half a mile, till the last projecting point had been rounded, I entered the valley of Kashmir. This "celebrated valley" did not at all come up to the expectations which I had formed from previous descriptions, and from the appearance of the termination of the valley of the Sind river. The first impression was one of considerable disappointment. It was by no means well wooded, and the centre of the valley along the river, being very low, had an unpleasant swampy appearance. The road to the town, which is about ten miles from Ganderbal, led over an elevated platform. There were several villages, and plane, willow, and fruit-trees were scattered here and there, though far from abundantly. The platform was in general covered with a carpet of green, now spangled with myriads of dandelions and other spring flowers. The mountains on the left, which at first were very low, gradually rose in elevation, and were throughout rugged and bare. As I approached the town I mounted an elephant, which formed a part of the *cortège* sent, according to the usual oriental etiquette, to receive an expected visitor; and I consequently saw the town to much better advantage than I should have done had I ridden through it on my little Ladak pony. Passing completely through the city, I was conducted to the Sheikh Bagh, a garden on the banks of the Jelam, at its eastern extremity, in a pavilion in the centre of which I took up my quarters.

The town of Kashmir is apparently of great extent, and seems very densely populated. Its length is much greater than its width, as it is hemmed in between the Jelam on the south and a lake on the north. The principal part of the town is on the north side of the Jelam, but a large suburb occupies the opposite bank, surrounding the Sher-Garhi, or fortified palace of the ruler of the country. The streets are in general so narrow, that there are but few through which an elephant can pass; and the houses, which have mostly several stories, are built with a wooden frame-work, the lower story of stone and those above of brick. There are no buildings of any great note; and the elaborate account of Moorcroft renders it unnecessary to enter into any detail. The river is crossed by many bridges, all built of deodar-wood.

The province or country of Kashmir consists of an extensive plain, surrounded on all sides by lofty mountains. It is the valley of the river Behat, or Jelam, which is separated from that of the Chenab on the south, by rugged and often snowy ranges, and from the basin of the Indus on the north, by the main axis of the Western Himalaya, which, originating in the peaks of Kailas, separates the basins of the Sutlej and the Chenab from that of the Indus. The mountains which surround the plain of Kashmir are very lofty. Those on the north are for the most part bare and rugged on their southern face, while those which lie to the south appear from the plain to be magnificently wooded with forests of pines and deciduous-leaved trees, descending almost to their base. On both sides of the valley the mountains rise above the level of perpetual snow, but those on the north side are considerably more lofty than the others. Numerous transverse valleys penetrate into these mountains, which are well cultivated in their lower parts, and, higher up, present superb mountain scenery. On the south side of the valley, many passes, varying in elevation from 10,000 to 14,000 feet, lead across the main chain to the Chenab valley and the plains of India. To the north there are only two frequented routes, that by the Garys pass towards Hasora and Deotsu, and that by the valley of the Sind river towards Dras. At the eastern end of the valley a high pass leads across the mountains to the valley of Wardwan, from which travellers can reach Kargil and the Indus on the left, and Kishtwar in the valley of the Chenab on the right.

The flat country or alluvial plain of Kashmir, which is 5300 feet above the sea, is about fifty miles in length, and not more than ten or twelve miles wide. It commences close to Islamabad, where the last spurs of the mountains at the east end of the valley disappear; and terminates at Baramula, where the ranges, branches of the opposite mountain chains, again advance close to the bank of the river. It is traversed in its whole length by the river Jelam, which rises at the east end of the valley, and winds from one side of the plain to the other, at one time washing the base of the northern hills, at another receding to a considerable distance from them. The Jelam flows with a tranquil stream, and, being navigable throughout the whole of the level country as far up as Islamabad, for boats of considerable burden, is the great highway for the traffic of the country, in which, notwithstanding its being perfectly level, wheel-carriages are unknown. At Islamabad it is a very small stream, but it gradually enlarges, by additions from both sides, as it descends. Near the town of Kashmir it is from fifty to a hundred yards wide, often very deep, and in few places fordable, even at the driest season.

The plain of Kashmir has evidently at one time been the bed of a lake, a deposit of fine clayey and sandy strata, more rarely partially indurated into a soft sandstone rock, occupying a great part of the surface. Soft pebbly conglomerate is also occasionally met with, and an indurated conglomerate, containing water-worn pebbles, occurs in many places in the lower course of the Sind river. This lacustrine formation forms elevated platforms, which are from fifty to one hundred and fifty feet or more above the level of the river. In many places, both on the Jelam and along the lateral streams which descend from the mountains to join it, the beds of clay have been removed by aqueous action. In such places the plain has a lower level, often very little above the surface of the river, and is covered with rice-fields or with marshy lands, undrained and not under cultivation.

The platforms of lacustrine clay are called, in Kashmir, "*karewah.*" They are often quite dry, and generally uncultivated, but where water is procurable they are highly cultivated, yielding luxuriant crops of wheat and barley. A proper application of artificial irrigation would, I believe, make the whole of these more elevated parts of the plain fertile, as the soil is everywhere well adapted for the growth of corn. These karewahs generally run parallel to the lateral streams which join the Jelam, and extend from the base of the mountains till they are cut off by the river. There are, however, in the upper part of the valley, several isolated patches, all horizontally stratified, from which I infer that they had originally been continuous. One of these, near Bijbeara, forms a table-topped hill of considerable extent, surrounded on all sides by low land. Several low hills near Islamabad, also, are evidently outlying patches of the same formation. The sands and sandy clays of these platforms are usually quite non-fossiliferous; but I determined the lacustrine nature of the strata by finding, on the flanks of Takht-i-Suleiman, a hill near the town of Kashmir, and close to the city lake, but at least thirty feet above its level, a bed of clay, which contained, abundantly, shells of the genera *Lymnæa* and *Paludina*.

The main chain of the Himalaya, north of Kashmir, consists, where I crossed it, by the Zoji pass north of Baltal, of metamorphic schist; and all its branches, which descend towards the plain of Kashmir, seem to be formed of the same rock. Along the north side of the valley, however, a series of hills of trap rise, almost isolated, out of the plain. Ahathung, near the Wulur lake, is, I believe, the most westerly of these, but I did not visit it, and only infer its structure from its conical shape and from its similarity in appearance to those further east. Near the town of Kashmir there are two of these isolated hills, composed of an amygdaloidal trap: these are Hari-Parbat, which is fortified, and Takht-i-Suleiman, which rises about eight hundred feet above the plain. The former lies to the north-west, and the latter on the north-east side of the town.

The lake or *Dal* of Kashmir lies to the north of the town, stretching from the base of these two hills to the more lofty mountain range which bounds the valley on the north. It is nearly circular and four or five miles in diameter, but is only open in its northern half, the end nearest the town being occupied by large islands, with narrow channels between them, in some of which there is a good deal of current. Its waters are discharged into the Jelam by a considerable stream, which, flowing from its south-east corner, runs to the westward in a course nearly parallel to the southern margin of the lake for nearly a mile, when it turns abruptly south to enter the Jelam in the middle of the town of Kashmir. This stream is evidently an artificial canal, and the embankment by which it is separated from the lake appears to have been constructed in order to keep the surface of the latter higher than it would naturally be. The stream at its point of exit from the lake flows through a narrow canal of masonry, and has, when the Jelam is low, a fall of several feet. A pair of flood-gates prevent the return of the stream in times of flood, when the waters of the river are higher than those of the lake.

The Wulur lake, below the junction of the Sind river with the Jelam, appears to be similar in appearance to that close to the town, and, like it, to owe its extent in part to artificial means. Its dimensions are, however, much greater. There are several large marshy tracts in different parts of the plain, which, by a little engineering, might also be converted into lakes: one in particular, near Avantipura, is quite under water in spring, though in summer and autumn it is only a swamp.

The climate of Kashmir is the same as that of the interior valleys of the Himalaya, but modified by its extreme western position, which brings it within the influence of the spring rains which prevail in Affghanistan and the countries on the lower mountain course of the Indus. There are at least four months of winter; and in general a good deal of snow falls. March and April are very rainy; the summer months mostly dry and fine. The periodical rains of India cannot be said to extend into Kashmir; but in July and August showers and thunder-storms are said to be frequent. The spring and autumn are unhealthy seasons. In the former, the cold rainy weather affects those who have already suffered from the malaria produced by the action of a powerful sun on neglected swamps. The abandonment of cultivation, in consequence of the long oppression of the country under a foreign government, has been the cause of the increase of marshy ground. The river in seasons of flood rises higher than the level of the lowest portion of the alluvial land, and is only excluded (as in Holland) by means of artificial works along the course of the river. By the omission to repair these *bunds*, or dykes, a large extent of country which might be under cultivation is left in a state of swamp.

There is no natural forest on any part of the open plain of Kashmir, and the cultivated trees are not numerous; the plane, poplar, and willow are all common, with numerous fruit-trees, chiefly walnuts, apples, apricots, cherries, and quinces. A mulberry is also common, the dried specimens of which are in no way distinguishable from those of the common white mulberry of Europe, with which I have compared it. The vines are trained up the poplar-trees, rising to their very tops, and hanging down from their summits. A species of *Celtis*, which is commonly planted around the town, is, I think, the most tropical of all the Kashmirian trees, being common in the warmer valleys of the outer Himalayas; it is, however, I think, *Celtis australis*, L., a species which is a native of western Asia and eastern Europe, and appears to find its eastern limit in the Himalaya.

At the time of my arrival in Kashmir, the fruit-trees were in full blossom; the wild vegetation had, however, made very little progress, only the earliest plants being in flower. The spring flora was eminently European in character; not only the genera, but many of the species, being identical with those of our own island. *Cruciferæ* were the most abundant natural order; and, among many others, I collected *Draba verna*, *Capsella*, *Erysimum*, *Alliaria*, *Turritis glabra*, and European species of *Lepidium*, *Thlaspi*, *Alyssum*, and *Sisymbrium*. Other common forms were *Lycopsis arvensis, Lithospermum arvense, Myosotis collina, Scandix Pecten, Ranunculus Philonotis, Anagallis arvensis, Euphorbia Helioscopia,* and several species of *Veronica.* None of the annual plants were Indian forms, though a few of them were such as occur commonly in the plains in the cold season. The shrubby vĕgetation was very limited: a Juniper (*J. communis*), a *Cotoneaster, Rubus, Rosa Webbiana, Zizyphus, Elæagnus, Daphne,* and two species of *Berberis,* were the most common. A few straggling trees of *Pinus excelsa,* which grew on the northern face of the low hill called Solomon's Throne, were the only pines which I saw in any part of the open valley.

CHAPTER X.

Environs of Kashmir—City lake—Gardens of Shalimar and Dilawer Khan — Pampur — Avantipura — Platforms of lacustrine clay—Mountain of Wasterwan — Ancient city — Clay, with shells and fragments of pottery—Ancient temple imbedded in clay—Lakes caused by subsidence—Islamabad—Shahabad—Vegetation—Vernag—Banahal Pass—Valley of Banahal—Tropical vegetation—Pass above Chenab Valley—Nasmon—*Jhula*, or Swing-bridge—Balota—Ladhe ke Dhar—Katti—Fort of Landar—Mir—Kirmichi—Tertiary sandstones—Dhuns—Seda—Jamu.

During my stay in Kashmir, besides the necessary ceremonial of complimentary visits, my chief occupation was visiting the principal places in the vicinity. From my residence in the Sheikh Bagh I had easy access to the river, as well as to the canal by which it communicates with the lake. A broad road, three-quarters of a mile in length, shaded on both sides by very fine poplar-trees, runs from the eastern end of the town, parallel to this canal, as far as the hill called the Takht, at the foot of which is situated the passage by which the lake discharges its waters into the canal. The weather was very favourable, the spring rains having terminated a day or two before my arrival. The Kashmiris are accomplished boatmen, a great part of the population living upon the water; and as most of the conspicuous objects around the town are only accessible by water, I gave pretty constant employment to a boat's crew whom I hired during my stay.

My first visit was to the lake, and to the celebrated gardens on its northern shore, which were the delight of the emperors who made Kashmir their retreat from the heat and cares of Delhi and Lahore. The southern part of the lake is very shallow, and I sailed along narrow channels, which separated large patches of tall reeds, among which a very narrow-leaved *Typha* and an *Arundo* were the commonest plants. Three or four species of *Potamogeton* were abundant in the lake, just coming into flower, but most of the water-plants were only beginning to vegetate. I saw three or four flowers of a water-lily (*Nymphæa alba*), and could just recognize *Villarsia nymphæoides*, *Menyanthes trifoliata*, and *Trapa*, all of which had been recorded by previous travellers as natives of Kashmir. I looked anxiously for *Nelumbium*, but saw no signs of it, except the withered capsules of the previous year, many of which I observed floating on the lake.

The gardens of Shalimar and of Dilawer Khan rise in a succession of terraces from the margin of the lake. They are laid out in a stiff formal style, straight walks crossing one another at right angles, and are irrigated by means of straight water-courses, branching from a long canal which passes down the centre, through a succession of ponds well built in masonry, and provided with artificial fountains, which are made to play on festivals and holidays. Pavilions of fine marble occupy the intersections of the principal walks. Magnificent plane-trees form the chief ornament of these gardens, which are now much neglected; straggling bushes and a wilderness of weeds occupying all the less conspicuous parts, while the main avenues alone are kept a little neat.

Although the chief beauty of the valley of Kashmir is undoubtedly the magnificent girdle of snowy mountains by which it is surrounded, the orchards and gardens, which are still numerous in the neighbourhood of the capital, are charming spots, and the more so from the contrast which they present with the barrenness of the surrounding country, and the absolute ugliness of the swamps in the centre of the valley. Nor should it be forgotten, when we compare the accounts given by early travellers with the impressions made upon us by the present appearance of the valley, that Kashmir is no longer in the same state as it was in the days of the emperors; a long continuance of misrule, under a succession of governors, whose only interest it has been to extract as much revenue as possible from the unfortunate inhabitants, having produced the only conceivable result, in abandoned cultivation, a diminished revenue, and an impoverished people.

On the 2nd of May I left the town of Kashmir, taking the route by the Banahal pass, towards Jamu and the plains of India. As my road lay for several days' journey along the course of the Jelam (or Behat, as it is always called in Kashmir), I engaged boats for the transport of my servants and baggage as far as Islamabad, travelling myself, however, generally by land and on foot, in order to see the country. My first halting-place was Pampur, seven miles from the town of Kashmir. After traversing the magnificent avenue of poplars, which runs north-west from the town, the road winds round the base of the Takht, the eastern face of which is only separated from the Jelam by a low swampy tract, a few hundred yards in breadth. East of the Takht a succession of rugged trap hills skirt the road, but beyond these the more distant mountains are evidently stratified. The road was grassy and quite level, and passed through much cultivation, the young wheat and barley being dripping with a heavy dew which had fallen during the night. A scarlet poppy and *Adonis* were common weeds among the corn.

Next day I travelled to Avantipura, seven miles further. The lacustrine formations, which had made their appearance on the bank of the river a little west of Pampur, continued to occur more or less constantly as we proceeded eastward, and the road traversed for some miles an elevated plain, quite bare of trees, and only partially cultivated, while the remainder was covered with grass. The surface of this plain was eroded by wide transverse valleys, formed by little streams which ran towards the Jelam: these were flat, and well cultivated, some of the wheat being already in ear. On the highest parts of the platform the cultivation of saffron is carried on, in beds four or five feet square, separated by deep ditches or furrows from one another. The plant, which flowers in autumn, was now in full leaf.

Behind Avantipura lies a high mountain, called Wasterwan, rising to a height of 10,000 feet above the sea by the determination of Jacquemont, or 4700 feet above the plain. It projects forward in an almost isolated manner, though it is connected by a narrow ridge behind with the general mass of the range on the north side of the valley. On the 4th of May I ascended to the summit of this mountain, which I found to be entirely formed of trap, partly homogeneous, and partly amygdaloidal. Several gigantic *Umbelliferæ*, already in full flower, were abundant in the lower parts of the open valley by which I ascended. One of these was *Prangos pabularia*, which formed dense thickets four or five feet high. From this open valley I got upon a sharp ridge, grassy below but very rocky above, along which I proceeded almost to the top; but being stopped by a precipice, I was obliged to enter a narrow rocky ravine, by ascending which I managed to gain the summit, which was grassy and rounded, and covered with a few patches of snow. On the northern face of the hill snow still lay in great quantity. The view from the top was very fine, the day being in every respect favourable: the greater part of the valley of Kashmir was seen spread out far below, and a complete circle of snowy mountains bounded the horizon. The mountains to the north were seen to be distinctly stratified.

The commonest plants on the ascent were a beautiful rose-coloured *Oxytropis*, and a tulip (*T. stellata*), the flowers of which, when fully expanded, spread out like a star. A few trees of *Pinus excelsa* were seen on the upper part of the ridge; and in a hollow close to the top there were about a dozen yew-trees. On the summit, though the vegetation was not generally alpine, most of the plants of the middle zone extending to the very top, there were many pretty little spring flowers, which did not extend far down. A *Primula, Pedicularis, Gentiana, Leontopodium, Corydalis,* and *Callianthemum,* were all in flower. On the northern slope of the mountain, a wood of deciduous trees, still bare of leaves, commenced a few yards below the summit. At first the trees were all birch, but lower down a cherry and maple were mixed with it; the former with young leaves, and just-formed racemes; the latter only recognizable by the last year's leaves, which strewed the ground. A few horse-chesnut trees were also seen near the top.

The neighbourhood of the village of Avantipura is one of the most interesting places in which the lacustrine strata of the Kashmir valley can be studied, as there is distinct evidence of the existence in that place of deposits much more recent than those which extend over the whole plain, and which were therefore formed when the valley was occupied by a large lake. Avantipura was formerly the site of a very large town, the capital, I believe, of the kingdom; built in the shape of an amphitheatre in a deep semicircular bay, enclosed by two low spurs, which project from the mountain Wasterwan, which rises immediately behind.

The ruins of the ancient town are still visible, consisting of heaps of stones, some of immense size, indicative of large buildings, but none of them showing the slightest traces by which the shape or structure of the edifices could be determined. These ruins extend all round the deep recess in the mountains, and terminate below quite abruptly, without any apparent cause, in a perfectly horizontal line along the mountain-side.

The mountain behind is an isolated peak, furrowed by numerous ravines, which are dry except immediately after rain. The place would therefore appear singularly inappropriate as the site of a large city, were there not, I think, sufficient evidence that a lake existed in front of the town, the surface of which was on a level with the horizontal line by which the ruins are abruptly terminated.

The ruins of the ancient city stand upon the lacustrine clay of the Kashmir plain, and are therefore posterior in age to the period when the valley was occupied by one large lake. Immediately in front of the ancient ruins, between them and the small modern village of Avantipura, which is situated on the banks of the Jelam, there occur beds of fine brown-coloured clay, containing in great quantity fragments of pottery, with here and there small pieces of charcoal and bone. In one place on the bank of a small ravine, which then probably carried a streamlet into the lake, I found the clay to contain, mixed with the broken pottery, numerous shells, some fresh-water and some land species, and all the same as are common at the present day in the river Jelam, or on the grassy hill-sides in the valley. The place where these shells occur is fifty or sixty feet above the river.

The appearance of this evidently very modern deposit is exactly that which would no doubt be exhibited, were the present lake close to the city of Kashmir dried up, and a section of its bed exposed. This lake contains abundance of shells, and in the neighbourhood of the town it is made the receptacle of refuse of every kind, broken pottery being particularly plentiful. In shallow places in the river, close to the town of Bijbehara, a similar deposit is accumulating, valves of a *Cyrena* being found to some depth in the fine mud, mixed with broken pots, charcoal, bones, and other refuse.

The most remarkable fact connected with this very recent lacustrine deposit is, that the ruins of an ancient temple exist on the plain above the Jelam, a little west of the modern village, partially buried in the clay. The upper parts of two temples, resembling in all respects the ruins on the elevated platform at Martand, near Islamabad, stand on the open plain, not far from the river, but perhaps twenty feet above its level, and certainly far below the level to which the clay containing pottery rises on the hill-sides. One of the temples is quite in ruins, the immense blocks of which it is built being piled confusedly on one another. The beautiful colonnade (exactly like that at Martand) by which it is surrounded, is evidently quite uninjured in any way; but it is entirely buried under the lacustrine clay, except a very small portion, consisting of three pillars, which were exposed by Major Cunningham in 1847. These three pillars may be seen in a cavity under the level of the present surface of the ground, and the clay in which they were imbedded contains fragments of pottery in profusion.

If these temples (the date of which I believe is approximately known to antiquarians) were contemporaneous with the ancient town, they must have been buried in the lacustrine silt at some period not very long subsequent to their erection, if I am right in supposing a lake to have existed at the same time with the town. Probably, therefore, they are anterior in age to the town, as they are imbedded in such masses of pottery as could only have been accumulated in the neighbourhood of a very dense population. Their present appearance, I think, helps to explain the nature and origin of the many lakes or marshy depressions which occur in all parts of the valley. It appears evident that at Avantipura, at some period subsequent to the building of the temples, a subsidence of the ground must have taken place during one of the many earthquakes which are well known to have convulsed the Kashmir valley. This subsidence, which must have been partial, and not co-extensive with the valley, converted the ground on which the temples stood into a lake. A fresh subsidence, or the gradual wearing away of the incoherent clay strata lower down the river, must at last have drained the little lake, and left the country round Avantipura in the state in which we now see it. Even now a marsh partly under water during the spring months extends from Avantipura for several miles up the river.

The occurrence of repeated partial subsidences in various parts of the Kashmir plain appears to me the only way in which the general appearance of the country can be explained. The abrupt, broad, and shallow depressions between the different platforms are seemingly much too extensive to have been formed by the trifling streamlets which now run along them, without the assistance of volcanic action. The lakes, too, are deeper than the present level of the river, a circumstance only explicable in an alluvial country on some such supposition; and as it is well known that violent earthquakes have at intervals convulsed this valley[1] for many centuries, this mode of explaining the phenomena becomes highly probable.

On the 5th of May I continued my journey to Islamabad, which is about eleven miles from Avantipura. The peak of Wasterwan is the termination of a long mountain ridge, which separates two large valleys from one another. Immediately to the eastward, therefore, the mountains recede from the river, and the road traverses a marshy tract, a great part of which, from the late heavy rains, was still under water, while the remainder was laid out in fields, prepared for the cultivation of rice. Further on, cliffs of lacustrine clay again rose perpendicularly from the river. Several streams joined the Jelam from both sides, some of them deep and sluggish, with straight banks like canals, while others were almost as large as the main stream, and broad and shallow, with a sandy bed and gently flowing current. Near Bijbehara, a considerable village, with many timber-built houses and a substantial bridge of deodar, the banks are beautifully wooded with shady trees. Above this village the Jelam is much smaller, often shallow, and the banks lower, though still eight or ten feet above the water, and not swampy, but either fringed with willow and mulberry trees, or bare and covered with fields of green corn, or of rape now in full flower. The bridge of Islamabad, which is the limit of navigation, is nearly a mile from the town, which is a considerable place, the next in importance to the capital, though very much smaller. It lies on low ground close by the river, but immediately behind it a long promontory of the lacustrine formation stretches back for several miles, rising abruptly out of the finely cultivated and well-wooded valley on the left, in steep, rugged cliffs, which are worn into irregular ravines by the action of rain. These formations attain here a thickness of at least 150 feet, and well deserve the particular attention of the geologist. The ancient temple of Martand, the most perfect of its class of ruins in the valley, is built on the upper and back part of this platform.

Leaving Islamabad, I crossed immediately one branch of the Jelam, which descends from the west. It had already lost the tranquil character of the stream lower down. There were pebbles in its bed, and it had a more rapid current. After crossing this stream, the country was for some distance quite flat, and entirely covered with rice-fields, now bare; some of them had been ploughed, but most were still just as they had been left after harvest. They were traversed by numerous ditches or canals for irrigation, in all of which a proportion of fresh-water shells, chiefly *Lymnææ*, were seen. Further on, the appearance of the country began to change: there were still plenty of rice-fields, but they rose in steps one above another, and the water in the irrigation canals flowed rapidly over pebbly beds. Crossing another branch of the Jelam, which had a broad channel full of large boulders, but shallow and easily fordable, the road began gradually to ascend a low range of hills covered with grass and bushes where it was dry, but still laid out in rice-fields wherever water was procurable. These hills, which are the termination of a long range which descends from the snow-clad mountains at the east end of the valley, are composed of a very hard limestone, the strata of which are much bent, sinuated, and fractured. On the south side of this ridge is the valley of Shahabad, which is watered by the principal branch of the Jelam. It contains numerous villages, surrounded with fine orchards, and its rice-fields are arranged in terraces. Water being plentiful, the whole valley is cultivated with rice, and the district appears to be one of the richest in Kashmir.

The general character of the vegetation continues the same as further west, and the more advanced season enabled me to recognize a few common Himalayan plants. The scandent white rose (*R. Brunonis*) was one of these, also *Lonicera diversifolia* and a shrubby *Indigofera*. I also observed *Viola serpens, Thymus Serpyllum, Lactuca dissecta,* and *Fragaria Indica*. Among the rice-fields several plains plants occurred, such as *Potentilla supina, Convolvulus arvensis, Mazus rugosus, Salvia plebeia,* and *Marsilea quadrifolia*. Nor were the plants of a Tibetan climate altogether wanting, for *Rosa Webbiana* was everywhere common, and a species of *Myricaria* grew plentifully among the boulders on the banks of all the streams.

From Shahabad I made, on the 7th, a short march to Vernag, a celebrated fountain near the bottom of the Banahal pass. Crossing the river, the road lay up the open valley of the Jelam, still among rice-fields, rising step by step behind one another, as the valley sloped upwards. Vernag lies close to the mouth of a little lateral valley, up which our further course lay. The fountain, which is built of marble, is large, contains many fish, and supplies a considerable stream. It is the reputed source of the Behat or Jelam, but the main branch of that river descends from the mountains a good way further to the south-west. The hills on both sides of the Shahabad valley are of limestone, the strike of which seemed to be west-south-west, or nearly in the direction of the valley. It is very much indurated, and its colour is bluish-grey; it has all the appearance of having been much altered by heat. The dip appeared different on the opposite sides of the valley: on the north it was east of north, on the other side southerly; the inclination of the beds varied much, and they were often very much distorted. I did not see any eruption of igneous rock on any part of the day's journey.

On the hills above Vernag there was a good deal of brushwood, consisting chiefly of *Fothergilla involucrata*, two species of *Viburnum*, *Cotoneaster*, *Lonicera*, and a few trees of *Pinus excelsa*, yew, and deodar. The opposite hills were bare and grassy. In the forests of Kashmir (as was first pointed out by Dr. Falconer) we do not find the oak, *Andromeda*, and *Rhododendron*, which are so abundant at similar elevations in the outer Himalaya. The appearance of the woods is, therefore, remarkably different, as these trees, which, in the temperate zone of the mountains near the plains, constitute almost all the forest, give the woods there a peculiar character.

On the 8th of May I passed from the valley of Kashmir into the basin of the Chenab, crossing the Banahal pass, the summit of which is not more than 10,000 feet above the sea: it is a very narrow ridge, separating two deep valleys. Starting through rice-fields, and passing at the upper limit of cultivation a few fields of barley and rape, I soon entered brushwood, the same as on the hills above Vernag. In the ravines on the left hand, snow descended below 7000 feet. Ascending rapidly on a ridge, the brushwood gave place to a fine wood of maple, horse-chesnut, cherry, hazel, and elm, all just bursting into leaf. The dip of the limestone rocks was exceedingly variable, at one time southerly, at another northerly, but the strike was, I believe, the same as the day before. The ascent continuing rapid, the shady side of the ridge was soon covered with snow; but the road kept on the southern exposure, which was sometimes bare of forest. Birch at last appeared among the other trees, and, as the elevation increased, it began to predominate. About the same time, the limestone gave place to a slaty rock, which was almost immediately followed by an amygdaloid, which continued to the summit. Both the slate and the limestone appeared to have been upheaved by the igneous rock, and I thought the slate seemed inferior to the limestone.

On the upper part of the ascent the birch gradually became more and more stunted; it was here almost the only tree, with the exception of a few specimens of *Picea Webbiana*, at the limit of forest a little below the summit. Here the hills were bare and rocky; but the forest did not cease on account of elevation, because on the opposite hill, which had a northern exposure, a shady wood, chiefly consisting of pines, rose to a level considerably higher than that of the pass, which was a depression in the ridge, considerably overtopped by the hills on both sides. The crest of the pass was undulating, and covered with green-sward, among which a few spring plants were in flower; these were a *Corydalis*, an *Anemone*, and *Primula denticulata*. A large patch of snow occupied the northern slope, just below the top.

The view from the summit would have been magnificent had the day been more favourable; but a thick haze rested over the more distant parts of the valley of Kashmir, as well as over the southern mountains in the direction of the plains of India. The southern slope of the range on which I stood was bare, scarcely even a bush being visible; and the Banahal valley, nearly four thousand feet below, appeared as a perfectly level plain, covered with rice-fields and scattered villages, marked by groves of trees. On the descent I followed a very steep rocky ridge. About half-way down, the amygdaloid was replaced by metamorphic slate, and for the remainder of the descent the rocks were alternations of slate, very hard conglomerate, and quartz rock. The dip of these strata was very variable, and on the face of several spurs, at a little distance, sections were exposed, exhibiting enormous flexures. I saw no limestone on the southern face of the pass, except in the valley of Banahal, where there was a good deal of a horizontally stratified limestone, very different in appearance from that on the other side, which, as it was confined to the bottom of the valley, and was there very local, appeared to be of much more recent origin.

After joining the Banahal river, the descent became more gradual. At first, the valley was almost level and quite covered with rice-fields, all under water. The villagers were busy ploughing, both bullocks and men knee-deep in soft mud. Further on, the valley contracted, and cultivation only occurred at intervals. In the narrower parts, the stream was fringed with trees, but the hill-sides were still quite bare. Round the villages there were very fine trees, chiefly walnut, horse-chesnut, and elms, with the ordinary fruit-trees; but the plane and black poplar do not occur, nor are any vines cultivated in the valley. The winter is said to be quite as severe as in Kashmir; and the elevation, so far as I could determine it by the boiling-point of water, is a little greater, the lower villages (in one of which I encamped) being about 5500 feet, while the highest fields are about 6000 feet. In the woods, *Fothergilla*, cherry, sycamore, and horse-chesnut were common, just as in Kashmir. The season was much further advanced than on the north side of the pass, all these trees being fully in leaf, and the horse-chesnut in flower. The greater part of the vegetation was identical with that of Kashmir, but I saw many more species, probably only from the more advanced state of the season. The *Zizyphus* and rose (*R. Webbiana*) of Kashmir were still common, and the white poplar was wild along the banks of the stream. I did not, however, see *Daphne* or *Myricaria*. In shady lateral ravines an oak was frequent, the more interesting as I had seen none in Kashmir; it was *Q. floribunda*, a species of the middle zone of the outer Himalaya, which usually occurs at higher levels than *Q. incana*, and lower than *Q. semecarpifolia*.

Though the river of Banahal is a tributary of the Chenab, yet the district has always been considered as a dependency of Kashmir, from which it is only a short day's journey distant, while for several days in descending towards the Chenab, the country is almost uninhabited. Halting one day at Banahal to change my porters, I made three marches to Nasmon, on the right bank of the Chenab, following the course of the Banahal river during the first and part of the second march, but afterwards leaving it, on account of its increasing ruggedness, to cross the range on the left hand by a pass about 8000 feet above the sea, which overhangs the valley of the Chenab. The bounding spurs which hem in the Banahal valley descend almost perpendicularly upon the Chenab, and dip at last very abruptly to that river. At first, large masses of snow were visible at the sources of all the lateral valleys, but lower down the elevation was not sufficient, and the hills were bare. After leaving the last village of Banahal, the bottom of the valley was for some time level and covered with fine forest, consisting chiefly of magnificent trees of *Celtis*, elm, and alder; the others were two species of *Acer*, *Fraxinus*, *Morus*, *Populus ciliata*, and a willow. *Fothergilla* now grew to a small tree, and *Marlea* made its appearance, the first indication of an approach to a hot climate. Soon, the banks of the river became rocky, and left no passage, so that the road ascended on the right bank, and lay at a considerable elevation on the hill-sides, looking down upon a richly wooded and often rocky glen. The hills were steep and generally bare, but the ravines were often well wooded. *Pinus excelsa* occurred occasionally; *Quercus floribunda* was common, and *Q. lanata* made its appearance.

Before leaving the Banahal river, I had got down to

about 4000 feet, meeting latterly with some familiar plants of the warmer zone: *Pinus longifolia* formed dry woods, *Cedrela Toona*, a fig, *Albizzia mollis*, and last of all, *Dalbergia Sissoo*. Still, most of the plants of the upper part of the valley accompanied me throughout; even the hoary oak had not disappeared, and the general appearance of the vegetation was very different from what it would have been at the same elevation further east, the plants of a hot climate being chiefly such as delight in a dry heat, and are capable of enduring a considerable amount of winter cold, provided the summer temperature be sufficiently elevated. It was evident that the temperature was considerably lower than it would have been at the same height in the Sutlej valley, and I drew the same inference with regard to the humidity, from the appearance of a number of dry-climate plants; for instance, a yellow spinous *Astragalus*, a *Dianthus*, and *Eremurus*, an Asphodeleous genus common in Kunawar, and other dry valleys of the Himalaya.

In the ascent of the lateral ravine, towards the pass above Nasmon, I encountered, for the first time, *Rhododendron arboreum* and *Andromeda ovalifolia*, the two trees which, with the hoary oak, form the mass of the Simla woods. The forest was now very fine, as I was on the northern slope of the range. On the upper part of the ridge by which I ascended, there was a grove of fine deodar-trees, and in the bottom of the dell a shady wood of horse-chesnut and sycamore. I had now entered a zone in which the flora was quite similar to that of Simla; *Fothergilla* being the only tree I observed, which is not common in that district. And it was curious that it was on the northern and most shady, as well as most humid exposure, that this identity of flora became first remarkable, and that the same trees which at Simla form the forests of the drier slopes and more exposed situations, grew in this valley low down on the hill-sides, in the most sheltered spots.

The ascent towards the ridge was latterly steep, with a good deal of silver fir and deodar. The trees rose to the very top of the northern slope, but, as usual, the summit was bare and grassy, though the tops of the trees were actually higher than the crest of the ridge, and obscured the view to the north. As the elevation was only 8000 feet, there was no peculiarity of vegetation, all the plants being those of the middle zone, except the silver fir, which descended to a lower level than it usually does in the Simla hills. There was some cultivation of wheat and barley within a very short distance of the summit, which overlooked the valley of the Chenab; and as the day was fortunately clear, there was a very fine view. The ravine through which the river flowed appeared everywhere rugged, more especially towards the plains, where a succession of steep rocky hills were seen, the nearest of which surrounded the mouth of the Banahal river. Across the Chenab, a high range, beautifully wooded, ran parallel to the river, rising into a snowy peak nearly opposite to me. This peak, which concealed all view of the plains beyond, lay on my road to Jamu, and was about 9000 feet in height.

The descent to Nasmon, which is only 2700 feet above the level of the sea, was very steep. At first it led along the face of a bare hill, but soon entered a shady ravine, filled with alder, oak, walnut, and *Celtis*, but without any of the superb horse-chesnuts which had been so abundant in the humid valleys on the northern face of the range; nor was there any *Rhododendron*. Crossing a considerable stream, the road ascended through fine forest to the crest of a ridge, beyond which there was a long and steep descent of at least 1500 feet, to the village of Nasmon, on which tropical vegetation made its appearance very abruptly. *Pinus longifolia* grew scattered along the sides of this hill, and *Daphne*, pomegranate, the olive of the Sutlej valley, *Vitex Negundo*, *Colebrookea*, *Rottlera*, *Sissoo*, *Adhatoda Vasica*, a thorny *Celastrus*, *Acacia modesta* and *Lebbek*, and *Bauhinia variegata*, made their appearance in succession, in the order in which I have named them. Most of these are the same as the shrubby forms common in the Sutlej valley at Rampur; but the *Celastrus* and *Acacia modesta* are plants of the plains of the western Punjab, and do not extend so far west as that river. The range parallel to the Chenab on the north, which I had just crossed, has probably a granitic axis, for boulders of granite were common on the upper part of the ascent on both sides of the pass, though I did not anywhere see that rock *in situ*. On both sides the first rock exposed was a fine-grained gneiss, with large crystals of felspar. Lower down, on the north face, I observed mica-slate, with garnets; and in the bed of the Banahal river ordinary clay-slate occurred.

Nasmon is a very large but scattered village, with much cultivation. It lies on a high platform of alluvium, considerably above the bed of the river. Plane, orange, apricot, and pear trees grew in the gardens, with *Melia Azedarach*, and a few trees of the European cypress (*C. sempervirens*), bearing apparently ripe fruit. The day was oppressively warm, the thermometer rising above 85° in the shade.

On the 13th of May, I crossed the Chenab by a bridge about a mile above Nasmon. The descent to the bank of the river was gradual, and very bare. Rocks of a black clay-slate and of conglomerate, in nearly vertical strata, formed the bed of the river, which was as large as the Sutlej at Rampur, and very much swollen and muddy. The bridge is the simplest form of *jhula*, a single set of ropes, from which a wooden seat is suspended, which is pulled from side to side by means of a rope, worked from the rocks on either side of the river. The banks of the river were adorned with a profusion of bushes of *Nerium odorum*, in full flower, and highly ornamental. The vegetation along the river exhibited the same curious contrast of tropical and temperate forms, which I have already described as characteristic of the dry valleys of the interior of the Himalaya, at elevations between two and four thousand feet; and the tropical plants were so similar to those which I observed on the Sutlej, that I need not particularize them. There was no forest in any part of the valley near the river, but a few trees of *Pinus longifolia* grew scattered on the bank; and on the stony ground which skirted the stream, there was a low jungle of the same tropical shrubs as had occurred on the lower part of the descent the day before. I saw also *Zizyphus nummularia*, a shrub which is eminently characteristic of a dry climate, being common in the most desert and rainless districts of the Punjab. The shrubby temperate forms were not numerous, being chiefly *Rosa Brunonis*, and the Himalayan pear, *Lonicera diversifolia*, *Myrsine bifaria*, and *Jasminum revolutum*, all plants which have a very wide range in the Himalaya.

Passing through the bush jungle which skirted the river, I entered a large tract of almost level cultivated land, covered with fields of barley, ripe and partly cut. One or two plantain-trees, and some buffaloes, were signs that we were still in a very hot region. Crossing a considerable stream, the road began to ascend rapidly on a narrow ridge. Passing some farm-houses, surrounded by fields, I entered a scattered wood of wild olive-trees (*Olea cuspidata*), mixed with *Zizyphus* and wild pomegranate. The young shoots and panicles of the olive were abundantly covered with a white floccose glutinous matter, the source of which I could not exactly determine; but I could see no trace of any insects by which it could have been formed, so that it was perhaps a natural exudation from the tree. Small woods of *Pinus longifolia* occurred at intervals, almost alone, for few plants seem to thrive under its shade. At 4000 feet, while the olive and pomegranate were still abundant, *Quercus lanata* appeared. At 4500 feet, which was about the upper limit of the olive, I re-entered a cultivated district, disposed in terraces on the slopes of the hills. The barley was quite ripe, and being cut, but the wheat, though in full ear, was still green. There were also a few fields of the opium poppy in full flower, and of safflower (*Carthamus tinctorius*), which was not nearly so far advanced.

I encamped at the village of Balota, elevated 5000

feet. Round the village were some very fine table-topped deodars, perhaps the relics of a former forest, though more likely planted by the villagers. The hills on all sides were richly cultivated, as far up as 6000 feet, above which elevation fine forest commenced; and the snowy top of the mountain behind, which I had seen from the pass of the 12th, was visible rising behind the forest. During the whole of the ascent from the Chenab, the rock was a coarse-grained sandstone, in highly inclined strata, generally of a reddish-brown colour, the surface of which rapidly passes into a state of decay.

The range of mountains to the south of the Chenab, by which that river is separated from the basin of the Tawi or river of Jamu, still lay between me and the plains of India. On the 14th of May, I crossed a spur from this range, descending into a valley watered by a tributary of the Chenab. This ridge, which is called Ladhe ke Dhar, rises a little above 9000 feet, that being the elevation at which the road crosses it. After leaving the cultivated lands of Balota, the ascent, which was steady, lay through fine brushwood and stunted oaks. On the banks of the stream, which occupied the centre of the valley by which I ascended, sycamore, horse-chesnut, and cherry, were abundant. On the slopes there were a few trees of *Pinus excelsa* and *Picea*, but the forest was not dense. About 7000 feet, on the north-western face of a spur, there was much cultivation of wheat and barley, hardly yet in ear. Here there was a fine view in the direction of the upper valley of the Chenab, of rugged mountains, scarcely wooded on the slope exposed to view, rising behind one another, the more distant still heavily snowed. Higher up, the forest was chiefly formed of the holly-leaved oak, but the latter part of the ascent was through a dark forest of silver fir, intermixed with a few fine yews. The underwood here was chiefly *Viburnum nervosum*, still in flower, though its leaves were almost fully developed. On emerging from this gloomy forest, in the upper part of which there was a thin sprinkling of snow, I found myself on the crest of the range, which was bare and rounded. Snow lay in large patches, and had evidently been till very recently continuous over the whole top, as vegetation was just commencing, and few plants were in flower. *Primula denticulata* was common, as well as a little gentian, which extended on both sides at least 2000 feet lower; the only alpine plant was the little *Callianthemum* which I had found some days before on the summit of Wasterwan in Kashmir. The distant view was unfortunately quite obscured by haze, so that I could not see, as I had expected, the plains of India.

In descending the southern face of this mountain, the road at once entered a forest of silver fir, in the upper part of which I saw one tree of *Quercus semecarpifolia*, a species which I had not met with on the Kashmir passes, or anywhere since leaving the Sutlej. About 8000 feet, the pines were replaced by the holly-leaved oak, forming open woods, in the glades of which patches of cultivation soon occurred; I encamped at about 7000 feet, at the village of Katti. During the day the sandstone rock occurred uninterruptedly, partly, as the day before, of a reddish-brown colour, partly grey, or nearly white. On the descent large angular fragments of this rock were everywhere scattered over the surface, almost always more or less imbedded in the soil: these had somewhat the appearance of a former moraine, but the surface was so much covered with wood, and the boulders were so much buried, that I could not trace their arrangement in a satisfactory manner.

Next morning I continued the descent, which was rapid, so that I soon arrived at tropical vegetation. There was but little forest, except in ravines, and the heat soon became very great. About three miles from Katti I passed the fort of Landar, built on an almost isolated cliff, overhanging the ravine; and a little further on I descended abruptly to a small stream, running towards the Chenab, the elevation of whose bed was about 3000 feet. The descent, which was almost precipitous, led down the face of a mass of clay, in some respects like the alluvial deposits so common in Tibet. Similar masses of alluvium, all table-topped, and very steep, and much worn by ravines, had occurred throughout the whole of the descent from Katti. A few pines grew on this steep bank, and all the shrubs which I had found on the banks of the Chenab at Nasmon were again met with. After crossing this stream, the bed of which was filled with large water-worn boulders, I again ascended to about 5000 feet, chiefly among cultivation, and encamped at *Mir*, a small village close to the crest of the main range south of the Chenab, the elevation of which was now very inconsiderable.

Next day, a gentle ascent of half an hour brought me to the crest of this range. The mountain slopes were bare and grassy, but in the ravines there was now and then some brushwood. *Andromeda ovalifolia* and *Rhododendron arboreum* were both noticed; and, much to my surprise, I observed at intervals a few trees of *Fothergilla*, for I had not expected to find this Kashmir tree so close to the plains, and in a district the flora of which was so completely that of the Simla hills. On the summit of the pass, which was not more than 6000 feet, I found a beautiful gentian (*G. Kurroo* of Royle) and a yellow spinous *Astragalus*, seemingly the same species which I had found at Nasmon, on the Chenab. It was curious to find a representative of the spiny-petioled group of this genus in so hot a climate and so near the plains; for in the rainy parts of the mountains, and in the more humid parts of the Indian plain, the genus is almost wanting, and this particular section entirely so.

From the summit I descended at once through a pine-wood to the bottom of a valley, the course of which I followed throughout the day in a southerly direction. It gradually widened as I advanced; villages became frequent, and were surrounded by extensive cultivation, and all temperate vegetation disappeared. I encamped at the village of Kirmichi, where the valley which I was following appeared to expand into an open plain of some width. Here oranges and mulberries were cultivated in gardens, and the toon and mango, pipal and banyan (*Ficus religiosa* and *Indica*) were planted in groves round the houses.

On the 17th of May, I continued my journey towards the plains of the Punjab. An open, somewhat undulating valley lay before me, appearing to stretch from east to west, and to be bounded by two ranges of hills which had the same direction. Trikota Debi, a curious three-peaked hill, the last culminating point of the range separating the Chenab from the Tawi, rose some miles to the westward. To the eastward the valley of the Tawi was open as far as Ramnagar, which was distant about twenty miles. In crossing this open plain, or *dhun*, I nearly followed the course of a little stream which had excavated for itself a deep channel in the soft sandstone of which the plain was composed. This rock was very different in appearance from the red or grey sandstone which had accompanied us from Balota; it was pure white, and almost horizontally stratified, while that was always highly inclined. During the latter part of my journey of the 10th I nowhere saw rock *in situ*, so that I had no opportunity of ascertaining the contact of these two formations, which are probably of very different epochs, the sandstone of the open plain being certainly the Sewalik tertiary formation, while the red sandstone of the higher mountains, which in the total absence of all organic remains is as yet of uncertain age, is perhaps the same as the gypsiferous and saliferous sandstones which skirt a great part of the western Himalaya.

One or two pine-trees, and some bushes of *Euphorbia pentagona*, were almost the only features in the vegetation which distinguished this open valley from the plains of India. On shady rocks along the stream three or four ferns were common; the oleander also grew near water; a dwarf date-palm occupied drier spots; and I saw a few trees of *Cassia fistula*. Crossing a broad shallow river which flowed to the eastward at the southern boundary of this *dhun*, in a depression faced by cliffs of sandstone, I entered among low hills covered with scattered trees of *Pinus longifolia*. This plant appears to grow luxuriantly on hot dry hills; the trees did not attain a great size, but appeared vigorous and healthy, with thick trunks and gnarled branches, exactly like the Scotch fir, except in the great length of the leaves, which are pendulous from the ends of the branches.

On the 18th, I crossed a sandstone range, in which the strata exhibited an anticlinal axis, dipping towards the plain on both sides. The ascent was easy, and the summit was not above the limit of tropical vegetation, as a banyan-tree grew on the top. The descent was much steeper and considerably longer, the valley to the south being a good deal lower. The road was good, being in the steeper parts paved with large flat stones, while in the more rocky parts the sandstone was cut into steps. A flat and well cultivated valley lay to the south of this range, in the centre of which flowed a river, in a wide channel several hundred feet below the level of the plain: it was very shallow, and was crossed by stepping-stones. Another hilly tract followed, covered with straggling bush jungle, and on the upper part with pine-forest: this was also of sandstone, very soft, and excavated by the various little streams which traversed it, into narrow and deep ravines. Even foot-paths, by constant use, were sunk four or five feet deep in the soft rock. The dip of this range was gentle, towards the plains of India.

I encamped on the 18th at Seda, under the shade of a superb banyan-tree, in a hollow in this sandstone range, and next day continued my journey to Jamu. Emerging from the hills after a mile or two, I entered a third valley, and followed the course of the little stream by which it was watered, to its junction with the Tawi, along which I travelled about four miles; to the town of Jamu, which is built on the outermost range of hills, at the point were the river Tawi finally quits the mountains. These hills rise very gently from the plains, their southern slope forming a long inclined plane, densely covered with a jungle of low thorny trees. The same sort of jungle usually skirts their base to a distance of two or three miles, or as far as the alluvial soil of the level country which lies beyond is covered with stones and shingle. It is principally composed of *Acacia modesta* and *Catechu*, and of two species of *Zizyphus*. The northern or inner face of this range of hills is very steep, often quite precipitous; and where they overhang the Tawi, they terminate abruptly in a line of cliffs facing the river. A similar range, but a good deal lower, descends from the eastward towards Jamu, and, like the other, presents a series of vertical cliffs covered with brushwood towards the river. The town occupies the gentle slope which faces the plains; it is a straggling and dirty place, but with some very good houses. The principal building is the residence of Maharaja Gulab Sing; at the time of my visit occupied by his eldest son. It is situated on the edge of the cliff, overhanging the river, and commands a fine view of the open valley of the Tawi below, and of the mountain ranges to the north and east, the more distant of which were still tipped with snow.

The outermost range of hills, which does not rise to any great elevation, consists entirely of loose conglomerate coarsely stratified, the beds dipping very gently towards the plains. The boulders of which it is composed are waterworn, and very various in composition, but all referable to the interior ranges; a few thin beds of sand and of a clay resembling pipe-clay, are interposed between the strata of conglomerate.

The very curious country through which I had been travelling since the 16th, had so much the appearance of a succession of valleys parallel to the plains, and separated by long ranges of hills, that it was difficult to avoid taking up that impression, which, notwithstanding, I believe to be an erroneous one. The gentle slope of the different tributaries which join the Tawi from the right and left, tends to keep out of sight the longitudinal ranges parallel to that river, from which the lateral ramifications proceed. When we obtain a detailed survey of the district, it will be found that the lateral valleys on each side of the Tawi do not correspond in direction, and are not quite opposite to one another, and that the apparent uniformity is caused by the great width of their valleys, when compared with the elevation of the bounding ranges. The Sewalik sandstone here attains a width of at least thirty miles, which is very much more than is found further west.

CHAPTER XI.

Leave Jamu to return to Tibet—Lake of Sirohi Sar—Vegetation of lower hills—*Dodonæa*—Ramnagar—Garta—Dadu, on a tributary of the Chenab—Camp at 10,000 feet—Badarwar—Padri pass—Descend a tributary of the Ravi—and ascend another towards the north—Sach *Joth*, or pass—Snow-beds—Camp in Chenab valley.

On my arrival in Kashmir, I had forwarded an application to the Indian Government, requesting permission to return to Tibet, for the purpose of visiting the mountains north of Nubra, which, from the advanced state of the season, I had been unable to do the previous year. Soon after reaching Jamu, I received intimation that the Governor-General, Lord Dalhousie, had been pleased to accede to my request. I had already determined, if permitted to return to Le, to take the route by Zanskar, which, though much frequented by the natives of the country, was quite unknown to European travellers; but as the season was far advanced, I chose a road through the higher hills, instead of taking that leading directly to Chamba, which would have obliged me to travel for at least a week through the hot valleys of the outer ranges.

I left Jamu on the morning of the 23rd of May.

After crossing the Tawi by a ferry immediately below the town, my road lay for three miles up the left bank of that river, along an open sandy plain, only very partially cultivated. I then turned to the right, and entered the low hills which skirted the plain on that side. The road generally followed the course of the ravines, which have been excavated out of the soft sandstone by the numerous tributaries which descend to join the Tawi. These streams are all of small size, with gravelly or sandy beds, and are separated by low ridges of some breadth, faced generally by perpendicular cliffs. An undulating country of this nature occupies the whole of the space which intervenes between the outer range of hills and that next to it, a distance, by the road along which I travelled, of about twelve miles. This second range is a branch given off by an axis, whose direction is nearly east and west. The road ascended to it by a very steep rocky path, after surmounting which I found myself on a considerable tract of nearly level ground, partly occupied by a pretty little lake, with grassy banks. On the banks of this lake, which is called Sirohi Sar, and is rather less than half a mile in length, I encamped on the 24th of May, in a grove of very fine mango-trees. The depth of the lake did not appear great, its margins being for a considerable distance very shallow, and producing an abundance of reeds and water-plants, among which the sacred *Nelumbium*, with its gay flowers, was conspicuous. The elevation of the lake, as deduced from the boiling-point of water, I found to be 2200 feet. It occupies a depression in the top of the ridge, being surmounted on both sides by low ranges of hills, rising only to the height of a few hundred feet. At the east end, a low flat plain, interrupted only by a few regular rocky knolls, seemed to indicate that the size of the lake had formerly been more considerable than at present.

The vegetation of the country between Jamu and Sirohi Sar was entirely of a tropical character. The rocky hills were in many places covered with thinly scattered pines, all of small size, and generally with much-contorted trunks, but apparently healthy and vigorous. In the cultivated grounds the plants were identical with those of the plains, but, as is usual in all hilly countries, the barren tracts produced a flora of a different character. *Nerium odorum* was abundant on the banks of streams, and I met with *Cassia fistula*, *Punica*, species of *Rhus* and *Casearia*, as well as the curious *Euphorbia pentagona*, and now and then the beautiful *Bauhinia Vahlii*. *Acacia modesta* and a *Zizyphus* were the most common trees. The lake produced a great variety of water-plants, but except an *Alisma* and *Dysophylla*, both of which were new to me, the species seemed all natives of the plains.

On the 25th of May, I proceeded along the side of the ridge in an easterly direction, passing several small flat-bottomed depressions, apparently the sites at a former period of small lakes, similar to that from which I had commenced my march. The road was rocky and rugged, and gradually rose several hundred feet to the crest of the ridge. Pine-trees were generally plentiful. On reaching the top, shortly after daybreak, a fine wide undulating valley was seen below, bounded on the north at the distance of about ten miles by a third range of mountains, and traversed by several streams, which had excavated for themselves deep perpendicular-sided ravines in the sandstone strata. All these streams had a westerly course to join the Tawi, which, issuing from a deep valley behind the third range, crossed the open plain in a south-west direction.

Leaving the ridge, the road descended gradually to the plain, and after crossing a deep ravine, with precipitous walls, continued through a fine level country to the village of Thalaura, about a mile from the third range of hills. The sandstone frequently contained a few waterworn pebbles scattered through it; and a bed of coarse conglomerate, with an indurated matrix, capped the cliff above this ravine. Some strata of indurated clay and soft slate also alternated, but rarely, with the sandstone. The plain was well cultivated, being chiefly laid out in rice-fields; and the people were all busy ploughing, sowing rice, and harrowing with a log of wood, drawn by bullocks and kept down by the weight of a man.

On the earlier rocky part of the road the vegetation was much the same as the day before. *Dodonæa* was common, as it is in most parts of this hilly tract, never, however, rising out of the tropical belt. I do not know how far to the eastward of Jamu this plant extends; but as it does not seem to occur to the east of the Sutlej, and probably stops much sooner*, it appears to prefer

* I have been told by Dr. Jameson that he has met with it in the Kangra hills, but that he has never seen it in Mandi.

a rather dry climate, and will, I think, be found limited to the drier portion of the Peninsula, from which it probably extends through Central India, and along the hilly country west of Sind. On the open plain the pines entirely disappeared, and the aspect of the vegetation was entirely that of the plains of India.

From Thalaura I marched, on the 26th of May, to Ramnagar, crossing the third range of hills, the ascent of which was at first very steep and rocky, over a made road, paved with large stones, in many places much out of repair. This range was also sandstone, dipping to the north at a gentle angle; some strata of indurated clay occurred between the beds of sandstone. These hills were precipitous to the south, and sloped gently towards the north, in the direction of the dip. The tree *Euphorbia*, which, with its stiff fleshy branches springing in verticils of five from the stem, forms a striking feature in the vegetation of the lower hills, was common on the ascent, and the yellow spinous *Astragalus*, which I had observed between the Chenab and Jamu a fortnight before, was frequent on both sides of this ridge; but even at the top, except one species of *Indigofera*, no plants indicating elevation were met with: on this account I omitted to determine the height of the range by the boiling-point of water, but comparing its elevation with that of Ramnagar, which was in sight, I estimated that it might be about 3600 feet. To the north lay another valley, considerably more rugged than that crossed the day before, and evidently much more highly inclined, as its eastern termination was not far distant. This valley was traversed by the principal branch of the Tawi, the source of which is in the mountains east of Ramnagar.

The descent from this range was very gradual, the road running obliquely to the eastward, among scattered pine-trees, over bare sandstone rocks, till it reached the bank of a small stream separated from the Tawi by a low range of hills. During the descent, a number of plants of Himalayan forms made their appearance, which had not occurred before: these were a berberry, *Rubus flavus*, and *Myrsine bifaria*. *Olea cuspidata* was seen lower down, and a species of alder grew in shady ravines along the edge of the stream. In the bottom of the valley, the mixture of the forms of the middle and lower zones was curious and interesting. *Pinus longifolia* occurred with *Phœnix sylvestris*, alder with *Rondeletia* and *Rottlera*, pear with *Sissoo*, and *Fragaria Indica* and *Micromeria* with *Trichodesma* and *Solanum Jacquini*. At the same time, it was evident that in this dry stony valley the tropical species, which formed the majority, were more at home than the stragglers which had descended from above.

After ascending for a short distance along the banks of the little stream, the road crossed it, and after a short steep ascent from the right bank, the remainder of the day's journey was nearly level, along the sides of hills, or over a high table-land to Ramnagar, a small town and fort, formerly the residence of Rajah Suchet Sing, since whose death the place has been rapidly falling to decay, most of the shops of its well-built bazaar being now empty. There were in the neighbourhood one or two large gardens, in which the trees and plants were nearly all Indian, *Sissoo* and *Melia Azedarach* being the most common. A single plane-tree was scarcely an exception; for though undoubtedly more at home at greater elevations, the plane (like the poplar and many of the fruit-trees of temperate climes) does not refuse to grow even in the plains, as is proved by the occurrence of a number of trees of it of considerable size and apparently healthy in gardens at Lahore.

Leaving Ramnagar on the morning of the 27th, I continued to ascend the valley of the Tawi for about three miles, the road running along the sides of the hills among rich cultivation at a considerable height above the stream. It then descended somewhat abruptly to the river, and soon crossed to the right bank, from which a steep ascent commenced at once, and continued, with one or two interruptions of level cultivated ground, to the end of the day's journey. The ascent had throughout a southern exposure, and was in consequence generally bare of trees, and dry and grassy. Much cultivated land was met with, wherever the ground was sufficiently level to admit of it. I encamped at a small village, or rather cluster of farmhouses, called Garta, at a height of about 5800 feet. From the bare grassy nature of the ascent and its hot sunny exposure, the number of species of plants which occurred was very limited, and the change of vegetation much less marked than in better-wooded regions of these mountains. A few oaks (*Q. lanata*) made their appearance about half-way up, or perhaps at 4500 feet.

During this day's journey, I believe that I passed the point of contact of the tertiary sandstone with the more ancient rock, for on the ascent after crossing the river, the strata were very highly inclined, and often bent into large curves. The rock was also more indurated, and different in colour and appearance from that of the outer hills. I did not, however, observe the place where the change took place.

Next day, the ascent continued equally steep and bare as the day before, and there was still much cultivation, wherever the surface was sufficiently level for the purpose, or could be made so by means of terracing. During the preceding day's march, the fields of wheat and barley had been for some time cut, but here, though generally ripe, they were still standing. On attaining an elevation of about 7000 feet, the steep spur which I had been ascending joined the main ridge, and the road, turning to the east, entered a thick forest of small oak-trees (*Q. lanata*) through which it continued, alternately descending and ascending a little, as it entered the recesses or advanced along the projecting ridges. The greatest height attained may have been about 8000 feet, and the summit of the range, which was frequently visible, did not seem to be above 1000 feet higher. After about three miles of forest, the hills again became bare, and continued so till the end of the march, which terminated by an abrupt descent of 600 or 700 feet to a ravine, and an equally steep ascent to the village of Pata, which was elevated about 7500 feet. Throughout the day, the vegetation, both in the forest and on the open tracts, was identical with that of the Simla hills. The forest consisted of oak, *Rhododendron*, and *Andromeda*. Pines were visible at the very top of the ridge, but did not cross to the southern exposure: they appeared to be *Picea Webbiana* (*Pindrow*). The village at which I encamped was of considerable size, with extensive wheat cultivation, very luxuriant and in full ear, but still quite green. Many trees of the glabrous holly-leaved oak were scattered among the fields, which, from the lateral branches having been lopped off by the villagers, rose to a great height with an erect poplar-like trunk, bearing only a small tuft of branches at the top, in a manner very foreign to the usual habit of the tree.

On the 29th of May I crossed the range along which I had travelled the previous day, and descended into a valley watered by a tributary of the Chenab, running towards the north-west. The ascent, which was bare and grassy, amounted only to about 1000 feet in perpendicular height. Close to the top, a few trees of *Picea* made their appearance, while I was still on the south face of the ridge, and on gaining the crest of the pass, I found that the northern slope was occupied by a fine forest of the same tree. As the range was not sufficiently elevated to produce any really alpine plants, the vegetation presented little worthy of note. *Viburnum nervosum* was the commonest shrub, and an *Anemone*, a *Ranunculus*, the common *Gypsophila* and *Trifolium repens* were the herbs which predominated at the top.

The road descended rapidly through fine forest. The sombre silver fir was, after a short descent, mixed with plenty of horse-chesnut and sycamore, and of the glabrous-leaved oak. Lower down, deodar and *Abies Smithiana* also appeared, and on arriving in the valley, the forest gave place to cultivated fields, with only a few oak-trees scattered among them. The road now ascended the valley, which was tolerably open and well cultivated. The stream ran through a deep ravine, with steep, well-wooded, often rocky banks, far below the level of the cultivation. I encamped at an elevation of about 6800 feet, at a village called Dadu, or Doda, situated on the edge of a small open plain, covered with luxuriant crops of wheat.

Near the village, and along the edges of the cultivation, were numerous apricot-trees of large size; and a willow, apparently the same which occurs in Kashmir (*S. alba*) was commonly planted. The general appearance of the place was very much that of the villages in lower Kunawar; and I was much interested to find that although the greater part of the vegetation was the same as is common in the outer ranges of the mountains, a few plants indicative of a drier climate were to be seen. I was particularly surprised to find that *Quercus lanata*, *Rhododendron arboreum*, and *Andromeda ovalifolia*, three trees which are everywhere most abundant in the outer ranges of the Himalaya in the temperate zone, had entirely disappeared. The Kashmir *Fothergilla* was not uncommon, and I noted at least four or five herbaceous plants, which I had first met with in that valley or in Kunawar.

On the northern face of this range, between Pata and Dadu, the sandstone, which had continued since I left the valley of the Tawi, was replaced by a succession of metamorphic slates, sometimes very micaceous. In the valley of Dadu, boulders of gneiss, with crystals of felspar from one to three inches in length, were common, but the rock did not occur *in situ.*

The range of mountains bounding the valley on the south, did not appear to rise anywhere to a greater height than between 9000 and 10,000 feet, and where I crossed it, was not, I should think, higher than 8500. Immediately to the east of this low pass, however, it began to rise rapidly, and at the head of the valley lay a high snowy mountain, evidently a projecting peak of a long range descending from the north-east, and forming the boundary between the basins of the Chenab and the Ravi. This range, which in most places must be upwards of 11,000 feet, and which in some probably rises to 14,000, must, I think, to some extent check the progress of the masses of clouds during the monsoon, and therefore tend to diminish the quantity of rain, particularly as the rain-clouds come from the eastward, on which account the lower altitude of the ridge to the south-west is of less importance.

Halting at Dadu on the 30th of May, my road on the 31st lay up the valley towards the snowy range to the eastward. Cultivation did not continue beyond the village; and after a steep, somewhat rocky ascent and descent over a bare spur, I followed the course of the stream as nearly as the precipitous nature of its banks would permit, through a forest of sycamore, walnut, alder, horse-chesnut, and holly-leaved oak. Pines also were abundant, of the four common species: namely, deodar, spruce, silver fir, and *Pinus excelsa.* After following the course of the river for about a mile, the road crossed a large lateral tributary descending from the right, and ascended a steep bare spur between it and the main stream for perhaps 500 feet, after which it ran for some distance through fields of wheat still green, at first at a considerable distance above the stream, the bed of which, however, rose so rapidly that a very short descent brought me again to its banks. I then re-entered a beautiful forest, principally pine, in which the *Pindrow* was now the most common tree, bearing in abundance its erect purple cones. As the road rose rapidly, the vegetation soon began to change: *Syringa Emodi*, a currant, and other plants of the sub-alpine zone, making their appearance. The most common shrubby plants were *Viburnum nervosum* and *Spiræa Lindleyana*, both of which occurred in vast quantity. For perhaps a mile and a half, the valley was extremely beautiful; the torrent being rocky and rapid, and the forest very fine. The road then crossed the stream by a good wooden bridge, and a steep ascent commenced. As the forest was confined to the bottom of the valley, I soon emerged on dry grassy slopes. The precipitous nature of the banks rendered it necessary to ascend nearly 1000 feet, after which the road was again level along the dry mountain slope facing the south. The bed of the stream rose very rapidly, so that the road soon re-approached it; and when nearly on a level with it, I again entered forest, in which *Quercus semecarpifolia*, the alpine oak of Himalaya, was the prevailing tree. After about a mile, having attained an elevation of 10,000 feet, I encamped on an open grassy spot in the forest. The ravines facing the north had for some time been full of snow, but I had got close to camp before any appeared in those on the right bank, along which the road lay. A snowy peak, the upper part of which was high above the level of trees, lay to the south-east.

In the lower part of the ascent, the rock was clay-slate; but near my camp it was succeeded by the same gneiss, with large crystals of felspar, which I had found (in boulders) around Dadu. In general appearance, this gneiss was very similar to that observed on the mountains north of Nasmon, on the Chenab; and as these two places have nearly the same relative position as the usual line of strike in the north-western Himalaya, it is very probable that the rock is the same in both.

On the morning of the 1st of June, I continued to follow the course of the stream, ascending now very gently. The valley was open, and the road lay over undulating grassy ground, the forest having receded to some distance on both sides. Round my camp I had noticed very little in the vegetation different from what was common one or two thousand feet lower; but almost immediately after starting, I found myself among numerous bushes of *Rhododendron campanulatum* in full flower, and many other alpine plants appeared very shortly afterwards: of these, perhaps the most lovely was the elegant *Primula rosea*, which was extremely plentiful in hollow marshy spots from which snow had recently melted.

The ascent continued exceedingly gentle till close to the end, when, turning suddenly to the left into a pine-clad ravine, a few steps brought me to the crest of the ridge over which my road ran,—a lateral spur from the great snowy mass, which (as is often the case) was a good deal lower where it branched off than at a greater distance from the main range. After gaining the crest of the ridge, I followed it for a few hundred yards previous to commencing the descent. I had unfortunately somewhat rashly concluded, the day before, that the ascent during the day would be very trifling, and therefore did not carry with me the means of ascertaining the elevation of the pass; I believe, however, that it a little exceeded 11,000 feet. It was still in the forest zone. The trees were mostly the alpine oak, with a few scattered individuals of *Pinus excelsa*. At a short distance, on the more shady slope, and still higher than the pass, *Picea* was plentiful. The highest level of trees only rose a few hundred feet above me, and the lofty snowy peak which lay to the southward, attaining a height of probably little under 14,000 feet, was quite bare.

I reached the summit of the ridge between nine and ten A.M., at which time a dense mass of heavy clouds filled the whole of the valley below, while the sky above was perfectly clear. Vivid flashes of lightning were seen, accompanied by loud thunder, and the clouds were in violent commotion, being driven about by violent gusts of wind; but in less than half an hour they had entirely disappeared, disclosing a most magnificent view, bounded only by the grand snowy range beyond the Chenab, stretching in both directions as far as the eye could reach. Much nearer lay a second range of snowy mountains, evidently that which runs parallel to the Chenab on the south. Still nearer were other ranges of mountains, which, from the elevation at which I stood, looked like gently undulating hills. Immediately below, lay the rich and fertile valley of Badarwar, to which the descent was extremely rapid, down the face of a projecting spur, densely covered for the upper half of the way with forest. At the top of the pass, there were here and there, on slopes facing the north, large patches of snow, especially under the shade of trees, but on the descent it appeared only in the most shady ravines. .As the elevation diminished, the same change in the forest was observed as during the ascent. The alpine oak and spruce gave place to horse-chesnut, sycamore, and holly-leaved oak, with deodar and spruce. Lower down, cultivation appeared, and the road, lying on the southern slope of the spur, was generally bare and grassy, with only a few scattered deodar-trees of small size. At the base of the descent, clay-slate rocks replaced the gneiss.

The town of Badarwar is of considerable size, containing, I should think, not less than from three to four hundred houses, all, however, small and without any indication of wealth. It lies at the elevation of 5800 feet, in the upper part of a valley watered by a tributary of the Chenab, from which it. is distant, according to Vigne, twelve or fourteen miles. Round the town the valley is two or three miles in width, and completely covered with fields, rising in terraces one above another. Some rice is cultivated, but millet and Indian corn, neither of which were yet sown, are, I was informed, the principal produce.

The vegetation of the valley of Badarwar was hardly at all different from that of the one which I had just left, and the few new forms which occurred were for the most part Kashmir species. *Quercus lanata*, and the trees usually associated with it, did not occur; but *Fothergilla* was plentiful in the woods on the hill-sides, and in open exposed sunny places a Kashmir *Daphne* and *Zizyphus* were common: both of these species, however, are natives of the Sutlej valley. In the shady ravines a species of *Philadelphus*, and the *Nima* of Hamilton, were met with. Vines were cultivated near the town, as well as a few trees of *Populus nigra*, and a rough small-leaved elm, which grew to a gigantic size.

From Badarwar two roads were open to me, by either of which I could reach Chatargarh on the Chenab, from which place there is a road into Zanskar. One of these follows the course of the Badarwar valley to its junction with the Chenab, and ascends that river by Kishtwar; the other crosses the mountains to the eastward, so as to get into the valley of the Ravi, and to join the road which leads from Chamba to Zanskar. Of these I selected the latter, which appeared to present the advantages of being less known, of leading through a more elevated country, and also (as I was led to believe) of saving several days.

I started from Badarwar on the morning of the 3rd of June, and proceeded up the valley in a south-easterly direction, towards the Padri pass, a depression in the range which separates the districts drained by the Chenab from those whose waters run towards the Ravi. At first the road lay through cultivation. The fields of barley were ripe, those of wheat still green, and considerably more backward than at the same height in valleys more distant from the snow. The elevation of the valley increased gently but steadily, and its breadth gradually diminished as I advanced, the fields becoming reduced to a narrow strip along the bank of the stream, and then ceasing altogether. The road lay on the right bank, and was generally open, but the opposite slopes and ravines were often prettily wooded. After three miles the road began to ascend the hill-sides on the north of the valley, for about a mile gently, but afterwards more steeply. The hill-sides were bare, but on the opposite side of the valley there was a fine forest; and as soon as the road had attained the crest of the ridge or spur, the same dense forest was observed to cover the whole of its steep northern face, stopping abruptly at the top. As the elevation increased, the trees and herbaceous vegetation exhibited the same gradual change which I had noted on the ascent two days before, and I met with very few species which I had not collected at that time. In the shady woods on the northern slope of the ridge, I found the little Kashmir *Hepatica*, another instance of the extension to the eastward of plants characteristic of that valley. Near the top *Thermopsis barbata* was plentiful, in full flower, on open stony banks. The ascent continued steep to the top of the pass, the height of which was 10,000 feet. The top was nearly level for some distance, and was covered with large patches of snow. The continuation of the range to the north was undulating and grassy, and the hills of very moderate elevation above the level of the pass. To the southward they rose abruptly to a considerable height, and the ravines were filled with forest. I encamped on a grassy plain close to the top. The morning had been cloudy, and after eleven A.M. it rained smartly till evening; the temperature at sunset was $47\frac{1}{2}°$.

Next morning, before commencing the descent, I ascended a ridge on the mountains to the south, to the height of about 1000 feet above the pass. The snow had evidently only just melted from the greater part of the surface; it still lay in large patches under the trees, and the spring plants were just bursting into flower. The forest, as is usually the case at that height, was principally the alpine oak. A rose, willow, currant, cherry, *Lonicera*, and *Viburnum nervosum* were bursting into leaf, and *Rhododendron campanulatum* was abundant and in full flower. The greater part of the herbaceous vegetation consisted of *Primula denticulata*, a yellow *Corydalis*, and species of *Thermopsis*, *Anemone*, *Caltha*, *Onosma*, *Potentilla*, *Valeriana*, *Trillium*, and *Gentiana*. I continued to ascend to the limit of herbaceous vegetation, stopping only where the ground was uninterruptedly covered with snow. The uppermost level of trees was still at least 500 feet above me. In descending I followed the course of a ravine full of snow, the sides of which were covered by a dense forest of silver fir.

After reaching the direct road from the pass, which I had quitted to ascend the hills in the morning, there was a short ascent over a low spur, and then a long and very steep descent, to the bottom of a deep rocky ravine, so narrow and sheltered from the sun's rays, that the stream was still covered with a great thickness of snow. Over this I crossed to the north side of the valley, down which the road ran for the remainder of the march, descending at first with great rapidity, but on the latter half much more gently. There was plenty of fine forest, but, as usual, it was for the most part confined to the south side of the valley. The road lay along grassy slopes, sometimes steep and rocky, at other times, where there was any extent of tolerably level ground, covered knee-deep with a rank herbage of dock, *Polygona,* thistles, and a variety of other plants not yet in flower. It was in general at a considerable height above the bottom of the valley, which was deep and gloomy, and filled with snow during a great part of the way. I encamped at a village called Langera, at the height of about 7600 feet, and was surprised to observe large patches of snow still lying on the banks of the stream, at least three hundred feet below me.

On the 5th of June, my road again lay on the left side of the valley, and usually along the hill-sides at some height above the stream, to which it descended only once or twice. The valley was very pretty, being generally deep and more or less rocky, and on the south side well wooded. For the first three miles, large patches of snow were seen now and then in the most shady parts, more than once covering over the stream. The forest presented a good deal of variety. Except *Picea,* all the common pines occurred, as well as horse-chesnut, cherry, elm, *Celtis, Populus ciliata,* and holly-leaved oak. *Fothergilla* was very common all along, and on the latter half of the march *Quercus lanata* and *Andromeda ovalifolia* made their appearance. The occurrence of these trees I regarded as a sure indication that the rains were somewhat more heavy than on the west side of the pass, and as a confirmation of the view I had taken when in

Badarwar, that the climate of that valley was considerably modified by the occurrence of a high and partially snowy range to the eastward. Throughout the day's journey there was a good deal of cultivation, always considerably above the stream; and at the village of Deghi, at which I encamped, at about 5800 feet, the fields of wheat were being cut, clearly showing that the climate was much milder on the east side of the pass than at the same elevation in Badarwar, where they had been still quite green two days before.

On the 6th of June, I again followed the course of the valley, at a considerable height on the steep but well-cultivated hill-sides overlooking a deep and pretty glen. The slopes along which the road ran were bare, or covered with scattered brushwood, trees only occurring in ravines, but the opposite bank was usually well wooded. I encamped at a small village called Buju (just below 5000 feet), considerably higher than the bottom of the valley. The vegetation was in most respects (except the occurrence of *Fothergilla*, which was plentiful) what is usual in the neighbourhood of Simla, at similar elevations. Several species of the sub-tropical belt occurred, mixed with the ordinary plants of the middle zone, such as *Marlea*, *Albizzia mollis*, *Olea cuspidata*, *Xanthoxylon*, and others, and in the neighbourhood of Buju *Pinus longifolia* was common on the south side of the valley.

From Badarwar to the summit of the Padri pass, and throughout the descent, clay-slate had been the prevailing rock. It varied much in appearance, and latterly it alternated with a conglomerate, and was often very fragile, splitting into thin shaly layers. Near the village of Dewar, a hard bluish limestone occurred in considerable quantity, close to the river.

The general direction of my journey, while descending this valley, had been south-east, the elevation of the mountains on my left hand having been too great to permit me to turn to the north. On this march, however, about three miles from its termination, at a village called Dewar, I left the road to Chamba, which there crosses the stream and proceeds direct over low hills to the Ravi, while the valley (and my road) turned suddenly to the north-east. A little below my camp at Buju, the river resumed its former direction, and, uniting itself with a large stream descending from the northward, took a southerly course, to join the Ravi.

Along the valley, which descended from the north, ran the road from Chamba to Chatargarh on the Chenab, and on the 7th I proceeded in that direction. The two streams, at their junction, flowed through an extremely deep rocky ravine, so that I had several fatiguing ascents and descents before I succeeded in passing into the valley which I wished to ascend. I was, however, gratified, at the highest part of the road, where I turned for the first time fairly towards the north, by a superb view of the snowy range, towards which I was now travelling. On the 8th and 10th of June (having halted on the 9th) I continued to ascend the valley, encamping on the latter day at 8000 feet. During both days, many parts of the road were very rocky and difficult, with frequent steep ascents. At other times, when it was more level, very long detours were necessary, to pass deep lateral ravines. The valley was in general open, and the hill-sides only sparingly wooded, though at intervals along the stream there was a fine and dense forest of oaks, horse-chesnut, laurels, and *Celtis*. The ranges of mountains on both sides were tipped with snow, and from my camp of the 10th the snowy range in front appeared so close, that I could scarcely give credence to the assurances of my guides that I was still a good day's journey from its base.

Since I had left Jamu, the weather had been very uniform. The mornings were generally fine, with a cloudless sky and little or no wind; towards the afternoon, or if not then, certainly in the evening or during the night, clouds collected, and it rained heavily. This was of daily occurrence; sometimes the rain lasted for several hours, but before morning the sky was always serene. The atmosphere was hazy, as is usually the case in the Himalaya during the dry season, before the accession of the rains.

On the 11th, I continued to ascend the valley. At the commencement of the march, the hills were bare and open, and the vegetation was still entirely that of the middle zone. There was a good deal of cultivation, and the wheat was still green. After crossing several ravines, the road began to ascend rapidly through a wood of small trees of holly-leaved oak, interspersed with numerous small patches of cultivation. Among the corn, *Adonis æstivalis*, and a number of other common Kashmir weeds, were abundant, and apricot-trees were commonly planted. By degrees, other trees were mingled with the oaks, and the forest became very dense, with luxuriant undergrowth of *Indigoferæ*, *Spiræa Lindleyana*, and *Philadelphus*, and a vine was common, climbing up the trunks of the trees. Numerous open glades, covered with a luxuriant herbaceous vegetation of dock and other rank plants, were met with in the forest, which, though not so beautiful, a good deal resembled that of Mahasu, near Simla. On the opposite and shady side of the valley, the forest seemed to be chiefly composed of pines. As the elevation increased, silver fir and alpine oak began to appear, and soon became the only trees in the forest. The ravines were now all full of snow, the oaks were still in flower, and there was little or no vegetation under their shade, except in swampy places, where a bright yellow *Caltha* and a pink *Dentaria* were in full flower. I encamped at 10,600 feet, on an open grassy spot overlooking a deep ravine full of snow, which lay between me and the snowy range in front.

On emerging from the forest, which extended close to my camp, I found myself surrounded by a truly alpine vegetation. *Rhododendron campanulatum*, which is certainly, when *en masse* and in full flower, the pride of our northern Indian mountains in early spring, was in vast abundance and great beauty. The hills around were covered with birch; *Rhododendron lepidotum*, *Gaultheria trichocarpa*, *Deutzia corymbosa*, willows, and many other alpine shrubs, covered the rocks, and the moist grassy sward of the open spots was adorned with the brilliant flowers of *Primula denticulata*, *Corydalis Govaniana*, *Gagea*, *Caltha*, and other plants. The sky was brilliantly clear, the very heavy rain of the preceding day having, for the time, quite removed the usual haze, and the view from my tent was superb. The last village in the valley was many miles behind, and no cultivation was anywhere in sight. The opposite spurs, which rose, like that on which my tent was pitched, abruptly from the snowy ravine, were beautifully wooded, up to the limit of forest, while all above was covered with snow.

On the 12th of June, I crossed the snowy range into the valley of the Chenab. At starting, the road lay through forest, which covered the precipitous face of the rocky hill overhanging the deep ravine above which I had encamped. After crossing the ravine, which was full of snow, the road ascended a bare steep slope, which was swampy and covered with *Caltha* and *Primulæ.* Every other part of the face of the hill was occupied by a dense jungle of shrubs, almost impenetrable from the prostrate position which their branches had taken from the pressure of the winter's snow. Very stunted bushes of *Quercus semecarpifolia* constituted the greater part of this shrubby jungle. With it grew *Rhododendron campanulatum*, a cherry, and a birch, whose silvery trunks rose conspicuous above all the others. This dense covering of shrubs being confined to the lower part of the slope, the road soon rose above its level, and continued obliquely along the face of the bare grassy hill, rising very gently, and by degrees approaching the line of snow. I observed that the line of the highest level of trees varied much according to the exposure, being more elevated on the shady side than on slopes exposed to the sun. The snow level, as might have been expected, was extremely indefinite, varying with the degree of inclination of the surface, with the absence or presence of trees, and especially with the exposure. On the slope facing the south, it was about 12,000 feet, while on that opposite it descended among the trees several hundred feet lower. Close to the snow, among rocks and in swampy places, the alpine vegetation was extremely luxuriant and beautiful.

After skirting the snow for perhaps half a mile, I descended a little to cross a ravine, and immediately after began to ascend rapidly over snow, which was hard and firm, so that it was traversed without difficulty. Throughout the whole ascent, there were at intervals steep slopes and masses of rock bare of snow, and even on the smallest of these spots vegetation was making rapid progress, under the encouragement of a powerful sun and abundant moisture. The plants observed were all alpine: among the number were several *Primulæ*, and species of *Draba*, *Potentilla*, *Sibbaldia*, *Ranunculus*, and *Pedicularis*. The ascent continued steady to the top of the pass, which was a mass of bare rock, quite free of snow, and elevated 14,800 feet. The pass (the name of which is *Sach Joth*) was a deep depression in the crest of the range, which rose on both sides to a considerable height. The ridge was a mass of black slate rock, in highly inclined strata, on which no snow lay, and which absorbed so much heat from the sun, that a number of minute plants were not only vegetating but in full flower. *Primula minutissima* and a yellow *Draba* were common, and a little *Ranunculus* and *Potentilla*, with one moss and a species of lichen, also occurred more sparingly. The view from the pass was extensive to the southward, but to the north entirely intercepted by lofty precipitous ridges, distant not more than a mile. The morning had been beautiful, but before I reached the summit, a high wind had sprung up from the south, drifting heavy watery clouds over the crest, from which there were slight showers of hail.

The descent on the north side was over snow, commencing a few feet from the rocky crest of the pass. After the first few hundred yards, the snow-bed was very steep, and perhaps covered a small glacier. Further on, the mountains on both sides closed in so as to form a narrow valley, the course of which I followed for many miles, before I could find a bare spot upon which to encamp. The valley was bounded on both sides by exceedingly steep rocky mountains, sometimes quite precipitous, which soon became bare of snow. After descending rapidly for a considerable time, patches of juniper appeared on the hill-sides, succeeded by birch, and soon after by a few pines, which, from their shape, were, I believe, silver fir. A little lower, pines became frequent wherever the mountain-sides were not absolutely precipitous; *Picea* and *Pinus excelsa* were first recognized, and a little lower down *Abies Smithiana;* deodar did not appear till I had nearly reached the end of the day's journey. I encamped at 8500 feet, on the first available bare spot, among a few pine-trees.

From the summit of the pass till within a few hundred yards of my encampment, snow was continuous in the valley along which I descended, covering the stream and the whole of the level portion of the valley for many miles after it had melted from the steep sloping hills on both sides, on which vegetation was already making rapid progress. This snow-bed was not in the least icy, but consisted of pure snow, much compressed and often dirty. Its slope followed that of the valley, and its surface was quite smooth till close to its termination, where it was broken up into fragments by the fall of portions into the stream below. The greater permanence of snow in valleys and ravines than on mountain slopes seems to be due to its accumulation there during the winter to a great depth by avalanches from both sides.

CHAPTER XII.

Marked change in the Vegetation—Bridge over Chenab—Pargwal—Description of Chenab valley—Asdhari—Chatargarh—Road turns up valley of Butna—Vegetation of Chenab valley—Chishot—Snow-beds—Camp at 10,500 feet—Ancient moraines—Glacier—Camp at 11,500 feet—Rapid ascent along glacier—Camp on moraine, at 14,600 feet—Change of weather—Ascent towards pass over glacier—Cross Umasi La—Descent—Immense glacier—Encamp in Tibet, at 13,800 feet—Open valley of Zanskar—Padum—Great change of climate—and in vegetation.

As a great part of my baggage and some of my servants did not reach camp till after dark, in the evening of the 12th of May, I halted on the 13th. I was encamped in a very narrow valley, on both sides of which lofty mountains rose very abruptly. The spurs which projected into this ravine were all of very peculiar configuration, their northern face being uniformly quite precipitous, while to the south, though still steep, they were green and sloping. I ascended on the southern slope of the spur, nearest to my tent, to a height of perhaps 1500 feet, without obtaining any extensive view of the valley of the Chenab, though I afterwards found that I was not more than two miles in a direct line from that river, but that the rocky mountains right and left, retaining their elevation till they were close to it, completely interrupted the view in every direction, except directly down the ravine, where a small portion of the snow-topped mountains beyond the river was visible.

From the great elevation of the mountains which I had just crossed, I was prepared to find a marked change in the aspect of the vegetation, and I was not disappointed. The steep slopes were covered with a most luxuriant herbage, above two feet in height. A tall panicled *Rheum* was very common, and numerous *Umbelliferæ*, *Silene inflata*, *Geranium*, and *Pteris aquilina* were abundant. The most remarkable plant, however, from the extreme quantity in which it occurred, was an Asphodelaceous plant (*Eremurus*, Bieb.), the long scapes of which, from four to five feet in height, covered the hill-sides in countless myriads. These scapes were clothed, for nearly half their length, with a profusion of elegant white flowers, very slightly tinged with a pale yellowish green. I met, during the day, with most of the characteristic plants of the Kunawar flora; as instances, I may mention *Ephedra*, *Dictamnus*, *Rosa Webbiana*, *Dianthus*, and *Scutellaria orientalis*. The arboreous vegetation was much the same as on the other side of the pass. The right side of the ravine was well clothed with pines, of all the four ordinary species; the left side was usually bare, the northern faces of the spurs, which are generally wooded, being too precipitous, but in the hollows there were a few small clumps of trees, principally pine, walnut, and sycamore.

On the 14th of June I resumed my journey. The

ravine in front was pronounced by my guides impracticable, and, as I afterwards saw, not without reason, as it gained the Chenab by running down an almost precipitous rocky slope between 1200 and 1500 feet in height. The road ascended the steep hills to the right rather abruptly, inclining to the north at the same time, till it gradually wound round the northern angle of the mountain range which formed the side of the ravine, when I found myself looking down on the valley of the Chenab from a height of about 3000 feet above the bed of the river. Unfortunately the day was foggy, with a light drizzling rain, or no doubt the view would have been magnificent. After rounding this rocky angle, the road ran parallel to the Chenab, but in a direction contrary to its course, and continued to rise very gently among shady forests, with scattered patches of snow. I conjectured at the time that an immediate descent was prevented by precipices below; and I afterwards ascertained from the opposite side of the river that such was the case. After about a mile and a half an extremely abrupt descent commenced, at first through dense forest, but afterwards among numerous fields and scattered houses, constituting a large village between 8000 and 9000 feet in elevation. Fruit-trees were abundant, principally walnut, of which there were many magnificent trees. The crops of wheat were not yet in ear.

Below the village lands the road entered a forest of deodar, and continued to descend rapidly. The deodars continued nearly to the river, a few hundred feet only at the lowest part being covered with high brushwood, principally consisting of *Fothergilla*. The Chenab (or

Chandrabhaga, as it is always called in the mountains) is a noble-looking, rapid stream, running through a deep rocky channel. It is crossed at a considerable height above the water by a good and substantial wooden bridge, from which the course of the valley could be seen both up and down, to a considerable distance; and in both directions the river flows between lofty ranges of mountains, generally very rocky and precipitous, and often finely wooded. I did not determine the elevation of the bed of the river, but believe that it may safely be stated to be about 7000 feet. After crossing the Chenab the road ascended very abruptly to the village of Pargwal, in which I encamped, at an elevation of about 8500 feet. On the lower part of the ascent the forest was much more luxuriant than on the opposite side, and than it usually is on slopes facing the south: this was caused by the great depth and narrowness of the ravine through which the river flowed.

This day's march was rendered unpleasant by rain, which commenced about seven A.M., and continued to fall steadily till near sunset; the sky being completely overcast, and the day nearly calm. It was, however, very gentle, so that the quantity which fell during the day was beyond a doubt much less than would have fallen with constant rain for an equal length of time in the outer ranges of mountains, where no snowy range is interposed to stop the rain-clouds. It did not rain again while I continued in the valley; still one day's experience would of itself be quite insufficient to warrant any conclusion, were it not that the inhabitants describe the climate as tolerably dry. Their account is, that the rains continue lightly at intervals for about a month from the middle of June, after which they cease entirely. I have already pointed out that the climate of lower Kunawar is precisely the same in character, and these two valleys are equally similar in situation with respect to the mountain ranges.

I had reached the Chenab at a point a good deal higher up than Chatargarh, from which place the most frequented road into the Zanskar valley turns to the north. There is, I believe, another pass a good deal more to the eastward, the road to which leaves the Chenab not far from the place where I crossed it; but I was informed that it is at all times extremely difficult, and that the season was still too early to attempt it. I therefore proceeded, on the 15th and 16th of June, down the right bank of the Chenab, through an exceedingly mountainous country, and generally at a great height above the stream, but with frequent descents to cross lateral torrents. The mountains to the north were generally crested with snow, and dipped very abruptly to the river. The north-west face of each ridge was invariably precipitous, so that all the descents along the road were abrupt, rocky, and difficult. Many villages were met with in the valley, and much cultivation usually high up on the sides of the mountains. Poplars (*P. nigra* and *alba*) and apricots were commonly planted, but the favourite fruit-tree seemed to be the walnut. I did not see any vines cultivated. On both days the scenery was extremely fine, varying with every turn of the valley; at times the view from the top of the scarped precipices, which were frequent, was of the grandest possible description. The south side of the valley, where not absolutely precipitous, was covered with forest, most frequently of pine; and on the north side, on which the road lay, though the upper parts were often bare and grassy, or only covered with brushwood, yet the banks of the river were usually well wooded, and all the ravines, which were deep and shady, were filled with a dense forest of deodar, horse-chesnut, hazel, sycamore, birch, and *Fothergilla*, with many other trees. *Pinus Gerardiana*, which may be looked upon as more characteristic of a moderately dry climate than any other tree, inasmuch as it will not flourish where the rains are at all heavy, was extremely common. On the 16th a great part of the road lay through an extensive wood, of a species of oak (*Q. Ilex*), which I had only before seen in Kunawar, where it is not uncommon.

On the 15th I encamped at the village of Asdhari, at an elevation of 8800 feet, and nearly 2000 feet above the river. On the 16th my halting-place was Shol, a large village close to the Chenab, with an extensive tract of cultivation, quite bare of trees, except a few cherries. The elevation of my tent was here about 6900 feet: it was not more than fifty feet above the river. Opposite the village, on the south bank of the river, under a cliff which screened it from the rays of the sun, there was a very large patch of snow.

The early part of my march of the 17th was still along the Chenab, through fine shady forest, for about three miles, rising to the height of about 1000 feet, and again descending close to the water's edge. The road then continued nearly on a level with the stream, and became very rocky and difficult, planks of wood or rough bridges being laid in some places from rock to rock to effect a passage. Below this narrow rocky part of the channel the valley widened out on the north side into an open sandy plain, watered by a large tributary stream, descending from the north. Close to this stream lay the small fort of Chatargarh, the residence of the Thannadar of the valley, and of a small garrison of soldiers. The Butna, which here joins the Chenab, and up which my road lay, is a large impetuous stream. I crossed it a short way above the fort, by a good bridge, and, following its right bank for about two miles through oak forest, encamped at the village of Liundi.

The flora of the valley of the Chenab, as far as my road lay along it, continued to agree in most respects with that of Kunawar. As I descended the river, there were some indications of an approach to the vegetation of the outer Himalaya; but the number of species belonging to that flora which appeared was not great. A *Zizyphus* common in the lower Sutlej and in Kashmir, the common pomegranate, and a shrubby *Desmodium*, were those noted. This gradual transition in the character of the vegetation occurs equally in Kunawar; and as both the Sutlej and the Chenab commence their course in an arid climate, and enter the plains under the full influence of the rains, it is quite in accordance with what might be expected to happen. The change is in both valleys extremely gradual, and appears to be directly proportional to the diminished elevation of the mountains which run parallel to the rivers on the south.*

* A species of vine was very common in the forests, climbing to a

On the 18th of June my road again lay up the valley of the Butna, usually close to the stream, partly through bare country, with scattered bushes of *Zizyphus* and *Daphne*, but mostly through very beautiful forest of oak, alder, horse-chesnut, and ash. The river varied much in character; but for the most part it flowed with great rapidity over a rocky channel, and in one place formed a cataract of some size. More than once, however, and always above the most rapid parts, it was tranquil, though still swift, and flowed between gravelly islands. The hills on both sides were steep and lofty, and after the first two miles, patches of snow occurred in every ravine. I passed several villages and a good deal of cultivation, and encamped at Chishot, at about 8200 feet above the level of the sea.

Next day, at starting, the road lay through pine-forests for about two miles, the elevation rapidly increasing. At about that distance, there was a very long rapid or cataract, with a fall of several hundred feet within a space of 150 or 200 yards. At the lower end of the rapid, the river disappeared under a snow-bed, which formed an arch across it from bank to bank. Above, the stream was wide and tranquil, and the pine-forest ceasing, the road entered an open valley, with much cultivation around the village of Himor. Along the water-courses by which the lands of this village were irrigated, there was

great height on the trees, which very closely resembled the common cultivated vine, from which it is not, I think, specifically distinct. At the same time, my specimens are scarcely distinguishable from *Vitis Indica*, L., a species of the plains of India, not uncommon in hot jungles, even at a considerable distance from the foot of the mountains.

a good deal of swampy ground, in which grew *Parnassia, Polygonum viviparum,* an *Orchis* not unlike *O. latifolia,* a *Triglochin,* and some *Carices,* all Kunawar species. Beyond the village, the valley continued open and bare, but was very rocky, and covered with large boulders. There was no wood, except in the ravines, which were occupied by groves of poplar (*P. ciliata*) and walnut; a few trees of the same and of birch being scattered over the hill-sides. No oak or Gerard's pine was seen during the day. The herbaceous vegetation on the open sunny banks was very luxuriant, and the species were mostly the same as I have recorded in a similar situation, and at the same elevation, on the 13th, after descending from the Sach pass. I must except the *Eremurus,* then so abundant, which was here entirely wanting. There were also a few novelties. Large tracts were covered with a tall fern (*Pteris aquilina?*). After passing through the cultivated lands of a second village, and crossing some snow-beds, the road entered a wood of stunted deodars, and, turning to the left, proceeded up the more northerly of two ravines, into which the valley here divided. That to the south, which in direction was a continuation of the valley, was filled with forest, but the one up which the road turned was steep and stony, and contained only a few scattered trees of birch, hazel, and poplar. After a march of about eight miles, I encamped on an open level spot, where there were a few fields, and one or two huts, at present uninhabited, at an elevation of 10,500 feet.

On the 20th, I proceeded further up the same valley,

ascending gently but steadily. The valley was open and bounded on both sides by steep rocky mountains, those on the right partially wooded with birch, on the other side quite bare. Behind, beyond the point from which I had the day before turned abruptly to the left, rose a lofty snowy peak, very steep and rocky; in front, only a very small portion of the snowy range which I was rapidly approaching could be seen. The stream was for the most part covered with snow, and the road crossed numerous snow-beds. At first, the hill-sides were rounded and covered with vegetation, but very soon the road became rocky, and was covered as yesterday with enormous boulders, evidently indicative of a former glacier. These were all gneiss, which rock also occurred *in situ*, as had been the case ever since I had left Chatargarh, where it replaced the clay-slate, which had been common on the banks of the Chenab. After walking for about two miles among these huge masses of rock, I suddenly emerged into open country, and, after descending a few feet, entered a level plain, nearly two miles in length and at least half a mile in width, partly covered with snow stretching down from the ravines on each side. This plain appeared to have been at one time the bed of a small lake; and as its lower end was crossed by an evident moraine, it seems probable that a glacier had at some former period crossed the valley and dammed up the channel of the stream. Small groves of willow of two distinct species, one twelve to fifteen feet high, the other not above two or three, were scattered over this plain. The surface, where free from snow, was usually grassy, and near the lower end very swampy. The snow had evidently very recently covered the whole surface, as few plants were yet in flower, except a bright blue gentian in the marshy parts, and a viscid *Cerastium* on the gravel. A species of rhubarb was abundant on the banks surrounding this plain, and its acid leaf-stalks were eagerly eaten by the men who carried my luggage. The road traversed the whole length of this level tract, and, at its upper end, crossed two low ridges of boulders, evidently moraines. Beyond these lay another plain, much more barren and desolate-looking than the previous one, the greater part being still covered with snow. Those parts from which the snow had melted were gravelly, with scarce a vestige of vegetation. I encamped on the last bare spot of this plain, close to extensive snow-beds, from below which the stream flowed, and about a mile from the end of a large glacier which filled up the end of the valley, but was cut off abruptly at the commencement of the open plain. The elevation of my tent was 11,400 feet. The plain on which I was encamped was surrounded on all sides by lofty mountains, all extremely steep and rugged. Those to the south and east were covered with snow to the very base, but to the north little or no snow was visible, the hills close at hand rising so abruptly that they entirely excluded the view of the ranges behind. The southern slopes from the base to the height of about 1000 feet were covered with birch-trees, still quite leafless, except a few on the edge of the plain, which were beginning to throw out buds, the snow having melted round their roots.

On the 21st of June I continued my journey over the

snow-bed close to which I had encamped, in the direction of the end of the glacier. While still several hundred yards distant from it, the road turned abruptly to the left, ascending a very steep stony hill, which formed the side of a lateral ravine descending from the north. When I had ascended a few hundred feet, I obtained an excellent view of the glacier which occupied the valley below. Its surface, from the great slope of the valley, was extremely irregular, and to all appearance quite impassable, from the numerous fissures which traversed it in every direction, and the irregular pinnacles of ice which rose above its surface. It was terminated abruptly by a perpendicular cliff, which projected more in the centre than on the sides, and was much and deeply fissured both horizontally and perpendicularly. The glacier was in parts covered with masses of boulders and gravel, on which lay a sprinkling of snow in small patches. The lateral moraines were well marked, being much higher than the surface of the glacier, and separated by a deep fissure from the rocky wall of the valley. Immediately in front of the termination of the glacier, the surface of the plain was free from snow; numerous boulders of large size were scattered over it, and large masses of ice, evidently fragments of the glacier, lay among them.

The ascent of the lateral ravine continued steep, sometimes over rock, often over what appeared to be an ancient moraine, and now and then over grassy sward, adorned with numerous alpine plants in full flower. Among these was a little *Iris*, which I had seen the day before in fruit, *Podophyllum*, *Fritillaria*, and a pretty rose-coloured *Pedicularis*. There were a few stunted bushes of birch on the first part of the ascent, but they were soon left behind. After ascending about 1500 feet, I passed a singular-looking little circular plain, perhaps half a mile in diameter, still covered with snow. The road lay on the left of this plain over a hill of boulders. It now ascended very rapidly, and soon reached another glacier, the termination of which was extremely oblique, being prolonged much further on the right or south-east side of the ravine than on the other. The slope of the valley was so extremely abrupt, that the surface of the glacier was fissured in a most extraordinary manner; and it was still partially covered with snow. The road ascended over the moraine which lay between the glacier and the wall of the valley, generally at a great height above the level of the ice. In the crevices of the stones one or two plants still lingered: *Primula minutissima* was in flower, and a little *Sedum* and a dwarf willow (*S. repens*, L.) were beginning to expand their buds. My day's march amounted to about five miles, and I encamped upon the moraine on a level piece of ground just large enough to hold my tent, and close to the glacier. The temperature of boiling water indicated an elevation of about 14,600 feet. All around was snow and ice, except one steep sloping bank facing the south, on the most sheltered corner of which my baggage porters established themselves. On this bank vegetation had already made considerable progress: at least a dozen species were in flower, of which the most abundant were a rose-coloured *Polygonum*, a *Potentilla*, and *Ranunculus*, and, most abundant of all, a beautiful blue *Gymnandra*.

The surface of the glacier opposite to my tent was much covered with debris, and many large boulders were imbedded in the ice, which was very much fissured, rising into sharp pinnacles. As the day advanced, it was traversed by numerous rills of water, and the sound of falling stones was heard in every direction.

I had hitherto been extremely fortunate in weather, considering the season; but just at sunset, a few light clouds having first appeared in the south horizon, the sky became suddenly overcast, and light snow began to fall. Very little fell during the night, but at daybreak on the 22nd of June, just as I was preparing to start, it began to snow rather heavily. I had unfortunately no choice but to proceed. The place in which I was encamped was not at all adapted for a resting-place during a heavy fall of snow; and arrangements had already been made for the relief of the baggage porters who had come with me, by a party of Zanskaries at the top of the pass on this day.

The first part of the ascent lay up the moraine parallel to the glacier, and was extremely steep for nearly 1000 feet of perpendicular elevation, up to the top of the very abrupt ravine in which I had been encamped. Beyond this, the valley widened considerably; and as its slope was now very gentle, the glacier was quite smooth, and the path lay over its surface, which was covered by a considerable layer (five or six inches) of last winter's snow, as well as by a sprinkling of that which had fallen during the night. The ice was a good deal fissured, but in general the fissures were not more than a few inches in width; a few only were as much as two feet. The road continued for two or three miles over the surface of the glacier, which gradually widened out as I advanced. Its upper part was expanded into an icy plain of great width, bounded by a semicircular arch of precipitous rocks, except where three ravines descended into it, down which three narrow glaciers flowed to contribute a supply of ice to the vast mass in the bay. On the smooth ice below, central moraines were very visible, and could be distinctly traced to the rocks by which the three smaller glaciers were separated. A great part of these central moraines were covered with snow; but now and then an immense detached boulder of gneiss was seen, supported by a column of clear blue ice, veined with horizontal white bands, by which it was raised high above the surface of the glacier, and the snow which covered it.

The three branches which united to form this grand sea of ice were very steep, and consequently much fissured and fractured. The road lay up that to the right, ascending by the moraine to the left of the glacier, the surface of the ice being quite impracticable. This ascent, which I estimated at the time to amount to at least 1000 feet, was exceedingly steep and laborious, as beneath a thin layer of fresh snow it was covered with hard frozen snow, on which the footing was quite insecure. On attaining the summit of this steep ascent, I found the surface of the glacier much more smooth, the inclination of the bed of the ravine having suddenly changed; it was now, however, covered with a layer of snow several feet thick, which probably tended to render small inequalities of surface unobservable. I was now in a wide valley or basin, the rocky hills on both sides rising precipitously to a height of from 200 to 1000 feet above the level of the snow. After perhaps two miles of gradual ascent, these rocky walls gradually closing in united in a semicircle in front, and the road passed through a gorge or fissure in the ridge, to the crest of which the snow-bed had gradually sloped up. This fissure, which was not more than two feet in width, was the pass, but when I reached it, snow was falling so thickly that I could not see ten yards in any direction. I therefore remained only long enough to ascertain that the boiling-point of water was 180·3°, indicating an elevation of at least 18,000 feet.

The commencement of the descent was very rapid down a narrow gorge, into which the fissure at the top widened by degrees. The fresh snow, which had fallen to the depth of at least a foot, was quite soft and yielding, so that great caution was required. After four or five hundred yards, the slope became more gradual and the ravine considerably wider. The road was now evidently over the surface of a glacier. The mountains on both sides were extremely rocky, rugged, and precipitous. Each lateral ravine brought an additional stream of ice to swell that in the central one; and on each lateral glacier there was a moraine which had to be crossed. Further on, the slope again increasing, the road left the surface of the glacier, and ascended the moraine by its side. This was at first covered with deep snow, both old and fresh; but as I advanced I found the old snow only in patches, but covered with a layer of new. At last I reached a point at which the snow melted as it fell, and not long after the glacier stopped abruptly, a considerable stream issuing from beneath the perpendicular wall by which it terminated.

Beyond the end of the glacier the valley continued very steep. It was several hundred feet across, and covered with loose stones of various sizes, over which the stream ran in a wide shallow channel. Lower down, the bed of the rivulet became contracted and rocky, and I crossed to its right bank over a natural bridge consisting of one large stone, ten or twelve feet long, which had fallen so as to lie across the rocky channel. Advancing a few paces beyond this bridge, I suddenly found myself at the end of the ravine, and overlooking a wide valley many hundred feet below, filled by an enormous glacier descending from the left. This glacier was completely covered with a mass of debris, which entirely concealed the ice, and from its enormous dimensions must have had a very distant source. I had no means at the time of determining with accuracy either its width or depth, nor do I find any estimate of it (except in superlatives) in my notes made on the spot; I cannot, therefore, at this distance of time, venture to give any exact dimensions: I can only say that it much exceeded in size any that I have before or since had an opportunity of seeing.

It was just at the termination of the upper ravine that the first traces of vegetation were observed: till reaching this point the rocks and gravel had been quite bare. The first plant observed was *Primula minutissima;* the only other in flower was a large purple-coloured *Crucifera* (a species of *Parrya*), but leaves of several others were beginning to expand.

The road did not descend at once into the large valley, but, turning abruptly to the right, ran parallel to the glacier but high above it on the rocky mountain-side, for nearly a mile, gradually descending so as to reach the bottom of the valley just as the glacier ended. The valley beyond its termination was wide and stony, and I encamped among a number of very large boulders about half a mile further on. The elevation of my camp was 13,800 feet, so that I had descended upwards of 4000 feet from the top of the pass. I found that the inhabitants on the two sides of the pass knew it by different names, those of Padar, on the south, calling it the Bardar pass, while to the Zanskaries it is known as Umasi La.

The morning of the 23rd of June was bright and clear, but intensely frosty. The valley in which I was encamped was enclosed by lofty mountains covered with much snow, though on the level ground there were only a few patches. The road lay down the valley, which soon became narrow and stony, and the descent somewhat rapid. The ground was at first quite bare, and devoid of any sort of vegetation, except here and there on the bank of the stream, where, close to the water's edge, a small patch of green was occasionally to be seen. The narrowest parts of the ravine were occupied by large snow-beds, entirely covering the rivulet, but at intervals the valley widened out into a gravelly plain. After about a mile, some vegetation began to appear, and after four or five miles it became plentiful. The banks of the stream, in the wide and gravelly parts, were fringed with dwarf willows just bursting into leaf. *Primula minutissima* was plentiful in the crevices of the stones, and I met with many plants scattered about, of which none but the very earliest were yet in flower. Two or three species only could be identified with the plants of the Indian side of the pass; the majority were quite different. *Lithospermum Euchromon* of Royle, and the *Parrya* first seen the day before, were among the commonest species; several other *Cruciferæ* were also seen, as well as a *Gentiana*, one or two *Astragali*, a species of *Meconopsis*, a small *Gagea*, *Ephedra*, and *Nepeta glutinosa*. Species of *Artemisia*, *Cynoglossum* and other *Boragineæ*, of *Polygonum* and *Rheum*, though not in flower, were recognizable, but the greater number of plants were only beginning to vegetate. As I descended, a few shrubs of *Lonicera hispida* and of *Rosa Webbiana* (the Tibet rose) were met with, but all very stunted.

The valley continued to descend, and the snow soon receded to some distance up the mountain-sides. At last I came to a single habitation, a little monastery inhabited by one Lama, and built under the precipitous rocks on the left side of the valley. A very small patch of cultivation lay on the bank of the stream just below it; the corn was not more than two or three inches high. A little further on, the road suddenly turned into a much larger and more open valley, watered by a considerable stream, which ran through a wide, open, gravelly channel, from which long and very slightly inclined gravelly slopes extended on both sides to the base of the mountains. The stream proved to be the western branch of the Zanskar river. To the north-westward of the point where I entered its valley, its upward course was visible for eight or ten miles, all the way through an open gravelly plain. Several villages and a good deal of cultivation were seen in that direction, on the slopes descending from the mountains.

My road lay to the eastward down the valley, partly through cultivated lands, partly over barren gravelly or stony plains, and often over grassy meadows on the banks of the river. Wheat, barley, and peas were the crops cultivated, all only a few inches in height. Round the fields and on the banks of the water-courses a luxuriant herbage was beginning to spring up, which contrasted strongly with the sterility of the stony plains. The fields were quite flat and generally unenclosed, the valley being too level to require terracing; small canals conducted water for irrigation to every field. The villages were all small and bare, and during the day I saw only a single tree—a small poplar—in a garden or enclosure at one of the last villages through which I passed, before halting for the day. I encamped, after a march of at least twelve miles, near the village of Markim, on a fine grassy plain close to the river, the banks of which were lined by a few bushes of *Myricaria* and *Hippophaë*. The elevation of my tent was 12,100 feet.

In the valley of the Chenab the prevailing rock had everywhere been clay-slate, but where I turned up the valley of the Butna it was replaced by gneiss, which continued to form the whole mountain-mass on both sides of the Umasi pass, so far as I could infer the nature of their structure from the boulders brought down by glaciers. On the earlier part of this day's journey, the gneiss gave place again to mica-slate and clay-slate; but in the wide valley, where no rock was seen *in situ*, the boulders were all composed of gneiss, and had probably, therefore, been transported from the upper part of the mountains.

On the 24th of June I continued my journey to Padum, which is considered the capital of Zanskar. My road lay still east, down a wide, open plain. The mountains on the north side of the valley were not to appearance very lofty, and were merely tipped with snow; those to the south were much higher and had a great deal of snow, which, however, did not come within perhaps 1500 feet of the plain. There was no snow in the plain itself, which had a width of from two to four miles. Cultivated tracts were frequent, occurring wherever water was easily procurable for irrigation, but the greater part of the surface was dry, barren, and stony, producing scarcely any herbage. The river ran through a wide, gravelly bed, and was divided into numerous channels. It was often fringed with low jungle of *Myricaria* and *Hippophaë*, two shrubs which, though not entirely confined to Tibet, are most abundant in every part of that country up to nearly 14,000 feet, in the gravelly beds of streams. In some places the banks of the stream were very low and swampy, and covered with turf. About half-way down the plain the different branches of the river united into one, which ran with a swift impetuous current over the boulders which formed its bed, the melting of the snow on the mountains having brought down a very large body of water. At this point it was crossed by a rope-bridge, leading to a large village on the left bank. A little further on I passed through a considerable village, with extensive cultivated lands, and a large well-built monastery, in which, I believe, Csoma de Körös resided while in Zanskar. The road then made a considerable detour to the south, to the base of the mountains, to reach a bridge over a lateral stream now so much swollen as to be unfordable. After crossing this stream by a good wooden bridge, the road entered an open grassy plain sloping imperceptibly from the mountains towards the river, at the south-east angle of which lay the town or village of Padum.

Padum, which was at one time the principal place in Zanskar, is, though now much decayed, still considered as such, probably both from its central situation and from the garrison of Gulab Singh's troops being established near it. It is built on a low hill lying at the south-east corner of a wide open plain which surrounds the junction of two large streams which here unite to form the Zanskar river. Of these, one descending from the south runs through a rocky and barren country, which contains, I was informed, but few and small villages. It is that to which Moorcroft, who crossed it near its source, has given the name of Zanskar; and as it appears to the eye the larger stream of the two, it will probably be found entitled to retain the name, although the district watered by the western branch, which runs gently through an open country, is much more fertile and populous. The junction of these two streams takes place four or five miles north of Padum. The plain is partly low and partly a platform nearly a hundred feet above the level of the rivers.

Entirely secluded by lofty ranges of snowy mountains from the approach of any moisture-bringing winds, the valley of Zanskar has an absolutely Tibetan climate. Tree vegetation is entirely wanting, and the mountains and plains are dry, barren, and desolate. At the same time, from the dryness of the summer, the powerful influence of the sun induces here, as elsewhere in Tibet, a much milder climate than prevails at an equal elevation within the influence of the periodical rains, for in no part of the Indian portion of the mountains does any cultivated valley exist at an elevation of 12,000 feet above the level of the sea. The extent of open country is more considerable in this portion of the Zanskar valley than elsewhere in the basin of the Indus. Villages also are frequent, particularly in the lower part, and the cultivated lands of many of them are extensive. The alluvial platforms are of great extent, and so nearly level, that no terracing is required for purposes of irrigation. On this account, and from the total want of fences, the appearance of the plain is remarkable, and very different from that usual around Tibetan villages. At the period of my visit, the crops were only a few inches in height, and the whole population were busy in the fields, irrigating them and keeping out straggling cattle. The inhabitants, in appearance, manners, and mode of life, are the same as those of Ladak; their language and religion too are the same, as far as I could learn.

The change of climate was, as a matter of course, accompanied by an almost total change of vegetation, which had assumed entirely the Tibetan character. Scarcely more than a fourth, on a rough estimate, of the species observed, were the same as grew on the Indian side of the pass. Of these, a very few were cosmopolitan or widely-diffused plants. Such were *Thymus Serpyllum*, *Plantago Asiatica*, *Taraxacum*, *Veronica biloba*, *Medicago lupulina*, and *Polygonum aviculare* or a closely-allied species. The greater number were species of the dry climate, which, from being capable of bearing a certain quantity of moisture, vegetate also in the first valleys on the opposite side of the pass, though quite incapable of living under the full influence of the rains: as instances, I may mention *Rosa Webbiana*, *Myricaria*, *Hippophaë*, *Ephedra*, *Aquilegia Moorcroftiana*, and several *Astragali*.

Excluding both these classes, more than two-thirds of the plants were entirely different from those which flourish on the Indian side. The season was early spring, so that a great part of the vegetation was still dormant, but it was making rapid strides under the influence of a powerful sun, particularly in the neighbourhood of the town of Padum, which appeared to be the warmest nook in the valley. The dry, barren tracts, which constitute the greater part of the surface, produced numerous, generally dwarf species of *Boragineæ* and *Cruciferæ*. Three *Potentillæ* were common, one of them *P. anserina*. Near the river there was a more luxuriant vegetation. Rank species of *Heracleum*, *Astragalus*, *Scrophularia*, *Matthiola*, and *Eurotia* were coming into flower under the shelter of walls and bushes. In richer soil a species of *Hyoscyamus*, with pale yellow trumpet-shaped flowers (*Belenia* of Decaisne), was common, while around the fields grew species of *Geranium*, *Cynoglossum*, *Nepeta*, and *Astragalus*. Except a little *Poa*, no grasses were yet in flower, but several small *Cyperaceæ* formed dense patches of turf. The meadows close to the edge of the river were invariably swampy, and had a peculiar vegetation of their own, consisting of two species of *Triglochin*, a white-flowered *Taraxacum*, a little *Primula*, *Ranunculus Cymbalaria*, and *Glaux*, with *Hippuris* and *Utricularia* in the pools of water.

CHAPTER XIII.

Rope bridge across Zanskar river—Tongde—Zangla—Road leaves Zanskar river—Takti La—Nira—Bridge over Zanskar river—Singhi La—Phutaksha—Wandla—Lama Yuru—Cross Indus river—Kalatze—Nurla—Saspola—Nimo—Le—Pass north of Le—Small glacier—Kardong—Kalsar—Vegetation—Diskit—Passage of Shayuk river—Upper Nubra—Vegetation of Nubra—Hot spring at Panamik.

I REMAINED at Padum two days, to make inquiries as to the road and arrangements for porters and supplies. On the 27th of June, I commenced my journey towards the Indus. The road lay down the valley of Zanskar, crossing the eastern branch of that river opposite the town of Padum, by a rather insecure-looking rope-bridge, high above the stream, which was deep, rapid, and muddy. The rope, as is usual in Tibet, was formed of willow twigs. After crossing this bridge, I followed the right bank of the stream in a north-easterly direction, principally over dry, desert, stony plains, considerably elevated above the river. These high banks were composed of fine clay, which was occasionally quite pure, but more frequently contained numerous fragments of a black slate rock. These were especially abundant where lateral ravines descended from the mountains, while in the intervening spaces the clay was comparatively free of them. The same black slate cropped out *in situ* in several places along the bank of the river; and from the numerous boulders everywhere scattered over the surface of the platform, it appeared to be the prevailing rock in the mountains on the right. The platforms usually terminated abruptly, being either scarped or sloping very steeply towards the river. A strip of low, wet, grassy ground, which was more or less covered with *Hippophaë* jungle, was generally interposed between the cliffs and the river. When this was absent, the steep slopes were barren till close to the water's edge. On the left bank of the river, after the first two miles, the table-land sank, an extensive low plain forming a tongue of land between the two branches. On this low land, close to the eastern river, and about two miles from the town of Padum, lay the fort occupied by the military force of the valley: a small square, with four round bastions. After marching nine or ten miles, I encamped at a small village called Tongde, among undulating clay hills, by which the view of the river and valley was excluded. Nearly opposite, a mile or two below the junction of the two rivers, was Karsha, at present the largest town in Zanskar: it lies in a ravine at a considerable distance from the river, and, from the steepness of the slope on which it is built, presents rather an imposing appearance. The level tract intervening between the town and the river was covered with cultivation.

On the 28th, I continued along the valley, but in a more northerly direction than the day before. The lofty snowy range to the south-west was now finely seen, forming a semicircle of rocky peaks behind Padum. The road lay again over dry plains, partly stony, partly hard clay; even the banks of the river were dry and stony, without a vestige of turf. The only species worthy of note which occurred during the day, in addition to the plants common on these barren tracts, was *Oxytropis chiliophylla*: it was very scarce at the beginning of the march, but before I had reached half-way it had become so abundant that at a distance the ground appeared of a bright red colour, from the immense abundance of its flowers. Several villages were passed on the road, and two considerable streams, both of which had excavated deep ravines in the loose conglomerate of which the plateau was formed. On the latter part of the march, the mountains which formed the right side of the valley approached close to the river, leaving no passage along the bank, so that the road made a short steep ascent over loose shingly debris and rocky ground, and continued for more than a mile along the face of the ridge. After that distance, it descended to a grassy, saline, very swampy plain, close to the river. I encamped at the village of Zangla, which lies at the base of the mountains, on the upper part of a steep stony slope, extending down to the river.

The alluvial platforms during this day's journey were generally of great thickness. This was especially the case around Tongde, where the clay formation formed considerable hills; and on the latter part of the march, where the mountains advanced nearly to the stream. Here high banks of clay were accumulated on the ridges, and were frequently, as in many other parts of Tibet,

2 B

worn into fantastic shapes by the melting of the snow. Near Zangla, too, detached masses were seen clinging to the sides of the mountains, at considerable heights, in positions which indicated great denudation.

The result of my inquiries at Padum had been, that the lower part of the course of the Zanskar river (which I had hoped I might be able to follow to its junction with the Indus) was so rocky and difficult as to be impracticable, and that at the present season, when the torrents were all swollen by the melting snow, the only practicable road to the Indus lay through the mountains, at a distance from the river. I was now approaching the point where the road entered the mountains, and could already see that the fine open valley through which I had been travelling was soon to have an end. At Zangla it had become sensibly narrower, and the mountains on both sides, still tipped with snow, were extremely rocky and rugged.

The earlier part of the march of the 29th of June was still parallel to the river, partly over table-land, at other times through a dense jungle of *Hippophaë*, which covered its low banks, as well as several islands in its channel. After about four miles, the road turned suddenly to the right, and, leaving the valley altogether, commenced a rapid ascent on the steep slope of the mountain. From the point at which the road turned off, the Zanskar valley ahead could be seen to narrow rapidly, by the closing-in of the mountains. A turn in its direction, at the distance of four or five miles, hid the further course of the river from view, but the steep scarped mountains, which seemed to rise almost perpendicularly from its bed, left no doubt of the difficult nature of the country through which it ran.

The first part of the ascent was very steep and bare. A prickly *Statice*, in dense round tufts, made its appearance after the first few hundred feet, accompanied by another very common Tibetan plant, which had not been met with in the open plain, a species of *Cicer*, described by Bentham as *C. microphyllum*, if indeed the Siberian *C. Soongaricum* be not the same species. This plant is remarkable, not only for a very viscid exudation, but also for its peculiar strong aromatic and pungent odour, which, except that it is very much more powerful, a good deal resembles that of its cultivated congener *C. arietinum*, the well-known *gram* of Upper India. It also recalls to mind the smell of the common black currant, which, however, is more aromatic and less pungent and acidulous. On the lower part of the ascent the prevailing rock was limestone, of a dark bluish-grey colour, extremely hard, containing many white veins and crystals of calcareous spar; it closely resembled the limestone of the Hangarang pass, and, like it, alternated with hornstone and cherty quartz rock, and with finely laminated slates.

On leaving the bare slope, the road entered a narrow ravine, and continued to ascend rapidly along the bank of the streamlet which trickled down it. The ravine was full of loose angular stones, and had on both sides high rocky precipices of limestone and slate. Close to the little rivulet, a willow, a *Lonicera*, and a rose grew in great plenty among the loose stones, forming a dense bushy mass of green, six or eight feet high, which contrasted strongly with the barrenness of the shingle remote from the water, and of the rocky walls on either side. The ascent was rapid, and ere long, as the elevation increased, the shrubby vegetation disappeared, and the only plants which grew among the loose fragments of slate were a few small alpine species: *Anemone, Corydalis, Thermopsis,* and *Androsace*, were the genera to which these hardy plants belonged. In the crevices of the rocks, a large fleshy-leaved saxifrage, of the subgenus *Bergenia,* was common: it was a different species from either of the two hitherto described from India, as well as from *S. crassifolia* of Siberia, and was particularly interesting as a connecting link between these two floras. Further on, the ascent became more gentle; a few small patches of snow were passed, and soon after, the road ascended a very steep and shingly slope on the north side of the ravine, to the crest of a ridge, the elevation of which I estimated at about 15,500 feet.

The top of the ridge was rounded, and had more soil, and, as a consequence, more vegetation, than the stony dell below. Several plants of the valley reappeared, particularly *Lithospermum Euchromon* and a species of *Cynoglossum*, both of which seem to have a wide range in altitude. A few new species of *Cruciferæ* and *Astragalus* were obtained on the ridge. There was a very good and extensive view to the north, of mountain behind mountain, all bare and desolate; but in every other direction ridges close at hand intercepted the view. The most distant ridge had much snow on it, and appeared very elevated: I supposed it to be that between the Zanskar river and the Indus. After leaving the ridge, the road gradually descended towards the north, down a ravine full of fragments of slate: the hills on both sides were low and rounded. On the descent, *Caragana versicolor*, the *Dama* of the Tibetans, occurred very plentifully; it is, however, in general, much less common in the north-west parts of Tibet than further to the south, where it is very luxuriant. Following the course of the ravine, after a considerable distance, I observed bushes of willow and *Lonicera* to appear in the dry channel, and almost immediately afterwards a little water was found trickling down it, so that I was enabled to encamp, after rather a fatiguing march, at an elevation of about 13,700 feet.

Next day I continued to descend the ravine. The hills were now considerably higher and more rugged than in the upper part, and were faced by cliffs of a clayey conglomerate, partly soft, but often indurated. A rapidly decaying yellowish slate, in highly inclined strata, was seen occasionally in the bed of the river. The stream was, as usual, fringed by willow and *Lonicera;* and a species of poplar, forming a small tree, occurred frequently. There was scarcely a single vestige of vegetation on the mountain-sides. After descending about two miles, I reached a large ravine, the slope of which was much more gradual. The banks were still composed of clay conglomerate, which rose in lofty precipices on both sides; after about three miles, however, this disappeared, and the ravine became very narrow and rocky. The road was now very rugged, ascending high on the mountain-side, and then descending to cross the stream. The limestone cliffs, which here approached within ten or twelve feet of one another, were marked with horizontal undulating grooves, perhaps indicative of the former existence of a glacier in this spot. As I advanced, after crossing to the right bank of the stream, the road became still more rocky and difficult, till at last the ravine in front became quite impracticable. I now turned suddenly to the right, and entered a narrow passage with perpendicular walls of rock, down which ran a very small streamlet. In this dark shady dell, which was so narrow that the light of the sun could not possibly reach the bottom, there were several large patches of snow. The ascent was at first rapid, but after a mile and a half the slope became more gradual and the ravine considerably wider. The usual shrubs then appeared on the water's edge, close to which I encamped, after a march of perhaps nine miles, at about 13,600 feet, very nearly the same elevation as the place from which I had started in the morning, and in an equally desert situation. The whole march was exceedingly barren, and without any cultivation or village. A few small bushes of juniper (*J. excelsa*) were met with about half-way, for the first time during my present journey.

On the 1st of July, I continued the ascent of the ravine, which was still extremely barren and stony, except in the immediate vicinity of the stream, where the usual vegetation of willow and *Lonicera* continued plentiful. A few birch-trees were seen on the road-side. After following the ravine for nearly two miles, I reached a point at which it divided into two branches. The luggage porters took that to the right, which was said to be easier, but longer, while my guide led me to the left, up a steep ravine, which, after a few hundred yards, contracted to a mere fissure three to six feet in width, with very lofty rocky walls, and full of loose shingle. In several places, large masses of hard smooth ice had to be passed, which, from the steepness of the slope, proved no easy task, and would certainly have been almost an impossibility for loaded men. After passing through this fissure, which, as usual, opened out in its upper part, the road turned to the left up a long steep shingly hill-side, to the top of the ridge, which was rounded. While in the ravine I saw no plants; but on the shingly ascent a number of alpine species made their appearance. One of the first was an *Anemone*, but by far the most abundant was a yellow species of *Thermopsis*, which was in full flower, and seemed to thrive best among loose stones. A small *Veronica*, with bright blue flowers, occurred several times on the ascent.

The pass over this ridge is called Takti La. Its elevation was, according to my observation of the boiling-point of water, 16,360 feet. The mountains to the right and left, rising perhaps 1500 feet higher than the pass, obstructed all view. Behind, the landscape was shut in by a lofty snowy mountain, not a mile off; and in front, part of the same snowy range which I had observed from the ridge two days before, was visible. There was a good deal of vegetation at the top, which was in part swampy round a small spring, where probably the snow had only recently melted. The plants were all alpine: *Bieberstcinia odora*, a well-known North Asiatic form, was very common, with several *Ranunculaceæ* and *Cruciferæ*, and one or two species of *Polygonum*.

On the steep shingly ascent which faced the south, I had met with no snow till close to the top, when I saw a few very small patches. On leaving the top of the pass, the road continued to run along the side of the mountain on the left hand, nearly level for about a mile. As I got more fully on the north face, I found snow lying in large patches, which were melting rapidly; and when fairly on the northern slope, I found that, though very steep, it was covered by a continuous bed of snow from the very crest down to about 15,500 feet, as near as I could guess. The view to the north, which, from the pass itself, had been very limited, was now extensive. The range in front was everywhere tipped with snow, and the road up to its crest, with the pass by which I was to cross it, were distinctly visible. Between this range and that on which I stood was interposed the deep ravine of the Zanskar river, the course of which could be traced for a long way, though from the precipitous rocks through which it ran, the stream itself could not be seen.

I find it extremely difficult to describe in an adequate manner the extreme desolation of the most barren parts of Tibet, where no luxuriant forest or bright green herbage softens the nakedness of the mountains, but everywhere the same precipices, heaps of rocks, and barren monotonous deserts meet the eye. The prospect now before me was certainly most wonderful. I had nowhere before seen a country so utterly waste. At the great elevation on which I stood I completely overlooked the valley, and the two or three villages which I afterwards found to exist were either seen as mere spots, or concealed by ranges of hills. Directly in front, across the Zanskar river, a rocky precipice, worn and furrowed in every direction, and broken into sharp pinnacles, rose to the height of at least 2000 feet, overhanging a deep ravine, while to the right and left mountain was heaped upon mountain in inextricable confusion, large patches of snow crowning the highest parts.

From the edge of the snow I descended rapidly to the village of Nira. On the earlier part of the descent, the ground was soft and miry from the recent melting of the snow, which still lay in the more shady parts in large patches. A bright yellow *Ranunculus*, with numerous petals, and the pretty *Lloydia serotina* were plentiful close to the snow. Further down, the road was extremely stony, and the descent very abrupt, but towards the end I followed the course of a small streamlet, the margins of which were skirted by a belt not more than a foot in width of vividly green turf. The village of Nira, in which I encamped, was 12,900 feet above the level of the sea: its cultivated lands were extensive, and both in the village and on the hills around juniper-trees of considerable size were common.

On the 2nd of July I crossed the Zanskar river to the village of Yulchung (13,700 feet). At Nira, besides the usual crops of barley, there was a good deal of buckwheat, which was just above ground. The fields were bordered, as usual, by a rank vegetation. A *Nepeta*, very like *N. Sibthorpiana*, was quite new to me, and a tall erect *Wahlenbergia*, with very large pale greenish-blue flowers, and coarse, somewhat fetid leaves, was very abundant, just coming into flower; the rest of the plants observed were the same as in the upper part of Zanskar. The stream which ran by the village had in some places spread out into a marshy meadow, in which a large pink-flowered *Cardamine* or *Dentaria* occurred plentifully, with *Orchis latifolia?* a white *Juncus*, and many common plants.

Below the village the descent was bare and stony, and extremely abrupt the whole way down to the river; the Tibetan rose was in full flower on the road-side. The river did not come into sight till it was close at hand, the bottom of the ravine through which it flowed being narrow and rocky. A common wooden bridge, without side-rails, forty or fifty feet above the surface of the water, was thrown over at the narrowest part, where the stream was hemmed in by high rocky walls, and was, I think, not more than forty feet broad. The current was rapid, and the water much discoloured. The course of the river at the bridge was easterly, but below, after a slight bend to the south of east, the valley seemed to take a more northerly direction, and above the bridge it came from the south-west. The banks of the river did not seem to be at all practicable, and I was informed that it was only when the river was frozen that travellers could proceed down it to Le. Accounts differed much as to the length of time required for the journey, and I could not discover that any of my party had ever travelled it, so that I presume the route is not very much frequented.

Immediately after crossing the river, a long, steep,

utterly barren ascent commenced over stones and shingle. A deep ravine, with a small stream at the bottom, lay to the right of the road, beyond which were the lofty rugged precipices which had been so conspicuous from the heights the day before. At about 13,000 feet I gained the summit of a projecting ridge, which rose, a little to the right, into a rocky peak, and then sank abruptly down to the ravine. The road then dipped into a hollow filled with large boulders and fragments of rock, perhaps of glacial origin, and rose again more gradually to a second ridge, in the hollow beyond which lay the village at which I had determined to encamp, its lowest houses overhanging the deep ravine on the right. The elevation not being materially different from that of Nira, the plants of the cultivated grounds were the same. *Potentilla anserina* was very plentiful, and remarkably luxuriant.

The rocks during the ascent were chiefly a very hard but very brittle quartz or schist, alternating with loose crumbly slates, and a little limestone. I diverged a little from the direct road, to visit an iron mine, and to see the process of smelting. The ore was yellow ochre, occurring in a breccia-looking conglomerate situated on the flanks of a steep narrow ravine. There were two smelting furnaces, built of stone, of a conical shape, three feet in height, and about six inches in diameter at the top. The fuel employed was charcoal, and no flux was mixed with the ore.

On the 3rd of July, I crossed Singhi La, the pass which I had seen so distinctly on the 1st. The ascent commenced at once from the village of Yulchung, over dry rounded hills, at the same time receding considerably from the deep ravine on the right. No rock *in situ* was visible on the earlier part of the ascent, the hills being entirely covered with coarse gravel and small stones, among which a spinous *Astragalus* and a species of *Polygonum* were the predominant plants; a glabrous *Artemisia*, a little *Euphorbia*, and the prickly *Statice*, were also frequent. After about 1000 feet of ascent, plants of the alpine zone began to appear. Afterwards the ascent was more gentle, over similar ground, till I attained an elevation of about 15,000 feet; at which height the road was for some distance nearly level, winding round a deep bay or hollow in the mountains, with high hills rising on the left hand, and the deep ravine still on the right. Several small streams were crossed, and many alpine plants seen, all familiar to me, except a species of rhubarb, which grew among the shingle in considerable quantity, and which is probably an undescribed species.

After completing the circuit of the deep bay, the ascent recommenced, but was not at all rapid, till within a few hundred yards of the top, when a short steep pull occurred. On the latter part of the ascent, from the loose, stony nature of the soil, vegetation was very scanty; and at the top, which was rounded, there was absolutely none. The elevation was 16,500 feet. Several large patches of snow occurred on the south side when close to the top, but not continuously. The view was extensive to the south, embracing a considerable portion of the great snowy range north of the Chenab, which, from the great elevation of the spot on which I stood, as well as of the intermediate ranges, and from the much smaller quantity of snow on its northern face, looked much less imposing than it does when viewed from the Indian side. Right and left were huge rocky peaks, and in front the view was obstructed by mountains close at hand, except to the north-west, in which direction a long gently-sloping valley was visible, running between two steep ridges, along which, I was informed, the next day's journey lay. From the top of the pass I attempted to form an estimate of the height of the neighbouring ranges, taking the quantity of snow as a guide, and it appeared to me that they were in general between 19 and 20,000 feet, a few isolated peaks only exceeding that altitude. Such guesses, however, are necessarily extremely vague.

Quartzy rock, slate, and limestone, alternated during the ascent; and near the summit of the pass the limestone evidently contained organic remains, perhaps coralline, though the traces were not sufficiently distinct to enable me to decide the point. The fossils were not observed *in situ*, but the angular fragments in which they occurred did not appear to have been transported from any distance.

On the north side of the pass a snow-bed commenced at the very crest, down which the descent was very steep for a few hundred yards. The snow was very soft, and was rapidly melting, but it possibly covered a permanent mass of ice, as it terminated abruptly, and the valley at its base was wide and but little inclined, with only a few patches of snow. The ground near the snow was swampy, owing to the rapid thaw. Here a little sweet-scented *Primula* was abundant, with one or two more alpine plants. The road followed the course of a wide arid valley, descending very gently. Two species of rhubarb were common, and a dwarf willow fringed the margins of the stream.

As I advanced, the valley gradually narrowed, and on the right high precipitous rocks ere long overhung the stream, so that I crossed to the left bank, and, instead of keeping on the bottom of the valley, proceeded horizontally along the hill-sides. A little further on, the stream, which had hitherto had a north-west course, turned suddenly to the north, and entered an extremely narrow rocky ravine, which to all appearance was quite impassable. Here the road turned abruptly to the left, and ascended to cross a low ridge. On attaining the summit an open valley was seen 1000 feet below, which at its lower extremity contracted into a fissure precisely similar to that just described; and as the two ravines were only separated by a narrow rocky ridge, which rose to the north into a high cliff, there can be no doubt that the two streams joined a mile or two below. Descending gradually into the valley, I encamped at the village of Phutaksha, at an elevation of about 14,300 feet.

Notwithstanding its great elevation, the valley of Phutaksha was partially cultivated. The fields formed a narrow belt parallel to the stream, along which they extended almost up to 15,000 feet, but the crops were scanty. The wild plants of the borders of the cultivated land were the same as those common in Zanskar, and grew with great luxuriance along the margins of the irrigation streamlets. Alluvial boulder clay was common in the valley; and I saw also a great deal of the fine cream-coloured clay, which I have elsewhere noticed as being probably of lacustrine origin. The occurrence of this clay at an elevation of upwards of 14,000 feet is rather uncommon, and here, as well as elsewhere, appears to be accompanied by such a conformation of the mountains as to render the former existence of a small lake probable. Below Phutaksha, as I have already observed, the ravine of the little stream is exceedingly narrow and rocky, and as likely as any other part of Tibet to have been blocked up by alluvial deposits so as to form a lake.

On the 4th of July my road lay up the valley. The banks of the little stream were lined with most beautiful green turf, producing all the characteristic plants already mentioned. I took the right-hand branch of two which here united, and, on looking up the other, observed that the snow-line on the northern slope of the mountains, at its head, was very considerably above the level at which I stood; its height, where lowest, seemed to be about 16,000 feet. In one small side-ravine there was an incipient glacier. After leaving the cultivated lands the valley became extremely stony and barren, fragments of a brittle limestone rock being everywhere scattered about. The vegetation changing to that of the alpine zone, several new species of *Astragalus* and *Phaca* were collected. Following the streamlet almost to its source, the road afterwards ascended to the top of a steep ridge, elevated probably a little more than 16,000 feet; this ridge was rocky, or covered with shingle of a dark slate, which had succeeded to the limestone. The yellow *Thermopsis* was almost the only plant which grew on the summit, from which I had a fine view of the pass crossed the day before, and of the range of mountains I had left; but to the north there was no distant view, the valley bending abruptly to the right.

From the top of the pass I descended rapidly along a deep valley, generally at some height above the stream, to the village of Hanupata, elevated 13,100 feet. This valley was throughout barren and stony, and became very narrow in the lower part. *Dama* was very plentiful, but otherwise there was little novelty in the vegetation, except along the bank of the stream in its upper part, where I made a rich collection of small alpine species. A large-flowered *Aster*, a white *Pyrethrum*, and a little *Pedicularis*, were the new species obtained. In the lower part of the valley willow and *Lonicera* as usual appeared; and when close to Hanupata, I met with a shrubby species of *Labiatæ* (perhaps a *Ballota*) which is an extremely common plant in the valley of the Indus from 7000 to 14,000 feet, but seems never to occur far from that river.

On the 5th of July I proceeded down the same valley to Wandla, a distance of about eleven miles. The fields of Hanupata occupied only a narrow strip along the bank of the stream, the sides of the valley being steep and rocky. The crops were much further advanced than any I had hitherto seen; the barley in particular was very luxuriant, and one field was already in ear. Along the margins of the field there was the same rank herbage as usually occurs in similar situations. Lucerne and melilot, both seemingly the common European species, were very plentiful. Poplars and willows were cultivated; and I observed some large juniper-trees. Beyond the cultivation the valley became very narrow. The bed and banks of the stream were gravelly, and on the latter grew a dense thicket of *Myricaria*, *Hippophaë*, willow, and rose. After two or three miles there was not left space even for these, the mountains coming so close together that in many places there was not room to pass between them and the water. The current was too rapid for fording, so that it repeatedly became necessary to ascend to a considerable height in order to effect a passage. One of these ascents was not much less than 1000 feet perpendicular, up a narrow lateral ravine, and then over a very steep bank of loose shingle, descending again with great abruptness to the water's edge. The road also crossed the stream several times.

In one place I observed a very remarkable natural tunnel, where the stream flowed below a solid mass of conglomerate rock, which formed an arch obliquely across it. The conglomerate was exceedingly hard, and rested on both sides on very soft friable slate, by the excavation of which, by the action of the stream, the tunnel appeared to have been formed. The original channel of the stream was still visible six or eight feet higher than its present level a little to the right. The ravine continued narrow and rocky for nearly seven miles, but during the last two of these the road lay high upon the mountain-side, and was tolerably level and good. Near the end the valley became wider, and several small patches of cultivation appeared, with a few apricot-trees; and a double yellow rose was planted near some of the houses. The last mile of the day's journey was entirely through very rich and luxuriant cultivation, which was further advanced than any I had yet seen.

The elevation of Wandla is only 11,000 feet, and the heat of the sun was very oppressive. On the latter part of the march, many plants of the Indus valley which were familiar to me from my journey of the year before, but which I had not seen during my present visit to Tibet, made their appearance. *Echinops* and *Nepeta floccosa*, *Mulgedium Tataricum*, a large and handsome yellow *Corydalis*, *Capparis*, and numerous *Chenopodiaceæ* were abundant. The leaves of *Tussilago Farfara* were common along the water-courses; in the corn-fields a little viscid *Cerastium* (*Lepyrodiclis*) was only too plentiful. By far the most conspicuous plant was the rose (*R. Webbiana*), which, in the rich and well-watered soil of the cultivated plain, grew most luxuriantly, forming dense almost spherical bushes, many of which were at least fifteen feet high, as much in diameter, and bushy down to the ground. They were now in full bloom, and the foliage was almost entirely concealed by the profusion of bright red flowers.

I was obliged to remain a day at Wandla, owing to the serious illness of one of my servants, who, though a native of a mountainous country, had suffered much more on the high passes than any of the inhabitants of the plains of India, and was now so much exhausted as to be unable to move. On the 7th, however, I proceeded towards the Indus, not a little glad to be at last within a day's journey of that river, as I was considerably later than I had originally calculated, not having made allowance for the very rugged nature of the country between Zanskar and Le.

The valley of Wandla, I was informed, contracted

again into a rocky ravine a very little way below the village. This ravine was not quite impracticable, but the stream had to be forded very frequently; and as it was at least four feet deep, I was recommended to follow another route, a little more circuitous, but free of difficulty. For the first mile I proceeded up an open valley, which joined at a right angle from the west that which I had descended on the 5th. I then turned to the right up a very sterile ravine, with much saline efflorescence; in a few places a small streamlet trickled among the stones, but for the first part the channel was quite dry, the water filtering underneath the gravel. The sides of the ravine were bare and shingly and without vegetation, except at the entrance, where a *Corydalis*, thistle, and one or two other plants occurred sparingly. On the most stony parts *Güldenstädtia cuneata*, Benth., was common, and here and there in the gravelly channel was a bush of *Myricaria* (not *M. elegans*, but a smaller and much less handsome species). After a gentle ascent of about two miles, I gained the head of the ravine, and crossing a stony ridge not high enough for alpine plants, descended another valley on its north side, which, though at first if possible more barren than the ascent, soon became somewhat green with willow-bushes and the ordinary plants. After descending perhaps a thousand feet, I reached an extensive tract of cultivation, just above which, in another ravine, lay the village and monastery of Lamayuru, of which a circumstantial account has been given by Moorcroft*. At this place, I joined the road

* Travels, vol. ii. p. 11.

from Kashmir by Dras to Ladak, which has been repeatedly traversed by European travellers, and is particularly described in Moorcroft's Travels.

Below this village the valley contracted, and was for some distance full of immense masses of lacustrine clay; lower down it became a narrow rocky ravine. The road descended with great rapidity till I reached the Wandla stream, which I had left in the morning; it was afterwards less steep, following the banks of that river through a winding rocky valley to its junction with the Indus, which was not seen till close at hand. The valley of the Indus, where I entered it, was very barren, with bare rugged mountains on both sides. A stony platform of alluvial conglomerate usually intervened between the mountains and the river, over which my road lay for about three miles up the river, to a good wooden bridge, defended on the north side by a small, very indifferent fort. By this bridge I crossed to the right side of the river, and a mile further on reached the village of Kalatze (or Kalsi, as it is commonly pronounced), at which I encamped.

In the lower part of the Wandla ravine, the clay-slate rock became much indurated, and alternated with a very hard conglomerate, the matrix of which had a semi-fused appearance, while the pebbles which it contained were all rounded. This rock is very similar to, and probably identical with, that of the Giah ravine north of the Tunglung pass, and of the upper Indus. A modern conglomerate, with an indurated sandy and calcareous matrix, in horizontal beds, rested unconformably upon the more ancient rock, but afforded no indications by which I could form an opinion of its exact age.

The elevation of my tent at Kalatze I made to be 10,400 feet; but I was encamped at the highest part of the village, and the bed of the river was not much above 10,000 feet. The cultivated lands, which are very extensive, lie on the top of a thick platform of alluvium, through which the river has excavated a deep broad channel. The lands of the village slope gradually from the base of the mountain to the edge of the cliff overhanging the river, and the fields are made into level terraces by walls of stones from three to six feet in height. Numerous streams of water are conducted through the fields for irrigation, upon which cultivation in Tibet entirely depends. The crops had an appearance of great luxuriance: they consisted of wheat and barley (both in full ear, the latter even beginning to turn yellow), buckwheat, peas, and oil-seed (*Brassica Napus*). Fruit-trees were abundant, chiefly apricots; but there was no deficiency of apples, pears, walnuts, and mulberries. Along the water-courses and on the edges of the fields grew plenty of wild plants, many the same as occur everywhere in Tibet, but, from the diminished elevation, numerous novelties were observed. A *Clematis*, with dingy brownish-orange flowers, straggled over bushes; a shrubby *Ballota* and a *Perowskia* covered the walls; *Iris, Capsella, Veronica biloba* and *agrestis, Lamium amplexicaule, Mentha, Potentillæ, Plantago Asiatica, Thalictrum*, and numerous other plants grew along the water-courses; while in the fields among the corn the weeds were much the same as are common in Europe and in the plains of India in the cold season; *Vaccaria, Silene conoidea, Stellaria media, Malva rotundifolia*, and *Convolvulus arvensis* being plentiful.

On the 8th of July, I marched to Nurla*, about eight miles up the valley of the Indus. After leaving Kalatze, the whole day's journey was quite barren, the road usually lying on the top of an alluvial platform. Just beyond Kalatze, a large stream had cut a deep ravine through the platform, showing it to be composed of large incoherent water-worn stones, mixed with gravel and clay. The mountains on both sides were steep, rocky, and bare. The vegetation on these platforms was scanty: *Boragineæ* and *Chenopodiaceæ* were the two prominent orders; *Nepeta floccosa*, a little *Hyoscyamus, Güldenstädtia*, a large and handsome *Corydalis*, a *Matthiola*, and several *Astragali, Cruciferæ*, and *Artemisiæ*, were also prevalent. Of grasses, *Stipa* was the most common, but several sub-tropical forms were observed, which were interesting and somewhat unexpected. A species of *Cymbopogon*, and an *Andropogon* allied to *A. Ischæmum*, grew among rocks close to the river. In similar places I met with two species of *Vincetoxicum*, one a twiner, and the other erect; *Tribulus*, too, was common on the most barren spots. At Nurla, the cultivated lands are very extensive: the crops and fruit-trees as at Kalatze; some of the barley was nearly ripe. The com-

* Written, I believe, *Snurla*, as Le is written *Sle*, and Nimo, *Snimo*, the initial letter being in all three mute. Many similar instances might be given, silent initial letters occurring very commonly in the written language of Tibet. It admits of much doubt whether the best mode of spelling be according to the pronunciation, or as the words are written: I have preferred the former, as less likely to mislead.

mon bean seemed a good deal cultivated, usually intermixed with wheat; *Lathyrus sativus* was also a common crop*.

Behind the village of Kalatze, rounded hills of moderate elevation were capped with incoherent beds of sand and boulders of considerable thickness, horizontally stratified; similar beds, sometimes indurated into a soft sandstone rock, occurred at intervals throughout the day. Boulders of granite were abundant in the alluvium and on the surface of the platforms, derived, I believe, from the axis of the chain separating the Indus from the Shayuk. These transported masses of granite were not observed anywhere between lower Zanskar and the Indus; it may therefore, I think, be inferred that the superficial alluvium (which, where the two occur together, generally covers the lacustrine clays) has been deposited since the present river system was in full operation, and is not, as I at one time conjectured, analogous to the drifts of Europe. The ancient rocks between Kalatze and Nurla were alternations of friable slate with indurated conglomerate and grey sandstone.

Between Nurla and Saspola, to which place (eleven miles) I marched on the 9th, the valley of the Indus

* I do not know whether or not to attribute to this plant a remarkable disease which, on my return down the Indus in September, I found in the village of Saspola. At least thirty people in that village, of all ages from a full-grown man to an infant, and of both sexes indifferently, had been attacked with paralysis within the last two years. The palsy was confined to the lower extremities, and differed much in degree. The sufferers were in other respects the most healthy and good-looking portion of the inhabitants. The people themselves were quite at a loss to assign a cause for this extraordinary affection, and, except in some article of diet, I was unable to think of any.

was narrower than before, as well as more rocky. The rock was chiefly grey sandstone. The road frequently ascended to some height in places where the banks of the river were too rugged to permit a passage. On the 10th of June I proceeded to Nimo, ten miles further. At Saspola the road leaves the banks of the Indus, to ascend a barren valley, among hills of loose conglomerate. At first, the banks of the little stream were green and turfy; but after about a mile I entered a dry stony ravine, along the bed of which the road gradually ascended. The rocks were clay-slate, conglomerate, and sandstone, and all the hills were capped with modern alluvial clay conglomerate. Granite boulders occurred abundantly, and marks of the action of water were seen on the rocks far above the reach of the present streams. At the summit, which must have been nearly 1000 feet above the Indus, I emerged suddenly upon a wide and open gravelly plain. To the right, a number of low hills concealed the course of the Indus; to the left, the mountain range had receded to some distance, and could be seen to be here and there tipped with snow. The road lay for several miles over this barren plain, which was entirely alluvial, descending afterwards very abruptly into a deep flat-bottomed hollow, excavated out of the soft conglomerate by a considerable stream. In this hollow, quite concealed till close at hand, was the village of Bazgo, with a long narrow strip of cultivation along the margin of its stream. Following the course of this valley till near the Indus, I then ascended its left bank, and emerged upon another extensive alluvial platform, high above the river, but parallel to it. At the east end of this platform was the village of Nimo, the termination of my day's journey.

From this place my journey of the 12th brought me to Le, about twelve miles. About a mile above Nimo the Indus is joined by the Zanskar river. The valley where the two rivers unite is very rocky and precipitous, and bends a long way to the south. The road to Le does not follow the river, but ascends among gravelly ravines behind the village, and emerges on a wide open plain, which, as on the previous march, is interposed between the northern range of mountains and the present channel of the Indus. The height of this plain above the river was at least 1000 feet; it was lowest in the centre, sloping up not only towards the mountains to the north, but to a range of round-topped hills of moderate elevation, which overhung the valley of the Indus, sinking on their south face very abruptly down to the river. The higher mountains were chiefly granite, with a few interposed beds of slate dipping at a high angle. The granite exhibited the usual tendency of that rock to decay in spheres, or rather in irregular-shaped masses with rounded angles.

In proceeding along this plain, the road at first rose almost imperceptibly, but after two miles I reached the highest part of it, from which it sloped down towards the east. From this point the course of the Indus in front of Le, and to the south-east for many miles, was finely seen. The river runs through a wide valley, but the range of mountains to the north sends down many rugged spurs, which, in the shape of low rocky hills, advance close to the river. On the south or left bank, on the contrary, a wide, open, gently-sloping plain extends to a considerable distance. From the highest level of the plain a long gradual descent brought me to the Indus, to which it was necessary to descend in order to get round one of the spurs just referred to. It is here a tranquil but somewhat rapid stream, divided into several branches by gravelly islands, generally swampy, and covered with low *Hippophaë* scrub. The size of the river was very much less than it had been below the junction of the river of Zanskar, the latter appearing to contribute considerably more than half the amount of water. At the point of the low spur lay the village of Pitak, on an isolated hill, surrounded by extensive deposits of cream-coloured lacustrine clay. From this village there is a gradual ascent of about four miles to the town of Le, which is built on a low hill at the upper corner of a wide open valley.

The bed of the Indus at Pitak, below Le, has an elevation of about 10,500 feet above the level of the sea, but the town is at least 1300 feet higher. Its sheltered situation, in a hollow surrounded by hills, and facing the south, compensates to a certain extent for this increase of elevation; still the crops are very much inferior to those on the banks of the Indus. There are but few trees, the apricot being the only fruit-tree cultivated, and it does not seem to thrive. Water is plentiful in the valley, and is conveyed through the cultivated lands in deeply-cut canals or trenches, faced with walls of stone. Natural meadows of tall grasses, intermixed with luxuriant lucerne and melilot, are common along the banks of the river, especially above the town.

The vegetation in the vicinity of Le scarcely differed from that of the Indus at Kalatze. The most abundant families of plants were *Chenopodiaceæ, Labiatæ,* and *Artemisiæ,* which covered the barren and stony tracts; the *Boragineæ,* so abundant throughout Tibet in early spring, had already quite dried up and disappeared. In the meadows tall species of *Thalictrum, Silene,* and *Heracleum,* were coming into flower, and in swamps *Veronica Beccabunga* and *Anagallis, Limosella,* and a yellow *Pedicularis,* were the most abundant plants.

At Le I had the pleasure of meeting Captain Strachey, who had spent the winter there, and had returned shortly before my arrival, from an exploring journey to the eastward. After a week's stay I set out for Nubra on the 19th of July, crossing the lofty chain separating the two rivers by the pass directly north of Le, which, during the summer months, presents no difficulty, and is therefore preferred as being the most direct. The pass is distinctly visible from the town of Le, to which it appears very close, though the distance is at least ten or twelve miles. I did not attempt to cross it the first day, but encamped as far up on the southern face as I conveniently could, so as to reach the top early in the morning. At starting, the road lay for about three miles through an open valley, partly cultivated, and with a good deal of swampy ground. Higher up, the valley contracted into a barren ravine, with a narrow strip of green along the margin of the stream. About half-way, the road left the bottom of the valley, and for the remainder of the march I proceeded along the bare side of the mountain, ascending very rapidly. There was a striking change in the vegetation as the height increased. On the lower slopes *Cicer* and *Statice* were abundant, with several *Astragali*; on the latter part of the ascent many alpine plants were observed, belonging to the genera *Corydalis*, *Elsholtzia*, *Potentilla*, and *Draba*. A very small violet was extremely plentiful in the crevices of the rocks, and among stones, after I had reached 15,000 feet. I encamped at about 15,700 feet, on a level piece of ground, a few hundred feet above the bottom of the valley.

On the 20th I crossed the pass, starting about sunrise. The morning was intensely frosty, and the stones and vegetation near the water were encrusted with ice. The path lay close to the stream, ascending somewhat rapidly among the green turf which grew along its margin, in which I found many little alpine plants, among which, a large-flowered *Aster* and a small poppy with still unexpanded flowers were the most conspicuous. The last part of the ascent was extremely steep, among immense angular granite boulders, with here and there a little snow in the crevices. Here a most elegant sweet-scented species of *Primula* was common, so firmly fixed in the frozen mud, that I could with difficulty procure a specimen. Except in very small patches, there was no snow till within two hundred yards of the top of the ascent, for which distance it was continuous, but very soft, and evidently melting rapidly. The crest of the pass was a narrow ridge of large spheres of granite, seemingly quite detached from one another, but which had probably been formed on the spot they now occupied by the peculiar decay characteristic of that rock.

The continuation of the ridge on both sides was for

some distance very little more elevated than the pass itself, the height of which was 17,700 feet. To the south, the view was very extensive, embracing a great extent of snowy mountains, with numerous lofty peaks, as well as a part of the Indus valley, and the town of Le, immediately below; to the north it was much more limited, as hills close at hand completely excluded all distant view, except directly in front, where one snowy peak could be seen a long way off, evidently beyond the Shayuk.

On the north side of the pass snow commenced at the very top, and continued for at least 1200 feet of perpendicular height. The descent for this distance was extremely steep, over a snow-bed, which appeared to cover an incipient glacier. About 1200 feet below the top I came to a small oval-shaped lake, completely frozen over; a little higher up I had passed a small bare piece of rock projecting through the snow, and perhaps thirty feet long, on which the beautiful blue-flowered *Nepeta multibracteata*, Benth., had already put forth its flowers. Beyond the frozen lake the descent became at once much more gentle, and was partially free of snow. The path lay over a vast accumulation of angular stones, which appeared to have fallen from the rocks above. Many parts of the valley were swampy, evidently from recently melted snow, and in such places the *Primula*, noticed on the ascent, occurred in great abundance, its scapes rising to the height of six to eight inches, and bearing large globes of deep rose-coloured flowers. Among the loose stones *Nepeta multibracteata* was common. About three miles from the top I passed the end of an exceedingly well-marked moraine, which must have been deposited by a glacier at a time when, from increased cold, these masses of ice stretched down much further than they do at present. The remainder of the descent was again more abrupt, but very bare, stony, and uninteresting. A single tree of *Juniperus excelsa* grew in one of the ravines, and below 14,000 feet a species of berberry, with very small leaves, was common on dry stony ground. I encamped at the small village of Kardong, at 13,500 feet. The cultivation round this village was on a level plain without any terracing.

On the 21st I proceeded to Karsar, a village on the bank of the Shayuk river, distant about nine miles. A few hundred feet above the village of Kardong the alluvial boulder clay had begun to occur in the valley, and around the village, which occupied the end of a lateral ravine, it was already very thick. From Kardong to the

Shayuk this alluvium continued in great quantity, forming elevated platforms, sloping very gently from the mountains, and faced by steep, often quite perpendicular cliffs. Where lateral ravines joined the main valley the

alluvium was deeply excavated by the little streams which traversed them, and the road descended abruptly by steep and curiously winding paths down the cliffs of clay, and among piles of boulders, to re-ascend to the platform beyond the stream. Such a ravine, of great depth, occurred just below Kardong. After crossing it the road lay over the surface of the clay platform, which was nearly level, and consequently at an increasing height above the bottom of the Kardong valley, which rapidly diminished in elevation. This platform was extremely barren, and quite devoid of water. Here and there isolated rocky masses rose up through the alluvium. The rock was peculiar, being very hard, and, as it were, porphyritic, with a black, basaltic-looking matrix, quite homogeneous, in which numerous white specks were diffused. In hand specimens and boulders, and even on a near view of the hills, this rock appeared quite an igneous rock, but when an extensive section was exposed, it could be seen to be distinctly stratified.

When within a short distance of the Shayuk valley, though still high above it, the road turned to the left, and, leaving the alluvial platform, proceeded among rugged rocky hills, in a direction parallel to that river, at the same time descending somewhat rapidly to a platform of modern lacustrine clay and conglomerate, which filled up the whole of a deep recess in the mountains facing the Shayuk, to a thickness of at least 1000 feet. The village of Karsar, at which I encamped, lies in a deep ravine, excavated out of the clay formation by a considerable stream, on both sides of which, for nearly a mile, there is a belt of cultivation, very narrow where the stream issues from the mountains, but gradually widening as it descends. Owing to the sheltered situation, from the great height of the cliffs of clay on both sides, the crops were exceedingly luxuriant, and fruit-trees were plentiful, principally apples and apricots. Some very fine walnut-trees also occurred.

From the same cause the herbaceous vegetation was particularly rich, and I met with many species which were new to me. The banks of the stream, from the point where it issued from among the mountains, were everywhere bordered by large bushes of *Myricaria elegans,* now adorned with masses of sweet-scented rose-coloured flowers. In the lower part of the village-lands there were shady plantations of poplar and willow, which seemed to be occasionally irrigated, in order that they might produce a rich natural pasture. In these groves *Euphrasia officinalis*, species of *Gentiana*, *Ranunculus*, *Potentilla*, and *Carum* grew most luxuriantly; a tall but very small-flowered *Pedicularis* was also very common. No less than three species of *Orchideæ* occurred, a family which more than any other dislikes dryness: these were *Orchis latifolia*, an *Epipactis*, and an *Herminium*. Many of the weeds of the cultivated fields were also new and interesting: a *Hypecoum*, an *Elsholtzia*, and some species of *Polygonum* were those I particularly noted.

The lacustrine formation of Karsar consists mostly of very pure white clay, horizontally stratified; but at the lower end of the ravine, where it is about to expand into the open plain of the Shayuk, a tolerably solid but still very friable sandstone, the strata of which were also quite horizontal, occurred under the clay. I saw no fossils, but when the clay is examined with care, they will probably be occasionally detected. At all events, as this clay formation is at least a thousand feet thick, if we take into consideration the open nature of the whole valley of Nubra, there can be no doubt that it must have been deposited from the same waters with the very similar clay which I found at Tertse, in lower Nubra, in October, 1847, and that it is therefore lacustrine. If this be admitted, it seems impossible to escape from the conclusion, that the deposits in the Kardong valley, (of which I have given an imaginary section in page 398,) though different in appearance, belong to the same lake. Now, these attain an elevation of 13,500 feet and upwards, as they commence above Kardong: the level of the surface of the Nubra lake can therefore hardly have been less than 14,000 feet; so that it must have extended up the Tanktse valley, almost as far as the low pass by which that district is separated from the Pangong lake.

From Karsar, I marched on the 25th of July, down the valley of the Shayuk, to Diskit. The earlier part of the road, after ascending abruptly out of the Karsar ravine, lay over the clay platform, which was perfectly flat; but after about four miles, it descended nearly to the level of the river, whose wide gravelly plain now extended on the south side to the very foot of the mountains, the lacustrine beds having been entirely removed. The plain was traversed by several small streamlets, apparently derived in a great measure from the river, the water of which seemed to sink among the gravel and sand of its bed, and to spring up again at a distance from the main channel. One of these streams ran at the extreme edge of the plain, close under the cliffs, which here rose almost precipitously to a great height. Its banks were very saline, and in the neighbourhood of Diskit a great part of the plain was encrusted with soda.

The cultivated lands of the village, which is of considerable size, lie on a sloping bank, rising rather steeply out of the plain. Many apricot-trees grow among the houses, some of which were large enough to afford a shade under which a tent could be pitched. The vegetation was in general the same as at Karsar, but a white-flowered *Allium* was new, as well as a species of *Chloris*, which was abundant in the pastures. A very small *Cyperus*, which grew in the water-courses, appeared to be a dwarf state of a species common in the plains of India, and, with the *Chloris*, which is a tropical grass, was interesting as an indication of the considerable heat of the summer climate in the valley of the Shayuk, notwithstanding its great elevation.

The village of Diskit is almost exactly opposite the place where the Nubra river joins the Shayuk from the northward. In October, 1847, I had crossed the Shayuk five or six miles above Karsar, and descended along its right bank, but during the hot months this route is not practicable, as there are no bridges, and the river is too deep to be forded anywhere except just at its junction with that of Nubra, where the wide gravelly plain of the Shayuk expands to its greatest diameter, and the river is divided into numerous branches.

The greater part of the 26th of July was occupied by the passage of the Shayuk, which was both tedious and difficult, the river being now nearly at its greatest height. The first branch was nearly two miles from Diskit, the intervening gravelly plain being partly swampy, with a few bushes of *Hippophaë*, *Tamarix*, and *Myricaria*. There were four large branches to be crossed, besides several of smaller size. Nearly a mile of sand separated the last large branch from the remainder, and the ford was a most intricate one, each branch being crossed obliquely and at a different point from the adjacent ones. The united breadth of all the streams could not, I think, have been less than half a mile. The velocity of the water was so great, that though the depth nowhere, I think, exceeded three and a half feet, and was more usually about two and a half, people on foot appeared to have the utmost difficulty in retaining their footing, and the loaded men had to be supported by one or two without loads on each side. In the more difficult parts, two men placed themselves on each side of my horse's head, to guide him in the proper road, and two more at each stirrup to give him support in case of need. When in the centre of the current, where, from the necessity of keeping my eye on the horse's motions, I had to look at the water, I found it impossible to avoid a feeling of giddiness, and an impression that horse and rider were being hurried upwards with extreme velocity in a direction contrary to the stream. These very rapid portions, however, were never more than ten or twenty yards broad; the remainder was more moderate and shallower.

After safely effecting the passage with all my party and baggage, I proceeded about a mile over loose sand, and encamped at the village of Lyakjung, situated at the border of the low plain of the river, at the point of union of the two valleys. The Shayuk valley is visible from this place as far as the large village of Hundar, about ten miles, the river running throughout that distance through a wide gravelly plain, but with high rocky mountains on both sides.

From the 27th of July till the 9th of August, I remained in the valley of Nubra, the necessary preparations for my further journey, which was to be entirely through an uninhabited country, requiring considerable time. During this interval, I moved from place to place in the valley, which is well inhabited and rather pretty. The river is in the hot months very large and rapid, and has its origin, no doubt, in the great snowy mountains to the north. I crossed it twice a little above the town of Chirasa, and found its current quite as strong as that of the Shayuk, and in many places as deep, but its breadth was considerably less. In one of the channels, a lad, carrying a light bundle, was carried away by the stream, and rolled over repeatedly in the water, after being separated from his load, before he was picked up by a number of men who hastened to his assistance. The difficulty of crossing was much increased by numerous quicksands, which made it necessary to proceed by a tortuous path, and which were evidently very liable to shift, as the guides proceeded very cautiously, and more than once abandoned a ford on finding the footing insecure.

The general appearance of the valley of Nubra is very agreeable, and superior to that of any other part of Tibet at the same elevation. The villages are well wooded, with orchards of apricot-trees, and with poplars and willows, which are either planted in rows, or scattered irregularly in meadows on the skirts of the cultivated lands: the willows, when not pollarded, attain a large size, and afford an ample shade. The fields are carefully enclosed with walls, or hedges of *Hippophaë*, or with a fence of the dead branches of that plant. Green and shady lanes, bordered by high *Hippophaë* hedges, full of *Clematis* and rose-bushes, lead through the village lands. The crops are chiefly wheat and barley, with a few fields of millet (*Panicum miliaceum*), buckwheat, and rape. There is also much pasture, particularly along the little streams, and in fields near the river, which are often swampy.

The beauty of the cultivated tracts is much enhanced by the utter sterility of the drier parts of the plain, which are either gravelly or stony, and utterly barren, except that occasionally from some peculiarity of soil or position there is a considerable extent of clayey soil not low enough to be swampy, but not remote from water, covered with short turf much encrusted with soda. These grassy plains are more common in the upper part of the district, and are perhaps connected with springs containing carbonate of soda in solution*.

Except from the more advanced period of the season,

* This view has been suggested to me by Dr. R. D. Thomson, who has paid much attention to the chemical contents of springs, and is at present engaged in examining the saline matters which I brought with me from Tibet.

the flora of Nubra differed but little from that of Le. Species of *Artemisia*, *Labiatæ*, and *Chenopodiaceæ*, were now in full flower on the more desert and stony tracts, in which a shrubby *Lycium* (which is not found on the Indus) was also common. *Chenopodiaceæ* had become extremely plentiful, and belonged to many different genera: shrubby species of *Eurotia* and *Caroxylon* were common, but the greater number were herbaceous, and belonged to the genera *Chenopodium*, *Ambrina*, *Salsola*, *Echinopsilon*, and *Corispermum*. A species of thistle grew on barren soil, particularly where the ground was saline; on the salt soil, *Glaux*, a little *Crucifera*, and a *Polygonum* were the most abundant plants. *Mulgedium Tataricum*, a *Galium* (very like *G. Aparine*), and a scandent species of *Vincetoxicum*, were frequent in hedges; and species of *Mentha*, *Erodium*, *Epilobium*, *Lepidium*, and *Matthiola*, all common plants at Le, being now in full flower, attracted notice more than at an earlier period. A very tall species of grass (*Melica?*) in large and elegant tufts, often six feet high, was one of the most ornamental plants in the valley; while as uncommon forms I may enumerate a prickly *Sophora*, *Orobanche*, *Parietaria*, and in ponds a little *Utricularia*, closely resembling a European species.

A small-leaved elm, which is common near Tagar, is apparently wild,—at least it is not acknowledged by the inhabitants as a cultivated tree. I have not observed this tree elsewhere in Tibet, but Mr. Vigne mentions that he met with an elm in the mountains between Shigar and Khapalu. It appears to be the same with a species common in the forests of the lower valleys of Kashmir.

About a mile from the large village of Panamik are the hot springs formerly visited by Moorcroft. They are two in number, and spring from the rocky mountain-side, about a hundred yards from the edge of the plain. The temperature of the water in the spring which I tried was 170·5°. It was faintly sulphurous both in taste and smell, but not perceptibly saline, and deposited a thick calcareous incrustation on everything within its reach.

To the south of Panamik the rocks of Nubra are chiefly black slate, but transported blocks of granite are everywhere common, and at that village the latter rock descends to the level of the river, and continues to form the whole mass of the mountains on the left side of the valley as far as I continued along it. On the right side there were indications of stratification on the steep sides of the mountains, and, from the colour, the rock there appeared to be partly granite and partly metamorphic slate.

CHAPTER XIV.

Start for Karakoram—Steep ascent out of Nubra valley—Meet a party of Merchants from Yarkand—View from summit of pass—Rapid torrent—Large glacier—Steep moraines—Alpine vegetation—Numerous glaciers—Lakes—Glacier on crest of Sassar pass—Sassar—Cross Shayuk river—Murgai—Limestone rocks—Ascend Murgai Valley to 16,800 feet—Singular limestone formation—Open plain above 17,000 feet—Recross Shayuk river—Karakoram pass—Return to Sassar—Glaciers of Sassar—Return to Le—Start for Kashmir—Lamayura—Phatu pass—Kanji river—Namika pass—Molbil Pashkyum—Kargil—Dras—Zoji pass—Kashmir—Lahore—Completion of journey.

Having at last completed the preparations necessary for a journey of twenty days through uninhabited regions, I started on the 9th of August from the village of Taksha. My first day's journey lay up the Nubra valley, which continued wide, though the alluvial platforms were destitute of cultivation, and quite barren. In several places (always opposite to ravines) they were covered with enormous boulders, which had all the appearance of having been brought to the position they occupied by glaciers. Two small villages were seen, both on the west bank of the river. Four miles from Taksha I crossed, by a good wooden bridge, a large stream which descended from the mountains on my right hand through an exceedingly

SKETCH MAP
of Route from
NUBRA TO KARAKORAM.
by Dr. T. Thomson
Karakorum Pass
35° 30'
Probable Glaciers
Probable Glaciers
35°
Aranuo
11 609
Glaciers are indicated
by curved lines
Probable position of Glaciers
by dotted curved lines

rocky gorge. After seven miles and a half, I found that I had reached the point at which the road followed by the merchants in travelling from Le to Yarkand leaves the valley of Nubra. It was too late in the day to attempt the ascent of the ridge to the right; I therefore encamped in a grove of willows, which formed a belt along the margin of a stream whose bed was now quite dry, its scanty supply of water having been diverted into an artificial channel for the irrigation of a couple of fields of indifferent barley not far off.

In the valley of Nubra, beyond this encamping ground, which is known by the name of Changlung, there are, I believe, only three small villages, the most distant of which appeared to be not more than five or six miles off. In the direction of the valley, which was still north-north-west, very lofty mountains were visible at no great distance, all with snowy tops, and generally with heavy snow-beds and glaciers in their hollows; and according to the statement of my guides, the river at the distance of less than two days' journey issues from beneath a glacier, by which all passage is stopped*.

On the 10th of August I started at daybreak, immediately commencing the ascent of the mountain range which enclosed the valley on the east. The mountain was exceedingly steep, indeed almost precipitous, and the road proceeded in a zigzag direction over bare granite rock, with scarce a vestige of vegetation. During the ascent I had a good view of the valley, and of the mountain

* Two months later, Captain Strachey ascended the Nubra valley till stopped by this glacier, which appears to be on a still more gigantic scale than those of the Shayuk to the eastward.

range which bounded it on the south-west; large patches of snow lay on its peaks, and here and there I saw a small glacier in its ravines. The upper part of the valleys by which these mountains were furrowed had a very moderate slope, but from about 14,000 feet down to the bottom they were extremely abrupt.

After about 3500 feet of extremely laborious climbing, I arrived at a small level plain, perhaps two hundred yards long and forty or fifty wide, evidently much frequented as a resting-place by travellers, a small pool of water being the inducement. I here met a party of merchants on their way from Yarkand to Le. Their goods were conveyed by ponies, apparently much exhausted by their long journey through desert country. I had noticed, on the way up the mountain, that the road was lined by numerous skeletons and scattered bones of horses; I had also seen one or two of the same animals recently dead, and the appearance of these loaded ponies enabled me to understand the cause of the great mortality. Many of the unfortunate animals appeared scarcely to have strength to accomplish the few miles of descent which still intervened between them and plenty of food. The main reliance of the merchants for the support of their horses is on corn carried with them, to which there must be a limit, otherwise they would carry nothing but their own food.

From this halting-place the remainder of the ascent was less abrupt, though still steep and extremely stony. There was, however, a little more vegetation than on the lower part, where the barren rocks, except at the very base, produced scarcely anything but *Ephedra*, a dwarf species of *Rhamnus*, and tufts of the hardy *Statice*. Higher up, several species of *Astragalus* and *Artemisia* were plentiful, with *Lithospermum euchromon*, *Dracocephalum heterophyllum*, and several *Chenopodiaceæ* and grasses. The top of the ridge had an elevation of 15,300 feet, but from its extreme aridity and rockiness, and its consequent elevated temperature, no alpine plants occurred. On reaching the top I was able to see something of the road before me, regarding which I had previously had little information, except in accounts of its extreme difficulty. These I had been inclined to consider exaggerated, but the prospect before me was undoubtedly far from tempting. Immediately below lay a narrow stony valley, to which, from the spot on which I stood, the descent was almost perpendicular. Opposite to me there was a range of mountains higher than that on which I stood, with here and there a patch of snow. The valley below me was partly occupied by a mass of loose alluvial conglomerate, through which the stream had excavated a deep ravine; its direction was south-south-west, and there could be no doubt that the stream which I had crossed the day before, about half-way, was that which drained the valley upon which I now looked down. On the top of the alluvial platform, on the opposite side, there was a narrow strip of green, indicating a small patch of cultivation, without, however, any habitation, the crop being apparently left to its fate till ready for the reaper. In every other direction, stones and snow were alone visible.

I descended obliquely into the valley, so as to reach it about a mile and a half higher up than the spot from which it was first visible. The descent was very laborious, a great part of it being covered with loose gravel or coarse sand, produced by the disintegration of the granite rocks. There was rather more vegetation than on the opposite face, and I collected a number of plants which I had not recently met with; a *Nepeta*, *Scrophularia*, *Cicer*, and *Heracleum*, and two shrubby *Potentillæ*, were the commonest species. One of the species of *Potentilla* (*P. discolor* of Jacquemont) was remarkable for exciting violent sneezing when touched or shaken; this curious property seemed to be owing to a very fine dust which covered the under surface of the leaves.

After reaching the surface of the alluvial platform overhanging the stream, about half a mile of gentle ascent among large stones brought me, after a journey of ten miles, to my encamping ground. This was a level spot, close to a lateral torrent, which had its source in a snow-bed in the mountains on the left, and was rushing in a most impetuous milk-white torrent over immense boulders, to unite itself to the main stream. The elevation of my camp was about 14,000 feet.

On the morning of the 11th, at starting, I crossed the torrent close to camp. Although much less considerable than it had been the previous afternoon, still, from its great rapidity and the number of boulders in its bed, the crossing was not accomplished without difficulty by the laden animals, who carried the greater part of my baggage. I crossed it myself by leaping from boulder to boulder, which would have been quite impossible in the afternoon of the previous day, when it was swollen by the action of the sun upon the snow. The road lay up the valley parallel to the river, among a most extraordinary accumulation of granite boulders of all sizes, from one to ten feet in diameter, piled upon one another in vast heaps, and evidently transported by a former glacier. After about half a mile, I crossed the river by a wooden bridge of two or three beams, which must have been brought from Nubra for the purpose, as no timber of any sort grows in the valley. The stream was very rapid and muddy. A mile further, a torrent descending from the mountains on the right was crossed, and soon after I got upon the bank of the main stream, now more tranquil and fordable. The road for the remainder of the march lay along its left bank, over boulders and gravel, ascending now and then a little way on steep sloping banks, entirely composed of transported materials. I encamped on a level, somewhat grassy spot of ground, which was evidently commonly used as a halting-place, having travelled only four and a half miles, an unnecessarily short day's work. I had throughout my journey had considerable difficulty in fixing the marches at proper lengths, the inhabitants having no measure of distance but the day's journey. In the present instance, my tent was pitched, and most of the party had commenced to cook, or were dispersed to collect fuel, long before my arrival, so that I was obliged to rest content for the day.

The course travelled during the day had been north-north-east, but I had evidently arrived nearly as far as was practicable in that direction, for about half a mile in front was the bluff end of a very large glacier, filling up the continuation of the valley. This glacier, which was nearly half a mile wide, was covered almost entirely with stones and earth, very little of its surface being visible, and the dirty black colour of its terminating cliff showing how much soil had been mixed up with it in its progress. The elevation of my tent was about 14,500 feet, and the termination of the glacier may have been 250 feet higher. All around the mountains were very lofty, their tops covered with snow, which nowhere came within 2000 feet at least of the valley, even on northern exposures. Granite was everywhere the prevailing rock, but on the higher mountain slopes, which were often precipitous, it was much intermixed with a dark rock, probably clay-slate.

During the day I had scarcely seen any vegetation, except when close to the edge of the stream. Among the boulders and on the bare stony ground there was frequently not a vestige of herbage. Near one of the ravines I found the white shrubby *Potentilla*, along with an exceedingly pretty prostrate plant, with bright rose-coloured flowers, belonging to the order of *Compositæ:* it was a species of the genus *Allardia*, described by M. Decaisne from the collections of Jacquemont, by whom it was found in Piti. One of the very few alpine plants which I saw during the day was a little gentian, common among the turf close to my tent. Round camp a species of nettle was plentiful, seemingly, like others of the genus, attracted by the nitrogenous nature of the soil of an encamping ground much frequented by shepherds with their flocks. The sting of this nettle, though rather faint, was quite perceptible. It was decidedly an alpine plant, which is rather uncommon, not only in the genus, but the order to which it belongs.

The journey of the 12th of August commenced by a steep ascent into a lateral valley descending from the eastward. The hill-side up which I climbed (apparently the bluff termination of an ancient moraine) was very stony and dry. When a sufficient elevation above my encampment had been gained, I obtained a commanding view of the glacier which occupied the continuation of the main valley. It was nearly straight, and, as I believe, at least five or six miles long; distances, however, are so difficult to estimate on snow, that this must be regarded as a mere guess. The inclination of its surface was considerable; but, while the distance remained doubtful, no just estimate of the height of the ridge from which it descended could be made. On each side, two or three lateral glaciers, descending from the mountains by which it was enclosed, contributed to increase its size, all loaded with heaps of stones, which had at the lower end of the central glacier so accumulated as completely to cover its whole surface.

After 800 or 1000 feet of ascent I found that I had attained the level of the lateral valley, along which the road ran, and that the remainder of the way was much more gentle, but exceedingly fatiguing, from its excessive roughness, and from the great elevation, which made the slightest exertion difficult. On both sides were high ranges of mountains, which had much snow on their summits, and in one or two ravines there was a small snow-bed or incipient glacier, but the distance from the crest of the ridge not being great, no glacier of any length was formed. On the left hand, the mountains were steeper and higher than those on the right, and several bulky glaciers on very steep slopes occupied their ravines. None of these entered the valley along which my road lay, but their moraines often projected to its very centre, forming immense piles of angular fragments of rocks, which attained, in more than one place, a height of several hundred feet, and indicated that the glaciers had at some former period advanced much further than they now do. The main valley was itself everywhere covered with boulders; in some places large blocks, ten to twenty feet in diameter, were arranged at moderate distances from one another, but more frequently the fragments were all small.

After the first steep ascent, the slope of the valley was uniformly gentle, except when a steep-sided moraine had to be passed. Latterly a few small patches of snow occurred in the valley. I encamped at 16,600 feet, on a level grassy spot of ground close to a small circular plain resembling the bed of a lake, and still partially covered with snow. The snow level on the mountains to the south had approached within less than one hundred feet of the level of the plain. Though the distance travelled during the day was only six miles, I felt a good deal fatigued, and suffered much from headache, caused by the rarefaction of the air.

From the great quantity of snow on the mountains all around, there had been throughout the day an abundance of moisture, and vegetation was in consequence much more plentiful than usual. The plants were all alpine, and being mostly diminutive, had to be sought in the crevices of rocks, and among the stones which everywhere abounded. The banks of the stream were frequently grassy, and there was a great deal of marshy ground. Most of the plants obtained were in full flower, and the colours were in general very bright, and sufficiently varied. By far the greater part belonged to the same genera which prevail on European mountains, such as *Draba*, *Saxifraga*, *Sibbaldia*, *Potentilla*, *Ranunculus*, *Papaver*, *Pedicularis*, *Cerastium*, *Leontopodium*, and *Saussurea*. The most remarkable forms were three species of *Allardia*, several *Astragali*, a one-flowered *Lychnis*, *Delphinium Brunonianum*, and a *Ligularia*. The alpine nettle was common on many parts of the road, chiefly near places frequented by the shepherds as halting-places.

Next day at starting I proceeded along the edge of the small plain close to which I had been encamped. On the right hand was an ancient moraine, which prevented me from seeing the road in advance. At the upper end of the plain I found a small streamlet running parallel to the moraine; and about a mile from camp I reached the end of a small glacier, from which the streamlet had its origin. Crossing the latter, which was still partially frozen, I ascended in a deep hollow between the left side of the glacier and the moraine. The icy mass had not yet begun to thaw, the temperature being still below freezing. After half a mile I ascended on the surface of the ice, and as soon as I did so, was enabled to see that the glacier had its origin in a ravine on the south, and entered the main valley almost opposite to me. The great body of the ice took a westerly direction, forming the glacier along which I had been travelling; but a portion formed a cliff to the eastward, which dipped abruptly into a small, apparently deep lake. At the distance of perhaps five hundred yards there was another glacier, which descended from a valley in the northern range of mountains, and, like the one on which I stood, presented a perpendicular wall to the little lake. Right and left of the lake were enormous piles of boulders, occupying the interval between its margin and the mountains, or rather filling up a portion of the space which it would otherwise have occupied. Into this very singular hollow I descended, on a steep icy slope, and passing along the northern margin of the lake, ascended on the glacier beyond; as before, between the ice and moraine.

On reaching the surface of the second glacier, I found that a similar but smaller depression lay beyond it to the east, in which also there was a small lake, with another mass of ice beyond it. This third glacier also came from the north, and was a much more formidable mass than those which had already been crossed. It was very steep, and was covered with snow, which was beginning to thaw more than was convenient. When at the highest part, I found that though apparently nearly level, it sloped downwards sensibly, though very slightly for nearly half a mile, in an easterly direction. It was evident that I had now reached the highest part of the ascent, and that the crest of the pass was covered by this glacier. I did not make any observation to determine its altitude, but the ascent from camp was very moderate, not, I think, exceeding a thousand feet. Assuming this estimate to be correct, the height of the pass would be about 17,600 feet, which I believe will prove not far from the truth.

On so icy an ascent vegetation could not be expected

to be plentiful; still, even in the depressions between the glaciers, the crevices among the boulders produced a few plants, mostly the same as those observed the day before, but three species of *Saussurea* were the most common of all. Before arriving at the first glacier, the beautiful *Primula* collected on the pass above Le was met with in great abundance.

For about half a mile, as I have said, the slope of the glacier was just perceptible; beyond that distance the descent was abrupt. On reaching the end of the level portion, I obtained an excellent view to the eastward, in which direction a wide valley was seen at a distance of several miles. Through this valley, from left to right, ran a considerable river, which proved to be the Shayuk. Beyond the river, rocky mountains were seen, apparently nearly as high as those near at hand, and perfectly barren. In descending from the pass, I soon left the surface of the ice, which, as soon as the slope became abrupt, was too rugged to be walked over. I then got upon the moraine; about half-way down, the glacier, which had latterly been almost entirely covered with debris, came to an end, but a moraine continued a long way down, and the remainder of the descent was very stony. I encamped at about 15,400 feet on a dry gravelly plain, close to the broad valley of the Shayuk, but at least 500 feet above it. To the right, in a very deep ravine, was a small stream, on the banks of which were patches of snow. The name of the ground on which I encamped, which is a usual halting-place, was Sassar, and the Turki merchants call the pass also by the same name.

2 E 2

From Sassar not more than three or four miles of the upward course of the river were visible, but within that distance three glaciers were in sight. Two of these stopped short of the valley, while the third, which was at the most distant point visible, appeared to descend to the river. An enormous precipice, which must have been at least 3000 feet in height, rose on the opposite side of the valley beyond the glaciers. Downward the valley of the Shayuk was seen for nearly ten miles, as a wide gravelly plain, with high rugged mountains on both sides.

On the morning after my arrival at Sassar, it was snowing slightly at daybreak, and continued to do so till near noon. The snow melted almost immediately on the level ground, but on the mountain-sides it lay all day, down as low as the level of my tent. The afternoon was dull and stormy, but no more snow fell. This unfavourable weather was of less consequence, because I had determined to halt in order to make fresh arrangements for my baggage, being advised not to take any cattle beyond Sassar, the roads in advance being very bad. I afterwards found that they were gravelly, which is more injurious than even rock to the unprotected feet of the Tibetan bullock.

The gravelly sloping hills round my encampment were covered with abundance of vegetation, but few of the species were alpine, and almost all were familiar to me. A species of *Allium*, with purple flowers and broad strap-shaped leaves, was the most plentiful of all. *Thermopsis* was frequent, in fruit; other common plants were species of *Artemisia*, *Cynoglossum*, *Cicer*, and *Draco-*

cephalum. The only new species were a very handsome dark purple *Nepeta,* which grew in large tufts among loose shingle, and a tall *Saussurea,* by far the largest species of the genus which I had found in Tibet, but I believe one of those described from Jacquemont's collections. A species of *Rheum* occurred occasionally on dry stony places, but it was the same which I had found several times before.

On the 15th of August I resumed my journey. The morning was misty, with a few flakes of snow at intervals, and the sky remained overcast all day, with high squalls of wind. My road lay across the Shayuk, but I found it necessary to ascend about half a mile on the high bank before I reached a place where it was possible to descend to its gravelly plain, which was more than half a mile wide, and quite destitute of any kind of vegetation. The river was running in several channels, with an average depth of about a foot and a half; in one place only it was as much as two feet. The current ran with considerable rapidity.

On the opposite side of the plain of the Shayuk, I entered an extremely narrow ravine, bounded by precipices of black slate, down which ran a small stream, which crossed at every turn of the ravine from one side to the other, generally close to the rocky wall, and had to be forded a great number of times. After a mile and a half, the road, suddenly quitting the ravine, turned to the right, and ascended by a steep pathway to a wide, very gently rising plain, bounded on both sides by snowy mountains. This plain was partly grassy, but mostly composed of hard dry clay. In a few spots where snow appeared recently to have lain, the clay was soft and treacherous, sinking under the feet. About a mile's walk over this plain brought me to the highest part of it, beyond which it began to slope to the eastward, at first very gently but afterwards more rapidly. Many large isolated boulders were observed on its surface. It was curious to observe that the gravel produced by the disintegration of the mountains (chiefly, I suppose, by snow-slips in winter) differed in colour on the two sides of the valley, and that the line of demarcation followed very closely the centre of the valley. The northern mountains, being granitic, produced a hard quartzy gravel, while those to the south, which were schistose, contributed a dark-coloured gravel of sharp slaty fragments. On the lower part of the descent, a small rivulet made its appearance in the centre of the plain, and I encamped, after nine and a half miles, close to an open valley of considerable size, whose course seemed to be south-east.

This encamping-ground is called by the Turki merchants Murgai, by the Tibetans, Murgo-Chumik; the former name being probably a corruption of the latter. It was the last place at which I was to expect a sufficiency of fuel, or even, with rare exceptions, of grass for my horse, which, though not often used, I was unwilling to leave behind, lest I should by any accident be disabled from walking. The temperature of boiling water here indicated an elevation of about 15,100 feet, but as the weather was stormy and threatening, this was probably several hundred feet more than the truth. A number of springs appeared to break out of the ground close to my tent, where there was a considerable extent of boggy pasture, much greener than is usual at so great an elevation. A few bushes of *Myricaria elegans* were the only shrubs, but tufts of *Artemisia* and *Eurotia* were sufficiently plentiful to produce an abundance of fuel. In the boggy meadow, a pretty little species of *Primula* was very abundant; the other plants observed were a white *Pedicularis*, two species of *Triglochin*, and some *Carices* and grasses.

The morning of the 16th of August was bright and beautiful, the clouds having been entirely dissipated during the night. The wide valley near which I was encamped descended, as I was informed, to the Shayuk, which it was said to join through a rocky gorge eight or ten miles lower down than Sassar. Along its course the merchants are in the habit of ascending at the season when the valley of the Shayuk is followed all the way from Nubra, which is only practicable in early spring and late in the autumn, at which times that river is fordable throughout. It is a fortunate circumstance for the trade that there is thus a choice of routes, for at these seasons the Sassar pass must be in a great measure blocked up with snow.

On my arrival at Murgai, I had observed that the mountains to the north were very precipitous, and had been puzzled to decide what direction the road might take. On starting, however, I found that it lay along the upward course of the stream which watered the valley before me, and which here issued from the mountains through a very narrow ravine with high precipices on both sides. At first I ascended to the top of a platform of conglomerate which lay at the base of the mountains. The ground was strewed with fragments of limestone, evidently derived from the mountains above; and about half a mile from camp I passed a calcareous spring which had deposited large quantities of tufa throughout the whole of the space between its source and the face of the precipice which overhung the river: the thickness of the incrustation was, in front of the cliff, from six to eight feet. A little further on, the road descended abruptly to the stream, and, after crossing it several times within a few hundred yards, ascended equally abruptly the steep stony slopes on its left bank, at a point where its course, which had previously been nearly north, turned rather suddenly to the eastward. On emerging from the ravine, two small glaciers came in sight almost directly opposite, in branches of a narrow and very deep gorge, which descended from the mountains to the north nearly in the original direction of the ravine. The road ascended to the height of at least 1000 feet, and then proceeded along the steep slopes, alternately ascending and descending over very stony ground, occasionally covered with loose limestone shingle. The stream was visible below, running through a narrow rocky fissure.

After about a mile and a half, the road again descended to the river, now a little wider, with a gravelly channel. Here I found that there were two roads. One of these, for loaded animals, ascended steeply on the north side, to the height of nearly 1000 feet, and again descended very abruptly. The other was in the bed of the stream, which was partially filled up with huge blocks of rock. The stream being almost dry, I took the lower road, which for pedestrians was only objectionable from its great roughness, and because it was necessary to cross the rivulet occasionally. After about a quarter of a mile, the ravine suddenly opened out into a gravelly plain nearly half a mile in width, traversed by numerous branches of the little stream: these were now almost dry, owing to the cloudy weather of the last few days having in a great measure stopped the melting of the glaciers by which they were supplied. Along this open plain I continued for nearly five miles. In one place only it contracted again for a few hundred yards into a gorge full of huge rocky masses heaped one on another, by which it was apparently quite blocked up; this however was avoided by a slight ascent among angular limestone fragments. On descending into the plain again, I observed a very small patch of grassy ground on a bank a few feet above the level of the stream, the only herbage seen during the day. About a mile further on I encamped, after a march of nine miles, on the south side of the plain, on a dry bank elevated four or five feet above its gravelly bed. There was a sudden change in the direction of the valley just at my encamping-ground, its further course being in a direction west of north. The elevation of my tent was very nearly 16,000 feet.

High, rugged, precipitous mountains, with snowy tops, rose on both sides of the road during the whole of this day's journey. The rock throughout the day was limestone, a few thin layers of slate excepted. It varied much in colour, but was generally very dark and highly crystalline, and often contained large masses of white calcareous spar. It was distinctly stratified, and occasionally exhibited obscure traces of what might be fossils, but which were too indistinct to be relied upon. The principal mass of snow seen was nearly due south of my encampment, but this was probably owing to the northerly exposure of the mountains on that side. The vegetation observed during the day was scanty in the extreme; *Eurotia*, a *Saussurea* with very viscid leaves, *Oxytropis chiliophylla*, and *Biebersteinia odora* being almost the only plants on the stony slopes and shingle during the first half of the way. On the gravelly plain there was no vegetation at all, but on its margins a few scattered plants were occasionally to be found, a *Pyrethrum* and two or three *Cruciferæ* being the species noted. The most remarkable plant observed during the day was a species of *Alsine* in dense hemispherical tufts, a foot or more in diameter. This plant (the moss of Moorcroft's visit to Garu, and of other travellers in and on the borders of Tibet) is a common Tibetan plant at very great elevations, 16,000 feet being perhaps not far from its lowest level*.

On the 17th my road lay entirely along the gravelly plain in a direction always considerably to the west of north. The plain gradually narrowed as I advanced, and came to an end by contracting into a rocky ravine, just as I halted for the day. The mountains on the left were still very lofty; one glacier was seen on that side. On the right the mountains were lower and quite without snow, but extremely rugged and rocky. The slope

* Excellent specimens of this singular alpine plant, each tuft of which must, I think, represent the growth of centuries, may be seen in the Museum of the Royal Gardens at Kew, collected by Dr. Hooker in Eastern Tibet.

of the valley was scarcely perceptible, but I found at the end of my day's journey, which amounted to twelve miles, that I had risen above 700 feet, the height of my encampment being a little more than 16,700 feet. The day was bright and sunny, and the stream, which, in the morning was quite insignificant, not three feet wide and scarcely ankle-deep, had increased much by the afternoon, and had become of a dirty red colour. It was twenty feet wide, and a foot and a half deep, where I crossed it just before halting. The vegetation was still more scanty than the day before, though most of the plants then noted were again seen occasionally. Small tufts of a little *Stipa* were not uncommon, constituting almost the only food for cattle, as patches of green grass, a few feet in diameter, were only seen twice during the day. Two very small *Saussureæ* formed dense tufted masses on the surface of the ground, and a little rose-coloured *Astragalus* spread itself prostrate over the gravel; indeed, this mode of growth seemed to be characteristic either of the climate or soil, as I found, though rarely, a species of *Myricaria*, with short thick wiry branches lying flat on the ground and spreading into patches a yard in diameter.

Not far from the point where the direction of the valley changed so suddenly, the blue or greyish massive but brittle limestone of the higher mountains gave place to a rock of a very different appearance. This was also a limestone, perfectly white, or with a very faint yellowish or greyish tinge, and either quite amorphous, with a saccharine texture, and often honeycombed, or composed of a congeries of very minute crystals. Occasionally, but rarely, rolled pebbles were seen in it. No traces of stratification were anywhere discoverable, in which respect it differed very strikingly from the limestone of the previous day, in which lines of stratification, much contorted, were well seen in many sections exposed at different heights. This remarkable limestone formed the rock on both sides of the gravelly plain during the greater part of the day's journey. In one place only metamorphic slate was seen below it, dipping at a high angle to the north-east. The limestone was extremely brittle, and the cliffs terminated above in sharp pinnacles of the most fantastic shapes, while at the base they were covered with heaps of angular debris*. A coarse conglomerate replaced the limestone during the last mile previous to my encamping.

On the 18th of August, after following for a few hundred yards the course of the stream through a narrow rocky gorge, the road turned abruptly to the right, up a dry stony ravine, ascending rather rapidly. The coarse conglomerate of the lower part of this ravine was succeeded by a coarse sandstone, and that again by an incoherent alluvial conglomerate with a clayey matrix. After a short distance, the ravine widened out into a narrow, gravelly, moderately steep valley, with low rounded hills on either side. By degrees, as I increased my elevation, superb snowy mountains came in sight to the south-west, and on attaining the top of the ascent an open, gravelly, somewhat undulating plain lay before me, while behind a grand snowy range was seen in perfection, forming

* I have no conjecture to offer regarding the age or nature of this very remarkable rock.

apparently a continuous chain, with a direction from south-east to north-west. The snow was to the eye perfectly continuous in both directions as far as the mountains were visible, and appeared everywhere to lie on the mountain-sides to three and four thousand feet below their tops. As I had passed through this apparent chain of mountains without rising above 16,000 feet, the continuity of the snowy mass was of course a deception. Many very lofty peaks rose above the others at intervals. The height of the more distant ones I could not venture to estimate, but I felt at the time fully convinced that a very high peak, just opposite to me, and distant, according to bearings taken afterwards, about ten miles (in a direct line) from the edge of the plain, was 6000 or 7000 feet higher than the ground on which I stood, or at least 24,000 feet above the level of the sea. I do not wish that any great degree of confidence should be placed on this estimate, but I think it right that I should state my impression at the time, formed without any wish to exaggerate.

The stream along which I had ascended during the two last days lay in a deep ravine far below the level of the plain. Its source was evidently not far distant, and it issued no doubt from a large glacier at the head of the gorge, though the slight upward slope of the plain to the west prevented me from seeing its precise origin. In a northerly direction the plain appeared to extend for six or seven miles, and beyond it lay several ranges of mountains running from east to west, but only very moderately patched with snow. Eastward the plain diminished slightly in elevation for four or five miles, at which distance there was a low range of hills, and immediately at their foot a small stream apparently running to the northward. Beyond these low hills were a number of lofty black peaks to the northward of the great mass of snow, on the further side of which the country probably dips to the eastward in the direction of Khoten. Every one of my guides positively denied the existence of any road in that direction; afraid, perhaps, that I might attempt to proceed by it; for I learned afterwards, on my return to Le, from a merchant of Yarkand, that there was an unfrequented path by which Khoten might be reached, if the Chinese authorities were willing to permit it to be used.

My road lay across the open plain in a direction very little west of north. The surface of the ground was covered with a few boulders and many small pebbles, for the most part rolled, and very various in composition; granite, greenstones of many sorts, amygdaloid, limestone, and different-coloured slates, being all seen. Many of these were encrusted with a calcareous concretion, and the whole plain had the appearance of having formerly been the bed of a lake. Skeletons and scattered bones of horses indicated with great exactness the road across this arid tract, which seemed to be almost destitute of either animal life or vegetation. The only living beings seen were a few ravens, a hoopoe, and a small bird somewhat like a sparrow. Tufts of the moss-like *Alsine*, referred to on the 17th, were the only vegetation, except in the bed of a little rivulet near the middle of the plain, which produced a few specimens of *Saussurea* and *Sibbaldia*. This streamlet rose in a large patch of snow about half a mile to the westward, and ran towards the east, turning afterwards nearly due north along the foot of a low range of hills mentioned above. The elevation of its bed, which was the lowest part of the tableland in the direction in which I crossed it, was 17,300 feet, and the lowest part of the plain was immediately under the low hills to the eastward, where it probably was about 17,000 feet.

There was no snow on the plain, except one patch close to its highest part, in which the little rivulet had its source, and a very few remnants on the shady side of a low undulating ridge, which crosses it near its northern border. After about five miles, having been ascending very gradually since leaving the banks of the stream, I passed through an opening between two low gravelly hills, and found myself looking down upon a wide valley, into which I descended very gradually along a dry ravine. Passing a small patch of swampy, grassy ground, at which I left my horse with a servant till my return, as there was no food for him further on, I arrived, about two miles from the point at which the valley just came in sight, at a small river about thirty feet wide and ankle-deep, running from east to west. According to the information of my guides, this was the river which runs past Sassar,—in fact, the Shayuk. None of them had followed its course, but they assured me that there was no doubt of the accuracy of their statement, which indeed is confirmed by the fact (which I mention on the authority of Yarkand merchants) that formerly travellers used to ascend the Shayuk from Sassar, in order to reach the Karakoram pass, instead of pursuing the circuitous route by which I travelled; but that about ten or twelve years ago the glaciers above Sassar descended so low as entirely to prevent any one passing in that direction, for which reason it became necessary to adopt a new road*.

The course of the Shayuk was visible for several miles, running nearly due west. Beyond that distance, it disappeared among rocky hills. Fording the river, I ascended a steep bank, to get upon a stony platform, over which I proceeded in a northerly direction, gradually approaching a small stream which came from the north to join the Shayuk. Passing a low rounded hill to the right, I descended after about two miles into the ravine excavated by this little stream, and, crossing it, encamped under low limestone rocks on its right bank after a march of twelve miles. I did not ascertain the elevation of this halting-ground, but, from the result of an experiment made at a place which appeared nearly midway (in point of elevation) between it and the bed of the Shayuk, where I got a boiling-point, indicating an elevation of 17,000 feet, I estimate the bed of the river at 16,800 feet, and my encamping-ground of the 18th at 17,200 feet. The plain all round seemed destitute of vegetation, so that, as on the two last days, there was a great scarcity of fuel, which had to be collected from a distance of many miles; and consisted only of the roots of a small bushy *Artemisia* or *Tanacetum*, which rose three or four inches above the ground. During these

* The itinerary of Mir Izzet Ullah shows that at the time of his journey from Le to Yarkand the direct road up the Shayuk was still open.

three days, I suffered very considerably from the effects of the rarefaction of the air, being never free from a dull headache, which was increased on the slightest exertion.

On the 19th of August, leaving my tent standing, I started to visit the Karakoram pass, the limit of my journey to the northward. The country round my halting-place was open, except to the north, where a stream descended through a narrow valley from a range of hills, the highest part of which was apparently about 3000 feet above me. All the rivers had formed for themselves depressions in the platform of gravel which was spread over the plain. At first I kept on the south bank of the river close to which I had halted, but about a mile from camp I crossed a large tributary which descended from the south-west, and soon after, turning round the rocky termination of a low range of hills, entered a narrow valley which came from a little west of north-west. At the foot of the rocky point of the range were three very small huts, built against the rock as a place of shelter for travellers, in case of stormy or snowy weather; and bones of horses were here scattered about the plain in greater profusion than usual.

I ascended this valley for about six miles: its width varied from 200 yards to about half a mile, gradually widening as I ascended. The slope was throughout gentle. An accumulation of alluvium frequently formed broad and gently sloping banks, which were cut into cliffs by the river. Now and then large tracts covered with glacial boulders were passed over; and several small streams were crossed, descending from the northern mountains through narrow ravines. About eight miles from my starting-point the road left the bank of the stream, and began to ascend obliquely and gradually on the sides of the hills. The course of the valley beyond where I left it continued unaltered, sloping gently up to a large snow-bed, which covered the side of a long sloping ridge four or five miles off. After a mile, I turned suddenly to the right, and, ascending very steeply over fragments of rock for four or five hundred yards, I found myself on the top of the Karakoram pass—a rounded ridge connecting two hills which rose somewhat abruptly to the height of perhaps 1000 feet above me. The height of the pass was 18,200 feet, the boiling-point of water being 180·8°, and the temperature of the air about 50°. Towards the north, much to my disappointment, there was no distant view. On that side the descent was steep for about 500 yards, beyond which distance a small streamlet occupied the middle of a very gently sloping valley, which curved gradually to the left, and disappeared behind a stony ridge at the distance of half a mile. The hills opposite to me were very abrupt, and rose a little higher than the pass; they were quite without snow, nor was there any on the pass itself, though large patches lay on the shoulder of the hill to the right. To the south, on the opposite side of the valley which I had ascended, the mountains, which were sufficiently high to exclude entirely all view of the lofty snowy mountain seen the day before, were round-topped and covered with snow. Vegetation was entirely wanting on the top of the pass, but the loose shingle with which it was covered was unfavourable to the growth of plants, otherwise, no doubt, lichens at least would have been seen. Large ravens were circling about overhead, apparently quite unaffected by the rarity of the atmosphere, as they seemed to fly with just as much ease as at the level of the sea.

The great extent of the modern alluvial deposit concealed in a great measure the ancient rocks. At my encampment a ridge of very hard limestone, dipping at a high angle, skirted the stream. Further up the valley a hard slate occurred, and in another place a dark blue slate, containing much iron pyrites, and crumbling rapidly when exposed to the atmosphere. Fragments of this rock were scattered over the plain in all states of decay. On the crest of the pass the rock *in situ* was limestone, showing obscure traces of fossils, but too indistinct to be determined; the shingle, which was scattered over the ridge, was chiefly a brittle black clay-slate.

On my return no plants were met with till I had almost reached the bank of the stream. The first species which occurred was a small purple-flowered *Crucifera* (*Parrya exscapa* of Meyer). Throughout the day the number of flowering plants observed was seventeen, of which three were grasses, three *Saussureæ*, and two *Cruciferæ;* there was also one species of each of the following genera, *Aster*, *Nepeta*, *Gymnandra*, *Sedum*, *Lychnis*, *Potentilla*, and *Phaca;* the dense-tufted *Alsine*, and a shrubby *Artemisia* with yellow flowers, complete the number. The only animals seen, besides ravens, were a bird about the size of a sparrow, a bright metallic-coloured carrion-fly, and a small dusky butterfly. Returning by the same road, I arrived at my tent a little after sunset, the distance from the top of the pass being about ten miles.

While travelling at these great elevations the weather was uniformly serene and beautiful. There was but little wind, and the sky was bright and cloudless. At night the cold was severe, and the edges of the streams were in the morning always frozen. On my return towards Sassar I found that the bright sunny weather which had continued since the 16th, had made a great alteration in the state of the stream in the wide gravelly valley along which the road ran. It was now impetuous and muddy, increasing considerably towards the afternoon, when it ran in several channels, which were not always easily fordable. In some places the gravel was throughout the whole width of the plain saturated with water, and gave way under the feet, so that it became necessary to ascend on the stony sloping banks on one side or other, instead of following the centre of the valley. At Murgai, on the evening of the 23rd of August, just after sunset, I felt three slight shocks of an earthquake. On that day the weather again became dull, and on the morning of the 24th there was a slight fall of snow for about an hour.

The remarkable open plain to the south of the Karakoram pass occupies a deep concavity in the great chain of the Kouenlun, which there appears to form a curve, the convexity of which looks northward. The main range to the eastward was distinctly visible, forming a range of snowless, but certainly very lofty, black peaks beyond the sources of the most eastern branch of the Shayuk; while the heavily-snowed mountains, the summits of which were seen further east, were probably also a part of the axis of the chain, which apparently bends round the sources of the river of Khoten, or of some stream draining the northern flanks of the Kouenlun. To the westward, no peaks rose behind the snowy ridge which terminated the western branch of the Shayuk a little west of the Karakoram pass, beyond which the surface probably dips, while the axis of the Kouenlun bends to the southward, towards the glaciers of the Nubra river.

In crossing the open plain on my return towards Sassar, I had the splendid snowy peaks to the south-west always in view, and was able to form a tolerable estimate of their appearance and elevation. The range was very heavily snowed, and from the lateness of the season but little additional thaw could be expected. What seemed the highest peak was very near, and its position could be determined by bearings with little risk of error. It rose abruptly in the midst of a great mass of snow, which filled the hollows and slopes of the range all around. The surface of the plain over which I was travelling sloped very gently up to the westward, and partly concealed the lower edge of the perpetual snow on the mountains behind, the limit of which was, I think, between 17,500 and 18,000 feet. To the northward and eastward the snow-line was certainly much higher. Here and there, where there was shade, there were patches below 18,000 feet, but even up to 20,000 feet there was no continuous snow. As the source of the snow-fall on these mountains is no doubt the Indian Ocean to the south-west, the gradual rise of the snow-level in advancing north-east, and the occurrence of the highest peaks, and of the greatest mass of snow on branches of the chain, and not on its main axis, are quite in accordance with what is usually the case throughout every part of the Himalaya.

The occurrence of a nearly level plain, six or eight miles in diameter, with a mean elevation of not less than 17,300 feet, is certainly very remarkable. The ridge or watershed of the plain appeared to me parallel to the deep ravine, excavated by the stream along which I had travelled on the 17th of August, and at no great distance from it, as the descent was abrupt. All the northern and western part of this level tract was composed of loosely cohering matters, and was possibly of lacustrine origin; but a much more accurate acquaintance with the outline, structure, and elevation of the plain will be necessary before any certain conclusion can be drawn as to its age or origin.

Before leaving Sassar, I visited the glaciers which descend into the valley of the Shayuk, a little to the north of that place. The path at first lay along the high platform on which I was encamped, which was precipitous towards the Shayuk; it afterwards descended to the level of the river, close to which I travelled for some distance over enormous boulders. The bluff ends of two glaciers were seen high above at the top of the precipitous alluvial bank, and after a walk of upwards of three miles, I arrived at a most superb glacier, which, descending a broad and deep valley in the mountains, and latterly in the alluvial platform, entered the bed of the Shayuk at the bottom of a deep bend, and fairly crossed the river, which flowed out below the ice. On the opposite side of the river, the mountains were precipitous a few hundred feet from the water's edge, but the stream of ice did not extend to the foot of the precipice, but stopped a very few feet up the opposite bank. I could of course only see the position of the ice at the edge of the glacier: how far it extended in the centre I could not tell.

The glacier was extremely rugged, being covered with huge sharp pinnacles of ice, and I was obliged to ascend a long way parallel to its side before I could find a place where it could be crossed. Near its lower extremity it rose high above the surface of the plain, and sloped rapidly down to the river: its sides were there scarped and inaccessible, but higher up it lay in a deep hollow in the alluvial conglomerate. A moment's reflection showed how impossible it was for clay and boulders to resist the friction of such an enormous mass; still I was much pleased to observe the glacier buried, as it were, in a groove of its own forming, from the light which was thereby thrown on the origin of the many broad, shallow, flat-bottomed valleys which occasionally occur in the modern alluvial and lacustrine formations in all parts of Tibet, as for instance at Karsar in Nubra, and at Bazgo below Le. An ancient moraine, deposited at a period when the glacier must have been much more bulky than it now is, skirted the edge of the high bank of alluvium, and prevented the ice from being seen till close at hand, and then only by mounting on the top of the pile of boulders. Down this moraine, which on the face towards the glacier was extremely steep and perhaps sixty feet high, I descended to the surface of the present moraine. The descent required great caution, many of the blocks being loose and easily displaced. When I had reached the surface of the glacier, the passage was not difficult. About a quarter of its width on each side was occupied by blocks of stone; the centre was almost entirely ice, extremely irregular, and here and there a little fissured. The pathway, which was only marked by the footsteps of two men whom I had sent the day before to select a place for crossing, at one time ascended to the top of a ridge of ice, at another descended into a deep hollow. At the time I crossed (about eleven A.M.) numerous streams of water had begun to flow in furrows on the surface of the ice. The whole width was close upon half a mile, and on the north side I ascended a steep moraine similar to that which I had previously descended.

From the top of the bank on which the moraine rested, a second glacier came in sight at the distance of a mile. My exploring party reported that they had been unable to find a point at which this glacier could be crossed, and as from the appearance of the mountains behind I felt certain that after crossing it I should only arrive at a third, I did not long persevere in trying to find a passage, but descended to its extremity in order to see whether or not I could walk round it, as it did not appear to enter the water. At the bottom of the valley it spread out in a fan-shaped manner to the width of at least a mile; perhaps indeed much more, for as I failed in getting round it, I was unable to ascertain precisely. At its south-east corner, where it was nearly a hundred yards from the river, a considerable stream, white with suspended mud, was rushing out from beneath an arched vault of ice, even before sunrise. To avoid fording this icy stream, the margins of which were thickly frozen, I crossed with a good deal of difficulty an angle of the end of the glacier. On its surface I found several small moraines, which had sunk down into grooves ten or fifteen feet deep, and had therefore been invisible from outside. Further progress on the ice was stopped by cliffs which were not accessible without ladders, so that I had to descend to the bank of the Shayuk. I walked along between the ice and the river, till my advance was stopped by the glacier fairly projecting into the water in such a manner that I could not see anything of what lay beyond. The icy wall being quite inaccessible, I could not get upon the surface of the glacier to attempt to advance in that way, nor could I ford the river, which was very deep.

The terminal cliff of the glacier varied in height from fifteen to thirty feet, and a talus of large stones lay in front, evidently deposited by it. Indeed, while I was there I saw several small stones which projected from the face of the cliff, drop out by the melting of the ice in which they were imbedded. Many cavities were seen in the ice, from which large stones must have dropped out no longer ago than the day before, and the stones which corresponded in size to them were seen lying close at hand. Before I left the front of the glacier, the heat of the sun having become considerable, rapid thaw had commenced; rills of water trickled down its face in every direction, and the sound of falling stones was to be heard on all sides. Now and then a report as loud as that of a cannon was heard, caused, as I supposed, by the fall of a very large boulder from one of the smaller glaciers, which stopped abruptly at the top of the high cliff of alluvium.

Before quitting finally these magnificent glaciers, I ascended to a height on the mountain-side in order to see whether or not there was any lake in sight corresponding to that laid down, from information, by Mr. Vigne as Nubra or Khundan Chu. The mountains were very steep and stony, and were covered above 16,000 feet with snow, which had fallen in a storm a few days before; I did not, therefore, get up to any great elevation, probably not beyond 16,500 feet, but at that height I could see nothing of the river beyond the second glacier, though its course through the mountains could be traced distinctly enough. It is, however, highly improbable that any permanent lake exists. Such could, I think, only be formed by the stoppage of the river by a glacier, an obstruction which could only be temporary, and would inevitably be followed by a terrific inundation, such as is known repeatedly to have devastated the valley of the Shayuk.

It had been my original intention, on my return from Karakoram, to follow the course of the Shayuk all the way from Sassar to Nubra, but on my return to the former place after visiting the pass, I found that there was no probability of the road along the river being practicable for at least three weeks, the depth of the stream, which requires frequently to be forded, being still much too great; I was therefore reluctantly compelled to return by the same route as that by which I had reached Sassar. Early in September, I found the crops in Nubra ripe, the barley being mostly cut; buckwheat and a few fields of millet, however, were still quite green. The Shayuk had very considerably diminished in size: one branch which in July had been three feet deep was quite dry on the 6th of September. On the 11th of that month I crossed the pass above Le, the state of which was a good deal altered. The little lake, which on the 20th of July was still frozen over, was now free of ice, nor was there any snow, except a very few small patches, below the steep snow-bank on the northern side. The snow, which had covered this steep descent, had melted away, exposing a mass of ice, which was not crossed without a good deal of difficulty and some little risk. Loaded cattle were unable to get to the top of the pass till the afternoon. The snow on the south face had almost entirely gone.

I reached Le just in time to escape some very unsettled weather, during which snow fell on the mountains down to about 13,000 feet. This was ushered in by very high wind, blowing in gusts from all points of the compass. Heavy clouds formed, but always high: on the 14th there was a good deal of thunder, and during the following night a smart shower of rain, which lasted about an hour.

The inhabitants were busy with the operations of harvest. A coarse knife or rude sickle was employed to cut the wheat and barley as close to the ground as possible; they were then tied into large bundles, each sufficient for one load, which were carried (usually by women) to the threshing-floors, not without considerable loss, from the ripeness of the ears and the great bulk of the loads, which were rubbed against every obstacle, particularly the narrow walls of the pathways between the fields. The grain was trodden out of the ear by cattle and asses, all muzzled, on small threshing-floors made of clay beaten hard. It was then winnowed, by being gently shaken out of flat vessels held as high as possible above the ground.

On the 15th of September I left Le for Kashmir. For five days my route was the same as that by which I had travelled in July. On the fourth day I reached Kalatze on the Indus, and on the 19th of September I encamped at the village of Lama-Yuru, close to which the road from Zanskar joins that along which I proposed to travel towards Dras. In the valley of the Indus a great part of the vegetation was already destroyed by the night frosts; *Chenopodiaceæ* were now the most numerous family, and these were rapidly ripening their seeds. In the narrow ravine of the Wandla river, on the ascent to Lama-Yuru, I found a few plants indicative of lower and hotter regions than those in which I had lately been travelling: a little wiry *Lactuca* with decurrent leaves, a spathulate-leaved *Statice*, and a small *Hyoscyamus*, all plants of the neighbourhood of Iskardo, were those which I noted.

On the 20th of September I crossed the Phatu pass, stated by Moorcroft to be 14,000 feet above the sea, but which Major Cunningham has ascertained to be only about 13,500 feet. The discrepancy is probably owing to some error in Moorcroft's manuscripts, from which the elevations given in his work were calculated by Professor Wilson. In the neighbourhood of Lama-Yuru lacustrine clay occurs in great abundance, and the ascent to the summit of this pass was gentle, up a gravelly valley, which was full of alluvium, almost to the very summit. The pass did not nearly attain the elevation requisite for alpine vegetation, still the flora was a good deal altered; two large-flowered thistles, *Caragana versicolor*, and several species of *Umbelliferæ* were observed, none of which had occurred in the hills to the north of the Indus; the prickly *Statice* was also common, but the *Chenopodiaceæ* of the Indus valley had entirely disappeared. The descent along the Kanji river to Karbu, at which I encamped, was long and gradual, down a wide valley skirted by gently sloping hills, which, at some distance on the left, rose into high mountains, but on the right attained only a moderate elevation, the Indus being at no great distance. Alluvium occurred throughout the descent, latterly indurated into a coarse conglomerate.

From Karbu I marched on the 21st to Molbil, crossing the Namika pass. The previous night had been very threatening, with violent wind, and at daybreak all the hills around were covered with snow; it was still snowing slightly, but none lay in the valley, and before nine o'clock it cleared, and the remainder of the forenoon was tolerably fine. For two miles I followed the banks of the Kanji river; afterwards the road turned to the left to ascend a clayey valley, to the rounded summit of a ridge separating that river from the Pashkyum on the left. The pass has been determined by Major Cunningham, who crossed it in October, 1847, to be 12,900 feet above the sea. The descent was long, but not rapid after the first mile. The upper part was desert, but lower down villages were frequent and cultivation extensive. At first the rocks were clay-slate, but these were replaced in the lower part by a hard limestone; alluvium was everywhere plentiful, forming, near Molbil, table-topped platforms of indurated conglomerate, horizontally stratified, and faced towards the stream by scarped cliffs. The afternoon was again stormy, and a good deal of rain fell during the night.

Next day I made a long march to Pashkyum, following the course of the river of that name. The descent was very gradual, and the road varied much in character, the valley being sometimes open, at other times narrow and rocky. The villages increased in numbers as the elevation diminished, and latterly for several miles cultivation was continuous. Pashkyum is not more than 8600 feet above the sea, and accordingly the season was much less advanced than it had been three and four thousand feet higher, the weather being much milder, and the summer heat no doubt much more considerable than in the neighbourhood of Le. The crops had long been cut, except the buckwheat, the fields of which were however quite ripe; the plants were being plucked up by the roots and laid down separately in the fields to dry, previous to removal to the threshing-floor.

A remarkable change had taken place in the appearance of the country during this day's journey. The banks of the river were frequently shaded with immense willows, and the trees of the cultivated lands were numerous and of great size. Many new forms of plants were also seen, though the general character of the flora was unaltered. Shrubby *Artemisiæ* were extremely plentiful, and the *Perowskia, Ballota, Echinops*, and *Iris* of the Indus valley were very abundant. The new plants were all species of Kashmir or Iskardo, such as *Verbascum Thapsus*, *Lappa*, *Valeriana*, *Swertia*, and *Gentiana Moorcroftiana*. *Trifolium repens* and *fragiferum* grew in the pastures close to the river, and tropical species of *Setaria* and *Amaranthus* were common weeds in the corn-fields.

In the immediate neighbourhood of Pashkyum the rocks consist of coarse-grained grey or white sandstones, often containing small water-worn pebbles, and alternating with dark crumbling pyritiferous shales. These rocks, which dip to the east or south-east, at an angle of not more than 15°, rise on the north side of the valley to the summit of a long sloping ridge, which appears to overhang the Indus. As these sandstones and shales contained, so far as I could observe, no fossils, their age is a matter of complete uncertainty. They were quite independent of the modern lacustrine formation, patches of which, perfectly horizontally stratified, and therefore unconformable to the other, were seen in several places resting on the sandstone. These sandstones perhaps reach as far as the Indus, but I was not able to determine how far they extended to the southward, in which direction high and rugged mountains, now covered with snow, skirted the valley at a distance of a few miles.

On the 23rd of September, I followed the Pashkyum river to its junction with that of Dras. Crossing, at starting, to the left bank of the river, the road lay for a mile through cultivated lands; it then ascended to a platform of alluvium, which blocked up the valley, while the river disappeared in a narrow ravine far to the right. Five miles from Pashkyum, I descended very abruptly from this elevated plain, to the village of Kargil, where the Pashkyum river is joined by a large stream from Suru, called by Moorcroft the Kartse; which I crossed by a good wooden bridge, close to a small fort, occupied by a Thannadar with a small party of soldiers. The cultivated lands of Kargil, which is elevated about 8300 feet, are extensive and well wooded; but immediately below, the valley becomes narrow and rocky, and continues so for more than a mile, till the stream joins the Dras river. Nearly due south of Kargil the stratified rocks of the mountains are replaced by igneous rocks, and the point of contact of the two is well marked on the precipitous face of a lofty peak. At first the igneous rock was dark and resembling greenstone, but it soon changed to granite, which, as I had observed in April, occurs everywhere in the valley of Dras, below Karbu.

I encamped on the right bank of the Dras river, about a mile above the village of Hardas. Henceforward my route was the same as I had travelled in April. On the 24th I travelled to Tashgong, and on the 25th I arrived at Dras. In most parts of the valley I found a great deal of alluvium, but I saw none of the fine clay which is characteristic of the purely lacustrine strata above the village of Bilergu, where I had observed it in April. Gravelly conglomerate was everywhere the prevailing form,—sometimes indurated, but generally soft and shingly. Most of these deposits were unstratified, but distinct stratification was far from uncommon. The alluvium often capped low hills in the open valley many hundred feet above the bed of the river, and it was observed at frequent intervals in every part of the valley, from the junction of the Pashkyum river to Dras itself.

The great extent and remarkable forms of alluvium which I had seen in the district through which I had travelled, between Kalatze and Dras, induced me to note with care the position and composition of the alluvial beds of the Dras valley. The known low elevation of the Zoji pass, between Dras and Kashmir, which is only 11,300 feet above the sea, made the great extent and continuity of these deposits very remarkable, and with difficulty explicable, unless on the supposition of the existence of a series of lakes separated from one another by extensive accumulations of alluvium, now to a great extent removed by denudation. The lacustrine clays of lower Dras, about Ulding, appear continuous with those of the Indus valley about Tarkata, but the clays of Pashkyum, which are separated from them by a very thick mass of alluvium, which occupies that part of the Dras and Pashkyum rivers immediately above the junction of the two, may have been deposited in an isolated lake. Further east again, at Lamayuru, there are beds of pure clay as high as the summit of the Zoji pass, so that the alluvial beds of the upper part of the Phatu ridge must have separated the lake in which these were deposited from the more western waters, which (it may be conjectured) at the same time covered the whole of the valley of Molbil and Pashkyum.

The vegetation of Dras was still very Tibetan, but transitional forms were becoming frequent. The *Chenopodiaceæ* (except *Eurotia*) had all disappeared, but *Artemisiæ* and *Umbelliferæ* were very abundant. The new forms were all Kashmirian, and indicated a considerable increase of humidity: a small white-flowered balsam was observed not far from Hardas, and *Prunella*, *Thymus Serpyllum*, an *Achillea*, *Senecio*, *Galium*, and *Silene inflata* were all seen below the fort of Dras. At that place the harvest was but just over; indeed, a field or two of wheat were still uncut.

On the 26th of September, I marched to Maten, along a road which, in April, had been entirely covered with deep snow. Part of the road was rocky, but in general the valley was open. During this day's journey, a very great change took place in the vegetation. Hitherto, Kashmirian plants had been the exception, the greater part of the species being Tibetan; to-day the reverse was the case, most of the plants seen being those common in the comparatively moist climate of Kunawar, or species new to me, but belonging to families or genera which inhabit a more humid climate than Tibet. Groves of dwarf willows lined the banks of the stream, and nearly sixty species of plants not observed in Tibet were collected during the day. *Vitis*, *Aconitum*, *Hypericum*, *Vernonia*, a prickly juniper, *Convallaria*, and *Tulipa*, may be selected as illustrative of the greatness of the change, which was particularly interesting from its suddenness. Numerous Tibetan forms no doubt still lingered, but principally such as extend into Kashmir. At Maten the barley was still uncut, notwithstanding that it is upwards of a thousand feet lower than Le, at which place harvest was nearly over at the time of my departure.

There can be no doubt that the sudden alteration in

the character of the vegetation is due to the great depression in the chain separating Tibet from Kashmir, at the Zoji pass, which is far below the usual level of the lowest parts of these mountains. The access of a great amount of humidity, which would have been condensed if the moisture-bringing winds had been obliged to pass over a lofty chain, makes the autumn partially rainy, and frequently cloudy, thereby diminishing the action of the sun's rays, and lowering the mean temperature of the summer.

On the 27th of September, I crossed the pass of Zoji La, which had now a very different aspect from that which it had presented in April. From Maten the road lay up a wide open valley with a scarcely perceptible ascent, generally along the edge of a small stream, but occasionally on the slope of the hill-sides. The valley was flat and often swampy; but the mountains on both sides, more particularly on the left, were high and abrupt, not unfrequently precipitous. On that side there were in most of the ravines large patches of snow, and in one there was a fine glacier, which stopped abruptly within a hundred yards of the main valley. Latterly a few patches of snow lay even in the open valley. The vegetation was almost entirely Kashmirian, not more than six or seven out of about 110 species being otherwise; the hill-sides were covered with brushwood, at first of willow and prickly juniper, but latterly principally of birch.

Five or six miles from Maten, the main branch of the stream was found to descend from a narrow ravine on the left, at the head of which there was perhaps a glacier. In the valley along which the road lay, there was scarcely any water in the bed of the stream, and about a mile further on, without any increase in the inclination, I came to a large patch of dirty snow, beyond which there was a very evident slope to the southward. The boiling-point of water here indicated an elevation of 11,300 feet. A few hundred yards further, I arrived at a large pond (it could hardly be called a lake), into which a very small rill of water was trickling from the north, while from the opposite end a stream ran towards the south. This little lake was not, as I had expected, on the crest of the pass, but undoubtedly on the Kashmirian side of it.

Beyond the lake, the descent became steep, and the valley contracted into a rocky ravine, full of snow, under which the little stream disappeared. The road was at first on the left side of the valley, but crossed on the snow at the commencement of the contracted part, and ascended rather abruptly a steep hill on the right through a very pretty grove of birch. The top of this steep ascent is usually considered by travellers as the pass, and is the place to which the name Zoji La properly belongs. The point of separation of the waters must of course, for geographical purposes, be considered as the actual pass, but this ridge, which, if not actually higher, is at all events on a level with it, and has in addition a steep ascent on both sides, has not unnaturally had that honour assigned to it. On reaching the shoulder of the ridge, the valley of Baltal came in sight, presenting, in the words of Moorcroft, "as if by magic, a striking contrast in its brown mountains and dark forests of tall pines to the bare rocks and few stunted willows to which we had so long been accustomed." The sight of a forest is certainly a great source of gratification to a traveller who has been long in Tibet; but the pleasing effect of the view from the Zoji pass is not owing merely to contrast; as the traveller looks down upon the bed of Sind river, more than 2000 feet below, and the forest in the valley is not too dense, but interspersed with open glades, while beyond rise high mountains tipped with snow. I do not think that I have anywhere in the Himalaya seen a more beautiful scene than that which then lay before me; but the effect was enhanced by the recollection of the appearance of the same spot in April, when the whole landscape was covered with snow, and I descended from the summit of the pass on a snow-bank which filled up the now inaccessible ravine, on account of which I was obliged to make a long detour. The descent was extremely abrupt, through a pretty wood, down to a log hut built for the accommodation of travellers a few hundred yards from the river, at an elevation of 9,200 feet.

The flora of the Sind valley at Baltal was very rich: the forest consisted chiefly of pine, poplar (*P. ciliata*), birch, and sycamore, intermixed with underwood of *Ribes, Berberis, Viburnum, Lonicera,* and *Salix*. The herbaceous vegetation had all that excessive luxuriance which characterizes the subalpine forests of the Himalaya at the end of the rainy season. Gigantic *Compositæ, Labiatæ, Ranunculaceæ,* and *Umbelliferæ* were the prevailing forms. There were several large patches of snow in the bed of the lateral torrent which descended from Zoji La, as low down as the log hut; and it was not a little curious to observe, that in spots from which the snow had only recently melted, the willows were just beginning to expand their buds, and the cherry, rhubarb, *Thalictrum*, *Anemone*, *Fragaria*, and other plants of early spring, were in full flower.

In descending the Sind valley towards Kashmir, my route was the same by which I had travelled in April. The mountains on the left were extremely precipitous and heavily snowed, and in a ravine a little below Sonamarg a glacier descended almost to 9000 feet. The lower part of the valley was one sheet of cultivation, chiefly of rice, which was almost ripe. In the neighbourhood of Kashmir, where I arrived on the 5th of October, the season of vegetation was almost at an end; species of *Nepeta*, *Eryngium*, *Daucus*, *Centaurea*, *Carpesium*, and several *Artemisiæ* being the most remarkable of the herbaceous plants remaining. In the lake there were vast groves of *Nelumbium* leaves, but the flowers and fruit were both past; *Salvinia* was everywhere floating in great abundance; while the other aquatic plants were species of *Bidens*, *Stachys*, *Mentha*, *Scutellaria*, *Hippuris*, and *Typha*, all European or closely resembling European forms.

Besides rice, which constitutes the staple crop of the valley, the principal grains cultivated in autumn appeared to be different kinds of millet, and a good deal of maize; Indian species of *Phaseolus* also were common, now nearly ripe. The wheat and barley, which are much earlier, were already above ground. I saw a few fields of *Sesamum* (the *Til* of India), and in drier spots a good deal of cotton, which was being picked by hand, but appeared a poor stunted crop, much neglected.

On the high platforms between Pampur and Avantipura the saffron was in flower, and its young leaves were just shooting up. This crop seems a very remunerative one to the Raja, who retains the monopoly in his own hands, compelling the cultivators to sell the produce to him at a fixed price. The bulbs are allowed to remain in the ground throughout the year, and continue in vigour for eight or ten years, after which the produce diminishes so much in quantity that the beds are broken up, and the bulbs separated and replanted. The flowers are picked towards the end of October, and carried into the town of Kashmir, where the stigmas are extracted.

Another very important product of Kashmir is hemp, which grows spontaneously along the banks of the river, forming dense thickets often twelve and fifteen feet in height, and almost impenetrable. It is only used in the manufacture of an intoxicating drink, and for smoking; and the plant is preserved entire, in store-houses, in the town of Kashmir, till required for consumption.

From Kashmir I proceeded towards the plains of the Punjab by the same route by which I had travelled in May. During my absence in Tibet, the second Sikh war had broken out, and as it was then at its height, it was not easy to reach the British territories. I was therefore detained a good while, first in Kashmir, and afterwards at Jamu, and did not reach Lahore till the 16th of December.

CHAPTER XV.

General description of Tibet—Systems of mountains—Trans-Sutlej Himalaya—Cis-Sutlej Himalaya—Kouenlun—Four Passes across Kouenlun—Boundaries of Western Tibet—Height of its mountain ranges and passes—Climate of Tibet—Clouds—Winds—Snow-fall—Glaciers—Their former greater extension—Elevation to which they descend—Snow-level—Geology—Lacustrine clay and alluvium.

The elevated country of Central Asia, situated to the north of the lofty snowy mountains which encircle India from Kashmir to Assam, is familiarly known to Europeans by the name of Thibet or Tubet,—most properly, I believe, Tibet. This name is also commonly employed by the Mohammedan nations to the north and west to designate the same country, but is not, so far as I am aware, known in the language of the Tibetans themselves, among whom different portions of the country are usually known by different names.

The whole of Tibet (as far as our present very limited knowledge of the south-east portion enables an opinion to be formed) appears to be characterized by great uniformity of climate and productions, and perhaps also of natural features, on which account it appears convenient to retain the name for the whole country, although, as has already been pointed out by Baron Humboldt*, it is naturally separable into two grand divisions. One of these, the waters of which collect to join the Sanpu, which in India becomes the Brahmaputra, is still scarcely known; the other, drained principally by the Indus and its tributaries, has been repeatedly visited by European travellers. The line of separation between these two portions lies a little to the east of the great lakes†, from the neighbourhood of which the country must gradually slope in both directions towards the sea.

If the whole of western Tibet formed (as it does, according to the popular opinion on the subject of the countries to the north of the Himalaya) an extensive plain bounded on the south by the great chain of the Himalaya, and on the north by the lofty mountains of Kouenlun, it would be an easy task to define its limits. This is, however, so far from being the case, that the greater part of the surface of the country is traversed in all directions by ranges of mountains in every respect similar to the Himalaya, of which in fact those south of the Indus are ramifications, while those on the north are branches of the snowy chain of Kouenlun.

If, again, the Himalaya formed an uninterrupted chain along the southern border of Tibet, broken only by the passage of the Indus at one extremity and by that of the Brahmaputra at the other, the mountainous nature of the interior would be no obstacle to the existence of a clear and distinct boundary. Unfortunately, however, for simplicity of definition, no such chain exists. A line

* Asie Centrale, vol. i. p. 14.

† Manasarawar and Rawan Rhad.

of high snowy peaks may doubtless be traced in a direction nearly parallel to the plains of India, but these are separated from one another by deep ravines, along which flow large and rapid rivers, and therefore afford no tangible line of demarcation between the two countries.

Between the river Indus and the plains of north-west India is interposed a mountain tract which has a breadth of about 150 miles in linear distance. This tract is everywhere (with one exception) extremely rugged and mountainous, nor is it at all an easy task to convey an idea of the extreme complication of the ramifications of the numerous ranges of which it consists. No wide plain (Kashmir alone excepted) is interposed between these ranges, so that the only feasible mode of division which appears to be applicable to them is afforded by the course of the different rivers which traverse them in various directions. If these be taken as a guide, the mountains will be found to resolve themselves into two great systems connected to the eastward, but otherwise independent of, though nearly parallel to, one another.

From the sources of the west branch of the Chenab or Chandrabhaga river, a range of very great elevation runs in a north-west direction as far as Kashmir, and, after reaching the north-east corner of that valley, assumes a more westerly direction so as to encircle the whole of its north side, bending at the same time gradually towards the south. This chain forms the line of separation between the waters of the Indus and those of the Chenab and Jelam. To the eastward of the Baralacha Pass it ramifies to a considerable extent, its different branches including between them several depressions quite unconnected with the general drainage of the country, and surrounded on all sides by ranges of hills which prevent any exit of their waters. The principal of these depressions is that of lake Chumoreri; another is occupied by the little salt lake first visited by Trebeck, and called by him Thogji*.

All these depressions, though at present unconnected with any of the river systems, have evidently at some former period been so. Chumoreri, as I am informed by Major Cunningham, is even now very slightly saline, though scarcely perceptibly so to the taste. It has evidently had an outlet at its southern extremity, where it is only separated from the valley of the Parang river by a very low range of hills which was crossed in 1846 by Mr. Agnew, and more recently by Captain H. Strachey. The outlet of the little salt lake of Thogji has evidently been near its north end, and its waters, previous to the change in the state of the country which interrupted their exit, in all probability flowed into that tributary of the Zanskar river which runs to the eastward of the Lachalang pass, and which is marked in the map accompanying Moorcroft's Travels as the Sumghiel. Major Cunningham, who travelled in 1846 by the same route as that previously followed by Moorcroft, informs me that no obstacle intervenes to prevent the waters of the lake taking that direction in case of their being raised in the lake itself to a height of two or three hundred feet above their present level.

If we consider the basins of these two lakes to be

* Moorcroft's Travels, vol. ii. pp. 47–50.

referable to the systems of drainage to which they appear to have formerly belonged, though now separated from them by accidental alterations of level, the course of the mountain chain which I am endeavouring to trace must be considered to run between the two. This is in fact the position of the loftiest part of the chain, which, skirting the north and east sides of Chumoreri, is thence continued in a south-east direction, forming that lofty but little-known range which separates the valley of the Sutlej from that of the Indus. This chain was crossed by Moorcroft on his visit to Garu, and appears to extend uninterruptedly as far as Kailas to the north of lake Manasarawar.

The mountain chain which lies to the south of the river Sutlej may also be considered to have its origin in the lofty country adjoining the lakes, but a little to the south and east of them. This chain, which separates the valley of the Sutlej from that of the Ganges and its tributaries (including the Jumna), sinks at last into the plains of India a little to the south of the town of Nahan.

The course of this chain has been admirably described by Captain Herbert in his Geological Report of the Himalaya*, a paper which contains exceedingly accurate

* Journal of the Asiatic Society of Calcutta, 1842, No. 126. Captain Herbert, who had travelled a great deal in the Himalaya, was the first to point out the impropriety of regarding these mountains as a single chain parallel to the plains of India. Jacquemont also arrived at the same conclusion, as will be seen from the following extract from his journal:—"Le langage de la géographie descriptive est théorique; c'est une grande faute si les théories qu'il rappelle sans cesse sont dénuées de fondement. Ainsi l'on dit que le Setludje *coupe* la chaîne centrale de l'Himalaya, que sa vallée est creusée au travers, etc., etc., et

general views of the mountains between the Sutlej and Jumna. He was quite unacquainted with the details of the mountains north of the former river, and therefore could not form any idea of their arrangement. Captain Herbert calls the chain south of the Sutlej the Indo-Gangetic chain, a very inappropriate name, for which, however, it is difficult to substitute a better. Perhaps the name of Cis-Sutlej Himalaya, though not exactly classical, is the best that can be devised, and if so, the chain which, commencing in Kailas, separates the waters of the Sutlej from those of the Indus, may not improperly be designated the Trans-Sutlej Himalaya*.

To these two great chains the whole of the mountains between the Indus and the plains may be referred. Both are of very great elevation, in the eastern half of their course more especially, but that north of the Sutlej is much less covered with snow than the other. This is owing to the moisture-bringing winds, which are entirely derived from the Indian side, being stopped by the chain to the south; and in fact, as soon as the elevation of the latter is so far diminished that it ceases to be covered with perpetual snow, the more northerly chain, without

l'on donne à penser par là que cette chaîne auparavant etait continue et que c'est par un effort des eaux que s'y est faite cette large trouée, comme si les montagnes avaient dû se former primitivement avec une continuité non interrompue" (vol. ii. p. 201); and again (at p. 269), "Le Setludje coule donc non au nord de l'Himalaya, mais entre deux chaînes à peu près également élevées."

* Captain R. Strachey, in his paper on the snow-level, proposes to call the more western part of the Cis-Sutlej Himalaya the Busehir range, a name which, though exceedingly appropriate to the portion to which he applies it, is not adapted for extension to the more eastern part.

any increase of elevation, becomes much more snowy, so as to merit the appellation of great snowy range, a term which, more to the eastward, is applied to the mountains south of the Sutlej. As several of the principal ramifications of the northern chain attain an elevation not at all inferior to that of the axis from which they are derived, they produce a similar effect upon the climate of the ranges to the north of them, being themselves covered with vast masses of snow, while the mountains which they shelter are in a great measure bare.

The northern boundary of Tibet is formed by the great chain north of the Indus, to which Humboldt, following Chinese geographers, has given the name of Kouenlun. Our knowledge of the appearance and course of this chain of mountains, by which Tibet is separated from Yarkand and Khoten, is so extremely limited that, except as to its general direction, very little can be said regarding it. The only conclusion which can be drawn from the scanty notices of it by travellers is, that it must be of extreme height and covered with perpetual snow. Many of the principal ramifications which it sends down towards the Indus are very elevated, and immense glaciers descend in their valleys, so that, except in a very few places, the main chain cannot be seen from the valley of the Shayuk, the mountains in the immediate vicinity of that river in general obstructing the view.

I am not aware of more than four places in which passes exist across the Kouenlun. The most westerly of these, called in Balti the pass of the Muztagh, lies at the source of the right branch of the Shigar river, a stream which joins the Indus opposite the town of Iskardo. The road over this pass to Yarkand was formerly frequented by merchants, but has for many years been disused, the reason assigned being the danger of plunder by the hordes of robbers beyond. As described to me by persons who had crossed it, the snow is reached after ten days' journey from Iskardo, and continues during three marches. It is said to be quite impracticable for horses, from which it may, I think, be inferred that there are numerous glaciers.

The second pass is that marked in Vigne's map as the Alibransa pass, at the head of a considerable tributary which joins the Shayuk river opposite Khapalu. The enormous glacier over which this road runs, by which, in conjunction with the lateness of the season, Mr. Vigne's attempts to cross the pass were frustrated, has been well described by that traveller*. I did not, while in Tibet, meet with any one who had crossed it, and I was assured by the inhabitants of Nubra that they were not acquainted with any road from the upper part of their valley, either towards Khapalu or towards Yarkand.

The third pass, and the only one now frequented, is that of the Karakoram, an extremely easy though very elevated one. The most easterly pass of which I find any notice occurs on the road between Ruduk and Khoten; it is mentioned by Moorcroft†, but without any account of the nature of the road, or the elevation of the mountains.

* Travels in Kashmir, etc., vol. ii. p. 382.

† Travels, vol. i. p. 361.

To the westward of Karakoram, the direction of the Kouenlun is seemingly as nearly as possible parallel to the Indus, but to the east of that pass nothing certain is known regarding it. In Humboldt's map it is laid down as running nearly from west to east, on the authority of Chinese geographical works. Its course is unquestionably to the north of the Pangong lake, but till it has been explored by European travellers its direction must, I think, be regarded as involved in much doubt. Another lofty range, however, unquestionably runs parallel to the Indus from south-east to north-west. This range, which is continuous with that by which the Indus and Shayuk rivers are separated, terminates (or more properly originates) in the still almost unknown mass of mountains which lies to the north of lake Manasarawar. Between this chain and the Kouenlun is situated a tract of country of unknown extent, which seems to be made up of a number of isolated lake-basins quite unconnected, not only with one another, but with the general drainage of the country by which they are surrounded.

If we except the basin of the Pangong lake, into which Moorcroft and Trebeck descended after crossing the range of mountains parallel to the Indus, every part of this country must be viewed as a *terra incognita*. It cannot, I think, be doubted, from the description of the Pangong lake given by Moorcroft and Trebeck, that the basin in which it rests had originally an outlet at its north-west extremity, discharging itself along the valley of Tanktse into the Shayuk. The country to the eastward is so totally unknown, that it is impossible to conjecture whether the little lake-basins of which it is said to consist, discharge themselves towards the Pangong lake, or southward into the Indus.

Western Tibet, then, is a highly mountainous country, lying on both sides of the river Indus, with its longer axis directed like that river from south-east to north-west. It is bounded on the north-east by the Kouenlun chain of mountains, by which it is separated from the basin of Yarkand. On the south-east its boundary is formed by the ridge which separates the waters of the Indus from those of the Sanpu. To the north-west and south-west its boundaries are somewhat arbitrary, unless the political division of the country be had recourse to, which, depending on accidental circumstances entirely unconnected with physical geography or natural productions, is so liable to change, that its adoption would be extremely inconvenient. The best mode of drawing a line of separation between India and Tibet, in those parts where mountain chains are not available for the purpose, appears to consist in regarding the latter to commence only at the point where the aridity of the climate is too great to support forests of trees, or any coniferous tree except juniper.

As limited by these boundaries, West Tibet includes the whole of the valley of the Indus and its tributaries, down to about 6000 feet above the level of the sea, a considerable portion of the upper course of the Sutlej down to between 9000 and 10,000 feet, and small portions of the upper course of the Chenab, of the Ganges (Jahnavi), and of the Gogra.

Every part of Tibet is traversed by ranges of mountains which have their origin either in the Kouenlun on the north, or in the trans-Sutlej Himalaya on the south. These mountain ranges are generally extremely rocky and rugged, but as a general rule it may be said that they are less so in the upper part of the course of the different rivers, than in their lower parts. This rule applies not only to the Indus and to the Sutlej, but with scarcely an exception to all the tributaries of these rivers. There are no extensive open plains in any part of the country, the only level portions being in the valleys of the rivers, the width of which is usually not more than one or two miles, and very seldom exceeds five miles.

To this general description of the surface of the country I have met with no exception in those parts of Tibet which I have had an opportunity of examining. I have not, however, had an opportunity of seeing the extreme south-west portion, my knowledge of the course of the Indus not extending further up than Hanle*.

The height of the mountain ranges which traverse West Tibet is in all parts pretty much the same, and, as a consequence, the depth of the valleys in the lower portion of the course of the Indus and of all its tributaries is very much greater than near the sources of these

* That Tibet is not an extensive plain, according to the usual idea, has already been pointed out by Humboldt (Asie Centrale, vol. i. p. 12). Chinese geographers, according to him, describe all parts of Tibet as 'more or less mountainous; the eastern portion of West Tibet (Gnari) as least so. Captain H. Strachey, in his account of his visit to lake Manasarawar, says expressly that "the surface of Gnari is for the most part extremely mountainous." In the lower Tibetan course of the Sutlej, the recent discoveries of Captain Strachey show that an alluvial table-land of considerable extent exists, intersected by deep ravines.

rivers. In the higher valleys therefore the mountains are apparently much less lofty; they are also frequently rounded and sloping, or at all events less rocky and precipitous than lower down, though to this there are many exceptions.

The elevation of the passes in a mountainous region represents in general the height of the lowest part of the chain. In the mountain ranges of Tibet the average height of the ridges does not exceed from 1000 to 2000 feet above the passes, many of which indeed are scarcely at all lower than the highest crest of the ridge in which they are situated. I believe that in estimating the principal ranges of mountains at 19,000 feet, and the minor ranges at from 17,000 to 18,000 feet, I approximate very closely to the truth. This estimate applies to all parts of the country, the height of the ranges being remarkably uniform; but peaks occur at intervals in every one of the principal mountain ranges, which considerably exceed the elevation just stated, rising very generally (so far as can be judged by the eye from known heights of 17,000 and 18,000 feet) to twenty-one or twenty-two thousand feet; some peaks appearing to exceed even this.

It is generally supposed that the great peaks of the Himalaya on the southern border of Tibet are much more lofty than the mountains of the interior of that country. I do not think, however, that the facts of the case are such as to warrant this assumption. West of the Sutlej, in which district only the mountains of Tibet may be said to be at all known, many peaks of the interior of that country are probably much more lofty than any of those near the plains of India, and if inaccessibility is to be any criterion, the chain of the Kouenlun is beyond a doubt a much more elevated mass than any part of the Western Himalaya. Of Tibet east of the Sutlej little is known, except that between Ruduk and Lassa no road into the interior of Asia appears to exist.

The climate of Tibet is in every part extremely arid, because it is surrounded almost entirely by ranges of mountains so elevated that the rarefied air which passes over them can contain only a very small proportion of aqueous vapour. Along the Indus, indeed, no mountain chains are interposed to obstruct the passage of moist air, but the lower course of that river lies entirely in a comparatively dry climate, so that the winds which blow over the plains of Sind and the lower mountains of Eastern Affghanistan cannot convey any excess of moisture to lower Tibet. In the few Tibetan valleys which, like that of the Sutlej, are traversed by rivers debouching on the plains of India in a rainy climate, the quantity of moist air which they can receive being limited to that which proceeds directly up the valley, the upward current, even when saturated with moisture at the commencement, being gradually rarefied by the increasing elevation of the river-bed, and meeting with descending currents of cold air in its course, it very early deposits its moisture, first in the form of light showers, afterwards of fog and mist, and in its further progress is just as dry as the air in the more interior parts of the country.

It will probably be long before lengthened registers of meteorological phenomena will be obtained from all the different stages between India and the central parts of

Tibet, so as satisfactorily to establish the gradual transition of climate. Till such shall be the case, the best evidence from which to deduce the fact of the alteration of climate, is afforded by the gradual change in the vegetation of the country as one advances towards the interior. Direct observation will probably at some future period fix the point in the outer Himalaya, at which the quantity of rain—always greater, *cæteris paribus*, among mountains than in level countries—is a maximum. I believe that in the Western Himalaya the greatest quantity of rain will be found to fall on mountains elevated from seven to nine thousand feet. Ranges of mountains which attain an elevation of from ten to eleven thousand feet have already (in the Western Himalaya) a very sensible effect in diminishing the quantity of moisture, as indicated by the vegetation; and when the mountain chains became sufficiently elevated to be capped by perpetual snow, they condense a very great proportion of the moisture of the air-currents which pass over them.

To a traveller who penetrates directly to the Tibetan interior from the plains of India, the change of climate is perceptible to the senses; most markedly so of course if his journey occurs during the Indian rainy season. Even during the rains, however, the irregularities which everywhere occur in the fall of rain provent the gradations of climate from being ascertained during a journey with the precision which a lengthened series of observations would permit; but the phenomena of vegetable life, which are dependent on the average seasons, are not affected by accidental irregularities, and therefore form an unerring guide.

Though the climate of the whole of Western Tibet may, in general, be characterized as extremely dry, it is by no means cloudless. The winter months in particular are often very cloudy, and a good deal of snow falls. During the summer the sky is either bright and clear, or overcast with very light clouds. These clouds, usually cirrhi, are in general elevated and extremely thin. The cirrhus, when it remains for any length of time, changes or increases into a uniform hazy stratum, which covers the whole sky; more rarely, and perhaps only by an optical deception, it is seen under the form of stratus. Cumuli are very uncommon. After several dull days the clouds generally accumulate, descend lower in the atmosphere, and rest on the mountain; as a few drops of rain fall in the valleys, the clouds disappear, and the highest peaks are seen to have received a slight sprinkling of snow, which is soon melted by the rays of the sun. It is only very rarely that the quantity of rain exceeds a few drops, or merits the appellation of a shower. The few occasions on which I have observed any fall of rain, at all deserving of being called by that name, have mostly been in early spring or in the latter part of autumn.

When the sky is clear, the sun, in all parts of Tibet, even at great elevations, but especially in the valleys at and below ten and eleven thousand feet, is extremely powerful. The shade temperature depends, of course, in a great measure on the elevation above the level of the sea, but also on the situation, exposure, and many other accidental circumstances. In the lower part of the Indus valley, at elevations of seven and eight thousand feet, it is said to be frequently very high*, the clear dry atmosphere allowing the full influence of the sun to be exerted on the bare, often black rocks. Even as far up as 11,000 feet, in narrow valleys, the heat is often great in the middle of the day, but the more open plains are generally very temperate in the shade, and the nights and mornings are always cool.

On the tops of the lower passes, and in the alpine valleys, the temperature of the nights and mornings is, in clear weather, very much depressed by radiation, so that the mornings, except when the sky is overcast, are intensely frosty, at elevations of 15,000 and 16,000 feet, or far below the level of perpetual snow. This is the case even in the month of August, which is the hottest of the year. The shade temperature at these high elevations rarely rises very high, even when the heat of the sun is oppressive, as it is moderated by the action of the violent winds which so generally prevail.

The periods of cloudy sky, which now and then alternate with the bright sunshine, which is the prevailing weather, are in the alpine regions extremely cold. The stratum of cloud, at first high in the atmosphere, gradually lowers itself, and the traveller is enveloped in a frozen mist, followed most commonly during the night by a fall of snow. The quantity of snow which falls is very small, seldom, so far as I have seen, more than an inch or two in depth, and it speedily disappears as soon as the clouds have been dissipated and the sky resumes its usual serenity.

* See some observations of the thermometer recorded by Mr. Vigne, at Iskardo, Khapalu, etc.

The whole of Western Tibet is subject to extremely violent winds, the course and direction of which could only be satisfactorily studied by a resident. From the great depth of the valleys, the wind in general follows their course, blowing at one time up them, at other times down. In unsettled weather the direction is extremely variable, often changing repeatedly in the course of the day, but in clear settled weather the direction of the wind is, during the day at least, more frequently up the valleys than in the contrary direction. I have not observed any constancy in the course of the wind on the passes, on which it would be principally important to be acquainted with it, but it probably varies in direction according to the period of the day, so that a traveller, whose time does not permit him to delay to register the changes as they occur, is not likely to be able to discover any general law.

The Tibetan wind, in the ordinary state of the atmosphere, commences after the sun has nearly attained the meridian, the mornings being in general quite calm. It increases in violence during the afternoon, sometimes till after sunset, ceasing to blow after dark, or at all events before midnight. This wind seems to be pretty constant over the whole country, from the upper Sutlej as far west as Rondu; and as a very similar wind blows in the valleys of Affghanistan, which have an identical summer climate in respect of moisture, it must, I presume, be caused by the influence of the sun, in heating the barren rocky plains and hills.

During periods of cloud, and throughout the winter, the wind is much less regular in its direction, as well as in the periods during which it blows. It frequently changes its direction very abruptly. About the equinoxes, or at the commencement and end of winter, at which times there seems to be generally a good deal of unsettled weather, it blows for some days with extreme violence. In March, 1848, at Iskardo, for several nights the wind almost amounted to a hurricane; its direction was from the south, or directly across the mountains. This was very commonly the case at Iskardo, in unsettled weather, during the winter, but never when the days were bright and cloudless.

The amount of snow-fall varies much, diminishing as we advance into the interior of the country, but being always much greater on the mountains than in the valleys at their feet. In the outer Himalaya, the amount at equal distances from the plains diminishes as we advance westward, but in the Kouenlun, where the source of moisture lies to the westward, the snow-fall diminishes rapidly from west to east. The same is the case in the valley of the Indus, where the amount of winter's snow, except in the most westerly parts, is quite insignificant.

It is probably owing to the absence of cumular clouds, and to the general uniform expansion of the condensed vapours over the whole sky, that the outward manifestations of electricity—thunderstorms—are of very rare occurrence in Tibet. I find only one instance of a thunderstorm recorded as having been observed while I was in a Tibetan climate. This was at Le, in September, 1848, at which time there was a good deal of cloudy weather for several days. From the extreme dryness of the air, electricity is evolved with great facility by friction: all articles of woollen clothing, blankets, and even the hair, emit sparks when rubbed in the dark. I have even observed this to be the case at the elevation of 15,500 feet, in cloudy weather, when snow was falling.

In every part of the Himalaya, and of Western Tibet, wherever the mountains attain a sufficent elevation to be covered with perpetual snow, glaciers are to be found. The occurrence of glacial ice is a sufficient indication of the existence of snow of more than one year's duration, and (setting aside trifling cases of masses of ice in deep and sunless ravines, which, indeed, are not an exception, as they have no motion,) it may be laid down as a general law, that every glacier has its origin in perpetual snow.

The converse of this proposition does not seem to be so universal. We have the high authority of Humboldt for the fact, that no glaciers occur in the Andes of tropical America, from the equator to 19° north latitude. Nor is it, I think, possible that the existence of glaciers should have escaped his notice, did they occur of such dimensions as would be indicated by the solitary and doubtful instance mentioned by M. Boussingault, to which Humboldt refers*, which is stated to have been seen at the same elevation as the town of Quito, or more than 5500 feet below the level of perpetual snow in that region of the Andes. The cause of the non-existence of masses of moving ice, in connection with the perpetual snow of the American tropics, must apparently be sought in the extreme uniformity of the seasons, and in

* Asie Centrale, vol. iii. p. 22.

the small quantity of snow which falls at any time of the year.

In every region of the earth, so far as is known to me, where the mean temperatures of summer and winter are very different, or where the climate is what is called excessive, perpetual snow produces glaciers. These rivers of ice, as they have most appropriately been called, vary very much in size and appearance. In the lofty chains of the cis- and trans-Sutlej Himalaya, and of the Kouenlun, whose peaks rise to a very great height, and collect in winter enormous depths of snow, they are of great length. In the central parts of Tibet, which are often lower, and even in their loftiest parts are less snowy than the bounding chains, the glaciers are of inferior dimensions, often of that kind which I have called incipient, where the snow-bed is at once cut off abruptly in an ice cliff, which can hardly be said to be in motion, or rather whose motion must be almost entirely from above downwards.

The general appearance of an Indian glacier seems in every respect to accord with those of Switzerland and of other parts of the temperate zone. It is only of late years, indeed, that they have been generally recognized in the Himalaya; but it must not be forgotten that it is only recently that the researches of modern investigators, and in particular the delightful work of Forbes, have familiarized the untravelled world with their appearance, and more especially with the fact and cause of their motion. It has also, singularly enough, long been the custom to look upon the Himalaya as a tropical range of mountains, in which it was, as a matter of course, regarded as impossible that glaciers could exist*.

The upper end or origin of a glacier seems commonly to be in an enormous snow-bed, occupying the whole space included by an amphitheatre of snowy peaks. The snow-slips and accumulations by which the snow-bed is added to during winter, must to a great extent remain concealed from human eyes; and in summer, when these icy fields are accessible, they are generally, I believe I may say always, covered by a thick layer of snow, which assists at the same time that it conceals the process by which the snow is converted into ice.

I have never measured the dimensions of any of the great glaciers of the Himalaya, nor is it easy to ascertain the length of any of them even approximately, as they are seldom traversed by roads, and are usually bent so that only a small part of their course can be seen. Many of them must considerably exceed ten miles in length; I have seen several which were more than half a mile broad; and the depth of the icy mass frequently amounts to hundreds of feet.

The appearance of the surface of a glacier seems to depend almost entirely on the inclination of its bed. Where the slope is gentle the surface is nearly uniformly smooth, or at most only slightly fissured. I have not had occasion to observe any fissures of more than a foot

* In the Map No. 65 of the Survey of the Western Himalaya, by Captains Hodgson and Herbert, the glacier of Gangutri is marked "Great snow-bed *or glacier*;" but whether this indication of a knowledge of the true nature of the mass is due to the surveyors or to the maker of the map in England, I have no means at present of ascertaining.

or two in width, so that, though often very deep, they are crossed without difficulty. In describing the icy surface as smooth, it is necessary to mention that such is only the case in the upper part of the glacier, where the moraines are small or only lateral. Whenever the surface supports rocky fragments in great quantity, it is extremely unequal till such time as the whole superficies becomes covered with stones, when the melting being uniform, the surface again becomes tolerably even.

On steeply inclined planes the glacier is traversed in every direction by enormous fissures, between which the surface is very irregular, rising into sharp icy pinnacles of the most fantastic shape and appearance. More than once I have seen extremely steeply sloping glaciers, which were terminated abruptly by a lofty precipice, at the bottom of which huge piles of boulders and occasional icy fragments sufficiently indicated the forward motion of the ice; at other times, the slope of the valley in which the glacier lies again becoming gentle, the ice ceases to be fissured and rugged, and is capable of being walked on without difficulty.

Moraines, which, on the larger glaciers and among mountains of easily decaying rocks, are of astonishing dimensions, form the margins of each glacier, and also occur longitudinally on different parts of their surface, increasing in number as the glacier advances, till at last the different series whose origin can long be traced to the different ramifications of the glacier, become blended into one. The nature, origin, and aspect of the moraines, the mode of melting of the ice beneath them, and the isolated pinnacles of ice which support large solitary boulders, agree so entirely with descriptions of glaciers in other parts of the world, that it is unnecessary to dwell upon them. The large glaciers are often a good deal lower in their central parts than where they are covered by a bulky moraine; and a curious ravine-like hollow, between the moraine and the bare ice, which makes the former appear as if entirely disconnected from the glacier, is of very common occurrence. There is, however, also very often an ancient moraine, not now resting on ice, which runs parallel to the glacier, and seems to indicate its former greater extent.

In every part of the Tibetan mountains, and in very many parts of the Indian Himalaya, I have thought that I could recognize unmistakeable proofs of all the valleys having been formerly occupied by glaciers at much lower levels than at present. At first sight it seems rather improbable, that in sub-tropical latitudes the present extension of perpetual snow should at any former period have been exceeded; but it would not be difficult to show that the mean temperature, and particularly the mean summer temperature, is very much higher in the Western Himalaya and Tibet than it might fairly be expected to be in such a latitude. In fact, in the more humid climate of Eastern Bengal, though at least four degrees nearer to the equator, the mean summer temperature at equal elevations in the mountains is probably considerably lower than in the mountains of North-west India, and the snow-level is certainly lower. It is fair, therefore, to conclude, looking back to a period when the sea washed the base of the Himalaya in the upper part of the Punjab, that at that period a very different state of atmospheric circumstances prevailed from that which we find at the present time.

Wherever I have seen glaciers in Tibet or the mountains of India, I have been able to trace their moraines to a level very considerably lower than their present termination; and when I find in those ranges of the Himalaya which do not at present attain a sufficient elevation to be covered with perpetual snow, series of angular blocks, evidently transported, because different from the rocks which occur *in situ*, and, so far as I can judge, exactly analogous in position to the moraines of present glaciers, I feel myself warranted in concluding that they are of glacial origin, and find it necessary to look about for causes which should render it probable that the snow-level should have formerly been lower than it is at present. In the rainy districts of the Himalaya, where forest covers the slopes of the hills, it is difficult to fix the lowest limits at which evident moraines occur, but in many places I have seen them at least three thousand feet lower than the terminations of the present glaciers. In the valley of the Indus, accumulations of boulders, which I believe to be moraines, occur in Rondu as low as 6000 feet.

Glaciers, as is well known, terminate inferiorly at the point where the waste by melting in any given time begins to exceed in amount the mass of solid ice which is in the same space of time pushed forward by the *vis à tergo*. In the mountains of Tibet the elevation of this point is very different in different places. It seems to depend principally on the mass of the glacier, as large glaciers invariably descend much lower than those of smaller size; the inclination of the bed has perhaps also some influence in determining the matter.

In comparing the glaciers of the Tibetan Himalaya with those on the Indian face of the same mountains, it will be found that, *cæteris paribus*, glaciers descend much lower on the Indian side, or in a moist climate, than in the dry and arid Tibetan climate. It is indeed impossible to ascertain with certainty that any two glaciers are of equal size, but it appears to me sufficiently accurate to compare the main glaciers on the opposite sides of the same pass. In the Umasi pass, which is situated in the main chain of the trans-Sutlej Himalaya, all the circumstances seem favourable for comparison. On the south side of this pass the principal glacier terminates at about 11,500 feet, while on the north side a much more massive glacier comes to an end abruptly at 14,000 feet. The difference then, on opposite sides of the same pass, where the pass coincides with the line of transition of climate, amounts to 2500 feet.

That I am justified in ascribing the cause of this difference to the change of climate appears from the fact, that in the interior of Tibet, where no such change is observed in crossing even very lofty passes, there is frequently a glacier on the north declivity when none exists on the south. This is the case, for instance, on the Parang pass, and on the pass immediately north of Le. It may therefore be inferred, that when glaciers occur on both sides of a pass, that on the northern exposure will, unless there be a marked alteration of climate, invariably descend lower than that on the south side. I have not had an opportunity of seeing glaciers on both sides of any pass in the most external ranges of the Himalaya, but I have been informed that in the range south of the Chenab river, glaciers frequently occur on the north sides of the passes, while none exist towards the south. If this were to be found universally the case, it would be an additional proof that the lower descent of glaciers on the south or Indian side of the mountain chain is an exceptional occurrence.

The glaciers of the southern slope of the Kouenlun appear, from the descriptions of travellers, to be on a still more gigantic scale than those of the Himalaya. Five mountain ranges of great height, separated from one another by rivers of great size, descend from the axis of that chain towards the Indus and Shayuk, and attain so great an elevation, that, with scarcely an exception, there is no passage from one of these lateral valleys to another. All these ranges rise far above the line of perpetual snow, and in their valleys enormous glaciers descend to a level which is gradually lower as we advance westward in the direction of the source of the rain- and snow-fall. The range east of the Shayuk has comparatively few and small glaciers, but to the west of that river the glaciers of Sassar terminate at about 15,000 feet. A little further west, a glacier, overhanging the valley of Nubra, terminates at 14,700 feet, and the great glacier of Nubra was found, by Captain Strachey, to terminate at 13,000 feet. In the range between Nubra and the Machulu again there are vast glaciers, but their height has not been determined, nor do we know precisely to what level those of the Shigar valley descend; though it is evident, from their proximity to the main valley, and their small distance from Shigar, which is not more than 7200 feet above the level of the sea, that they must descend very low, perhaps to 10,000 feet. In the valley of Gilgit, I am informed by Mr. Winterbottom, the glaciers descend as low as 8000 feet.

In the mountains further east than the Shayuk it would appear that the snow-fall is so very small that the level of perpetual snow recedes to an enormous height. This has been found to be the case on the passes north of the Pangong lake, many of which were crossed by Captain H. Strachey. The great height of the mountains without snow, east of the Karakoram pass, confirms the fact; and it is probable, so rapidly does the snow-level rise in advancing eastward, that if we could penetrate a very short distance beyond the eastern extremity of the Pangong lake, an absolutely dry country might be reached, in which rain or snow never falls.

So much error has unfortunately taken place regarding the height above which the mountains of North-west India are covered with perpetual snow, that it appears necessary that travellers should put upon record the results of their observations, however limited. It is for this reason, and not because I expect to throw much additional light on the subject, that the following remarks are hazarded. The recent paper of Captain R. Strachey* has furnished facts which had hitherto been wanting, while the theoretical considerations which have been laid down by Humboldt are so accurate and com-

* On the Snow-level in the Himalaya, in the Journal of the Asiatic Society of Calcutta.

prehensive, that the undoubted mistake into which he has fallen is the more to be regretted.

The Indian and Tibetan Himalaya, west of Nipal, lies entirely within the temperate zone, and from that circumstance has its year divided into summer and winter. The periodical rains, which it is well known are principally confined to the outermost parts of the mountains, being derived from the Bay of Bengal, are excessive in the easternmost part of the chain, and gradually diminish as we advance westward; there is no reason, however, to believe that the winter monsoon, which is particularly dwelt upon by Captain Strachey in the valuable paper to which I have had occasion to refer, is so. Probably indeed it is the reverse, though I have no detailed observations to refer to in corroboration of this opinion; I may however recall to mind, that the winter is the season of heavy snow, and the spring of heavy rain, throughout the north of Affghanistan, and that in the Punjab frequent cloudy weather and rain occurs during the cold season, while in the plains of India the weather seems to become at that period less unsettled as we advance eastward.

The quantity of rain which falls during the summer in the outer Himalaya has necessarily a very material influence on the sun's action during the time in which he has most power, and therefore on the mean temperature of the summer months, which at corresponding elevations, notwithstanding the northing of the chain as we advance from east to west, must be higher to the westward. In the interior or Tibetan portion of the Himalaya, this difference is not observed, the climate being the same, or nearly so, from east to west of the region under consideration.

In the most western part of the Himalaya, in Kashmir and Balti, the winter's fall of snow commences about the beginning of December, and continues on the highest ranges nearly to the beginning of May. The supply of moisture from which the snow is condensed is evidently derived from the Indian seas, and I suppose principally from the south-west, that being the general direction from which I observed snow-storms to arrive at Iskardo. The fall of snow must therefore, equally with that of rain in the rainy season, be greatest in the outermost (snowy) ranges, and very much less in all those in the interior. In the lower parts of Tibet on the Indus the snow-fall during winter is very considerable, though during summer the climate is as dry as elsewhere in Tibet. This difference seems to be explained by the westerly point from which the winter's wind blows, and by the much greater moisture of the atmosphere at that season over Affghanistan and Sind, so that the south-west wind advances loaded with vapour up the valley of the Indus. The increase of elevation in the bed of that river of course causes all the excess of moisture to be deposited without penetrating to any great distance, so that the more eastern parts of the country are not affected by this cause.

The snowy season in the highest mountains is probably in every part of the range very much the same. On the low outer ranges, which do not attain the height of perpetual snow, it is gradually lessened in duration as the elevation diminishes, ceasing entirely, in average years, at about 4000 feet. When the winter is at an end, the influence of a powerful sun and gradually increasing temperature is at once brought to bear on the mass of snow which has fallen; on the inner ranges where the summer is dry, this action proceeds uninterruptedly till the commencement of the next winter, but on the outermost snowy ranges it is modified by the access of the rainy season.

On the outer ranges of the Himalaya, the crests of which rise to between five and ten thousand feet, the powerful sun soon dissipates all snow. It is in the inner ranges, which rise nearly to the height of perpetual snow, and where the river-beds are from six to eight thousand feet above the level of the sea, that the snow remains for a great length of time. When the valleys are open, the plain on the banks of the stream becomes first of all bare of snow, then the banks which face the south, and lastly the northern slopes. It is not so, however, in the deep narrow valleys and ravines through which the Himalayan rivers generally flow. In these the bottom of the glen is so much sheltered from the sun that a dense mass of snow, the result of accumulation from the avalanches of the winter, remains for a very long time after both slopes are quite bare of snow. These *snow-beds* have nothing of the nature of a glacier in them, but are simply firm, hard snow. I have, in the month of June, descended along one of them from 13,000 feet (above which height there was perhaps a glacier beneath), to 8500 feet, a distance of seven miles without a break. It was entirely confined to the bottom of the ravine, both banks being throughout all that distance free of snow, and often covered with a most luxuriant herbage.

Similar snow-beds are to be seen in every ravine which is not too wide to be choked up by snow in winter. Their occurrence so universally is probably in a great measure the reason why glaciers were not recognized in our Indian mountains till so recent a period. These beds being so clearly transitory in existence, it was assumed that all masses of snow and ice were equally so. A visit to one of the great glaciers at the end of autumn would of course at once have indicated the dissimilarity.

In many narrow ravines remains of these snow-beds may be seen at surprisingly low elevations throughout the year, their permanence depending much more on the amount of the winter's fall of snow, and of the accumulation in that particular locality, than upon the mean or summer temperature of the place. At Baltal, in the upper part of the Sind valley in Kashmir, the little stream which descends from the Zoji pass was still arched over by a bed of snow several feet thick, in the end of September, at an elevation of not more than 9500 feet. This was not, as might have been expected, in a very shady spot, but fully exposed to the action of the sun; it was, however, in a place where the fall of snow during winter is very great.

The causes which are enumerated by Baron Humboldt as affecting the snow-level are numerous, but several are of only local effect. Two in addition to the latitude seem more important than the others, namely, the amount of fall during winter, and the amount of solar heat during summer. Captain R. Strachey regards the diminished amount of the winter's fall of snow as the main cause of the greater height of the snow-line in the interior of the

Himalaya, but I feel disposed to believe that both causes co-operate equally to produce the effect.

Captain R. Strachey has estimated (from the mean of several observations) the snow-level on the southern slope of the cis-Sutlej Himalaya at 15,500 feet. This elevation is, no doubt, as near as possible correct. Captain Herbert, in his geological report, had fixed upon 15,000 feet, which is a little too low even in the district of Baschir, to which his estimate, I believe, refers. In the trans-Sutlej Himalaya, from the diminished amount of summer cloudy weather, the snow-level is probably a little higher, but we are not yet in possession of any accurate determinations of heights in that range in those parts which are in close contact with the plains of India. Two of its ramifications are extremely well adapted for determining the height of perpetual snow. First, the Chumba range, which, as has been pointed out to me by Major Cunningham, is barely snow-tipped throughout the year; and second, the Pir Panjal range south of Kashmir, the northern slopes of which have perpetual snow and glaciers, while on the south side the snow has entirely melted before the end of summer. The elevation of the Pir Panjal has not been determined with accuracy, the heights given by Baron Hügel and by Mr. Vigne being estimated from their measurement of the pass over which they crossed*.

In the interior of north-west Tibet every principal range attains the elevation of perpetual snow, but only

* The thermometric results obtained by these two travellers do not agree with one another. M. Hügel's thermometer indicated 6300 feet for the elevation of Kashmir, a result which is known from the barometric observations of Jacquemont to be 1000 feet in excess.

a few peaks rise much above it. There is therefore no very great mass of snow during the summer months to lower the temperature of the air, and consequently circumstances are the most favourable possible for the elevation of the snow-line to an extreme degree; a dry, stony, desert, treeless country, violent winds, clear sky, and powerful sun, being all combined. In the most central part of the country, the Lanak pass, near Hanle, and the Sabu pass, near Le, both elevated as nearly as possible 18,000 feet, are without perpetual snow, but the Parang pass, between 18,400 and 18,600 feet, has a glacier on its north face, and therefore exceeds in elevation the snow-line. The snow-level in central Tibet must therefore be sought between these heights, but nearer that of the Parang pass, which has no perpetual snow towards the south: it is, therefore, certainly not below 18,000 feet.

In the Kouenlun, on the northern border of Tibet, where the mountains are again much more elevated, the snow-level descends no lower. Even on the 19th and 20th of August, the mass of snow, which was on the northern face of its highest peaks continuous down from 20,000 feet and upwards, did not descend below 17,500 feet, and the open level plain of the upper Shayuk had at that height only trifling patches of snow. On the Karakoram pass (18,200 feet) there were only large patches of snow, the south face of the ridge being quite bare for some distance in both directions.

Mr. Vigne's thermometer, when tested by Moorcroft's barometric results at Le, errs considerably in the opposite direction. In neither case do I know the mode of calculation employed, the results only being given.

The *vexata quæstio* of the difference of the level at which snow lies on the north and south slopes of the Himalaya, affords a singular instance of misconception. Enunciated originally in an obscure and somewhat incorrect form, when little was known of the structure of the inner part of the chain, the fact has been repeatedly contradicted by those who thought they found it contrary to their experience. Both parties were to a certain extent right. On each individual range the snow-level will at all times be found lower on the north face than on the south, except when the range which we are crossing happens to coincide with a very marked and abrupt change of climate, which will only be the case when it is extremely elevated. When this is the case, the proposition, otherwise true of the mountains *en masse*, or the inner ranges compared with the outer, becomes applicable to a particular range. This is probably the case in the very pass in Kamaon (I know not which it was) from which the law was first inferred. It is certainly so in the great passes north of the Chenab, where, on the Indian face, I found in June snow at 11,500 feet, while on the north side, only twenty miles distant, it had already receded beyond 15,000 feet.

From the rapid nature of my journey, and the great number of objects to which I was obliged to devote my attention, the geological observations which I was enabled to make were much more imperfect than I could have wished. It appeared, however, desirable, hurried as they were, to enumerate them, for the purpose of drawing the attention of future travellers to the subject; and for the same reason I shall here recapitulate the general conclusions which appear to result from the facts observed.

The greater part of Tibet consists of plutonic and metamorphic rocks; and from the gigantic scale on which the sections are exposed, and the general bareness of the mountains, which enables their structure to be seen, that country probably presents the finest field in which these classes of rocks could be studied. Granite occurs in great abundance, sending immense veins in all directions into the metamorphic rocks, which are seen to be everywhere upheaved and dislocated by the injected mass. In the immediate vicinity of the plutonic masses, all traces of the direction of the strata of the superposed rocks are lost; but elsewhere, with every variety of dip, it is very generally found that the stratified rocks strike in a direction which varies between north-west and south-east, and north-north-west and south-south-east. As all my observations were made roughly and unconnectedly, and without my discovering this identity till after my return to India, the strike is probably very uniform throughout a great extent of country.

It is not a little remarkable that a belt twenty miles wide, in the direction of this line of strike, drawn from Iskardo to the Niti pass, would cover every place south of the Indus in which limestone has been observed in Tibet. It would pass through Molbil on the Pashkyum river, the limestone districts of Zanskar, and the Lachalang pass, where limestone was found by Gerard. It would also cover Piti, Hangarang, and Bekhar, all well-known limestone tracts. Of course the limestones of Nubra and the Karakoram on the one hand, and of

Kashmir on the other, cannot in any way be connected with this line.

The sandstones, slates, and conglomerates, which so closely resemble in appearance those rocks which in Europe are chiefly members of the old red sandstone and greywacke series, appear to assume also the same direction. I bring forward these coincidences of direction only as a remarkable fact, worthy of investigation, without attaching any great weight to them, as more careful observation may show that they are merely accidental, and that rocks of very different ages exist among the limestones and associated rocks of the northern Himalaya.

The great extent and development of a very modern alluvium-like formation, composed of great masses of clay with boulders, and occasionally of very fine laminated clay, constitutes one of the most remarkable and striking features of Western Tibet. In every part through which I have travelled, and at all elevations, except on the highest passes, I have found these deposits in greater or less quantity. In their most common state they consist of loose earthy or clayey unstratified masses, containing boulders either angular or rounded. Very fine clay, distinctly and horizontally stratified, is also common; sandstone and hardened conglomerate are more rare, but also occur occasionally.

That some of these beds are of lacustrine origin, the occurrence of fresh-water shells appears to prove very clearly; and though here and there small portions may be terrestrial and of glacial origin, it cannot, I think, be doubted that the great mass of the boulder clay was deposited under water.

In the structure of Scotland at the present day we have a state of circumstances which appears to me capable of throwing much light on the nature of these deposits. We find there a series of narrow arms of the sea, stretching far into the land, and separated by rugged and generally steep ranges of metamorphic or plutonic rocks. They are all more or less silted up by sedimentary matter, and near their mouths, especially where, as is often the case, they are much contracted, we generally find a bar, shallower than the remainder. At various elevations above the sea-level again there is a series of fresh-water lakes, differing little in aspect from the arms of the sea. We find also in many parts of the Highlands of Scotland long valleys, nearly level, which are filled with incoherent sedimentary deposits, and bounded like the lochs by steep mountains. If these were formerly arms of the sea, which by the elevation of the land have been converted into dry land, then the fresh-water lakes probably occupy those parts of the narrow channels which were originally deepest, or which, being wider than the rest, have remained unoccupied by sedimentary matter at the time of the elevation. In conformity with this view we find that at the lower end of these lakes the mountains generally approach very close to one another.

If we were to suppose the gradual elevation of Scotland to continue till the mountains attained an elevation equal to that of the Himalaya, it is evident that a continued series of marine sedimentary deposits would extend from the summit to the sea-level, unless removed by the action of streams or other ordinary causes. Some of the valleys would be of considerable width, and would contain marine fossils in great abundance; but in the narrower mountain valleys the gravel and boulders would be quite destitute of fossils. Here and there fresh-water formations of partial extent would occur, but they would be separated from one another by large tracts filled with marine beds. The gradual elevation of the land would bring to bear upon these incoherent strata the powerful action of running water, which would remove portion after portion, till at last deep valleys would be excavated, and small patches only of the gravel and clay would remain where the action of the streams was least powerful. Such I conceive to be the present state of Tibet, but a much more detailed investigation of that remarkable country would be necessary, before this view can be regarded in any other light than an hypothesis.

The causes by which the metamorphic rocks, which must have been brought into their present remarkable state at a great depth in the interior of the globe, acquired their present configuration of mountain and valley, form a question on which I am not now prepared to enter. One continued process of elevation seems inadequate to produce the observed effects; but however numerous the alternations of elevation and depression may have been, it is evident that the alluvial deposits at present existing must all be referable to the last period of elevation, as such incoherent strata could not withstand the continued action of the sea.

INDEX.